Bret Harte

BRET HARTE
PRINCE AND PAUPER

Axel Nissen

University Press of Mississippi/Jackson

This book is published with the generous assistance
of the Research Council of Norway.

www.upress.state.ms.us

08 07 06 05 04 03 02 01 00   4 3 2 1
∞

Library of Congress Cataloging-in-Publication Data

Nissen, Axel.
    Bret Harte : prince and pauper / Axel Nissen.
        p. cm.
    Includes bibliographical references (p.) and index.
    ISBN 1-57806-253-5 (alk. paper)
        1. Harte, Bret, 1836–1902. 2. Humorists, American—19th
century—Biography. 3. Authors, American—19th
century—Biography. 4. California—Gold
discoveries—Historiography. 5. Western
stories—Authorship. I. Title.

PS1833.N57 2000
813'.4—dc21
    [B]   99-048552

British Library Cataloging-in-Publication Data available

To the memory of my grandparents,
to my parents, my brother Alf, and his wife Kari,
and to my lifelong friend, Edith Halvorsen,
do I dedicate this book.

He was indeed a prince, a fairy prince in whom every lover of his novel and enchanting art felt a patriotic property.

William Dean Howells,
"Bret Harte," *Literary Friends and Acquaintance*

Where have you lived? Nobody knows. Your own people do not know. But I know. You have lived in the Jersey woods and marshes and have supported yourself as do other tramps.

Mark Twain on Bret Harte,
The Autobiography of Mark Twain

CONTENTS

Acknowledgments xi
Introduction xiii

Part I. Going to Meet America 3

1. A Perfect Furore 5

2. The Shadow of the Temple (1836–1854) 13

3. Over the Trackless Past (1854–1860) 31

4. Waiting for His Chance (1860–1868) 58

5. The Rise of Bret Harte (1868–1871) 87

6. Age of Innocence (1871–1875) 113

7. "How am I to live?" (1875–1878) 139

Part II. The Cherished Exile 163

8. The Vanishing Consul (1878–1885) 165

9. Lord of Romance (1885–1892) 194

10. The Scent of Heliotrope (1892–1898) 222

11. No Time for Dying (1898–1902) 243

Abbreviations 267
Notes 269
Bibliography 305
Index 315

ACKNOWLEDGMENTS

In writing this biography I have had the assistance and encouragement of numerous individuals and institutions, whom I now gratefully wish to acknowledge: Sandra Bailey; Nicola Beauman; Sean, Jane, and Peter Byrne; Paul N. Christensen; Hunter M. Cole; John W. Crowley; Siri Dick-Henriksen; Donald Glover; Joan D. Hedrick; Patricia E. Kell; Nickole Kerner; Annette Kolodny; Rolf Lundén; Jay Martin; Mr. and Mrs. Anthony Pull; Pamela, Ian, and Catherine Roberts; the late Chester P. Sadowy; Cynthia H. Sanford; Gary Scharnhorst; Hans H. Skei; Seetha A-Srinivasan; Marian Collins Surtees; Per Winther; the Norway-Oxford Committee; the Norwegian Fulbright Committee; the Research Council of Norway; and last but not least, my home institution, the University of Oslo.

I am especially grateful to my first readers, Liv Glad Nissen and Orm Øverland, and to John Bret-Harte for his friendship and for permission to quote from his father's and great-grandfather's papers.

I would like to thank the staff of the many libraries and archives I have worked in. Special thanks to Claude Anspach; Michael Bott; Daniel Bourgeois; Mark Nissen Brown; Lesley Douthwaite; Maxime La Fantasie; (Dom) Philip Jebb, O.S.B.; Jennifer B. Lee; Jennie Rathbun; J. F. Russell; Raymond Wemmlinger; and the staff of the Faculty of Arts Library, University of Oslo.

For permission to quote from letters in their collections, I am grateful to Bancroft Library, University of California, Berkeley; Department of Special Collections, University Research Library, University of California, Los Angeles; Houghton Library, Harvard University; Bret Harte Collection (#5310), Clifton Waller Barrett Library, Special Collections Department, University of Virginia Library; Yale Collection of American Literature,

Beinecke Rare Book and Manuscript Library, Yale University; Rutherford B. Hayes Presidential Center; University Library, University of Southern California; and Harry Ransom Humanities Research Center, University of Texas at Austin.

I am grateful to His Majesty King Harald V of Norway for awarding the dissertation on which this biography is based His Majesty's Gold Medal in 1997.

Finally, I want to thank everyone who ever showed an interest in this book, not least of all my large and loving family, my colleagues in the Department of British and American Studies at the University of Oslo, and my friends. Mark Hildebrandt makes everything possible.

"Now death has come to join its vague conjectures to the broken expectations of life, and that blithe spirit is elsewhere. But nothing can take from him who remains the witchery of that most winning presence. Still it looks smiling from the platform of the car, and casts a farewell of mock heart-break from it. Still comes a gay laugh across the abysm of the years that are now numbered, and out of somewhere his sense is rapt with the mellow cordial of a voice that was like no other." He who remained was William Dean Howells, who ended his tribute to Bret Harte with a more than thirty-year-old memory of the youthful author waving goodbye as his train pulled out of a Boston railway station. Harte was at the height of his American fame then, in 1871; it was before all the troubles began, and Howells chose to embalm this image of a friend he had not seen in twenty years.

History is written by the survivors and in that sense Bret Harte was not a survivor. It would be up to other men of his generation—William Dean Howells, Mark Twain, Henry Adams—to sit down and throw a long last look back. To them was granted the leisure of a contemplative and retrospective old age in which to record their version of the past. It is interesting, then, that the memory of Bret Harte should remain so firmly engraved on the minds of these most representative men. On the day the newspapers made Harte's death known, Howells sat down to write to his old Boston friend Thomas Bailey Aldrich: "Stockton was bad enough, but Bret Harte! He belonged to our youth which was glad, and knew it, and I find that he had a hold upon my heart which I have no logic for. You must be feeling as I do, and words are vain."

"Broken expectations," "winning presence," "a gay laugh," "a voice that was like no other," these were the words Howells grasped when it was time to put Bret Harte to rest in the pages of *Harper's Monthly* in December 1903. We know he did not think it an easy task. "What is to be done in such cases?" he asked Mark Twain. "Of course I could have written, though not more sincerely, things that would have left blisters on his fame; but after all, such things had better be left to the Judgement Day, which I see more and more use for as I live along." Twain had written Howells as soon as he had read the piece, saying: "You have written of Harte most felicitously—most generously, too, & yet at the same time truly; for he *was* all you have said, although he was more & worse, there is no occasion to remember it & I am often ashamed of myself for doing it." Twain had been reading of Harte's breakthrough in the bound *Blackwood's Edinburgh Magazine* for 1871, when Howells's article appeared: "In the one night I saw him born; I saw him flit across the intervening day, as it were, & when night closed down again I saw him buried. It was weird & impressive." Twain's shame at thinking ill of his former friend did not prevent him from throwing several shovelfuls of dirt on Harte's grave some years later, when he was writing his memoirs. When Twain was done, he paused and sighed magnanimously: "By ancient training and inherited habit, I have been heaping blame after blame, censure after censure, upon Bret Harte, and I have felt the things I have said, but when my temper is cool I have no censures for him. The law of his nature was stronger than man's statutes and he had to obey it."

Who was Bret Harte, this man who evoked such strong and conflicting feelings in those who knew him? To Howells, Harte was a blithe spirit, who burned his candle at both ends. To Twain he was "the most contemptible, poor little soulless blatherskite that exists on the planet today." Henry Adams thought him one of the most brilliant men of his time. Ina Coolbrith, poet and San Francisco friend, thought him "one of the most genial, unselfish, kind, unaffected and *non*-conceited of all the writers I have known." To a reviewer of an early biography, he was "a fugitive from the home." To the bigot, he was a "Hebrew"; to the average dresser, he was a fop; to the pious, he was a purveyor of "moral filth." To the world, Bret Harte and Mark Twain were the most famous American writers in the second half of the nineteenth century.

Today Bret Harte is known primarily as the author of a handful of classics of the American short story. Although he was also a poet, dramatist, parodist, lecturer, editor, literary critic, and diplomat, he is remembered today for the stories he wrote for the *Overland Monthly* between 1868 and 1871. In stories such as "The Luck of Roaring Camp," "Tennessee's Partner," and "The Outcasts of Poker Flat," Bret Harte reinvented the American short story and laid the foundation for the Western. As Donald Glover has pointed out, his chief innovation was the coupling of the short story with local material. Patrick Morrow observes that "Harte led the Nineteenth Century reading public into realizing that a well-crafted and moving story about a particular locale was more meaningful than a didactically moralistic or sticky-sweet romantic short story." "Waves of influence run from the man," wrote Henry Seidel Canby, "and indeed the literary West may be said to have founded itself upon the imagination of Bret Harte."

To a writer in the *New York Times Saturday Review of Books and Art,* Harte was "the first American realist." To Hjalmar Hjorth Boyesen, he was "the last American novelist of any eminence who can be classed as a romanticist." At the remove of a century, most would probably side with Boyesen and place Harte in the romantic camp, yet this was not the way he was initially perceived. Despite their frequently fantastic plots and picturesque characters, Harte's early stories were read by his contemporaries as realistic portrayals of California life during the gold rush. As Theodore Watts-Dunton has pointed out in comparing Harte and Dickens: "though they were both by instinct idealists as regards character-drawing, they both sought to give their ideals a local habitation and a name by surrounding those ideals with vividly painted real accessories, as real as those of the ugliest realists." Another reader, George Meredith, wrote to a friend in 1872: "I love Browning and claim my right to criticize him. Moreover, will you believe it? the artistic that I am rejoices in shaggy realism enough to read 'The Luck of Roaring Camp' with envy of the writer's power." In a passage in his notebooks, Twain grudgingly credited Harte with widening the range of characters and situations an American author could bring before his audience. We have had Frank Norris and Stephen Crane, Theodore Dreiser and Hamlin Garland, Kate Chopin and Constance Fenimore Woolson since Bret Harte, but we must not forget that

Harte wrote his major works when some of these writers were not even born.

Following his sensational breakthrough in the late 1860s, Harte became a prime example of a self-made literary man, a Midas of the pen to satisfy the materialistic spirit of the Gilded Age. Through the force of his example—his popularity and renown—he heightened both the respect for the profession of authorship and its material rewards. In the early 1870s, no American writer had ever received so much for writing so little. The image of the writer starving in a garret, which had haunted Bret Harte's early life and made him turn to authorship only as a last resort, was replaced in the public imagination by the image of the prosperous, fêted figure of the author mixing with the cream of society and cashing fat royalty checks.

Harte was the first American author-celebrity in the age of mass newspapers, a time when fame could become worldwide fame. His stories were reprinted all over the world, his doings and sayings were reported in newspapers large and small, and his image adorned their columns and was sold over the counter. It is possible that his renown did not come home to him until he began to lecture in the first half of the 1870s and traveled all over North America. On a lecture tour of the Midwest in October 1873, he wrote to his sister in New York that he had had a wearisome trip, "although being in the country of 'Bret Harte' collars and 'Bret Harte' hats, and with a settlement named after me in the next township, I am among friends and admirers." While riding across a bleak prairie one afternoon and meeting an emigrant train, Harte had a singular experience: "one of the young men, after riding beside me for a few moments, suddenly asked me if I weren't 'Bret Harte.' I answered 'yes' and asked him why he asked the question. He said I looked like my picture, and produced it with the greatest naiveté from his pocket, greasy with handling. He said all my books were in the wagon, and to my great astonishment repeated nearly everything I had ever written."

Bret Harte was a famous author and celebrity with a large circle of friends and acquaintances, including most of the literary establishment on both sides of the Atlantic. With the notable exception of Mark Twain, people remembered him for his charm, wit, and modesty, and in his maturity he would move in the highest circles of English society with a grace and aplomb that masked his innate shyness and native reserve. Despite his personal popularity and the many lives he touched, it is possible to ask if anyone really *knew* Bret Harte. It would seem that with each of the major moves of his life he reinvented himself and buried a part of his past he would rather forget. To many of his friends, he remained an enigma. Howells speaks, for example, of "the Bret Harte Mystery . . . which used to puzzle us all." Bret Harte was born under a cloud, and he carried the truth of his mixed racial heritage with him throughout his life as one of his most closely guarded secrets.

As his life went on, there were other secrets and troubles that cast a shadow over his name. When his influential friends finally got him posted to an obscure commercial agency in Germany in the late 1870s, it was with a sigh of relief on their lips. Ironically, this very move brought about the major irregularity of Harte's life: the separation from his wife and children for the remaining twenty-four years of his life. While most of his American friends and contemporaries—Mark Twain, William Dean Howells, John Hay, to name but a few—lived lives of quiet and well-regulated domesticity, Bret Harte was the one who got away. In an age when the family became a quasi religion and the home a shrine, Bret Harte left his family behind in the United States and ultimately moved in with a Belgian diplomat, his wife, and their nine children. Despite earning large sums of money, he never had a home of his own.

It is our task as scholarly biographers to shape the narrative re-creation of a life in such a way as not to falsify the evidence, to allow others to understand the basis for our conclusions, and to give meaning to a heterogeneous mass of facts and details. On the first two points, we are presently at a high level of development. Contemporary scholarly biographies are largely dependable in their relation of the facts and provide us with a scholarly apparatus of notes and "works cited" that allow us, if we so should wish, to follow the biographer's process and check the validity of his or her conclusions against the evidence. It is possibly because of the emphasis on reliability and thoroughness that there has been little experimentation in the area that is to lend the facts meaning—the biography's form.

In one of his Alexander Lectures at the University of Toronto in 1956, Leon Edel remarked: "Biography, in its fear of fiction, has not studied sufficiently, it seems to me, the possible technical borrowings it can make from that characteristic literary form. There remains much room for trial and experiment." Forty years later, one might claim that there still remains much room for trial and experiment. "What one chiefly notices in modern biography," Robert Skidelsky remarked in 1988, "is how professionally it is done, not that it is experimental in style or arrangement, or that it seriously challenges accepted judgements. Nearly all biographies still start with ancestors, move on to birth, and then through birth to leading events, and so on to death, in much the same way as of old, and at about as funereal a pace."

In a book from 1981 devoted to the idea that "fiction is not needed to make interesting the life of even the most obscure human, but 'fictional' techniques are needed," Dennis Petrie asks: "How is one to exorcise the feeling of both biographers and critics that style, or any part of 'design,' constitutes a 'design' against the historical, factual integrity of a literary biography?" Petrie concludes that "both biography and fiction are *ultimately narrative*." Had he turned to the third mode of writing that is also ultimately narrative, namely history, he might have found a way out of biography's apparent epistemological impasse.

For more than twenty years there has been a discussion within the discipline of history concerning the epistemic status of narrative. The relevance for "the philosophy of biography" of discussions within the philosophy of history lies simply in the fact that history and biography share the same methodology and the same aims (though on a different scale). As biography is historical narrative, the conclusions of historical theorists such as Hayden White cannot fail to be of significance also to biographers. This is not the time or the place to give a detailed account of White's ideas about "The Historical Text as Literary Artifact," but their essence is the recognition of the participation of historical narrative in some of the same patterns of storytelling that govern fictional narrative.

As in all modes of historical narration, the epistemology and aesthetics of biography are intimately connected; what one discovers and what one is able to convey to the reader is determined by the way in which the narrative is shaped. "Facts do not speak for themselves," Hayden White notes, "in the unprocessed historical record and in the chronicle of events which the historian extracts from the record, the facts exist only as a congeries of contiguously related fragments." Biographies, like the histories White considers, "gain part of their explanatory effect by their success in making stories out of *mere* chronicles." White identifies the transition from chronicle to history as one of "emplotment," that is, "the encodation of the facts contained in the chronicle as components of specific *kinds* of plot structures." Emplotment is basically no different in fictional and factual narrative. The repertoire of available plot structures is the same and the same rules of coherence and correspondence apply. Just as with a history, a biography does not become a biography unless this emplotment takes place.

A biographical/historical method consists of more than simply "investigating the documents in order to determine what is the true or most plausible story that can be told about the events of which they are evidence." The ideas about plausibility, causality, and human character that we bring to this investigation will themselves determine what events we perceive, how we perceive them, and finally how we narrate them. In this view, the question of a biography's form is not just a question of rhetoric, that is, what form will best clothe some preconceived and independent notion of biographical content? Rather, how are the questions I ask and the answers I find determined by my conception of the genre's innate possibilities and, inversely, limitations? If I believe that it is my primary task as a biographer to give an introspective account of how it felt to be a certain person at a given time in his or her life, I will probably not be greatly concerned with hunting up sources that give me an external point of view on the subject. If I believe that it is most important to show how the individual's life was shaped by historical forces, I will spend time trying to re-create the economic, intellectual, and social environment in which he or she moved. If I want to explain how the life of a writer influenced his or her work and vice versa, I will probably devote much time during research and in the text to his or her writings. Ideally, of course, a biography should do all these things, but in practice, the biographer often opts for a certain type of emphasis.

Positioned as a discourse between fiction and history, biography shares the methodology of narrative history and can, if it wishes, share at least some of the stylistic innovations of the novel. There are things a biography cannot do or should not do—such as employ dialogue when there is no primary source material to base it on—but to a greater degree than is presently the case, biography should be open to the forms of narrative that have been developed during the last century. As concerns the consequences of Hayden White's ideas for historical (and hence biographical) *practice,* I would see them as an eloquent plea for a greater awareness of the "fictional," constructed nature of all historical discourse. Ira B. Nadel concludes that "[w]hat gives biography its impact is not the point of view of the biographer, as Strachey emphasized, nor the 'inner myth' of the subject, as Leon Edel stresses, but the linguistic expression, narrative technique and mythical elements employed by the author to tell his story." Park Honan makes an important point when he writes that a key requirement of a literary biographer today "is that of having patience to devise new, special, less limiting methods and forms for presenting evidence that one comes to know closely."

One of the potential strengths of biography as a mode of historical understanding is that, through the focus on the individual life and its tangencies with other lives, it brings into play a vast array of buried signifiers and displays the richness of the decipherable past. By having the potential to be as specific in time and place as it is possible to be in historical narrative, biography serves to remind us how much we have forgotten. One important way to gain, shape, and communicate biographical insight is through "dramatization"—the representation of specific moments in the subject's life in a scenic mode of discourse. This basic approach is not new; Leon Edel developed it famously in his multivolume biography of Henry James, and behind him we can, of course, discern the novelistic principles and practices of the Master himself. I differ from Edel in claiming that the scenes to dramatize are not necessarily the most dramatic moments in the subject's life but are rather those about which we have numerous sources and thus more certain knowledge. Another basic difference between his "scenic method" and mine is one of form. Edel uses the term loosely to denote any (usually brief) attempt at a re-creation of a specific historical situation involving several people. The biographical "scene," as I construct it in the following, is a situation in which the subject is alone with his or her own thoughts and is thus a form of monologue. While the lack of sources on which to base dialogue makes social scenes between several people almost impossible to depict without stretching the evidence, the nature of our most frequently used primary sources—letters and diaries—makes them an ideal basis for transformation into *narrated monologue* (what Dorrit Cohn has defined as "a character's mental discourse in the guise of the narrator's discourse"). While such materials are usually either quoted directly or paraphrased, they may equally be transformed into *free indirect style* and, in combination with information from other sources, form the basis of a scene. The narrated monologue allows the biographer to do three things: it allows him to give a detailed account of the who, what, where, when, and how of a given situation; it allows him the choice of a specific perspective outside himself; and it allows him to let the subject speak in his or her own words, while avoiding the stylistic disharmony and incongruity of the often used "mosaic method" (where sources such as letters are briefly quoted in the main text).

"Of the various techniques for presenting the mental life of third persons," Dorrit Cohn writes in a recent article, "the one that prevails in biography is obviously psycho-narration, 'the narrator's discourse about a character's consciousness.' " In proposing that we allow ourselves to move beyond psychonarration—"this most distanced of the fictional modes of [thought] presentation"—and what John Updike has referred to as the " 'must-have' school of biography," I am *not* proposing that we start fantasizing freely about "how things really were" but rather that we try to (re)construct a single moment in time on the basis of the historical evidence. While the moment to dramatize is the biographer's choice and discovery, the scene comes to life only at the point where the various sources intersect. The scene is conjectural and imaginative only to the extent that the concatenation of the sources is not given; they must be brought together by the biographer.

The biographical scene is meant to supplement rather than supplant the customary use of various forms of summary. In a narrative that is to give a detailed account of all the important aspects of a life of maybe seventy or eighty years in four or five hundred pages, summary is, of course, inevitable and necessary. While a biography consisting entirely of scenes is conceivable, it would probably be hard to follow. It is in the alternation between a scenic mode of representation and summary that the rhetorical and epistemological gain is to be made. Summary also allows us to fill in any gaps created by the scenes.

Another novelistic technique that I feel may be useful to biographers is what Boris Uspensky refers to as "consistent narration." "Here," he explains, "the position of the narrating observer is essentially real: the author describes the behavior of the characters in literature just as an ordinary person, in any ordinary situation, would describe the behavior of another person. In consistent narration, the author belongs to the same world as the characters and is not distinguished in any way from them." What this means if used in a biographical narrative is that the biographer for a time steps into the story world; he abdicates omniscience for a time, taking on the role of the casual observer. Consistent narration allows the reader to see the subject as he or she might have appeared to a stranger.

When I advocate letting the distribution and nature of the source materials more directly determine the form of the narrative, it is not to return to an outmoded ideal of letting the subject "speak for himself." That ideal led to the lack of synthesis and overarching perspective in the many Victorian "life and letters" biographies. Rather, the varied nature of any biographer's sources should inspire him to find new and innovative narrative strategies, reflecting varying points of view on the subject, from that of the subject himself to that of his family, his friends, and people who did not even know him personally. One of the more exciting discoveries I made during my research was a detailed description of how Bret Harte had appeared in his youth to a young man who was not personally acquainted with him. This allowed me to see Harte from a stranger's point of view in chap-

ters 3 and 4. In the final section of chapter 7, I mimic the epistolary novel and let the juxtaposition of extracts from seventeen
letters placed in chronological order tell the story of Harte's last
year in America. Though aspects of my technique are new, my
basic biographical attitude is not. James Boswell referred to this
kind of strategy as "an accumulation of intelligence from various
points," Virginia Woolf called it "hanging up looking-glasses at
odd corners," and Lytton Strachey, attacking one's subject "in
unexpected places."

Bret Harte

PART I

Going to Meet America

"Who knew Bret Harte?"

"I."

"And what did you know about him?"

No answer.

They are ready enough with their "I's," these old residents who watched the name of Frank Bret Harte, only thrice capitalized, grow to FRANCIS BRET HARTE, capitalized from end to end, within the pages of San Francisco's directory. They are ready enough, those who have watched that name arise to still higher letters in America's literary muster.

But when you ask these ready "I's" to prove their claim to acquaintance, alas for their memories.

The truth of the matter is, nobody ever knew Bret Harte.

San Francisco Chronicle, May 25, 1902

CHAPTER 1

A Perfect Furore

CAMBRIDGE, MASS.

FEBRUARY 25–MARCH 4, 1871

Did you like Bret Harte's face? There is a perfect furore in cultivated society now about Bret Harte. All the young ladies are in love with him—but it is of no use—he is married.

Elinor Mead Howells to her sister-in-law,
Aurelia H. Howells, January 29, 1871

On the second Saturday in January 1871, the cover of the artsy Boston illustrated journal *Every Saturday* featured the portrait of a romantic-looking young man with thick black curls, a straight manly nose, a black Dundreary mustache, and a faraway expression in his dark eyes. Readers in the East scrutinized the sketch with particular interest, for they were seeing for the first time the face of Bret Harte, author of such instant classics as "The Luck of Roaring Camp" and "Plain Language from Truthful James." So great was his popularity, stated the article inside, that "we suppose hardly any one who takes up this paper will fail to remember his name, or to cry out at sight of his likeness on the first page, 'Oh, *that's* he, is it?' " "We believe," wrote the journal further, "that everybody will be very glad to look upon the face of one who has already done so much to please and surprise the world; and we hope that all will note its refinement, strength, and distinction. There will be in it a good wholesome disappointment for all cockneys everywhere, who think that a Western face must be a rough one. . . . [A]cquaintance with this face cannot but heighten the enjoyment with which they [his readers] will turn again to his stories and poems."

One can readily imagine small, almost inaudible sighs passing out of the half-open mouths of young eastern girls, as they scanned the columns for information on Bret Harte's marital status, of which the paper said nothing. One such young admirer was Miss Sara Sedgwick—only she knew Mr. Harte was married and the father of two children no less. She knew this because she was a friend of Mr. and Mrs. William Dean Howells, who had been in communication with the author for some time. He had sent them his portrait last November. It was that picture that formed the basis for the sketch on *Every Saturday*'s cover. Not only that, last summer Mr. Howells, who was assistant editor of the *Atlantic Monthly,* had invited Harte to stay at his home in Cambridge when he came east. On Friday last, Miss Sedgwick had been thrilled when she opened an envelope from Mrs. Howells and saw that it was the following invitation: "Mrs. Howells requests the pleasure of Miss Sedgwick's company on Monday evening Feb. 27th at 8 o'clock, to meet Mr. & Mrs. Bret Harte. Berkeley St. Feb. 23." Miss Sedgwick had been too excited to write a formal reply.

Had the twenty-seven-year-old Henry James Jr. glanced at the *Boston Advertiser* on the day of the party, he would have been able to read that "Mr. Bret Harte arrived in this city about eleven o'clock Saturday forenoon, and went immediately to the residence of Mr. W. D. Howells in Cambridge." James had had to decline an invitation to visit a friend, writing: "A destiny at once cruel and kind forbids my acceptance of your amiable proposition for Monday evening. I am engaged to meet the Bret Hartes at Mrs. Howells's. An opportunity to encounter these marvellous creatures is, I suppose, not lightly to be thrown aside. . . . Primed with your compliment, and your father's, about the P[assionate] P[ilgrim], I shall really quite hold up my head to the author of the Heathen Chinee."

In his newly leased house on Berkeley Street, we find William Dean Howells, happy and probably not a little relieved that the visit is going so well. Since the Hartes had started from San Francisco on February 2, he had been able to follow their journey across the continent almost day to day. Their progress eastward from California had been telegraphed almost hour to hour, as if it were the progress of a prince! He had even started to wonder if maybe he had not overreached himself in inviting them; becoming doubly apprehensive after reading about the scandal in Chicago, when Harte failed to appear at a dinner in his honor because a carriage had not been sent for him. Not taking any chances, he had hired one of Pike's carriages and driven to fetch the Hartes at the station in the handsomest hack and livery Cambridge could afford. This was quite a measure in a place where everyone from Henry Wadsworth Longfellow to James Russell Lowell rattled along in the horsecar.

The big arrival had taken place on Saturday morning. The ride from Boston was very pleasant, and Howells had quickly gotten on friendly terms with the family. They had all just fit into the carriage—the boys interested in all the novelties they saw on the way and their parents commenting freely on how refined everything seemed to them compared to California. Since then Bret Harte had dined with the Saturday Club, where he met just about every major star on Cambridge and Boston's literary firmament: Louis Agassiz, Longfellow, Ralph Waldo Emerson, Oliver Wendell Holmes, Lowell, Richard Henry Dana, and James T. Fields. On hearing of all the famous names residing in the area, Harte had exclaimed in the manner of one of his own rustic characters: "Why, you couldn't stand on your front porch and fire off your revolver without bringing down a two-volumer."

After getting his invitation to the Saturday Club from Fields in January, Harte had written: "I would this had been put off until the tidal wave of my present popularity has subsided, or until I had done something more worthy—say, my tragedy in 5 acts or that great epic poem as truly American literature for which the world is anxiously waiting—but my daemon wills otherwise and I go three thousand miles to be found out." In the same letter Harte had thanked him for the prose sketch in *Every Saturday* and complained jokingly that the portrait was too idealized and that he would be taken for an impostor when he arrived. It was true, Howells thought, the photograph he had sent had not shown that the skin of his face was deeply pitted with smallpox scars. After an initial look, though, one forgot all about it. Rather, one noticed that Bret Harte had a most fascinating thrust to his lower lip and from between those lips passed the most winning voice and laugh in the world. One also could not help but notice that Harte was a child of extreme fashion. According to Mrs. Howells, all the young ladies were in love with Bret Harte, and Howells had seen several young women in fashionable tie-back dresses flitting back and forth before the house.

Harte was a most charming companion and delightful guest. When the caterers had finished setting up in the dining room, Howells had invited the guest of honor to come and have a look at the decorations. Harte had spluttered with delight at the lofty epergnes set up and down the supper table and had circled it several times to get the full effect of their towering forms. He had also jokingly commiserated with his host for the disparity between the caterer's utensils and china and "the simplicities and humilities of the home of virtuous poverty." From what he had seen of Harte so far, this was rather typical of his humor—mostly ironical, with an agreeable coolness even for the things he evidently admired.

Howells discovered that they had a common interest in Heinrich Heine, whom Harte described half-humorously as "rather scorbutic." When he spoke of literature, it was usually criticism of a general nature, but Howells found that he seemed to prefer to talk about little matters of common incident and experience. Altogether Harte was not much of a talker, yet now and then he had a way of dropping the fittest word and with a friendly glance or smile expressing his appreciation of someone else's apt remark. Though you never could be quite sure of him, Howells had never met a man who was less of a poseur, and Harte had the blessed ability to be able to laugh at himself. Success had clearly not spoiled him.

Two miles from the Howellses' on Berkeley Street, at his ancestral home, Elmwood, on the River Charles, we may imagine James Russell Lowell sitting in his study after the party and thinking of the young westerner who had burst so suddenly and spectacularly in upon them. We know he thought about his name: Bret *Harte*. Whether it was "Harte" from the German "Herz" ("heart") via English or rather from "Hirsch" ("hart" or "malehind"), to Lowell the name sounded Jewish. Regardless, to his way of thinking there was no doubt that Bret Harte had a great deal of merit, and Lowell believed that in time he would do even greater things. He feared, though, that it might have been a mistake for him to leave California. The chief value of his work was, after all, in its "local color."

At the Howellses' party, they had discussed one of Lowell's recent poems, "The Cathedral," which Harte had given a bad review in the *Overland Monthly*. Harte had repeated that he found the phrasing of some of the verses overliterary. By way of positive criticism, though, he had added that he thought Lowell had written one of his finest lines in the *Biglow Papers,* when he described how the boblink "Runs down, a brook o' laughter, thru the air." Lowell might have thought it funny he should mention the *Biglow Papers.* Talking with his old friend Howells earlier that week, Lowell had told him that witnessing Harte's recent overnight success had reminded him of the time, twenty-five years before, when his own satirical verses in dialect had been all the talk. Bret Harte was only a boy back then.

Apart from what Elinor Howells recorded in a letter to some friends, we have no record of what Bret Harte was thinking after his momentous reception at the Howellses'. Mrs. Howells could report that her guests "said they had a pleasant evening and seemed to like Cambridge people." "We liked Mr. Harte exceedingly," she added, "and Mrs. Harte too. He is bland, modest and good natured—quite elegant in his manners, and Mrs. Harte is stylish, dignified and sensible to a degree. Of course they are not quite au fait in everything, but they give you the idea of polished, cultivated people. . . . Mr. Harte is not as good looking as the pictures make him out, and Mrs. Harte is positively plain."

After sitting up with his host discussing the party and the guests, a talk which quickly degenerated into delicious giggles, we may imagine that Harte stopped by the nursery on the way to his room. Standing over his sleeping boys—Wodie, seven, and little Frankie, who would be six the following Sunday—he might have thought of his own childhood. Meeting his childhood friend Andrew Anthony at the party that evening, now a well-known engraver and a married man like himself, would certainly have brought back memories of his early years in New York.

Maybe Bret Harte thought of his dead brother as he went to bed that evening. What would Henry have thought if he could have seen his little brother Frank the guest of honor at a large party, with the literary elite of Cambridge and Boston coming out to meet him? Maybe Harte thought of his father, dead for over a quarter of a century, who had struggled so hard to support his family as a schoolteacher. Here his son had just been offered the most lucrative contract in the history of American literature. James R. Osgood was willing to pay him ten thousand dollars for the exclusive publishing rights to the poems and stories that he wrote in the course of the coming year. They would be published in the oldest and most respected literary journal in the country, the *Atlantic Monthly*.

At unhappy times, Harte had dreamt as a boy of making a three years' journey and returning home changed beyond recognition with a great deal of money in little bags marked twenty thousand and thirty thousand dollars. He would drive home in a carriage, just as his Uncle Ned had done when he came back from Europe, and create a sensation and have his aunt bring out the pie that she only gave to company. Then he would say, "Behold, your long lost nephew!" or words to that effect and immediately drive away, leaving them petrified with astonishment.

In a sense, Bret Harte had finally made that journey, and now he had come home to reap the rewards. When he arrived in New York by train on February 20, 1871, it was exactly seventeen years to the day since he and his little sister Maggie had left the city aboard the prophetically named *Star of the West,* bound for California. There had been time for a reunion with his older sister Eliza, her husband of twenty years, Fred Knaufft, and their large brood, but they had soon been off again to come to Boston and the village of Cambridge, the navel of literary America.

On the day of his arrival, among the many literary celebrities present for the customary midday dinner of the Saturday Club, Harte had the pleasure of meeting Oliver Wendell Holmes, whose poem "De Sauty" had inspired one of his own early satirical excursions and popular successes, "To the Pliocene Skull." The Howellses' party on Monday had been only the beginning of a whole series of entertainments. He had dined at Lowell's Elmwood on Tuesday; Howells had accompanied him to Longfellow's on Wednesday and to a dinner at Professor Agassiz's home on Quincy Street on Thursday. Louis Agassiz, the noted Swiss naturalist and professor at Harvard, had greatly amused him at the Howellses' party by approaching him over the coffee cups quoting a passage from one of Harte's dialect poems, "The Society Upon the Stanislaus." Yet, the opportunity to get to know Henry Wadsworth Longfellow was the finest experience of the week in Cambridge. They had met several times—at the Saturday Club, at the Howellses, at Agassiz's dinner party on Thursday, and Longfellow had twice been his host—but it was the walk they had together after Lowell's dinner party on Tuesday that Harte would always remember. It was then he felt he had verily begun to know the man.

For Bret Harte, it must have been almost unutterably strange suddenly to be surrounded by the names and faces of the great American poets he had known and loved since he was a boy and to be an honored guest in their homes. Only five years before, when he wrote to Holmes, he had not published a single book. Three years ago, the *Californian* had folded and he had only had the precarious prospect of the editorship of a new West Coast literary magazine to look forward to. The *Overland Monthly* had been the making of him, and Harte could honestly say that he had been the making of the *Overland.* As Howells had so graciously written: "When Messrs. Roman & Co. established The Overland Monthly, Mr. Harte was naturally and obviously the fit editor for it, and in his charge it has achieved all its enviable distinction. Without him it would be—the phrase forces itself upon us—Hamlet with the part of Hamlet left out." It was in the *Overland* Harte had begun to publish the poems and sketches of California life that had so captured the imagination of his readers. *The Luck of Roaring Camp and Other Sketches* was selling in the tens of thousands in book form, and his volume of poems was also doing very well. Though he could hold up his head to Longfellow, Lowell, and Holmes, he was determined to do greater things yet. Just think, he said to a friend, of the degradation of going down to posterity as the author of such trash as "The Heathen Chinee"!

The visit came to an end on Saturday morning, when the guests were driven back to the station in the same "vehicular magnificence" as had marked their coming. They arrived in time for the train, which was no small wonder, as their illustrious guest was chronically late. Looking back, Howells could not count the number of times they had rushed out to the carriage with Harte still half out of his dinner jacket. However late they were, he would arrive smiling at their destination, serenely jovial, radiating a bland gaiety from his whole person, and exhibiting a magnanimous willingness to ignore any discomfort he might have occasioned.

On the morning of his departure, they had been sitting reminiscing in the parlor car when Harte suddenly remembered he had forgotten to buy cigars. They both rushed to the cigar counter of the station restaurant, and when they returned, the train had already begun to pull out of the station. Harte climbed the steps of the rearmost platform, and his host did the same to be sure he was safely aboard. When Howells jumped back down to the platform, he missed by a hair's breadth being crushed to death as the train moved through an archway. William Dean Howells would never forget looking up to find Harte waving to him from the departing train, with a cigar in one hand and an expression of mock-heartbreak on his face.

CHAPTER 2

The Shadow of the Temple
(1836–1854)

New York, New York, early 1840s

Frank held his father's hand as they walked down a busy street. They were much farther downtown than the child could ever remember having been before, much farther than he would have been allowed to go on his own. The street was called Wall Street, and as he looked up a huge white building on the right hand side caught his attention. It had a long open gallery with two-story Grecian columns along the front, and if he pushed his head way back, he could just see the Stars and Stripes flapping in the wind from the rooftop. They stopped in front, and Frank's father told him this was the new Merchant's Exchange, built to replace the old one, which had burned down in the big fire of 1841. It covered the entire block bounded by Wall Street, William Street, Exchange Place, and Hanover Street.

After going up a flight of stairs, they entered a large room with two parallel rows of columns running lengthways through it. The room was full of gentlemen wearing high stocks, swallow-tail coats, and tall, black chimney-pot hats, and what was more extraordinary, some of them were jumping up and down and shouting with their hands waving in the air, as if they were trying to catch someone's attention. Frank's father explained that all these men were stockbrokers, who came there every day to buy and sell stocks and that that was what all the shouting was about. They were bidding. When he was lifted up, the little boy could see that there was a raised platform at the opposite end of the room with a balustrade around it. Behind that there was a man standing with a gavel in his hand. He was saying things in a loud voice and banging his gavel on the table. Next to him sat a cheerful-looking old man with big dark eyes, a strong nose, and long white hair. He was busy writing something in a book. When Frank asked what the man was writing, his father answered patiently that he was making a record of the transactions, of who bought and sold what and at what price. He told his little son that the old man with the quill was his grandfather. Then they went away.

On Thursday, July 19, 1855, Bernard Hart died at 23 White Street in New York, the home he had shared for the last eight years with his wife Rebecca, his congressman son Emanuel B. Hart, and those of his other children who were not married. His long life—he was in his ninety-first year when he died—had been one of remarkable success and achievement. Born in London on Christmas Day 1764, he had come to the United States in 1780 and settled in New York. There he started in business, though hardly more than a boy, by representing the interests of the large and thrifty Canadian branch of the Hart family, with whom he had been living since leaving England at age thirteen. For the next three-quarters of a century, Bernard Hart would be actively involved in the commercial and social life of the city. In 1792— now a broker at 55 Broad Street—we find him among the twenty-four signatories of the first agreement between the city's stockbrokers signed on May 17 of that year that laid the foundation for the New York Stock Exchange. Three years later, during the fearful yellow fever epidemic of 1795 in which 732 people died, his heroism was so remarkable that it was remembered seventy years later when Joseph Scoville began writing his work *The Old Merchants of New York City*. On August 13, 1806, Hart married Rebecca Seixas, eighteen years younger and one of the eight daughters of fellow stockbroker Benjamin Mendes Seixas. Hart installed his wife at 141 Pearl Street and there they started to raise the family that would finally consist of no less than eleven children—seven sons and four daughters—eight of whom lived to maturity, the youngest being born when Hart was sixty-three and his wife forty-five years of age. Hart became the secretary of the New York Stock Exchange Board in 1831. It was a post he would hold until within a year and a half of his death.

Bernard Hart was highly respected in the community and the very model of the upstanding citizen and family man. His friend, Assistant District Attorney Jonas B. Philips, wrote of him on his death: "A distinguished trait in the character of our friend was his scrupulous regard to truth—falsehood could find no existence in his heart, or utterance from his lips." Despite his reputation for honesty, Bernard Hart had been harboring a dark secret for more than fifty years. What the world would not know for another half-century and what his wife and children would never know, was that when he married Rebecca Seixas in 1806, he already had a six-year-old son.

In his letter to William Dean Howells of January 24, 1871, Bret Harte thanked Howells for the biographical sketch in *Every Saturday* and particularly for handling "with your usual delicacy a very commonplace history." Either Harte was exercising his customary modesty or he was trying to nip in the bud the inevitable speculations in the press about the facts of his early existence. To Howells he said only that he was "both amused and gratified at your gentlemanly doubts of certain newspaper reporters' facts—or rather their statement of facts—and the kindly way that you gave me the benefit of those doubts." Apparently at no point did he provide his fellow author with any biographical facts of his own. "Upon the hearsay of the newspapers," Howells had written in his low-key article, "he [Harte] was born at Albany, New York, in 1837; and we believe his family is in part of Dutch origin."

A closer examination of the origin of Harte's "commonplace history" will show that it was as romantic as any fiction Bret Harte would ever create. It all began with the liaison of Bernard Hart and a young woman named Catharine Brett. Legend has it that Hart met Catharine Brett during the yellow fever epidemic of 1795. Brett came of a fine upstate New York family and she was a Gentile, born and raised in the Dutch Reformed Church. Catharine's great-grandfather, Roger Brett, was descended from Sir Balliol Brett, Viscount Esher, and had come to New York as a young navy lieutenant and friend of the provincial governor, Lord Cornbury, about the year 1700. Catharine's great-grandmother, for whom she was named, was the daughter of the twelfth mayor of New York, Francis Rombout, and inherited enormous forest estates on the Hudson River from her merchant father.

According to legend, the young couple married in 1799. The marriage of a Jew and a Christian woman was an almost unprecedented event in the America of the late eighteenth century, and Catharine's family apparently threatened to disown her. A son, Henry, was born to the couple on February 1, 1800. After a year, or less, of marriage, they separated. Catharine went away with her boy, possibly to her family at Kingston.

This is the version of the story Bret Harte's biographer Henry C. Merwin had from Harte's older sister. As it turns out, Brett family records show that Catharine Brett (who was born in 1770) married Thomas Jackson of Dutchess County, New York, in 1786. Between that year and 1792 the couple had two sons and two daughters. Catharine Jackson presumably became a widow during the mid-1790s and was then free to marry Bernard Hart. No record of this marriage has ever been found. However they actually met and whatever the nature of their relationship, they had a son in 1800. Sixteen years later, Henry—now grown into a "well-built, athletic-looking man, with rather large features, and dark hair and complexion"—entered Union College at Schenectady, New York, as a member of the class of 1820. Henry Hart, who was to become the father of Bret Harte, stayed in college until his senior year and passed all his final examinations but failed to graduate because a bill amounting to ninety dollars had not been paid. Receipts at Union College show that the previous bills were paid by "Catharine Hart." It is possible that Bernard Hart had ceased to support his first wife and son; if so, it was an ironic twist of fate that his mother's money should have run out just as Henry was about to obtain his bachelor's degree.

Sometime during the mid-1820s, Henry Hart met Elizabeth Rebecca Ostrander, possibly at the Bretts' home in Kingston. She

came of a solid Dutch and English farming family living at Co-
lumbiaville in upstate New York. Her father, Henry Philip Ostrander, was a farmer and surveyor; his ancestors had settled at
Kingston on the Hudson in 1659. Her mother, Abigail Truesdale, was the daughter and granddaughter of officers who fought
in the American Revolution.

The couple was married in Hudson, New York, on May 1,
1827. In 1831 their first child, a daughter, was born and baptized
Elizabeth Cornelia Thorne Hart. Two years later, we find the
family settled in Albany. There Henry Hart taught reading, writing, rhetoric, and mathematics at Albany Female Academy, the
town's leading higher school for girls. The growing family
boarded with Mrs. Pease, wife of a wood measurer, at 289 North
Market Street, and there their second child and first son, Henry,
was born early in 1834.

By 1835 the Hart family had moved to a house down by the
Hudson River, at 15 Columbia Street, where Henry Hart opened
a school of his own. Though a number of buildings from the
middle of the last century have been preserved further up on
Columbia Street, where it rises toward Eagle Street and the capi-
tol building, the house where Bret Harte was born is long since
gone, the river end of Columbia Street having given way first to
the railroad and more recently to Route 787 of the freeway. To
judge from the houses that have survived, Henry and Elizabeth
Hart's third child was born in a small, two-story, Georgian, sash-
windowed row house on August 25, 1836. The Hartes' youngest
son was given the name Francis Brett Hart; Francis Brett for his
paternal great-grandfather and great-great-grandfather.

Frank, as he would be known to his family throughout his life,
was not destined to have his boyhood in Albany. Within a year of
his birth, his father's school failed in the panic of 1837, and the
family left the city. They returned to Hudson, where Henry Hart
became the principal of an academy. This position was apparently also soon lost or surrendered. A daughter, Margaret, was
born the day after her father's thirty-ninth birthday. For the rest
of Henry Hart's brief life, the family would lead an itinerant existence, moving from place to place, Hart opening and closing
schools of his own, working in those of others, tutoring, and
translating. In the late 1830s and early 1840s, they are known to

have lived in New Brunswick, New Jersey; Philadelphia; Providence, Rhode Island; Lowell, Massachusetts; and Boston. One of Bret Harte's earliest memories was of a thrilling feeling when he trod across the green slopes of Boston Common and dipped his bare feet in the frog pond.

Shortly before her death, Harte's mother, Elizabeth, read a biography of the educator and reformer Bronson Alcott and remarked that the privations endured by the Alcott family bore a striking resemblance to those she and her children had undergone. Alcott had made a number of school ventures in the late 1820s and 1830s, which often failed because of his radical and liberal teaching methods. It is uncertain if Henry Hart's lack of success as a schoolteacher was owing to his teaching practices or, as has been commonly believed, to some "want of balance in [his] character" that "prevented him, notwithstanding his undoubted talents, his enthusiasm, and his accomplishments, from ever obtaining any material success in life." It is also possible that parents objected to having a person of Jewish origin, even if he was not a practicing Jew, teaching their children.

The family finally moved to New York City in the mid-1840s. It was of New York that Bret Harte had most of his childhood memories, or at least those he chose to share with others. His father, who was apparently "a man of warm impulses and deep feeling," threw himself wholeheartedly into the presidential election of 1844, to the exclusion of all other employment, and campaigned on the side of the Whig candidate Henry Clay.

The addition of an "e" to the family name, making it Harte, dates from this period. According to family tradition, this was done to distinguish Henry Hart from a man with the same name who was also taking part in the campaign, probably on the opposing, Democratic side. That this man could have been Henry Hart's then twenty-seven-year-old half-brother Henry is entirely possible. Bernard Hart's eldest son with Rebecca Seixas, Emanuel B. Hart, had a distinguished career in the Democratic party, helping to elect Andrew Jackson president in 1828 and serving as alderman in New York, congressman, surveyor of the port under Buchanan and Lincoln, and commissioner of immigration. It is not unlikely that his younger brother was involved in the tumultuous election of 1844 on the Democratic side. In addition to the practical explanation for the name change, Bret Harte's father might have had good reason for wanting to separate himself from a father who denied his existence.

Family legend has it that when Henry Clay surprisingly lost to James Polk, Henry Harte lost all will to live. For whatever reason—the medical cause of his death is unknown—he died in 1845, the year his second son turned nine. He left his wife and four children with no means of support, and for the next eight years they would be dependent on money from Elizabeth Harte's family.

What was Bret Harte's childhood like? In most respects, we will never know the answer to that question. Harte made few references to his earliest years, and when he did harken back, it was seldom to the earliest period of his life. Fortunately, there were other budding authors growing up at the same time who have written something of what it was like to be a boy in America in the 1840s. From the autobiographical narratives of such writers as Mark Twain, William Dean Howells, Henry Adams, and Thomas Bailey Aldrich, all contemporaries of Bret Harte, we can piece together a composite picture.

From the time a healthy American boy was five or six and had exchanged his infantine dress for little shorts and leather booties, his life outside of school hours was an outdoors one. Whatever the weather or the season, his days were filled with games and activities in the streets, fields, and forests, on and in the lakes and rivers of his neighborhood or town. His life was one of constant physical activity; swimming and fishing in summer, skating and bobsledding in winter, and playing a plethora of games all the year round.

Both physically and mentally, it was a rough time in which to be growing up. William Dean Howells describes vividly the harsh and often violent interaction of the boys and their gangs and the terror of being a newcomer to the neighborhood. A boy's life was governed by an unspoken, almost tribal, code. According to this code, a new boy would have to fight any number of his peers to secure a place in the local hierarchy and to be accepted by a gang. Going home and telling his mother about any injustice suffered was the lowest thing a boy could do. It would stamp him as a "crybaby" and would lead to torment and ostracism.

The house was the sphere of influence of his mother and the place where his sisters played, and was shunned by the boys. If he showed his face at home, there was always the danger that he would be asked to perform some chore, such as weeding the garden, or worse, he might be asked to help entertain the ladies that came to call on his mother. Mothers who forced their sons to do the latter were a disgrace, and the appropriate way to right such a wrong, and others equally grave, was to run away.

Both Mark Twain and William Dean Howells indicate that for boys coming to consciousness in the 1840s, the Mexican War was the major historic event of their childhood. Howells remembered how hard it was to be the son of a Henry Clay Whig and the grandson of an abolitionist when the majority of his friends came from families who supported the war. Just as in Hamilton, Ohio, in the little town of Hannibal, Missouri, they raised a company of infantry, and "when that company marched back and forth through the streets in its smart uniform—which it did several times a day for drill—its evolutions were attended by all the boys whenever school hours permitted." Sixty years later Twain could still picture the scene and feel the consuming desire he had had as a boy to join in the struggle against the Mexicans. But they had no use for boys of twelve or thirteen.

They did, however, have use for Frank's twelve-year-old brother. The first dated episode from Frank's childhood takes place on May 13, 1846, when Henry Harte Jr. comes rushing into their mother's room shouting, "War is declared! War is declared!" and announces that he is going to fight for his country. The next four to five months are tense, as Henry tries to sign on with every captain whose ship is even going near Mexico. Finally a friend of Mrs. Harte tells Navy Lieutenant Benjamin Dove about the boy, and he is taken aboard his ship. A new uniform has to be specially made to fit him. On the way to Mexico the ship goes aground on the Island of Eleuthera, eliciting a remarkable account of the accident from the delighted boy to his mother in New York. Subsequently Henry is aboard Commander Tatnall's ship during the bombardment of Vera Cruz in March 1847 and is wounded in the fort at Tuxpan. Commander Tatnall, who was also wounded, wrote Mrs. Harte that on being hit, Henry had exclaimed "Thank God, I am shot in the face" and that he had hidden to prevent them dressing the wound out of fear that there would be no scar to show for his exploits. He returned home a hero when the hostilities ended with the capture of Mexico City in September 1847.

While his valiant big brother sailed for the Gulf of Mexico, Frank stayed home with his recently widowed mother and his two sisters. He was a weakly child and recalled being sent to a seaside village "at a sickly, callow age to be preserved in brine." His sister told one of his early biographers that from his sixth to his tenth year he was "unable to lead an active life." As there were many books in the house, it is natural he should have turned to them, following his older brother's example. Legend has it that he first encountered the magic of Dickens when at age ten he began to read *Dombey and Son*. He read much of Dickens as a child and in this he was no different from other studious boys from "cultured" homes. Henry Adams recalled that adults would read Longfellow and Tennyson aloud to their children, while "the children took possession of Dickens and Thackeray for themselves."

Among the older American writers, Frank read Washington Irving, the widely popular chronicler of his parents' upstate New York part of the world and the region where Frank himself spent a few precious summer vacations with his mother's relatives. He had a clear childhood memory of attending a service in an old, yellow, Dutch-brick church with the delicious fragrance of clover blowing in at the window. Through the glass, he could see the broken tombstones, the yellow dandelions, and the distant Catskills all in one glance. Many years later, while staying with friends at a country house in Staffordshire, he remarked mournfully in a letter to his wife that the rural English countryside was lovely, but he would give much for a breath of the Catskill mountain air.

Of his religious life as a child, we have only fleeting glimpses. While Frank's father, though raised in the Dutch Reformed Church, had converted to Catholicism shortly after leaving college, his mother was an Episcopalian, and it seems likely that the children were raised as Episcopalians as well. We know little Frank went to Sunday school, at any rate. Toward the end of his life, he wrote to a friend who had sent him a copy of *The Holy*

War as an Easter gift that he would read and value it, but as a boy, he had never been able to take John Bunyan seriously. This would prove to be one of Harte's most dominant character traits—an inability to take anything seriously.

Religious allegories clearly had no hold on him. What truly captured his youthful imagination was a satiric novel such as Cervantes's *Don Quixote* or a classic romance such as Alexandre Dumas's *The Count of Monte Cristo*. The latter book would be one of his favorites all his life. He also read much heavier fare as a child; at least he told Annie Fields that he was a lover of Michel de Montaigne at age nine. Fields noted in her diary after a visit from Harte that "Horace and Montaigne are so associated in his mind" and that Bret Harte was "a true appreciator of Hawthorne."

When there was company, Frank would recite Felicia Hemans's stirring poem "Casabianca," based on the story of the young boy who stayed at his post when his father's ship took fire and perished in the subsequent explosion. At age eleven, he secretly submitted a poem of his own called "Autumn Musings" to the New York *Sunday Morning Atlas*. He would never forget the thrill of going to a newspaper stand near his house a week later and finding his poem on the front page. He bought the paper and rushed home with it, but as he exhibited it to his family by cautious stages his hopes sank lower and lower. There had been a general lamentation, he recalled in 1894; his family considered him to be "lost" when he showed the signs of an artistic temperament. Influenced by his family's disapprobation, he had suddenly seen himself in the lean, miserable, and helpless guise of "The Distressed Poet" of his dead father's book of Hogarthian drawings. Harte would later reflect that it was a wonder he ever wrote another line of verse.

Despite apparently being traumatized by his family's negative reaction to his first literary effort, it did not long deter Frank from further attempts. At the age of twelve he wrote his first tragedy. A quarter of a century later, he jokingly observed in a letter to his friend Bessie Ward how this first play foreshadowed the point of view of his later fiction: "[E]ven at that tender age I forecast those great moral truths which my later works have exhibited. In my Play *Gilded Vice* was triumphant and *Simple*

Virtue and *Decent Respectability* suffered through five acts at my hands—as they have ever since done, so the critics say." Harte's sister recalled that when he was about sixteen, he wrote a long poem entitled "The Hudson River." His mother, who was an educated woman by the standards of her day and who apparently had a keen critical faculty, wrote out a lengthy criticism of the poem at her son's request.

Apart from this early incident, we know next to nothing about the relationship between mother and son. It is interesting that when Harte concludes his description of the time he ran away as a child, it is his aunt whom he depicts on his return as rushing up to him and kissing him frantically with cries and sobs. It is his aunt's special pie for company he mentions, and it is her reaction and that of his Uncle Ned he wonders about when he runs away: What will they do with his old clothes? Will they put anyone else in his little bed? Who will they get to repeat "The boy stood on the burning bridge"? Based on this evidence, it would seem probable that at some point, probably while Henry Harte was still living, he and his wife left Frank with their relations in New York—Mrs. Harte's younger sister May and her German-born grocer husband, Henry Kutzemeyer. What Frank felt at the early death of his father we have no record of. In the hundreds of surviving letters, there is only a single reference to his father. This reminiscence also involves his big brother, Henry, and it is the only mention of him in Harte's papers as well: When Henry was a baby he had apparently been given an overdose of a sleeping draught or some other medicine, and his father had had to carry him through the streets of New York showing him the shop windows to keep him from a dangerous sleep.

Many of Frank's childhood hours were, of course, spent in school. His schooling probably began at home, both his parents being well qualified to undertake it. He would later refer to attending the Ellington Institute during the middle years of the century, which would make it the last school he attended. His formal education ended at the relatively early age of thirteen, for reasons unknown. There may have been a reversal of fortunes at the end of the forties, which made it necessary for him to pay his own way. Of his school experiences, we know very little, but chances are he did not have too easy a time of it. A shy, delicate, bookish boy, not overly tall and of slight build, he was sure to have seemed a sissy to the more robust boys. We get one revealing glimpse of his youth from a conversation he had in the late 1860s with his good friend, the Californian poet Ina Donna Coolbrith. She had wondered if he had "bewailed" a bad attack of smallpox having "spoiled" his beauty. He answered whimsically that, no, he had not greatly regretted it and continued: "You see I was a little sensitive, and having been blessed in youth with a girlish pink-and-whiteness of complexion, my companions had got in the habit of calling me Fanny!" It was surely as a young man that he developed the classic defense of the brainy but not brawny: a stinging wit.

After leaving school, Frank was put to work in a lawyer's office, where he remained for about a year. From there he went to work in a merchant's counting room. At midcentury, the Harte family was breaking up. Henry, who had been restless at home since his triumphant return from the Mexican War, was taken on a voyage around Cape Horn by a family friend in late 1849. He finally ended up in San Francisco just after his sixteenth birthday, where he was taken in charge by a relative. In 1851, Eliza, then twenty, married Frederick Ferdinand Knaufft, a leather merchant twenty-one years her senior with three daughters. Toward the end of 1853, Elizabeth Harte, who had been a widow for eight years, went west to California with a party of friends and relatives. On the day of her arrival she married Andrew Williams, who had attended Union College with her late husband. Her youngest son, Frank, who was seventeen, and his little sister, Maggie, were left behind in New York for a few months. They probably lived with their married sister at 21 Irving Place, near Gramercy Park. Not quite three weeks after Maggie's fifteenth birthday—on February 20, 1854—Frank and Maggie embarked on *Star of the West* from Pier Number 2 on the North River, to follow their mother and older brother to California.

"Had he been born in Jerusalem under the shadow of the Temple and circumcised in the Synogogue by his uncle the high priest, under the name of Israel Cohen, he would scarcely have been more distinctly branded, and not much more heavily handicapped in the races of the coming century, in running for such stakes as the century was to offer." Thus Henry Adams chose to describe his own situation upon being born an Adams in Boston, Massachusetts, in 1838. It was a curious choice of analogy for one of the most anti-Semitic American intellectuals of the nineteenth century.

In a more real sense than Adams, Francis Brett Harte was born under the shadow of the same temple. Though his given names rang of a noble English and proud Flemish ancestry and his surname had been altered to distance it from its Jewish origin, there can be no question that the circumstances of Bernard Hart's liaison with Catharine Brett cast a long shadow over the lives of his father and of himself. Henry Harte would live the life of an outcast son and would have to confront the situation, difficult in any age, of having a mixed racial background. His solution was to distance himself from his father and to seek refuge in a religion alien both to his Protestant mother and his Jewish father.

His children, being only a quarter Jewish, were raised without any connection with their Jewish roots, either religiously or familially, and could, if they wished, conduct their lives without reference to that part of their heritage. This was the path Bret Harte chose to take. Throughout his life he told only a handful of people outside his own family of his Jewish ancestry. Ethel Bret Harte, the author's youngest daughter, could relate that her father "never made a secret, in the home circle, of the fact that he had a Jewish grandfather." Yet, in relation to the outside world, it was as if Bernard Hart had never existed. The best evidence we have of Bret Harte's desire to keep his Jewishness from the world is the letter he wrote to the noted psychologist Havelock Ellis in 1889. The latter, taking "a general interest in the ancestry of genius," had written to him to ask him about his family background. Harte answered promptly: "I am afraid I have not given that attention to my ancestry which distinguishes my republican fellow countrymen in Europe but in reply to your inquiry I think I am safe in saying that, to the best of my knowledge, my *mother* and her immediate ancestors were descended from the Early Dutch (Holland) settlers in America, while my *father* and his immediate ancestors were as distinctly English in origin." Harte's heritage was, of course, considerably more "mixed" than he let on. Though Harte told no untruth, we may agree with Ellis's response (on finding out from another source about Harte's Jewish ancestry) that his reply to Ellis's inquiry was "decidedly incomplete." Yet, as Ellis astutely observed, the letter "remains of interest as the account he wished to present to the world." In 1878, Mark Twain had noted in a letter to William Dean Howells that "he [Harte] hides his Jewish birth as carefully as if he considered it a disgrace." Mark Twain was one of the few friends Harte had confided in, probably in the mid-1860s when they first became friends in San Francisco and before the fame that was to come had visited either of them. It was that fame that would ultimately force Bret Harte to confront his heritage and to decide whether to deny or accept it in the face of the world.

In the United States during the last century there was a marked ambivalence in people's attitudes toward Jewish Americans. At early century, when there were relatively few Jews in the United States, prejudice could flourish through simple ignorance, caused by a lack of contact with them. When, in the 1870s and the following decades, the influx of Jews became large, they would be perceived as a threat. Throughout the century, there can be no question that there was very real prejudice against them in America, be it on religious or secular grounds. The perception of the Jew as Christ-killer would in Bret Harte's own generation be supplemented and partly displaced by other popular misconceptions, such as the Jew as the "quintessential parvenu" and as the evil and powerful international money broker who was about to take over the world.

The latter was only a contemporary development of the age-old Shylock image. It was this image that struck fear in the hearts of even some of the most intelligent and learned men of the age, men such as James Russell Lowell and Henry Adams. On a journey down the Nile in January 1898, John Hay—a longtime friend of both Harte and Adams—found Adams "clean daft over the Dreyfus affair" and "was amazed to see a sensible man so wild." Adams was still fuming in March that same year, when Hay wrote to a mutual friend that Adams "now believes the earthquake at Krakatoa was the work of Zola and when he saw Vesuvius reddening the midnight air he searched the horizon to find a Jew stoking the fire."

James Russell Lowell's anti-Semitism, which was curiously

mixed with an admiration for the Jews' often marked artistic abilities, manifested itself in a mania for unearthing hidden Jewish origins, which many people noticed. One such observer, Virginia Woolf's father, Leslie Stephen, described Lowell's "ingenuity in discovering that everyone was in some way descended from Jews." William Dean Howells recalled that at their initial meeting in Boston in the early 1860s almost the first question Lowell asked him was about the origin of his name, which, being thoroughly Welsh, afforded no cause for further examination. One wonders if Lowell asked Bret Harte about his name when they first met in February 1871 and, if so, what Harte answered. We can be certain that Lowell wondered about it. Howells recalled years later that "Lowell owned the brilliancy and uncommonness of Harte's gift, while he sumptuously satisfied his passion of finding everybody more or less a Jew in finding that Harte was at least half a Jew on his father's side; he had long contended for the Hebraicism of the name." Knowing that his continued success was at least in part dependent on being one of the boys among the literary oligarchy in the East, Bret Harte was perhaps not unwise in being reticent about his Hebrew origins.

We may wonder what was Harte's own attitude toward the people whose blood flowed in his veins. It must have been a strange experience growing up trying to reconcile his one brief impression of his hoary, rubicund Jewish grandfather with the images he encountered in his reading. If at Sunday School he was exposed to the much used and representative textbook by Sarah Peabody, *Sabbath Lessons,* he would find there numerous references to the "perverse Jews." In Shakespeare there was Shylock, the murderously vengeful moneylender; in Dickens's *Oliver Twist* there was Fagin.

In the letters from Bret Harte that have come down to us, even those to his wife and children, there is no mention of his Jewish heritage. In fact, there is nary a mention of Jews at all, save a passing reference to "these lying Jew publishers!" in a letter from 1880. This seems to indicate that in relation to certain persons Harte felt inclined to make use of the current racial slurs. We gain little further enlightenment about his real attitudes if we go to Harte's writings. In the twenty-five volumes of his own collected works there are no Jewish characters, and this despite the fact that Jewish peddlers were common in the midcentury California world he depicted. Yet this avoidance of part of the reality he was describing may not have been deliberate. Neither Mark Twain, who also wrote of the West and was not anti-Semitic, nor the other major western writer, William Dean Howells, include a single significant Jewish character in their many literary productions. New England authors such as Longfellow preferred to revive forgotten legends of Jerusalem's mythic past. Altogether, major American writers of the nineteenth century showed little interest in the realities of contemporary Jewish-American life.

Yet there is one incident that can tell us something of Bret Harte's feelings about his Jewish heritage. In late June 1877, a poem entitled "That Ebrew Jew" appeared in the *Capital*, a Washington newspaper, and was reprinted around the country. The stanzaic structure of the poem's eleven verses was strikingly like Harte's classic satire "Plain Language from Truthful James," and the poem was indeed written by him. While "The Heathen Chinee," as it came to be popularly known, was a veiled attack on anti-Chinese sentiment, "That Ebrew Jew" satirized prejudice against Jews. The title is an allusion to Falstaff's remark in *Henry IV, Part I*, when he is telling a skeptical Henry, Prince of Wales, of a large party he captured almost single-handed. Falstaff exclaims: "You rogue, they were bound, every man of them; or I am a Jew else, an Ebrew Jew," thus playing on the age-old racial stereotype of Jews as a lying and conniving race. But the satire of Harte's poem was more topical than the title might lead us to believe; it was written in response to an incident that had taken place that summer.

Readers of the *New York Times* on June 19, 1877, found half the front page taken up with the scandal that had just broken in the popular upstate New York resort of Saratoga Springs. At the fashionable Grand Union Hotel there, the well-known New York banker Joseph Seligman had been refused rooms for himself and his family. The hotel's proprietor, Judge Henry Hilton, had instructed his manager that "no Israelite shall be permitted in future to stop at this hotel," the reason being that business had been poor last season and there had been a large number of Jews at the hotel. Evidently the class of customer that the Grand

Union wished to attract did not desire to be in close contact with Jews, and in Judge Hilton's opinion "the wishes and prejudices of the only class of people who can support a hotel like this must . . . be consulted and followed." Further, Seligman belonged to a class not of Hebrews but of Jews who had "brought the public opinion down on themselves by a vulgar ostentation, a puffed-up vanity, an overweening display of condition, a lack of those considerate civilities so much appreciated by good American society, and a general obtrusiveness that is frequently disgusting and always repulsive to the well-bred."

Harte had a field day with Hilton's obtuse distinction between Jews and Hebrews, suggesting that the following might be the true basis for making the "subtle distinction 'twixt Ebrew and Jew" in American society: " 'For the Jew is a man who will make money through / His skill, his *finesse,* and his capital too, / And an Ebrew's a man that we Gentiles can 'do.' " Addressing the originator of this new "doctrine," Harte asked pointedly: "Now, how shall we know? Prophet, tell us, pray do, / Where the line of the Hebrew fades into the Jew? / Shall we keep out Disraeli and take Rothschild in? / Or snub Meyerbeer and think Verdi a sin?" He chose to end the poem with a reminder that the "King of the Jews," Jesus Christ, had died for them all when there was no place for him in his world. It is significant both that Harte wrote this poem and that he did not choose to include it in the Chatto and Windus edition of his complete work, which began appearing in 1880, nor in any later complete edition. "That Ebrew Jew" is the only overt sign that Bret Harte felt a sympathy with the people to whom he partly belonged.

The clear evidence of rising anti-Semitism in the 1870s, particularly among the "cultivated classes," makes it easier to understand why Harte was reluctant to let his part-Jewish ancestry become public knowledge. On the other hand, there were certainly educated people in nineteenth-century America who evinced a sympathetic attitude toward Jewish Americans. Lydia Maria Child wrote a passionate defense of the Jews in 1855 as part of her magnum opus, *The Progress of Religious Ideas through Successive Ages.* Only five months before Harte's arrival in Cambridge, in October 1870, the *Atlantic Monthly* published a lengthy essay by James Parton, the biographer of Benjamin Franklin and

Andrew Jackson and husband of the popular columnist Fanny Fern, entitled "Our Israelitish Brethren," which was an informed and positive account of the way of life and religious practices of contemporary Jewish Americans. It made a concerted and convincing effort to dispel current misconceptions about the Jews by explaining the historical and religious determinants of their prominence in the financial world and expressed a great deal of admiration for their artistic talents and strong family ties, concluding that "America can boast no better citizens, nor more refined circles, than the good Jewish families of New York, Cincinnati, St. Louis, Philadelphia."

To such a family Bret Harte both did and did not belong. Living at 16 Fifth Avenue in New York in the early 1870s, he could easily have walked two blocks over to Seventh Avenue, knocked on the door of his sixty-two-year-old uncle, stock broker and alderman Emanuel B. Hart, and said, "Behold, your long lost nephew!" just as he had dreamt of doing to his maternal aunt when he was a child. Yet he never did. During his and his father's lifetime not by a single word or deed was Bernard Hart's secret revealed to Rebecca Hart and her children. They went to their graves not knowing that they were closely related to one of America's most famous authors.

Over the Trackless Past
(1854–1860)

Over the trackless past, somewhere,
Lie the lost days of our tropic youth,
Only regained by faith and prayer,
Only recalled by prayer and plaint:
Each lost day has its patron saint!

Bret Harte, "The Lost Galleon"

In London, the cold gray mist lay heavily over the parks and lawns and architectural distances on this Sunday in December 1893. Before crossing yet another silent and deserted street, Henry Dam paused to take stock of the house he was headed for. Like a gorgeous chunk of white-iced wedding cake, 109 Lancaster Gate was the eastern culmination of a row of equally gorgeous townhouses, haughtily pulled back from the Bayswater Road. A penguin-clad footman responded not overhastily to the peal of the bell, and, having stated his business, Dam was led to a cheerful room on the first floor and duly announced.

The shrouded light of the morning sun was filtering in through the glass panes, and the heaped up coals in the grate cast flickering shadows over the book-lined walls. The silhouette of the man who rose from the spindle-legged writing table by the window was just over medium height and slender. As he came closer, Dam could see that he was dressed in an expensive tweed morning suit of the nattiest cut, with a pattern of large checks. The man's blanched white hair, cut in a fashionable dome, parted precisely in the middle and artfully combed forward, was in striking contrast to the darkness of his full, well-trimmed mustache. At his neck was an impeccably white, imperiously high, and almost cruelly stiff shirt-collar and a bow tie. A rose on his lapel, an artfully folded handkerchief in the upper left-hand pocket, and a heavy platinum watch chain threaded through the bottom buttonhole of a light-colored waistcoat completed the impression of a studied nicety in dress that bordered on foppishness. Dam had to remind himself that he was indeed face-to-face with the legendary chronicler of the no-less-legendary California gold rush, one of the wildest periods in American history. The Bret Harte of actuality was about as far removed from the Bret Harte of popular fancy as was the St. James Club from Mount Shasta. Motioning him to a chair, Harte resumed his seat at his desk, on which was ranged an incalculable visitation of Christmas cards, and the interview began.

It did not take long for the conversation to come around to the question Dam knew would interest his readers most. Over his cigar, with a gentle play of humor and a variety of unconscious gestures that were always graceful and never twice the same, Harte spoke of the impressions made upon him by the first sight of gold hunting in California. He had left New York for California when he was scarcely more than a boy, he began, going by way of Panama. After a few months working in San Francisco in the spring of 1853, he set out for the gold country, his particular choice being Sonora in Calaveras County. "Here I was thrown among the strangest social conditions that the latter-day world has perhaps seen," he continued. "The setting was itself heroic. The great mountains of the Sierra Nevada lifted majestic snow-capped peaks against a sky of the purest blue. Magnificent pine forests of trees which were themselves enormous, gave to the landscape a sense of largeness and greatness. It was a land of rugged cañons, sharp declivities, and magnificent distances. Amid rushing waters and wild-wood freedom, an army of strong men in red shirts and top boots were feverishly in search of the buried gold of earth. Weaklings and old men were unknown. It took a stout heart and a strong frame to dare the venture, to brave the journey of three thousand miles, and battle for life in the wilds."

Dam asked him if he had been taking notes for future literary work at this period. "Not at all," Harte replied, "I had not the least idea at this time of any portion of the literary fame that awaited me. I lived their life unthinking. I took my pick and shovel, and asked where I might dig."

He had not been a success as a gold digger, and it was conceived that he would answer for a Wells Fargo messenger. "A Wells Fargo messenger," he began to explain, "was a person who sat beside the driver on the box-seat of a stage-coach, in charge of the letters and 'treasure,' which the Wells Fargo Express Company took from a mining camp to the nearest town or city. Stage robberies were plentiful. My predecessor in the position had been shot through the arm, and my successor was killed. I held the post for some months, and then gave it up to become the schoolmaster near Sonora."

To what extent were the characters and incidents in Harte's stories drawn from life? "To a greater or lesser extent," answered their creator thoughtfully, and this statement, like every other expression of opinion from him, was very emphatic, but very polite, in fact, almost deferential in tone. Dam reflected that Bret Harte was as firm in his own conclusions but as gentle in differing with you as an oriental potentate, who might beg you with tears in his eyes to agree with him and complacently drown you if you did not. "I may say with perfect truth," Harte added, "that there were never any natural phenomena made use of in my novels of which I had not been personally cognizant. My stories are true not only in phenomena, but in characters. I believe there is not one of them who did not have a real human being as a suggesting and starting point."

Toward the end of the interview, the talk turned to Harte's experiences on the lecture circuit. "Those lectures were an amusing experience," he said laughingly. "What the people expected in me I do not know. Possibly a six-foot mountaineer, with a voice and lecture in proportion. They always seemed to have mentally confused me with one of my characters. Whenever I walked out before a strange audience there was a general sense of disappointment, a gasp of astonishment that I could feel, and it always took at least fifteen minutes before they recovered from their surprise sufficiently to listen to what I had to say."

As Harte talked his hands became eloquent. The gestures were quiet and graceful, but arms, wrists, hands, and fingers came into continuous play. And when he finally lit upon his grievance—like every other man of note, he had a grievance—he became particularly earnest and the gestures were slightly more emphatic. "I don't object to being written about as I am," he said, "but I particularly dislike being described as I am not. And, for some strange journalistic or human reason, the inventions concerning me seem to have much greater currency and vitality than the truths."

Under the title "A Morning With Bret Harte," Henry Dam's interview was published first in the *New York Herald* on April 8, 1894, and later in *McClure's Magazine* for December, 1894. The thirteen-page interview, richly illustrated with portraits of Harte himself, illustrations from his stories, and even a picture of his two daughters, was a bit of a sensation. It was the first and only detailed account Harte would give of his life and, more particularly, of his seminal years in California.

In the incipient age of mass newspapers, the public was given a constant diet of the minutiae of the daily lives of well-known figures. Famous authors were twinkling stars in the constellation of fame and fortune, serving a function not far different from the movie stars of today. Among these Victorian stars, Bret Harte was for forty years one of the biggest and brightest, yet holding out as well as he could against the constant attempted invasions of his privacy.

Throughout his life, Bret Harte was an intensely private person. One indication of this was his adamant refusal to write post-cards or even to have friends send them to him. He once wrote to a friend on this subject, remarking that he had never sent a postcard in his life and "should as soon think of shouting to you in the street as of taking the General Post-office into my confidence with you." To the never-ending demands for biographical information from fans and the press, he would respond by referring them to some standard biographical dictionary or to the introduction to his *Collected Works,* saying that he had very little to add. When he was approached about being written up in the first edition of *Who's Who* in 1896, he responded with characteristic charm that he quailed at being the only American included: "There are so many of my fellow-countrymen equally, if not more, worthy of a place that I fear they might think that the charming compiler of 'Who's Who' did not, in his American selection, know 'What's What.' "

At the time of Henry Dam's interview, in December 1893, Harte was going on fifty-eight and had been an international literary star for well nigh a quarter of a century. We may wonder what finally made him decide to break his lengthy silence. One explanation is a purely pecuniary one. Harte was sure to have been paid handsomely for his unaccustomed openness, and the interview may have been part of a deal with the McClure syndicate, which had been buying his stories for six years and had just bought his latest novel, *Clarence,* for syndication in the United States. In addition, times were changing. Authors were beginning to come alive to the importance of public relations, of keeping their name before the public, and even if Harte was reluctant to acknowledge this fact, his literary agent would not have let him forget it.

Another possible explanation for Harte's uncustomary openness is that he thought it was time to set the record straight. Harte's reticence with regard to his past experiences, and particularly concerning the time he spent in California, had led, not surprisingly, to a plethora of misinformation. Yet, if Harte wished to correct mistakes in the public record, it is surprising that the interview contains so many factual errors. Granted, he was reminiscing about events as far back as the 1850s, but as both contemporary letters and stories indicate, his memory of his early years was becoming clearer rather than cloudier as he neared sixty. He wrote to his youngest daughter, Ethel, in 1889, after recalling the circumstances of her birth and the death of his mother fourteen years before: "Dear me! I dare say I am getting very old for things of thirty years ago are much more vivid to me than storys [sic] of last year."

Harte's errors in remembering places and dates are not as significant as those instances when he enlarges on his personal experiences beyond the bounds of historical accuracy. These cases lead us to the question of his active participation in the creation of his own legend. One who knew him late in life tells us that "[a] very singular characteristic of one so distinguished as a limner of wild life was his extreme modesty in relating the part borne by himself amid the scenes he so doughtily de-scribes." The same person then goes on to repeat, on Harte's own authority this time, the persistent myth that his hair turned grey under "the continued influence of fear while a rider with Yuba Bill," the latter being the sharp-tongued stagecoach-driver character Harte created. Again we are told that several of Harte's expressmen predecessors had been shot. On the other hand, the historian Hubert Howe Bancroft points out in his *History of California* that stagecoach robberies did not begin to take place until 1859, which was after Harte's brief experience riding on the box seat. This is a typical example of how a truthful starting point, when combined with the stirring portrayals in Harte's fiction, would lure the author into a romantic half-truth, meeting his readers halfway in the complex complicity of hero worship.

Further examples make it apparent that despite his innate modesty and dislike of pretense, Bret Harte could not help but be implicated in the creation and re-creation of his own myth. The famous English actor John Hare, sharing his reminiscences with the readers of the *Strand* in 1908, recalled a dinner party in the late 1880s where Harte was present. "Bret Harte," Hare writes, "was a very abstracted and reserved man until he was drawn out of himself. He sat very quietly until the dinner was half over, when his geniality got the better of him and he blos-somed forth as a brilliant conversationalist, delighting everybody by his graphic descriptions of things he had seen." Though twenty years had passed and he had never seen the story in print, Hare remembered vividly Harte's description of a scene he had witnessed in his younger days when a journalist or a tax collector. It concerned a Creole woman who shot the sheriff to save her horse-thieving husband from the claws of death. Captured, she was about to be hanged, when her bravery in the face of death made her captors reconsider and let her go.

As it turns out, in January 1878, Harte had published a sketch in the *New York Sun* called "With the Entrées," which satirizes just this type of society dinner party. In this sketch, one of the guests, an unpolished Nevada mining mogul, tells a story similar to the one Harte related at Hare's dinner party. "With the En-trées" is a good illustration of the interplay between the roman-tic ideas and expectations of cultivated society and the way the westerner—adventurous or not—becomes implicated in perpetuating them. It also describes the role Harte would unwillingly have to play for the last thirty years of his life.

After relating some of Bret Harte's California experiences, Harte's friend and first biographer, T. Edgar Pemberton, commented in 1903: "Many of his later friends must have marvelled, as I have done, to hear a man whose one idea of life was the quintessence of refinement, relate the rough adventures, and almost squalid surroundings of his youthful Californian days. He had undergone far coarser experiences than he ever put into his stories, or than I can relate here." When Harte was evidently so ill-fitted to playing the role of the quondam gold miner and adventurer and when we are told on good authority that he was "sincere; never a poseur, and with little sympathy for those who pretended to be other than themselves," we may wonder why he clung so tenaciously to the idea that the characters and incidents of his stories were based exclusively on his own experiences in California.

To the modern way of thinking, Harte's active participation in and personal experience of the world he describes is not of great importance; he might as well have conjured up the "Bret Harte Country" from a loft in Greenwich Village as from direct observations in the field. This is because our age values imagination over observation; we marvel at an author's ability to create characters and incidents we realize he or she can have no personal cognizance of. We also read fiction for somewhat different reasons today than did the more serious-minded and influential portion of the Victorian reading public. Unlike them, we read more for identification than information and more for enjoyment than for enlightenment. From this perspective, psychological realism, however outlandish the situations or far-fetched the characters, will always win hands down over strict "slice of life" historical realism. Today the intense and prolonged discussion during the end of the last and the beginning of this century about whether Bret Harte gave a historically accurate portrayal of life during the California gold rush and, concomitantly, whether his stories were based on places he had seen, people he had known, and things he himself had done, seems a barren one. As long as his characters live, and surprisingly many of them do, doubts as to the verisimilitude of the Pike County dialect he created or niggling criticisms about the poppies being the wrong color or the moon being in the wrong part of the sky do not seem of great pith and moment.

More to the point, Bret Harte's Victorian readers took quite another view of the matter. To their way of thinking, a serious writer had a moral obligation to tell the truth and to base his fiction on the solid ground of personal experience. The most influential perpetrator of this view, which was prevalent if not unanimous, was the novelist and founder of the Society of Authors, Sir Walter Besant. Besant stated in no uncertain terms in his *The Art of Fiction* (1884) that "First, and before everything else, there is the Rule that everything in Fiction which is invented and is not the result of personal experience and observation is worthless." An adjunct to this was an increasing concern with realistic character portrayal and mimetic accuracy in the picturing of facts and events. During the late nineteenth century, "unnatural" became a frequent term of abuse in relation to both situations and characters. Portrayers of distant lands and peoples would be taken seriously only to the extent that their fiction could be seen as a realistic and informative picture of a specific region during a certain historical period. Thus it was shocking to William Dean Howells that Harte could not recognize an azalea bush, when he had his drunken hero Sandy Morton lying comatose under one in the very first sentence of "The Iliad of Sandy Bar." Equally, readers simply could not believe, insisting for years that it must have been a printing error, that Harte portrayed his cheating "Heathen Chinee" cardplayer with twenty *packs* up his sleeves, when it was a well-known fact that only the *jacks* were valuable in euchre. Despite these occasional lapses in verisimilitude, which contemporary reviewers delighted in pouncing on, Bret Harte was chiefly valued as the chronicler of the California gold rush of the late 1840s and 1850s. It was the same with his follower, Rudyard Kipling, who was highly regarded as the faithful recorder of facts about Anglo-Indian society at the end of the century.

With his incredible plots and outlandish characters, Harte was ever teetering on the edge of implausibility and the critical condemnation this would bring with it. On the background of the ruling Victorian aesthetic ideology I have just outlined, it becomes clear why Harte insisted so strongly on the documentary rather than the imaginative value of his work. If he were not to lose credibility, he himself *had* to be the guarantor for the truth value of his own stories, and realizing this goes far to explain the web of half-truths and untruths he became entangled in. It was necessary for his professional survival to reinforce ever more strongly the idea summed up in an article in *Belgravia* in 1881, that "Bret Harte wrote of things he had seen, of men he had known; wrote, as is so rarely done, of what he had felt or experienced."

When we left our hero, the year was 1854, the month February, Frank Harte was seventeen and a half years old and bound for California with his little sister, Maggie. On this journey he did not go by way of Panama, as he told Henry Dam, nor did he run away from home and cross the prairie on a wagon train, as he told Mabel Haskell in 1892, when she asked him if his latest novel, *A Waif of the Plains,* was based on his own experience. Frank and Maggie Harte went by sea, the first lap to Nicaragua with the *Star of the West.* After an arduous trek across the isthmus, they boarded the steamer *Brother Johnathan* at San Juan del Sur on March 8, 1854, and eighteen days and one broken-down boiler later, they landed at the Jackson Street Wharf in San Francisco. There they were greeted by their mother and their new stepfather, Andrew Williams. Williams, bearing the honorary title of "Colonel," was a lawyer who had arrived in California in 1852. Though Colonel Williams's office was in town, the couple had recently made their home across the bay in Oakland. There they had built a new house at Fifth and Clay Streets, the first dwelling in the area in which lath and plaster were used. It was a handsome one-story house. Its arched wraparound porch was supported by four slender columns and the roof was topped off by a pergola. For more than a year, until the property was lost in a long and costly court battle, this would be Harte's home. His mother and stepfather would live in Oakland for the next six years. Williams embarked on a political career in his fifties and was elected Oakland's fourth mayor in 1857. According to one contemporary witness, "Colonel Williams would never believe that Harte amounted to much as a writer, but he had neverthe-less a great affection for him." During the first six years in Cali-fornia, when he was down on his luck and unable to support himself, Harte would always find a home in Oakland.

Frank Harte had come to California because he had nowhere else to go. His older brother and mother were already there, and he did not get along with his sister Eliza's intensely practical husband. Fred Knaufft chided his young brother-in-law for his artistic pretensions and, together with his wife, was fully occu-pied with their rapidly growing family. In the long run, there was no room for Harte or his sister at Irving Place. So Harte went to California. In his own words, it was "with no better equipment . . . than an imagination which had been expanded by reading 'Froissart's Chronicles of the Middle Ages,' 'Don Quixote,' the story of the Argonauts and other books from the shelves of my father."

In the mid-1850s, Frank Harte was without prospects and vir-tually trapped in a provincial town not yet five years on the map. He did then as he had done as a child: he retired to the world of his books. The tiny pergola room—described by a later occupant as "a skylighted locker"—became his retreat, where he would withdraw to familiarize himself with his growing library. No one was allowed to enter this sanctuary, not even Harte's mother, who brought down a veritable storm upon her head when she broke the rule to go on much-needed cleaning forays. Legend has it that Harte bought volumes of Dickens on an installment plan, paying ten cents a week to a bookseller who took an inter-est in him. He had something of a knack for carpentry and built himself a bookshelf in his room. Later, when the family had moved to a broad, low-roofed bungalow in another part of Oak-land, Harte was responsible for constructing the whitewashed fence.

There is little evidence that he was doing anything systematic to pursue a career during these years. Unlike so many other young men, Harte did not go to California with any express idea of mining for gold. He said himself that "It was only in the lack of other employment that I ever cared to handle the pick and shovel. I never had the faith of a gold seeker. Even the glamour of emigration to a distant and unknown country, did not include the hopeful vision of picking up golden nuggets in the streets of San Francisco." Harte had been given a rudimentary education that fitted him for no specific trade or profession, except maybe that of a schoolteacher, when coupled with his own independent study. Mary Tingley, who used to spend weekends in the house next to where Colonel Williams lived, got acquainted with Frank Harte and cannot remember him doing anything in particular at this period of his life. Family tradition has it that he worked in Sanford's drug store in Oakland.

We have one vivid description of Harte from his Oakland years. At age seventeen, Henry Kirk Goddard was an observant young lad, boarding at the Brayton School and preparing for admission to the second class of the College of California in Oakland. Though he never knew Frank Harte to speak to, nearly half a century later he could still remember first noticing him in the cabin of the old-time ferryboat *Contra Costa* that ran between San Francisco and Oakland. The trip took an hour if the tide was high enough for the ferry to pass over the bar at the north end of the creek. If the boat stuck fast, it could take two to three. Goddard had ample time to observe Frank Harte and his mother:

> It was not possible that I should fail to note such a mother and son as they sat in the crowded stuffy cabin or walked the decks in pleasant weather. She had been in earlier years a singularly pretty woman, for she still retained traces of her charms. I remember well her mode of dress, and was often attracted by a shawl of delicate fabric and color which she wore in a style that was very becoming. In striking contrast was her gifted son. Plain in attire, with a face of regular features, but strongly pitted with ravages of smallpox, without a particle of style in bearing and withal modest to excess, there was nothing in his appearance then to cause one to take a second glance.

In the fall of 1856, we find that Harte has finally gotten himself out of Oakland and gone twenty miles across the hills to the San Ramon Valley. There he is tutor to the four eldest sons of Abner Bryan, the fifty-five-year-old owner of a substantial cattle ranch near the town of Alamo. The first known letter from Harte's hand, dated October 8, 1856, and written to his sister Maggie, describes his new home and the family:

The house is stuck in a deep canyon with high hills on either side
. . . a mere shanty that might be a hunter's cabin in the wilderness
. . . As Mr. Bryan (father of the boys I am teaching) is not a farmer,
but a drover, there is nothing of the rural character of a farm, saving
the corral at the bottom of the field and the haystack at the top, and
the whole place is as wild as the God of Nature made it . . . Mr.
Bryan is a very religious man. The four boys are named respectively,
George, Wise, Tom and Jonathan. They are tractable and docile.
George has religion; Wise is a mighty hunter; Tom, mischevious, and
rides a colt as wild as himself; Jonathan, a natural mathematician.

Tom was thirteen, Wise fourteen, Jonathan sixteen, and George
was Harte's own age or maybe a little older.

Harte's experiences in Contra Costa County and particularly
his eldest pupil, George, made a vivid impression on him. While
working in the U.S. Surveyor-General's office in 1862, he wrote
a story entitled "Notes by Flood and Field," which in its use of
names, setting, and character types has interesting parallels to
Harte's personal experiences as a tutor to the four sons of Abner
Bryan. The hero is George Tryan, the dashing son of a Sacramento Valley rancher. Joseph Tryan, George's bigoted old father,
"thumbing the leaves of a Bible with a look in his face as though
he were hunting up prophecies against the 'Greaser,' " is clearly
a portrait of the elder Bryan. To make the parallel to the Bryan
family even more clear, in the story George is given two brothers
called Tom and Wise.

In this first-person narrative, Harte casts himself as a land surveyor, who encounters George Tryan when he is out on a job.
George offers him his own bed, and the nameless narrator falls
asleep "with the pleasant impression of his handsome face and
tranquil figure soothing me to sleep." In the second half of the
story, the big Sacramento Valley flood of 1861–62 inundates the
region and the narrator returns to try to find George. He is mo-
mentarily elated when an engineer on one of the rescue vessels
indicates that a young man named Tryan has just come aboard:
" 'He's a sweet one, whoever he is,' adds the engineer, with a
smile at some luscious remembrance. 'You'll find him for'ard.' "
Yet it turns out to be George's brother Wise. The narrator later
discovers that George has drowned and mourns over his body
together with George's sweetheart, Pepita. This story would make

it seem that Harte cherished George Bryan's memory and was pondering his fate when the Sacramento Valley was flooded in 1861–62. For reasons unknown, Harte stayed only a short while with the Bryans. By the end of 1856, he was again unemployed.

One bright spring morning, something quite out of the ordinary could be seen on an open country road in Calaveras County, passing in the direction of the Stanislaus River and Tuttleville. It was a thoughtful-looking young man, dark-haired, with large puppy-dog eyes and an incipient mustache on his upper lip. This in itself was not extraordinary. No, what attracted the mirthful attention of a gang of Chinese "coolies" was the youth's getup. Even covered as he was in red dust, indicating a lengthy trek, they could see he was wearing what had once been a white "boiled shirt" and other appurtenances of gentlemanly apparel. In one hand was a pair of varnished leather shoes, looking much the worse for wear, and on his feet nothing but some half-hearted bandages made out of handkerchiefs. His "pack" consisted otherwise of a faded morocco dressing case and a silver-handled riding whip, in ludicrous and jostling juxtaposition with a badly rolled, coarse blue blanket and a tin coffee pot. The revolver at his waist, obstinately refusing to swing properly at his hip, had worked itself around until it was now hanging down in front like a Highlander's dirk. At the onlookers' evident amusement, the young man tried to affect a lofty indifference, but not long after, he plunged headlong into the woods and disappeared.

Thus Frank Harte made his weary way to the mines. He had lost his job as the master of a small rural school when two families—"representing perhaps a dozen children or pupils"—moved to a more prosperous and newer district. Down on his luck, far away from San Francisco and with only seven dollars to his name, he had decided to walk forty miles to the diggings to seek out a miner he had once met in the city. "With only his name upon my lips I expected, like the deserted Eastern damsel in the ballad, to find my friend among the haunts of mining men." In the end he did not find him but came across another miner instead, with a claim and a cabin on Jackass Hill. This young man in his mid-twenties was none other than Jim Gillis, who would play host to Mark Twain some eight years later and inspire "Jim Baker's Bluejay Yarn" and other of Twain's classic tall tales. Utterly exhausted, Harte sank down on the only chair in the cabin and stammered out his story. He ended up staying with Gillis for four days, possibly making a halfhearted effort at pocket mining. At the end of that time, Gillis gave him a twenty-dollar gold piece and sent him on his way back to San Francisco.

What I have just recorded is one possible version of Harte's mining experience. My narrative is a conglomerate of various sources, none of them 100 percent reliable. The main source is a sketch Harte wrote toward the end of his life, entitled "How I Went to the Mines," which was published in the *Youth's Companion* on November 23, 1899. With the exception of the interview with Henry Dam, from which it differs in some details, it is the only direct account he ever gave of his own personal experience in the California gold mines. The ending of Harte's sketch differs most substantially from my reconstruction in that he writes that he finally found his friend's claim and three of his partners but that his friend had just given up and returned to San Francisco. Harte then describes how he was offered to come in with the three men—"two . . . graduates of a Southern college and . . . a bright young farmer"—as a partner in the "Gum Tree" claim. He mined with them for three weeks, even staking out a new claim called the "Tenderfoot" but with negligible success, and there the sketch ends. According to Harte, "How I Went to the Mines" was "a very literal transcript of my own personal experience."

I combine this quasi testimonial from Harte himself, with some other sources to come up with my own account. Jim Gillis's brother Steve would later record that Harte had showed up at Gillis's cabin out of the blue one day, "dusty and tired and hungry and dead broke." He had come to Jackass Hill from somewhere in Calaveras County, by crossing the Stanislaus River at Melones. Jim lent him the money to get back to San Francisco and he departed, never to return. Steve Gillis's testimony is supported by the memoirs of Mark Twain, who would spend three months at the cabin in the winter of 1864 and probably heard about Harte's visit from Jim himself.

That the visit actually took place seems likely, that it is depicted in veiled form in "How I Went to the Mines" seems fairly clear, but the question is when it occurred. George Stewart claims on the authority of Jim and Steve Gillis's brother Bill, that Harte showed up at the cabin in December 1855. Charles Murdock, who knew Harte well in the late 1850s, seems to be of the opinion that he had gone to the mines late in 1856, after losing his job as tutor to the Bryan boys. Neither Harte's description in "How I Went to the Mines" of setting off on a "bright May morning" nor an acquaintance with the climactic conditions in the Sierra foothills makes it seem likely that he would have made the journey in the dead of winter, nor was there any mining activity at that time of year. A further clue is provided by the way in which Harte summed up the year's events in his diary on the last day of 1857: "I have taught school, played the Expressman for a brief delightful hour and have travelled some." When we take into account that he was almost certainly back in San Francisco by March 1 or April 5 and that he left for distant Humboldt County that summer, remaining there for the remainder of the year and, finally, that he told Henry Dam that he tried his hand as an expressman *after* failing as a miner, it would appear to place both his mining and expressman days squarely into the early spring of 1857. Riding up front with the driver and taking on the responsibilities of an expressman may well have been how he got home from the mines, with or without the twenty dollars from Jim Gillis.

The whole question is compounded and ultimately made impossible to answer in any authoritative way by the fact that we have no direct accounts from contemporary witnesses or other historical sources. From the time Harte stepped off *Brother Johnathan* in late March 1854 until the publication of his first poem in the *Golden Era* nearly three years later, we have no documentary evidence relating to his life whatsoever, except the one letter to his sister in October 1856. In the introduction to "How I Went to the Mines," which was cut when the sketch went over the 3,500-word limit, Harte states that he does not think he spent more than a total of three months in actual gold digging, and that not consecutively. Thus we have given the maximum amount of time he spent gold mining in various places. On the other hand, it is possible that he never actually mined for gold at all. Though the detailed and idiosyncratic nature of a sketch such as "How I Went to the Mines" would seem to indicate that it is at least in part a true account, Harte might perfectly well have spent a little time in the mines without handling a pan himself. Steve Gillis was sure he had not done any mining with his brother on Jackass Hill, and, in fact, there has never been a single individual to come forward and say he panned for gold with Bret Harte.

Uniontown, California, Thursday, December 31, 1857

It was New Year's Eve and he was all alone in the house. He preferred it that way, having just barely got over his Christmas follies and forebodings. Today had been just like any other day, though there had been no school. In the morning, he had gone out shooting and bagged a widgeon. In the evening he had done some writing, had given Jenny her lesson and listened to the boys read aloud. In the gathering gloom, bent over the slim, oblong black ledger that contained his diary for 1857, Harte paused to take stock of his situation at the close of the year. He was presently employed as a tutor at a salary of twenty-five dollars per month. Last year at this time he had been unemployed. Last year he thought he was in love; this year he thought he was the same, though the object was a different one. (On second consideration he went back and crossed out the words "in love.") He had added to his slight stock of experiences and suffered considerably. Ah! Well did the cynical Walpole say life was a comedy to those who think, a tragedy to them who feel. He both thought and felt. His life was a mixture of broad caricature and farce when he thought of others, it was a melodrama when he felt for himself. In those 365 days he had again put forth a feeble assay toward fame and perhaps fortune. He had tried literature, albeit in a humble way, successfully. He had written some poetry (passable) and some prose (good), which had been published. The conviction forced on him by observation and not by warm enthusiasm, that he was fit for nothing else, must impel him to seek distinction and fortune in literature. Perhaps he might succeed; if not he could at least make the trial. "Therefore," he concluded with a flourish, "I consecrate this year—or as much as God may grant for my device—to honest heartfelt sincere labor and devotion to this occupation. God help me, may I succeed."

Frank Harte wrote these prophetic words in his twenty-second year, on a farm half an hour north of Uniontown, near the Mad River. He had come to the tiny town of some five hundred people, with its one brick building and about a hundred wooden houses clustered on the northern end of the Humboldt Bay during the summer of 1857. In his own lofty words, he sought "a change of clime." He had grown weary of San Francisco, "of the endless repetition of dirty streets, sandhills, bricks and mortar. The smiling but vacant serenity of the morning skies, the regular annoyance of the afternoon gales and evening fogs." More likely than not, he had come there because he had nowhere better to go and nothing better to do. And then his sister Maggie was there. Married at eighteen to a purser from Maine called Benjamin Henry Wyman, she was already pregnant with her first child.

It was true, as he wrote in his diary, that he had "put forth a feeble assay toward fame and . . . fortune." He had sent half a dozen "Letters from 'Icabod' " to the *Humboldt Times,* published in Uniontown, and they had printed them. On March 1, 1857, he had had the pleasure of seeing his first poem in print in the *Golden Era.* The *Era* was a weekly journal leaning toward the literary. Published every Sunday in San Francisco, it was read by people all over the state. "The cradle and grave of many a high hope," as one contributor would aptly describe it, by the mid-1850s it was the largest journal of its type, both in size and circulation, in California. Harte's poem "The Valentine" was a mock-heroic trifle. It consisted of eleven disjointed couplets about an expectant lover tearing open a letter he believes to be from his "dear girl" only to find: " 'Dear Sir:—The Amount that stands charged to your name, / You'd oblige us by calling and settling the same!' "

The budding poet was probably not a stranger to debt; in Uniontown he had trouble finding a job. As one contemporary put it years later: "He was simply untrained for doing anything that needed doing in that community." The problem finally solved itself in the fall, when a prosperous resident, Captain Charles Liscomb, took him on as a tutor to his two young sons. As his diary records, Harte "commenced school" on Monday, October 19, 1857; present were Charles H. Liscomb, aged fourteen, and Frank M. Liscomb, aged thirteen. On a regular day,

school would start at 8:30 in the morning and be dismissed at
12:30. There was a separate schoolroom set aside for the purpose, which Harte tried to make as comfortable as he could.
There would also sometimes be lessons in the evenings, when he
would teach the Liscombs' twelve-year-old Indian servant,
Jenny—nicknamed "Irving"—to read and write.

Each day he would conscientiously record the day's lessons in
his diary, in addition to his own quotidian activities. One day was
much like the other: school in the morning Monday through
Saturday, a trip to town in the afternoon or a shooting expedi-
tion, alone or with one of the boys. During the five months Harte
kept the diary, he painstakingly recorded every duck, meadow-
lark, teal, widgeon, and ring-necked and buttheaded plover he
brought down. It was almost an obsession. Rain or shine, sick or
well, he tramped out to the marshes with his gun after school,
sometimes also in the morning before breakfast. On December
10, for example, he recorded that he shot a duck ("but couldn't
get him"), a teal, and a snipe, and remarked with evident satisfaction: "I am improving in my skill, and of late have made good
success [one word illegible] shooting. However I must try to persevere in other things." His hunting expeditions were an escape
from the claustrophobia of living among strangers and gave him
time to think. He got himself a dog, Bones, to keep him company.

The diary gives us an impression of a sober, serious-minded,
industrious, and critical young man—early to bed and early to
rise—thoughtful and a mite restless in his country isolation.
When it got too bad, he would walk into town and visit his sister
or the Martin family or Captain Bull's saloon. In the evenings
there would be piano-playing, cards, and conversation. He held
himself largely aloof from his peers, preferring instead the company of older men such as Maggie's brother-in-law, Justus
Wyman, or the Liscombs' bachelor neighbor, Colonel James
Boutelle. On Sundays, he would most often come into town to
go to church (though he found the sermons "vapid," "trite,"
and "commonplace"), socialize in the evening, and spend the
night at his sister's place, returning to the Liscombs' in time for
school the next morning. The cultural offerings of Uniontown
were limited for the most part to the occasional lecture. Harte

received the *Golden Era* every week. In October 1857 he could read his own "A Trip Up the Coast" in their columns. It was the first bit of prose he ever published. The cosmopolitan Liscombs subscribed to the *Illustrated London News* and *Harper's Monthly*. Most evenings he would read—he got through about eleven books that first fall and winter—and write a little. He spent his small salary on clothes, books, stationery, tobacco, and the occasional meal at Captain Bull's.

But there was also a darker side to his existence. The diary gives ample evidence of depression and even despair. Only a few days after moving in with the Liscombs, he came home from Sunday service "*very blue* and discontented." A month later, on Thanksgiving, there was a dancing party in town. Everyone was there; Harte tried to dance, found he couldn't, and was "very much annoyed." He came home "incontinently" in the pouring rain and spent a restless night. Christmas Day was even worse. He helped Maggie prepare the meal, and they had Christmas dinner with the Martins and her in-laws. He was feeling quite melancholy by this point, and attendance at a dance in the evening only made it worse. "What the d——d am I to do with myself," he scratched down desperately in his diary, "the simplest pleasures fail to please me—my melancholy and gloomy foreboding stick to me closer than a brother. I cannot enjoy myself rationally like others but am forced to make a gloomy spectacle of myself to gods and men." The "thermometer of my spirits," as he analyzed it that day, had started at 40 degrees temperate in the morning, risen to eighty by 3 P.M., fallen all the way down to zero by 9 P.M., and by 1 A.M., he was still awake and twenty below.

His melancholia is not hard to comprehend. He was going on twenty-two in a badly paid job with no prospects, stuck in an isolated settlement in the hinterlands of northern California. With his book learning, his store-bought "boiled shirts" and pantaloons, his manners and his mannerisms, his poetry and his sketching, he must have had an overwhelming sense of not fitting in in such an intensely practical and hard-nosed environment. Young Frank Harte was the sort of fellow who wrote "d——d" rather than "damned," disapproved of card playing for money and refused an invitation to go shooting with Captain

Liscomb on account of it being a Sunday; it was "a matter of conscience," he wrote. No fish was ever more out of water.

Contemporaries in Uniontown remembered him well. Charles Murdock, who was five years younger and a friend of the Liscomb boys, recalled the many evenings Frank Harte came to play whist at their home. Genial and witty, but rather quiet and reserved, he was fond of a practical joke and something of a tease. He bore the marks of good breeding, education, and refinement, Murdock wrote in his autobiography, and held himself aloof from "the general." These traits, combined with his extreme fastidiousness, did not make him especially popular among his peers. Jacob Hartley, who knew Harte in Uniontown in 1859, recalled that he always dressed better than the other young men of his class and that neatness was his most pronounced characteristic. He was never so happy, Hartley ventured, as when he could make someone make a fool of themselves. From a different point of view, Sarah Whipple Root recorded in the *Overland Monthly* in 1932 that Frank Harte had made quite a place for himself in the social life of the community. Though he never spoke, he was particularly interested in meetings of the Lyceum, where they would debate such searching topics as "Which is the stronger passion—love or anger?" or "Is intemperance in the use of intoxicating drink a greater evil than War?" Based on her father's recollections, Root tells us that young Harte "was popular, played a good game of whist and while friendly with the young women of the town paid them but little serious attention."

As for Harte's determination to "persevere in other things," the *Golden Era* published two more of his letters in the winter of 1857. On October 29, he wrote the opening lines of a new poem, which he finished two days later. The next day he went in to town and read it to his sister. Despite her youth, Margaret Wyman had taught school and knew her way around a poem. She had contributed to the *Era* before her brother and was probably the one who encouraged him to send them his poems. His latest effort, "Dolores," was an earnest though not particularly profound interrogation of the motives of the fair young nun of its title. It was full of pathos, archaic diction, and a vague sense of Spain, and ended with the poor damsel precipitating herself over the convent wall, to death or new life, we wot not which. After adopting a few of Maggie's emendations, Harte decided to send the poem off to the *Knickerbocker Magazine* in New York. The *Era* had already published ten of his poems, so it was time to aim for greater things. Lo and behold, the poem duly appeared in the *Knickerbocker* in January 1858, marking his debut in a magazine of national circulation.

That same month, Harte's intrepid big brother, Henry, who was living across the bay in Eureka, came for a visit. They all had a regular family dinner at Maggie's place, and afterwards George Tilly came and showed them some daguerreotypes, including one of "a might pretty girl" called Annie Daw, resident at Iowa City. Ten days later Henry returned to San Francisco. On February 2, 1858, Harte was enjoying the company of some young ladies and gentlemen at Captain Bull's—there was "skylarking and nonsense"—when he was called out by Mrs. Bull, who said Maggie was "sick" and wanted Mrs. Martin. Mrs. Martin wasn't home, so he sought out Maggie's sister-in-law, Mrs. Wyman, and got her to come down with him at about quarter past eleven. Not long afterward, Harte became the uncle of a healthy baby girl. She was named Florence and would be known as Floy. Harte was growing restless at the Liscombs', and when the storekeeper and druggist in one, Mr. D'Amour, needed a replacement for a couple of weeks, he jumped at the chance to mind the store for fourteen dollars a week and board. It would make for a change, and he would be able to live in town.

From the time of his last diary entry on March 5, 1858, until October 24, 1858, when his "Patagonian Lyric" was printed in the *Golden Era*'s "Answers to Correspondents," Frank Harte again disappears from sight. He publishes no prose or poetry and makes no other feints against oblivion that might give us a clue about his whereabouts and activities. On the evidence of people who knew Harte during his Uniontown years, it appears probable that he became the master of a private school in or near Uniontown sometime in 1858, after he left the Liscombs and finished his stint in the drugstore. When interviewed by George Stewart in the late 1920s, Mrs. Jas. Todd could distinctly remember having Harte as a teacher in a one-room schoolhouse around the year 1858. Charles Murdock writes in his memoirs,

A Backward Glance at Eighty, that Harte found occasional work in a drugstore and for a time had a private school.

When, much to the chagrin of its citizens, Uniontown lost the *Humboldt Times* to Eureka across the bay, it was determined to found a new weekly newspaper. The proprietors were Charles Murdock's father, Albert H. Murdock, and Stephen G. Whipple, the latter also taking editorial charge of the paper. The first issue of the *Northern Californian* saw the light of day on December 15, 1858. It was a fairly innocuous four-page weekly, containing a little news, a little gossip, a few poems, advertisements, and obituaries. The newspaper office was right on the plaza in the center of town. In addition to the editor, the *Northern Californian* employed a printer, who did the composition and the presswork, and a printer's assistant, whose chief duty was to help distribute the type and to ink the "forms" on the Washington handpress while the foreman pulled off the respective outside and inside forms of the paper.

The latter job of "printer's devil" went to Frank Harte, at a salary of sixteen dollars a month. In his own recollection, Charles Murdock had been slated for this berth on his father's paper but manfully gave way to Harte, whose need was greater. Justus Wyman had brought him to Whipple's attention as a young man ideally suited for the position. In truth, it was a very dirty job for such a fastidious young man. Harte insisted on bringing his own towel to the office when the cleanliness of the one that hung there did not come up to his rigorous standards, and "Harte's towel" soon became a standing joke. In "Wanted—A Printer," Harte described the toil of a printer, "a mechanical curiosity, with brain and fingers—a thing that will set so many type in a day—a machine that will think and act, but still a machine." This passage is typical of the pieces he wrote for the paper. "Our Rooster" on February 9, 1859, is the first we can identify as his. It would be followed by many more items of local interest and passing impressions and reflections, with titles such as "Ducking Extraordinary," "Whiskey," "Geology of Humboldt County," "Honor," and "What Is 'Care and Decency'?" When he had the chance, Harte particularly enjoyed aiming pointed verbal arrows at the rival *Humboldt Times* across the bay.

Realizing that he had a bright young man on his staff, Editor

Whipple let Harte have more and more responsibility. He wrote his first editorial in March of 1859, and when Whipple, whom Harte referred to half-humorously as "my Senior," went out of town on business, he stepped in as editor. He was in charge at the end of October and early November 1859, writing no fewer than four editorials for the October 26 issue and two on November 2, and he was in charge again in late February the following year. As it turned out, one of the two editorials he wrote on February 26, 1860, dealt with a much more explosive issue than the telegraph, schools, or hunting.

We find Bret Harte in the full flower of self-mythologizing in a scene he depicts about halfway through "How I Went to the Mines." Having discovered that his friend's claim is two miles on the other side of the settlement, Harte enters the saloon of the "Magnolia Hotel" to procure some refreshment. While he is standing at the bar about to taste of the drink he has just sheepishly ordered, the crowded room is instantly emptied. At the same moment a shot is fired from the street through the large open doors and answered from behind the bar. No fewer than six shots ring out in total, a mirror is smashed, and part of the rim of Harte's glass is carried cleanly away and the contents spilled, all while Harte stands calmly by, the smell of gunpowder in his nose, anxious only not to reveal his youth and inexperience. Taking up his broken glass, he says somewhat diffidently to the barkeeper: "Will you please fill me another? It's not my fault if this was broken."

As he leaves the saloon, a bearded stranger who has witnessed the scene and noticed the blistered state of Harte's feet, arranges to have him driven to the "Gum Tree" claim. As they part, he claps his hand on Harte's shoulder, saying enigmatically, "You'll do!" Without realizing it, Harte's unwitting grace under fire has made him the hero of the local miners.

It is fairly safe to say that this is not a truthful transcript of an actual experience. That it happened somewhere, sometime, to someone is possible, but probably not to Bret Harte. The sketch "Bohemian Days in San Francisco," written about the same time as "How I Went to the Mines" and published in the *Saturday Evening Post* in January 1900, dramatizes a slightly later period in

Harte's life, but significantly, it contains a scene much similar to the one just mentioned. This time it is set in the saloon of Harte's cousin in San Francisco. Harte again portrays himself as the guileless greenhorn fretting about his youth and inexperience, but the ruffians who have sworn to "shoot each other on sight" never actually come to blows. The cunning saloon owner deliberately spills coffee on one of the belligerents to be able to lure him away upstairs and avoid a confrontation with his sworn enemy, who is about to enter the establishment. By virtue of being less incredible and being set in a more specific and identifiable locale, this latter version is probably closer to the truth of Harte's actual experience.

More important is what the scene in "How I Went to the Mines" reveals about Bret Harte. Throughout the sketch we get an impression of a shy, intensely proud young man, desperately anxious about how he will appear to those about him. This extreme self-consciousness ironically leads to the protagonist becoming accepted as an equal member in the community, as symbolized by the miner's "You'll do!" The point is that during his youth there never was a burly miner to put his hairy paw on Harte's slender shoulder and pronounce these words of approval. Frank Harte would emphatically *not* do in the eyes of the "rougher element," as contemporary witnesses attest. In the *Northern Californian* for October 19, 1859, we find him trying to make light of a prank, which may not have been as genial as he wishes to make it appear. He begins by wishing to thank his friends, who favored him with a serenade one Tuesday evening. "The sentiment was touching—very," he continues. "In fact, we modestly protested against such expressions of friendship. We have frequently been termed by fond and foolish young women—'good looking,' but we do not think even the most loving hyperbole could express our lips as 'roses,' or the potent crucible of love transmute our eyes to 'stars.' For this reason, and from the fact that we have an indistinct recollection of being invited to rest on somebody's 'bosom,' we reluctantly adopt the belief that our friends had mistaken the window." As a young man in Oakland, Uniontown, and San Francisco, Frank Harte was never one of the boys. Despite the ironic distancing and humor in "How I Went to the Mines," it is poignant to find him, forty years later, at over sixty years of age, making himself "hero for a day" and still longing for the masculine admiration of his peers.

Frank Harte did have one brief, shining moment in California. It would mark the end of the 1850s, the end of his time in Uniontown, and, in a sense, the end of his rambling, aimless, haphazard youth. At midnight on February 25, 1860, a small group of white men armed with axes, clubs, and knives murdered more than sixty Indians. The massacre took place on Indian Island, in Humboldt County, where the native residents had invited tribes from the neighboring Mad and Eel Rivers to take part in a peaceful religious festival. The victims, mostly women and children, were either clubbed to death, stabbed, or had their throats cut. The attack was without provocation.

The following Sunday, in addition to a condemnatory editorial, the *Northern Californian* carried an article entitled "Indiscriminate Massacre of Indians / Women and Children Butchered." Both pieces were penned by Frank Harte. In the editorial he commented on the "humiliating fact that the parties who may be supposed to represent white civilization have committed the greater barbarity" and concluded: "We can conceive of no palliation for woman and child slaughter. We can conceive of no wrong that a babe's blood can atone for." His flying in the face of manifest destiny, however warped an interpretation of it, was not universally well received in Uniontown. Charles Murdock recalled that though sustained in his outrage by the better part of the community there was a violent minority that "resented his strictures." He was, in Murdock's words, "seriously threatened and in no little danger." Had he been in mortal danger, though, he would probably not have written yet another article only a week later. There he stated that if the only result of the new Indian Bill in Congress was to propose that they arm themselves against the Indians, they had better stop complaining. This would be his penultimate contribution to the *Northern Californian*. A month after he had written the inflammatory editorial there appeared a notice in the paper stating that "Mr. F. B. Harte . . . who has been engaged in this office from the commencement of the paper, left for San Francisco a few days since, where he intends to reside in the future." Editor Whipple wrote further: "In addition to being a printer, Mr. Harte is a good writer. He has often contributed to the columns of this paper, and at different times when we have been absent, has performed the editorial labors. He is a warm-hearted, genial companion, and a gentleman in every sense of the word."

It seems strange that with this potentially dramatic experience to relate, Harte should have chosen to resort to more or less fabricated episodes of witless bravery, such as in "How I Went to the Mines." During his own lifetime, his plainspoken defense of the Native Americans in the face of brutal aggression and at risk to his own personal safety did not become part of his legend. Bret Harte told very few people about the Indian massacre, it seems. Pemberton makes no mention of it in his two biographies, nor do any other of Harte's friends in their numerous memoirs and commemorative articles.

A likely explanation for Harte's reticence on this occasion, apart from his inborn modesty, was that Native Americans continued to be held in so low regard throughout the remainder of Harte's life that having risked his own safety to defend them against the white man's predations might appear to many people a hopelessly naive act, if not a sadly misguided one. The fact that Harte did not use this particular experience as a basis for any of his stories would also have made it easier to keep to himself. There would have been none of the customary prodding as to the basis for this or that dramatic incident or whether or not this or that thrilling episode was a transcript of his own lived experience.

Bret Harte's swan song in the *Northern Californian* would not be the last time he made his voice heard on the side of tolerance and justice. His broad humanitarian and liberal tendencies would make themselves directly felt in his journalistic writings during the next decade and indirectly in his fiction throughout his life.

It was a fortuitous twist of fate that dropped this quintessentially urbane creature into an uncongenial environment where he could be but an observer, never a full participant. While other men were busy doing, Bret Harte waited on the sidelines, watching and listening, unconsciously storing up a treasure trove of vivid images, romantic tales, and local lore—"[a] great mass of

primary impressions" that not until years afterwards would become "sufficiently clarified for literary use." The qualities that
best fitted him for the creative task ahead were his keen powers
of observation, his empathy, and his uncanny ability not only to
grasp the extraordinary visual contrasts before him but also to
see how the very fabric of daily life in California in those heady
years was indicative of some of life's essential contrasts. Greed
and self-sacrifice, innocence and experience, life and death, god-
liness and sin, love and hate, nature and culture—all were symbolized by the ever-changing, unrelenting human procession
that paraded before his eyes, bent on what was thought to be a
march of progress. Bret Harte's lived experience in California in
the 1850s—in San Francisco, Oakland, the San Ramon Valley,
the Sierra foothills, and Humboldt Bay—would form the basis
for the literary work of the next forty years.

Waiting for His Chance
(1860–1868)

In love with words, he married a girl older than himself,
Settled in carpet-slippers, played Papa a bit,
Went out alone nights,
Watched, waited for his chance.
Lawrence P. Spingarn, "The Journey of Bret Harte"

Had anyone happened to be walking down Second Street where it crosses Harrison Street on the morning of the Fourth of July 1861, they might have noticed a slender young man on the roof of one of the houses, his thick dark hair blowing in the perpetual San Francisco breeze. He was busy attaching a sturdy pole to the balustrade that ran around the top of the house. Fastened to that pole was a large American flag flapping eagerly in the wind, a Union flag, complete with thirty-five stars and thirteen stripes. It was the first summer of the Civil War, and as long as it lasted, rain or shine, the flag would fly from the roof of the family that owned it.

Rincon Hill was a good neighborhood in the early 1860s. It is now entirely gone, blasted and carted away for landfill, but back then you could see the whole city from its top. The charming little two-story house at 315 Second Street almost entirely occupied the small triangular lot it stood on, with a low brick wall against the street and a tiny patch of lawn before it. It was octagonal—a popular shape at the time, as it was believed that it allowed for the maximum amount of sunlight—and had an open veranda running around the first story. Shutters, decorative balustrades, and a single chimney completed its exterior appointments.

This house was Frank Harte's first real home in San Francisco. He had boarded in various places after moving to the city in the spring of 1860, but early the following year, he had moved in with Maggie, who had also left Uniontown for the metropolis. Her husband was away a lot—he had a new job as purser on the PMSS *Cortes*—and she could not very well live alone with her little daughter, especially as she was expecting again. Floy was three and a half that summer, and eleven days after they celebrated the birth of the nation, they would celebrate the birth of her sister Maud. The extended family gained a new member. The previous year they had lost one. Henry Harte Jr. died of consumption in Sacramento on January 17, 1860. He was twenty-six years old.

As the Fourth approached, Frank and Maggie had noticed with dismay the number of Confederate flags that were brazenly flying from the rooftops. Eager to assert their own loyalty to the North, they had tried to purchase a Union flag for themselves, only to find that they were sold out. This did not deter them. If they could not buy a flag, they would make one. Frank got hold of the correct measurements, but failing to get hold of any bunting, they had set to work with red, white, and blue flannel instead, of the kind used to make shirts for the miners. They worked all through the night of July 3, Frank cutting and Maggie sewing, and by morning the flag was ready. Admittedly, the stars were somewhat irregular in shape, but there were the right number for 1861 and from a distance no one would notice their homemade quality.

He was nearly twenty-five years old that summer, and the fifteen months since he left Uniontown had been eventful ones for Frank Harte. Not long after removing to San Francisco, he had gotten a job on the *Golden Era* as a "compositor" at ten dollars a week. The editor, Joe Lawrence, had also offered him a dollar a column to write some sketches for the paper, and Frank had been working there less than a month when his first sketch appeared. "My Metamorphosis" was a rather urbane, risqué little piece about a young man getting caught by surprise while swimming in the buff and posing as a Greek statue to avoid discovery.

By the end of May, Frank Harte had his own weekly column called "Town and Table Talk," consisting of chatty, informal reflections on goings-on about town or other matters that struck his fancy. In the pose of "The Bohemian" he invented a whole fictional life for himself, rather in the manner of Addison and Steele, with make-believe friends called Alexis Puffer, Jefferson Brick, J. Keyser, and Constantina the Peerless. These satirical pieces, with titles such as "The Bohemian at the Fair," "The Bohemian Does the Cheap Shows," and "The Bohemian on Muscle," would be his stock-in-trade for nearly three years. "Town and Table Talk" gave way in mid-February 1861 to the "Bohemian Feuilleton" and later to the "Bohemian Papers."

Neither was he neglecting his muse. Frank would publish some new verses in the columns of the *Era* nearly every month, and there was a story going around town that he set up his poems at the case without a manuscript. This particular legend does not jibe well with the memories of his colleagues on the paper. According to Rollin M. Daggett, one of the two founders of the *Era* in 1852, you could not make Harte hurry: " 'If it came time to make up the forms, and a hole *had* to be filled in a jiffy, Harte wasn't worth a!' " Daggett roared in later years. " 'Why, he would waste more time over a two stick item than I would take for a column." Noah Brooks recalled finding in his own wastepaper basket three of Harte's failed attempts at writing him a simple dinner invitation. Diary entries from his early years in Uniontown also indicate that he would write and rewrite his pieces several times before he was satisfied.

Fate brought two people to San Francisco in the spring of 1860 who would exert a greater influence on Bret Harte's life than anyone outside his family. One was a preacher, the other a society lady. Thomas Starr King was born in New York in 1824. Fatherless at age fourteen, he had had to give up his college plans to support his mother and five younger siblings as a clerk in a dry goods store. At eighteen he became a teacher in a Medford, Massachusetts, grammar school, and after a stint as a bookkeeper in the Charlestown Navy Yard, he took up preaching in his early twenties. Without any formal theological training, he nevertheless became the minister of the Charlestown Universalist Church at age twenty-two. During the eleven years prior to his call to San Francisco, he had been the pastor of the Hollis Street Unitarian Church in Boston, all the while building up a reputation as a lecturer that by the late 1850s put him on par with Wendell Phillips, the Universalist preacher E. H. Chapin, and Henry Ward Beecher. With his wife, Julia, and their eight-year-old daughter, Edith, King arrived in San Francisco on April 30, 1860, and took up his duties at the First Unitarian Church on Stockton Street the very next day. On May 4, he gave a newly written lecture entitled "Substance and Show" at the Mercantile Library Association. Among the large and enthusiastic audience it is quite possible we would have found Frank Harte.

One who certainly was present and no doubt casting no small degree of her own reflected glory on the occasion was Jessie Benton Frémont. Jessie Frémont, wife of "the Pathfinder" John Charles Frémont, explorer, soldier, and quondam state senator, was effectively the first lady of the state of California. The daughter of Senator Thomas Hart Benton of Missouri, she had eloped with Frémont when she was seventeen. Their eighteen-year married life had gyrated with the ups and downs of John Frémont's military and political career. Elected a senator from California in the early 1850s, he had been the Republican candidate for the presidency in 1856 only to be soundly defeated by James Buchanan. In later years, Frémont had devoted himself to running his vast estate, "Las Mariposas," in Mariposa County. Finding the climate in Bear Valley intolerable, Jessie Frémont had taken her three children to live in San Francisco not long before King came there from the East.

Jessie Frémont's new home was set in one of the most idyllic spots in the city. Eggleton's Cottage was one of five houses clustered on a hundred-foot height covered with the dark shrubs that gave it its name—Black Point. At the tip of the point, the property had a commanding view on three sides of the Golden Gate, Alcatraz, the bay, and the hills and mountains beyond. Of modest size, shrouded in shrubbery and clambering trellised roses, the cozy Gothic Revival cottage sat on thirteen acres of land, including a private beach. Jessie Frémont wasted no time in making improvements, adding a glassed-in veranda on three sides, enlarging the parlor, and building a summerhouse. The latter would become a favorite refuge of Thomas Starr King's

when he needed peace and quiet to write his sermons and lectures.

In January 1861, Jessie Frémont wrote to King: "As my hands
are empty I have taken a young author to pet." Toward the end
of her life she would recall that she had first become aware of
the existence of Bret Harte through his pieces for the *Golden Era*.
Being a friend of Joe Lawrence, she had asked him about the
identity of "Bret," as Frank frequently signed himself then, and
the editor of the *Era* could tell her that it was a young man
named Frank Harte. "I had to insist this very shy young man
should come to see me," she wrote in her autobiography in
1897, "but soon he settled into a regular visit on Sundays, his
only time of leisure, and for more than a year dined with us that
day, bringing his manuscripts; astonished by the effect of some,
at times huffed by less flattering opinion on others, but growing
rapidly into larger perceptions as he saw much of various people
to whom I made him known. Chief of these was dear Starr King."

We can imagine that Frank drove out with Jessie Frémont in
her carriage after the 11 o'clock service at the Unitarian church,
which both attended, though originally Episcopalians. At "Porter's Lodge"—thus King had renamed the cottage because of its
commanding view of the Golden Gate—it would often just be a
small family party: Harte, King, Jessie Frémont, and the children,
the Colonel spending most of his time in Bear Valley. The boys,
Charley and Frank, were nine and five. Lily Frémont was eighteen.

After the small-town oppressiveness of Uniontown, to Harte
these Sundays must have seemed like a bit of heaven. Both thirty-
six and in the prime of life, Thomas Starr King and Jessie Frémont were forces to be reckoned with. Highly cultivated and intelligent, they were passionately interested in literature and the
arts and could both wield a pen to great effect. King had written
on subjects as diverse as Plato and *The White Hills, Their Legends,
Landscapes, and Poetry* (1860), while Jessie Frémont, besides
doing much to publicize her husband's exploits, had more or
less "created" Kit Carson as a figure of romantic frontier legend.
Harte could have asked for no more perceptive an audience for
his work.

Among the stories he brought with him out to Black Point

that year were several that would ultimately find their way into his first landmark collection, *The Luck of Roaring Camp and Other Sketches*. "The Man of No Account" was a low-key sketch about a man called David Fagg. "He came to California in '52," the story opened, "in the 'Skyscraper.' I don't think he did it in an adventurous way. He probably had no other place to go to." It was Harte's first attempt at using the California of the 1850s as the scene for a story and was published in the *Era* in October 1860. Early the next year he published "High-Water Mark," a dramatic story about a young woman saving her baby from the ravages of a flood. It was set in Dedlow Marsh, Harte's fictionalized version of the Humboldt Bay area in which he had spent nearly three years of his life. Most significant of the manuscripts Harte read aloud to his small but select audience was "The Work on Red Mountain," a story in four parts that ran in the *Golden Era* during December of 1860. It would be better known under the title of "Mliss," after the name of its young heroine Mliss Smith, daughter of Bummer Smith, a drunken down-and-out miner in Smith's Pocket who ends up committing suicide. Mliss, with her coarse language, her gumption, and her unfailing ability to raise Cain, was in striking contrast to the gentility, piety, and general insipidness of the run-of-the-mill heroine of the 1860s. It would have been interesting to observe the reaction of Jessie Frémont to the girl's antics, not least of all the fact that eleven-year-old Mliss ends up leaving town hand in hand with her schoolmaster.

As 1860 drew to a dark close—with the election of Lincoln to the White House and the secession of South Carolina, soon to be followed by six other southern states—the conversation must have tended more and more toward politics, another of Jessie Frémont's passions. The Bentons were ardent abolitionists and refused to own slaves. Thomas Starr King, a political radical, was also rigorously abolitionist and favored the admission of African Americans into the military. As it turned out, these friends would do more than talk. With Jessie Frémont at his back, egging him on to ever greater heights of eloquence and conviction, the slight, unprepossessing, boyish-looking preacher would in the course of 1861 become the driving force behind the pro-Union movement in California. "Though I weigh only 120 pounds," King said humorously, "when I am mad I weigh a ton!" His ally in battle he described in aptly military terms as "a She-Merrimac, thoroughly sheathed, and carrying fire in the genuine Benton-furnaces." Thomas Starr King's lecture on "Washington and the Union," given in Tucker's Music Hall on February 22, 1861, was only the first of countless of his ardent appeals for the preservation of the United States and for money to help the sick and wounded. During late 1860 and early 1861 a strategy was laid over the dinner table and in the garden at Black Point that would ultimately put California squarely behind the Union cause and bring in hundreds of thousands of dollars for the victims of the Civil War.

To the vast projects and grand designs of his mentors, Frank Harte was at this point only an eager observer. After his year of Sundays at Black Point, we can perfectly well understand the patriotic fervor with which he laboriously cut out the flannel stars and stripes for his homemade flag. Jessie Frémont, who might have instructed him on how it should look, did not get to see it. In early June, her husband had been appointed Major-General and assigned to the Western Division of the Army; they were to be stationed in St. Louis. Two weeks before the flag was flown for the first time from the roof of the Second Street house, Jessie Frémont and the children had sailed for the East. As a parting gift to her protégé, in May 1861 she had secured him a position as a clerk at the U.S. Surveyor-General's Office, which was headed by her good friend, General Fitzhugh Beale. "A man cannot live on praise as a hummingbird does on honey-dew," she said, and left Harte with the princely salary of one hundred dollars a month. He never saw his benefactress again.

After a little over a year as a clerk in the surveyor-general's office, Frank Harte was promoted to a position in the U.S. Marshal's office in the fall of 1862. It was likely this new position and an increased salary that allowed him to make an even more fundamental change in his life. Two weeks shy of his twenty-sixth birthday, on August 11, 1862, Francis Bret Harte married Miss Anna Griswold in the Methodist Church of San Rafael, with Reverend Harry Gilbert officiating.

Of Harte's sexual history up until the time of his marriage, we know next to nothing. In his writings we find recorded various romantic longings, or memories of them, of a more or less commonplace and idealized nature, as if his idea of love was mostly based on books, which it probably was. We can read how as a boy he had felt silent rapture when gazing on the round, red cheeks and long black braids of a "peerless creature" in his class and how after buying a highly colored lithograph of a fair Circassian sitting by a window, he felt that somewhere a young and fair Circassian was sitting by a window looking out for him. At fifteen he had almost fainted from nervousness when on his way to pay a New Year's call on "Psyche—my soul," a girl "so light and etherial [sic] . . . that I remember cautioning her from standing near the chimney lest the draft might take her up." In 1856, when Harte was twenty, it seems he felt drawn to George Bryan, a boy of his own age and the oldest of his pupils in the Sycamore Valley. In Uniontown, he appears to have had a crush on Cassie Martin, a thirteen-year old schoolgirl, eight years younger than himself. In San Francisco, the trail is not very distinct, but we find him on friendly terms with at least two or three young ladies. There was Lily Frémont, a plain girl with a slight stammer inherited from her father and passionately devoted to her mare, Chiquita. She would recall Frank Harte as being "brilliantly clever and intensely shy." Then there was Augusta Atwill, the eighteen-year old daughter of Joseph Atwill, who had a music store on Washington Street. On a visit to Augusta's home on the corner of Powell and Clay on September 18, 1860, Frank wrote no less than two poems in her autograph book. One was entitled "Lines by an Ex-Schoolmaster" and ended charmingly: "I'm like the native born of Maine— / My capital's *Augusta*!" No less charming was a letter he wrote to a Miss Wills upon returning from a week's holiday in the countryside. He was bursting with eagerness to tell her of his trip, how many fish he had caught and how much game, and of his symptoms (he was "an invalid" when he went down), and he closed the letter with a sketch of Crystal Springs done in his "usual spirited manner."

Then, almost before we know it, Frank Harte is a married man. The ideal of the "fair Circassian" or the "simple, guileless figure" of a girl admired from afar has been transformed into the considerably more substantial reality of a woman, her dark hair strictly parted in the middle and gathered in a bun at the back, her eyes mournful and downturned, her mouth uncommonly wide, and her body primly swathed in a deluge of heavy woollen cloth. Anna Griswold is twenty-seven, decidedly plain, and well on her way to spinsterhood.

We can only imagine how Frank graduated from a largely platonic and idealized worship of adolescent ingenues "both young and fair" with "Dewy eyes and sunny hair" to marrying a homely, full-grown woman a year older than himself. There remains no record of their courtship whatsoever, with the exception of a poem Anna Harte claimed her husband had written to her while they were "a courting." Entitled "My Soul to Thine," the poem was published in the *Golden Era* on February 17, 1861, and was a comic description of a San Francisco lover serenading his beloved with the fog drifting wildly around him, damp in his throat, sand in his eye, and suffering from neuralgia. Apart from these brief verses, which reveal a more humorous than amorous attitude, all we know is that by 1862 Frank was a frequent visitor to the organ loft of the First Unitarian Church after services, Anna being the church choir's contralto. Henry Goddard regularly attended services in King's church and remembered observing Frank Harte in the gallery looking decidedly bored, except when he would whisper a word or two to his companions and set them off on a fit of barely suppressed giggles. If we venture a bit further, we might imagine that once Jessie Frémont had left town and his Sundays were no longer spent at Black Point, maybe Harte and Anna would walk home together after church. Anna lodged on Bush Street with her sister and brother-in-law and, it would have been on Harte's way to Maggie's house on Second Street. When he moved to lodgings at 524 Sutter Street he was only four blocks away from Anna.

As for the bride, who was she? Anna Griswold was the daughter of Daniel S. Griswold of New York City and his wife Mary, née Dunham. She was born in Florida on January 9, 1835, and went to California sometime in 1860, where her older sister Georgiana was living with her English husband Stephen W. Leach. Georgiana was the soprano and her husband the director of the Unitarian church choir of which Anna became a member. They all gave music lessons to supplement their income and shared lodgings at 518 Bush Street. Anna also had another sister, Mattie, living in San Francisco and married to L. T. Zander, a clerk with

Wells, Fargo and Company. They may all have come out to California together. As for her parents, it would appear that her mother was dead by the time Anna was fifteen. The 1850 New York Census lists her father as a New York lawyer living with two of his sons, Henry, also a lawyer, and Charles, a boy of ten. Also living with them is Caroline Dunham, who we can presume was Anna's maternal aunt.

This is about all we would know of Anna's family and early life, if it were not for the inquisitiveness of Elinor Mead Howells. When Anna was visiting in Cambridge, her hostess managed to get out of her that her father had been teaching in a girl's boarding school in San Francisco at the time of her marriage and that she was one of fourteen children. She also learned that Anna's brother-in-law, Mr. Starrington, was King's predecessor as minister of the First Unitarian Church. Mrs. Howells got the name wrong, though, it was in fact Joseph *Harrington*. He was the first regular pastor of the church and died of Panama Fever on November 2, 1852, only two months after his arrival in California. With the discernment of the "petite bourgeoise," Mrs. Howells was of the opinion, regarding the Hartes and the Griswolds, that "her family . . . was superior to his."

Regardless of whose family was superior, and they were probably more or less on the same social footing in the democratic San Francisco of the early 1860s, neither family approved of the match. Harte's mother was known particularly not to approve of it. His friends were surprised that he would be attracted to such a plain woman, with a personality that seemed no more appealing. Admittedly, she had a beautiful singing voice, and they shared the same sense of humor, but that was the limit of her attractions to their eyes. On the other hand, there were those who were surprised Anna would risk marrying a man who, despite a steady income, never seemed to have any ready money. She had no money of her own.

That it was an *amour folle,* a case of all-consuming passion, does not seem likely. Love letters from the period of their courtship, if there were any, have not been preserved, but the tenor of the hundreds of existing letters from the forty years of their married life is remarkable for being without romantic or sexual content of any kind. Their marital relations seem to be symbolized quite strikingly by the recurring final injunction from Harte: "Kiss the chickens for me, Nan, and 'don't worrit.' " In the only reference he ever made to his courtship, Harte once wrote apropos his unfamiliarity with horses: "[I]n California I used to ride a mule. That probably prevented me from marrying an heiress. It was a mule that eventually delivered me into the hands of Mrs. Harte." In this connection, we may recall what Mark Twain once remarked about his lifelong friend and enemy: "The higher passions were left out of Harte; what he knew about them he got from books." Exaggerated as this no doubt is, we shall see that Twain is at least to some extent borne out in his assertions by Harte's subsequent relations with his wife and children.

If we can more or less rule out mutual passion and pecuniary motives, we are left with companionship, security, and the force of custom as possible explanations for this union. For a young man with a secure income who is approaching thirty, the regular thing to do would be to find a wife. In Ellen K. Rothman's words, all young Americans at midcentury "wanted to fall in love, and men especially seemed to feel a sense of obligation, even of desperation about it." A lady of small means, on the wrong side of twenty-five who did not relish the prospect of supporting herself for the rest of her life would certainly try to find a husband. Thus it seems, Frank and Anna found each other and determined to make a go of it together.

The newlyweds moved into a house on the north side of fashionable Union Square, which was probably more expensive than they could afford. Within the year, they had moved to a new house in North Beach, where their first child was born. As was fashionable then, he was given his mother's maiden name as his first name and christened Griswold Harte. In a family fond of nicknames, he would always be known as Wodie. On hearing that Harte had become a father, Jessie Frémont wrote to her friend King: "I can't realize Mr. Harte's baby. Tell him I can see him eyeing it critically & taking it to task mentally poor little mannikin—he is not of the *species pater*."

For fifteen months after he got the job at the surveyor-general's office, Harte published nothing. His last "Bohemian Feuilleton" was printed on May 5, 1861, and then the columns of the *Golden Era* knew him no more. Jessie Frémont's plan for securing him a job that would give him more time to write had apparently backfired. But he returned with a vengeance during the summer of 1862, having finally discovered how he could do his bit for the Union cause. On July 20 he made his comeback as a war poet with the stirring lyric "A Volunteer Stocking." It was followed by "Our Privilege" in September. In that poem Harte assured his "brothers by the farther sea" that while it was not the Californians' privilege "To meet the charge that treason hurls / By sword and bayonet," "The same red blood that dyes your fields / Here throbs in patriot pride." Thomas Starr King included it at the close of his letter of October 14, 1862, to the *Boston Evening Transcript*, with the prophetic words that his friend, "Mr. F. B. Haste [sic] . . . will be known more widely in our literature." It was the first mention of Frank Harte in an eastern newspaper.

After Jessie Frémont left California, King had kept up his friendship with Harte. He got him involved in the work of the church, including a committee to raise funds for the families of fallen volunteers. As it turned out, King would also have ample use for Harte's literary talents. At the close of one of his impassioned appeals for contributions to the Sanitary Commission, he would as often as not pull out a piece of paper from his inside pocket, fix his lustrous eyes on the audience, and say he could not resist the chance to give them a royal treat. He held in his hand, he said, some verses contributed by a gifted poet that were too good to keep to himself. Then he would read "Our Privilege" or "The Copperhead" or "How Are You, Sanitary?" in a sonorous voice, bringing out the strong points with just the right emphasis. Harte's words and King's voice were a powerful combination. Over forty years later Henry Goddard would remember the great meetings in old Platt's Hall during the war as some of the most striking experiences of his life. In his opinion, Harte's poems would often do more to bring in money than the fervid words that preceded them. When the final tally was made, the people of California had contributed over one million dollars to the sanitary commission, one-quarter of the national total. Half the contributions came from San Francisco; an average of five dollars for every man, woman, and child in the city.

The most popular of Harte's Civil War poems was "The Reveille." When King read it at a mass meeting in early 1863 it was an instant hit and was subsequently published on the front page of the *Boston Evening Transcript*. Besides "Plain Language from Truthful James," it is probably Harte's most well known poem. At the beginning of World War I it was reprinted in the London *Times* and copied in nearly every newspaper in the United Kingdom. It begins sonorously: "Hark! I hear the tramp of thousands, / And of armèd men the hum; / Lo! a nation's hosts have gathered / Round the quick alarming drum,— / Saying, 'Come, / Freemen, come! / Ere your heritage be wasted,' said the quick alarming drum." Though he was young and patriotic, Harte did not heed this call himself. Even if he had, it is not likely that he would have seen active duty. The sixteen thousand volunteers from California were largely assigned to garrison duty within the state. But if it is true that the pen is mightier than the sword, then Frank Harte struck a powerful blow for the North during the war years, writing no less than thirty-five pro-Union poems between the middle of 1862 and the close of 1865.

In the midst of his new domestic life, his new job, and his poetry, Frank still somehow found time to write prose pieces for the papers. On October 5, 1862, he started a new column in the *Golden Era* called the "Bohemian Papers," which was a more polished version of "Town and Table Talk" and the "Bohemian Feuilleton"—breezy, half-humorous, half-serious reflections, "musings without method" set off by an observation from his window or on the streets of San Francisco. In addition to these almost weekly articles and his many war poems, Harte published "Notes by Flood and Field" in 1862 and an expanded version of "The Work On Red Mountain" in 1863 called "The Story of M'liss."

On May 2, 1863, the merchant Robert Bunker Swain was made superintendent of the United States Branch Mint in San Francisco. It so happened that Swain was the moderator of the First Unitarian Church, a good friend of Thomas Starr King, and through King he also knew Frank Harte, who had been a neighbor on Sutter Street. Harte was given a job as a clerk at the mint, again with the view to his having more time for his literary labors. From the windows of his office on Commercial Street, he could look across to Clayton's, a fancy restaurant run by a distant English cousin of his. Frank had lived in a small room at the top of the building when he first moved to San Francisco, and there he had some of the picturesque experiences he would later elaborate on in "Bohemian Days in San Francisco," including the near shoot-out only prevented by his cousin's cunning. By the summer of 1863, he had been promoted to the position of secretary and head of the general department, with twelve men working under him and a salary of $180 a month. It was raised to $217 a month in December. Harte would keep this position for six years.

The crowning event of 1863 was the publication of a story by Harte in the illustrious *Atlantic Monthly*. Jessie Frémont had not forgotten her young protégé in the West, and she and Thomas Starr King made up their minds that they would make a collective attack on the editor, James T. Fields, and get Frank Harte into his highly respected Boston journal. King made the first approach in January 1862, Fields being an old friend from his Boston days. "I am sure there is a great deal in Harte," King wrote, "and an acceptance of his piece would inspire him, and help literature on this coast where we raise bigger trees and squashes than literati and brains." In October, Frémont followed up. In her opinion, "his is a fresh mind filled with unworn pictures, & having the great advantage ... of cultivated perceptions. I should like," she added, "to be the one to announce any pleasant fact to him. I covet the post of bearer of good tidings, and it will be such to him to have your approval & to be admitted to a place of honor in the Atlantic." But there were as yet no pleasant facts to report. Fields returned the submitted pieces to Jessie with the words: "Your young friend fails to interest. He is not piquant enough for the readers of the Atlantic."

But Jessie Frémont did not give up. In the course of the next year, she wrote at least three more letters to Fields, drawing his attention to Harte's war poems being reprinted in the *Boston Transcript* and *Littell's Living Age*. Harte, she said in February 1863, "has something flaming in preparation for you." This flaming thing was a story called "The Legend of Monte del Diablo," based on a Spanish legend of the meeting of a devout priest and the devil on a mountain in the Sierras. Father José Antonio Haro, a Jesuit priest at the Mission San Pablo in the mid-eighteenth century, dreams of "a new Spain rising on these

savage shores," but the devil foretells the decline of Spanish influence in California in the next century and the incursions of
the coming gringo gold diggers. If Fields wanted something less
contemplative, Jessie wrote, "something to make Beacon Street
say Fie! & rush up stairs to read uninterrupted," her young
friend could manage that too: "You pays your money & you takes
your choice." Fields finally settled for the genteel Spanish legend, which was published in the *Atlantic* for October 1863.

Had you been a resident in San Francisco in the mid-1860s you
would probably have noticed a pensive-looking man with an aquiline nose and a sweeping Dundreary mustache, if for no other
reason than the fact that, even with what looked like limited
means, he made an effort to dress as fashionably as possible. You
might spot him on Montgomery Street on a chilly day in an elegant overcoat with an astrakhan collar lying high against his neck
and turned over with a great show of fur. You would have noticed
that he seemed to delight in being observed but that he scarcely
ever stopped for a friendly word with any of those whose admiration he seemed to covet. He would just peep at them out of the
corner of his eye to see if they were looking and hurry on. At the
Occidental Hotel you might spot him standing against the wall
while others played billiards or you might come across him
drinking alone at Barry and Paton's, the popular bar in Montgomery Street.

If you asked someone who he was, you would be told it was
Frank Harte, secretary of the superintendent of the mint and
author of the clever "Condensed Novels" for the *Californian*. He
was one of the favorite "poets of the day," and while he could
always be depended on to write good verse, the funny thing was
he would do anything to get out of reading the poems himself.
When Reverend King was alive, he often used to do the honors.

Frank Harte did not like people, you would hear. He wasn't
"a good fellow." People who worked beside him in the same
office or lived beside him on the same street didn't know him.
Mostly he kept to himself and was supposed to be quite the family
man. He wrote poems and sketches about his boys in the *Californian* and someone had gone to his house once and found him
on his hands and knees playing funeral with his kids, with a

feather duster fastened upright on his back to represent the plume of a hearse. It was also said by sharper tongues that he borrowed money and didn't remember to pay it back. He had a good job at the mint and no one could figure out where all his money went. His homes—he moved almost once a year—were reported to be simple in the extreme, almost threadbare, so the money didn't go in that way.

Frank and Anna Harte were in fact finding it difficult to make ends meet, especially now that they had two children, and Anna would complain of it openly. One observer put part of the blame on her, saying that she employed more servants than her husband's salary warranted. The couple would also at times be extravagant in their choice of address, if not in the interior embellishments of their home. When their second son, Frank Jr., was born on March 5, 1865, they were living on the ultrafashionable 600-block of Folsom Street, with the mansions of the banker John Parrott and former senator Milton S. Latham just down the street.

As for the couple's social life, despite the rumors, Frank Harte was shy rather than reclusive. If he seemed aloof when you met him on the street it was only because he deplored "the peculiar habit of stopping friends in the street, to whom we have nothing to communicate, but whom we embarrass, for no other purpose than simply to show friendship." Harte would later put the blame for their limited social life on his wife, writing to Ruth Watrous in 1880: "I think you have misunderstood Anna. I believe she *was* glad to see you and would always be glad to see you. Her not returning your call meant nothing—she seldom does return calls. Indeed I really know no one that she appears to care to be intimate with beyond the *members of her family*. As *I* never liked them,—and did not always believe that she did—for they often quarrelled dreadfully—this peculiarity was always distressing[?] to me." This passage may refer mainly to their married life in the 1870s, but the reference to Anna's family members (many of whom lived in San Francisco) would also seem to indicate that her social malaise may have extended even further back.

Among the couples the Hartes did socialize with were the Watrouses, who would be lifelong friends. Frank had first met

Charles Watrous in 1862. Watrous was then U.S. Mail agent for the Pacific Coast and worked at the post office across from the surveyor-general's at Washington and Battery, and they lodged near each other on Sutter Street before Harte got married. There was also Bob Rogers, a wealthy lawyer and his wife, Lydia, and Dick Ogden, a merchant, and his wife, Isabella. Among fellow journalists, Harte was closest to George Barnes, the editor of the *Call*, and Sam Williams, the editor of the *San Francisco Bulletin*, whom he would later refer to as "one of the best of fellows and the most loyal of friends," and he was friendly with Noah Brooks, the managing editor of the *Alta California*, and the journalist George B. Merrill.

New friends could not make up for the loss of Thomas Starr King. Ever since he came to San Francisco in 1860, King had been working himself to the bone. When he fell ill in late February 1864 with diphtheria complicated by pneumonia, his body had no defense. He died on March 4 with the words of the Twenty-third Psalm on his lips—"Yea, though I walk through the shadow of the valley of death, I shall fear no evil"—and was buried with a military guard the following Sunday next to the new Unitarian church on Geary Street, which had been consecrated only two months before. On his breast lay a tiny bouquet of violets from Jessie Frémont, the same flowers he had given her when they parted forever. The magical threesome had irrevocably been broken up, and even the site of their Sunday communions was no longer. The entire Black Point had been confiscated by the government in October 1863 and turned over to the military to be developed as part of the bay fortifications. Porter's Lodge was leveled, the remaining homes converted into barracks and offices, and the whole area renamed Fort Mason.

Harte was perhaps not aware of how serious his friend's illness was. Only two days before King died, Harte wrote a letter to Reverend E. B. Walsworth accepting an invitation to read a poem before the California College on commencement day, June 1. He wrote that he would probably avail himself of the offer of King to read it for him, "not only because I am an indifferent reader, but that in the charm of the Orator's voice Criticism may overlook the demerits of the Poet."

Only a few days later, Frank would be writing a commemorative poem to Thomas Starr King, dead at thirty-nine. Entitled "Relieving Guard—March 4th, 1864," it is one of his more touching poems because, unlike so many of his verses, it seems based on genuine feelings. He would write two further poems about his mentor, "At the Sepulchre—T.S.K. / Sunday, October 9th, 1864" for the dedication of the marble monument and "His Pen" in 1865, and he would name his second son, Francis King Harte, after him. Though he would sever nearly all his ties with California and Californians when he left in 1871, Frank would never forget Thomas Starr King.

The *Dramatic Chronicle* was a daily theater program distributed free of charge throughout the city and financed by advertisements. It also contained a small amount of reading material, almost entirely of a satirical nature. Harte did not usually publish in the *Chronicle*, but on July 4, 1866, there was a poem by him on the second page entitled "The Executive Committee to the Colored Population." It was a pointed attack in the best *Dramatic Chronicle* tradition on the decision of the Fourth of July committee not to allow blacks to participate in the parade. Harte couched his attack on the injustice of this decision partly in the form of a letter in verse from the committee to the applicants. This is the second stanza: "You'll do to fight our battles with, but not / To celebrate the victory when won. / At Petersburg it was your happy lot / To blend your life streams and our blood in one; / But that was War. In Peace mankind are prouder / Than when each hero's face was black—with powder." The decision, the committee averred, had only been made "to save from shame and slight the colored population"; they might come to harm if the prejudices of "Judas Copperhead" and his like were not considered. No, it was far better, Harte concluded, to "withdraw / Till that great day of your prophetic dreaming, / When eyes now blind shall open wide with awe / On that procession that, with banners streaming, / Leads on the martyrs to that heavenly city / Wherein there is no need of this Committee."

We recognize in this satire, the keen sense of justice of the young "junior" in Uniontown who came to the defense of the Indians, the man who in 1869 would unmask anti-Chinese sentiment in his most famous and popular poem, and who would write "That Ebrew Jew" eleven years after that. If there was one thing the young, the middle-aged, and the aged Bret Harte could not stand, it was cant and hypocrisy. Given the time and the opportunity, he would burlesque any point of view he found wrongful, extreme, or ridiculous. Much more than the sentiment and the melodrama he would later be known for, the satirical was his most basic attitude. He could not help but embody the prejudices of his age to some extent—he would later refer to blacks as "this quaint, utterly original, and utterly useless people"—but when it came to social injustice, incompetence, and insincerity, he was color-blind and objective. There were several aspects of the Californian society of the 1860s that would grate on him, and the midyears of the decade was when he let off the most steam in the form of satirical poems and sketches.

The medium for these controlled and cold-blooded outbursts would be the new literary journal the *Californian*. The *Californian* was the brainchild of Frank Harte and another writer on the *Golden Era,* Charles Henry Webb. Two years older than Harte, Webb had come to California in April of 1864 as a correspondent for the *New York Times,* soon becoming the literary editor of the *San Francisco Bulletin* and the *Golden Era*'s most highly paid contributor. Writing under the pen name of "Inigo" or "John Paul," Webb's mode of writing was irreverent satire and his specialty was punning. He once referred to the local Midas, Sam Brannan, as "a thing of booty and a bore forever." In a bravura piece on the actress and fellow contributor to the *Era,* Adah Isaacs Menken (best known for her role as Mazeppa, where she rode nearly naked across the stage), he noted archly that "she is best in her line—but it isn't a clothes-line" and added that her play "rested upon a stable basis."

This expert punster and Frank Harte came up with a concept for a new magazine, which saw the light of day on May 28, 1864. The *Californian* was aimed at a more sophisticated and cosmopolitan audience than the ubiquitous *Golden Era,* and despite its title it was very much a metropolitan literary journal, planning to be to San Francisco what the *Round Table* was to New York. Issued every Saturday morning and with a subscription rate of five dollars a year, it was printed on "prodigally fine" white imperial paper, with three wide columns of large, clean type, and contained sixteen pages in all. "The 'Californian' circulates among the highest class of the community," Samuel Clemens wrote home. Ironically, its very existence was made possible by the increased wealth, luxury, and spirit of materialism that the paper would disparage in its columns.

Harte published his last piece for the *Golden Era*—a Christmas story entitled "The Mysterious Drum"—on January 3, 1864, and then the two men set to work in an office at 728 Montgomery Street, which incidentally is the only one of the many buildings Harte lived and worked in still standing in San Francisco. Among the items on the front page of the first issue was a sketch entitled "Neighborhoods I Have Moved From / By a Hypochondriac / Number One" and "The Ballad of the Emeu." Unsigned, as were all contributions in the beginning, both pieces were by Frank Bret Harte. In the sketch he gave a humorous rendering of the house in North Beach where Wodie was born; he would follow it up with two further sketches on the neighborhood around Union Square and the Second Street house he had lived in with his sister Maggie.

The core of the *Californian* was to be local, humoristic, impressionistic sketches of this kind, written by Harte and Webb themselves as a carryover from their respective columns "Bohemian Papers" and "Things" in the *Golden Era*. Harte wrote some of his finest informal essays for the *Californian,* including "On the Decay of Professional Begging," "Complete Letter Writing," and "A Few Operatic Criticisms." In the first, he regretted that the new Benevolent Association threatened to make "Professional Mendicancy" one of the "Lost Arts," in the second, he gave mock-serious advice on elegant letter writing, and in the third, he made fun of operatic conventions, asking why baritones were "always either unsuccessful in love or inimical to its expression" and why the chorus was "always so unanimous in their expression of sympathy." A final passage from a piece called "On a Vulgar Little Boy" gives a good sense of Harte's high burlesque style. The narrator describes how he first became acquainted with his protagonist when one day the driver of a passing vehicle cut at him sportively with his whip: "The vulgar little boy rose to his feet and hurled after his tormentor a single sentence of invective. I refrain from repeating it, for I feel that I could not do justice to it here. If I remember rightly, it conveyed, in a few words, a reflection on the legitimacy of the driver's birth; it hinted a suspicion of his father's integrity, and impugned the fair fame of his mother; it suggested incompetency in his present position, personal uncleanliness, and evinced a skeptical doubt of his future salvation."

In addition to local observations of this kind, there were poems and factual articles but no local fiction. There was to be no whiff of the pioneer about the *Californian,* no frontier parochialism; in fact the paper expressed nothing but contempt for the pioneer ethos and the fundamental principles of the pioneer's credo, making the editors unpopular among certain factions. The consequence for Harte was that he abandoned the writing of fiction almost entirely during these years and, more specifically, the pioneer scenes and settings he had just begun depicting in stories such "The Man of No Account," "Notes by Flood and Field," and "Mliss." In line with what Franklin Walker has observed as a general trend in the literary development of the West Coast, Harte devoted himself to informal essays and parodies in prose and verse.

It was the prose parodies that would be his most lasting achievement during the mid-1860s. Harte had done a couple for the *Golden Era* when he started writing for the paper again in the fall of 1862, and in the *Californian*'s second year he picked up where he had left off. Between July 1865 and June the following year, Harte wrote no fewer than thirteen parodies of famous novelists. The authors burlesqued included T. S. Arthur, Belle Boyd, Mary Braddon, Emily Brontë, Wilkie Collins, James Fenimore Cooper, Charles Dickens, and Alexandre Dumas. The "Condensed Novel," as a brief parody of a contemporary novel came to be called, was a popular form during the decade, and in this genre Harte was preeminent. He had a keen sense of the salient aspects of an author's style and a pronounced imitative faculty, which he also exhibited in a series of verse parodies. Called "San Francisco, By the Poets," he there parodied Edmund Spenser, Thomas Gray, Sir Walter Scott, Edgar Allan Poe, and Lord Tennyson.

It was obvious that two men could not fill the pages of the *Californian* alone. In September 1864, Frank Harte hired a former writer for the Nevada *Territorial Enterprise,* who had moved to San Francisco in late May and tried his luck as a reporter for the *Morning Call* but had been fired after a few months. George Barnes, the editor of the *Call,* had brought him along to Harte's office at the mint, which was housed in the same building as the newspaper. "His head was striking," Harte would later recall. "He had the curly hair, aquiline nose, and even the aquiline eye ... of an unusual and dominant nature. His eyebrows were thick and bushy. His dress was careless, and his general manner one of supreme indifference to surroundings and circumstances." This "young man," who was in fact nearly twenty-nine at the time and a year older than Harte, was introduced as Samuel Clemens. Thus began a tumultuous relationship that would end with an acrimonious and permanent parting of the ways fourteen years later.

Harte hired Samuel Clemens to write one article a week for fifty dollars a month, the same terms Clemens had received from Joe Lawrence when he did some writing for the *Era* the year before. He wrote ten of these weekly articles during October, November, and the first half of December 1864 before heading off for the Sierra foothills to stay with Jim Gillis on Jackass Hill. When he came back three months later, Clemens brought with him a cache of stories and tall tales, including one about a frog, which he vividly recounted to Harte in his office. Harte and others who heard it, including the comedian Artemus Ward, encouraged him to write it down. When it was finished, Clemens decided to send it off to the East to be included with a volume of humorous sketches by Ward, but it arrived too late and "The Celebrated Jumping Frog of Calaveras County" was finally published in the last issue of the *Saturday Press* on November 18, 1865. Clemens continued to write for the *Californian* until he sailed for Hawaii to write travel letters for the *Sacramento Union* in March of 1866.

In addition to Samuel Clemens, Harte established two other close friendships through the *Californian.* In the early 1860s, poems had begun to appear in the *Golden Era* under the signature "Pip Pepperpod"; Pip for the hero of Dickens's *Great Expectations* and Pepperpod for the sake of alliteration. Behind the fanciful nom de plume was Charles Warren Stoddard, a clerk in

Chileon Beach's bookstore in Montgomery Street who was not yet twenty. Stoddard was an inveterate autograph hunter, and sometime in 1863 he induced Frank Harte to write some verses in his album. The result was "Mary's Album" and the beginning of one of Harte's most fun-filled friendships during his California years. When Harte became cofounder of the *Californian*, Stoddard became a regular contributor of poetry to its pages.

Josephine D. Smith had divorced her abusive husband in Los Angeles in 1861 at age twenty and shortly thereafter resurfaced in San Francisco as Ina Donna Coolbrith. She supported herself by teaching English at Professor J. Mibielle's language school, keeping house for her mother and stepfather, and publishing the occasional poem in the *Era*. Ina Coolbrith became another of the regular poetic contributors to the columns of the *Californian*—writing torrid love poems under the name "Ina"—and the third angle in a triangle of friendship with Frank Harte and Charles Warren Stoddard that would only get closer as the decade progressed.

It is somewhat ironic that up until his breakthrough in 1868, Frank Harte was more famous for something he had *not* written than for what he had. Sometime in the spring of 1865, the publisher and bookseller Anton Roman had dumped a bundle of yellowing newspaper clippings in his lap and asked if he would not consider editing a representative volume of the best of the young state's poetry. Harte had accepted and set to work, selecting from the pile, which consisted largely of pre–Civil War material, picking from the matter that poured in once news got out what he was getting together, and making choices from among poems in the *Californian*. He also asked Ina Coolbrith and Charles Warren Stoddard to give him some of their poems for him to choose from.

The result was a slim, elegant volume entitled *Outcroppings; being Selections of California Verse*, which was published in early December 1865, in time for the Christmas trade. The anthology contained a total of forty-two poems by nineteen poets, from Edward Pollock to Isadora Duncan's father, Joseph Charles Duncan. Ina Coolbrith was represented with four poems, Charles Warren Stoddard also with four, and Charles Henry Webb with five. Harte included none of his own poems, and his name was not given as the compiler of the book.

Harte's poetry anthology met with a landslide of vituperation from newspapers all over the state. "*Outcroppings* is the offspring of a mutual admiration society," wrote one local rag. It was "a Bohemian advertising medium for Webb, Harte & Co.," wrote another, and as a collection of California poetry, "beneath contempt." The book was doubtless a financial speculation, wrote the *San Francisco Bulletin*. The chief criticism was that the collection was not representative: Where was Frank Soulé? Where was Joe Goodman? Where were John Swett and Colonel Baker? And why was John R. Ridge represented by one of his least effective poems? *Outcroppings* hardly contained any work by early poets, with the exception of Pollock and Lyman R. Goodman. Names of countless deserving poets not represented in the volume were thrown at the editor "a good deal in the manner of epithets," Harte wrote just before Christmas; he was "pelted with fragments of verses, as though they were decayed cabbages—a resemblance not entirely inconsistent with their material."

The most lengthy and negative reviews came from the *Sacramento Union* and the Nevada *Territorial Enterprise*. According to the *Enterprise,* Harte was totally disqualified for the job he had taken on because he did not know the poetry of the state well enough. Joe Goodman, who probably wrote the review and was one of the discarded poets, summed up by calling Webb's poems "the very trashiest of the trash constituting the staple of *Outcroppings*." The *Union*'s chief complaint was that the anthology contained little poetry that dealt with local subjects. This last criticism was, strictly speaking, correct. In putting the book together, Harte had clearly followed his own taste and made his selection based on a rarified, genteel, and ultimately East Coast aesthetic. It is also notable that the reception in the East was largely positive, though many reviewers found the contributions not far advanced in style and sophistication.

But the root of the conflict went deeper than wounded personal or local pride. The *Outcroppings* scandal was basically about what direction poetry in the region should take. Should it attempt to emulate an Old World and basically European sensibility or should it strike out on a brave new trail of its own, reflecting the unique California scenery and society? The *Californian,* in the person of Harte and Webb, was clearly of the first opinion. As Franklin Walker has pointed out, in the mid-1860s they were unable to take the idea of a "Western epic" seriously. By the end of the decade all that would, of course, change.

By the spring of 1866, the *Californian* was in deep water financially, and the stalwarts of the crew were bailing out. Clemens went off to Hawaii in March. Webb decided to leave California for good and went back to New York in May. By fall, Harte had transferred his allegiance to the *San Francisco Bulletin,* a quality daily, and the *San Francisco News Letter and California Advertiser,* the most successful and widely circulating of the satirical journals and the "bad boy" of San Francisco journalism. His literary production in these organs was limited almost entirely to poems, often satirical in nature, such as "Mrs. Judge Jenkins / Being the Only Genuine Sequel to 'Maud Muller' " for the *News Letter,* or occasional and commemorative poems, such as the "Ode" delivered on the "Occasion of the Laying of the corner-stone of the California Deaf, Dumb and Blind Asylum" in September 1867 and printed in the *Bulletin.* Though the outlets were different and more various than during the *Californian* years, Harte continued to stay within much the same genres, still eschewing fiction.

In early 1866, Harte had got an even more direct medium for voicing his disapprobation of certain aspects of California society and an opportunity to write topical essays on the contemporary western scene. At about the same time, Samuel Bowles of the *Springfield Republican* and Warren Sawyer of the *Christian Register* had asked him to become the California correspondent for their respective papers. From the spring of 1866 till the end of 1867, Harte would write letters from California, sometimes once a week, sometimes once a month, for these two eastern papers, as Thomas Starr King had done for the *Boston Transcript* at the beginning of the 1860s. By the time he stopped writing them, Harte had contributed nineteen letters to the *Republican* and eighteen letters to the *Christian Register* on topics ranging from the climate of California to the visit to San Francisco of Queen Emma of the Sandwich Islands.

As California correspondent, Harte was in the position to bring some of his fellow San Francisco writers to the attention of eastern readers, and so it was that he wrote one of the first notices of "Mark Twain" in a national publication on November 3, 1866, when he devoted a long paragraph to Twain's "most entertaining lecture on the Sandwich Islands" and wrote prophetically that he recognized "a new star rising in this western horizon." When it came time to collect some of Clemens's sketches, including "The Jumping Frog," into a book, Harte helped him revise the story. Charles Henry Webb published the volume in April 1867, and Clemens, who was lecturing in the East and about to sail for the Holy Land, dashed off a note to Harte to the effect that the book was "full of damnable errors of grammar and deadly inconsistencies of spelling in the Frog sketch because I was away and did not read the proofs." Knowing Harte to be a perfectionist, Clemens begged him to "be a friend and say nothing about these things." When his hurry was over he would send Harte a copy "to pisen [sic] the children with."

Harte published two books of his own in the second half of 1867. The first was *Condensed Novels and Other Papers,* which appeared in early October. To make a sizable book, Harte had gathered together fifteen prose parodies from the *Era* and the *Californian,* and added twelve "Civic Sketches" from the *Californian* and a number of Spanish-Californian "Legends and Tales," including "The Legend of Monte del Diablo" from the *Atlantic.* The manuscript was forwarded to an agent of Anton Roman in New York, who placed it in the hands of G. W. Carleton. Carleton engaged to publish it at his own expense and pay the author ten cents per copy on all copyrighted copies. When Clemens heard about it, he wrote to Stoddard that Harte was "publishing with a Son of a Bitch who will swindle him," adding, "I don't know how his book is coming on—we of Bohemia keep away from Carleton's." This outburst, though it would prove justified, was undoubtedly fueled by no small degree of personal animus. Only a few months before, Clemens had had no scruples about publishing with Carleton's and had personally gone to see the publisher with his collection of sketches. Carleton had not accepted it.

Though Harte got his book published by Carleton, he would soon sincerely wish he had not. The physical appearance of the volume had been left entirely to the discretion of the publisher, and when it appeared it was a slipshod affair with so-called comic illustrations by a certain Frank Bellew. Webb, who saw the book before it reached California, could report to Stoddard that "Harte's book is out. A copy came to me today. Poorly printed, on wretched paper, with most *beastly* illustrations."

Harte was mortified that he should make his publishing debut in such a manner and that the format of the book would deflect attention from its contents. He even felt impelled to write to friends and potential reviewers to explain how it came to look as it did, stressing that he utterly repudiated the vulgarity of the illustrations and that he thought the book had much in it "that is inconsistent with its outward show." The *Atlantic*'s reviewer found the illustrations "in every way vulgar and inappropriate" but praised the parodies and found the miscellaneous essays "imbued with much original humor." Harte wrote to thank the editor, James T. Fields, for his kindness toward him and his work, particularly the book that Carleton "malformed in its birth."

As a continuation of the *Outcroppings* controversy, the most negative reviews appeared in the *Sacramento Union* and the *Territorial Enterprise*. The *Union* found the humor "of a somewhat coarse texture." The *Territorial Enterprise* made veiled accusations of stylistic plagiarism and lack of originality. "His taste fetters him to the classical models of the language," the paper wrote. "He seems to think it incumbent upon him to issue his productions on the collateral security of some acknowledged author." The *Californian* came to Harte's defense, quoting a reviewer in the *New York Evening Mail*, who found the collection "characterized by 'a delicacy and good taste which makes a pleasant contrast with the usual broad and coarse character of burlesque imitations.'"

In addition to the volume of prose, five days before Christmas, Towne and Bacon of San Francisco published a volume of Harte's poetry entitled *The Lost Galleon and Other Tales*. The book contained a selection of the poems Harte had written during the 1860s, including several of his Civil War lyrics. Harte had learned from his mistakes and this time the book was a delicate little edition in a purple binding, which the *Californian*'s reviewer assured its readers was the most elegant volume ever printed in California. The reviewer found that "One of the author's most powerful literary instincts seems to be a horror of the exaggerated, the unreal, and false in sentiment and passion"; he hoped that the book might "find a place on every center table in the State."

At the heart of the collection was the title poem "The Lost Galleon." It was written for the fourth annual meeting of the Associated Alumni of the Pacific Coast on June 5, 1867. Henry Goddard was in the audience when it was read in the hall on the Twelfth Street campus in Oakland and would remember it as one of the "Red Letter Days" of his life. The weather was beautiful, the hall was packed, and a "brilliant" oration by A. L. Stone was followed by the event of the day: Horatio Stebbins reading Harte's poem "The Lost Galleon." Stebbins, who had succeeded King as pastor of the First Unitarian Church, was an accomplished elocutionist. "When the pathetic ending came," wrote Goddard over forty years later, "Stebbins folded his manuscript and stood a moment in silence. He then lifted his face with streaming eyes turned toward the 'Golden Gate' and finished the impressive 'moral' from memory." Some of Harte's friends found the poem "the very best thing of the kind ever attempted." The *Nation* found it "labored." The paper said further of his poems in toto that Harte did not shine in the serious, patriotic pieces—"How are you Sanitary?" being the most successful—but excelled nearly everyone else in comedy: "[I]t seems as if he would do best for himself and his readers if he would forswear unmixed sentiment and make satire and fun his mainstay."

By the mid-1860s, Frank Bret Harte had become the recognized leader of literary men on the West Coast. Samuel Clemens wrote to his mother and sister on January 20, 1866, that though he himself was generally placed at the head of the "breed of scribblers" in San Francisco, he felt compelled to add that "the place properly belongs to Bret Harte." This qualification was not just a spasm of modesty on Clemens's part; there was no question that as a poet, editor, and literary artist, Harte's reputation at the time was further advanced than Clemens's, who never would be a poet, had as yet only published one story, and whose reputation rested chiefly on journalistic pieces for the *Era* and the *Californian*.

When Clemens came back to San Francisco in the spring of

1968 to make his impressions of "The Quaker City Pleasure Excursion to Europe and the Holy Land" into a book, it was Harte who spent many hours revising the manuscript to make it ready for publication that summer. Clemens wrote the entire account in sixty days, averaging three thousand words a day, and had every reason to be grateful for the editorial services of his friend. A few years later he would write to Thomas Bailey Aldrich that Harte "trimmed and trained and schooled me patiently until he changed me from an awkward utterer of coarse grotesqueness to a writer of paragraphs and chapters that have found favor in the eyes of even some of the very decentest people in the land."

CHAPTER 5

The Rise of Bret Harte
(1868–1871)

> The fateful year of 1870 was near at hand, which was to mark the
> close of the literary epoch, when quarterlies gave way to monthlies,
> letter-press to illustration, volumes to pages. The outburst was
> brilliant. Bret Harte led, and Robert Louis Stevenson followed. Guy
> de Maupassant and Rudyard Kipling brought up the rear, and dazzled
> the world.
>
> Henry Adams, *The Education of Henry Adams*

Had we been in the vicinity of Clay Street near Portsmouth Square in San Francisco on July 1, 1870, we might have observed two striking-looking men approaching No. 619, a three-story italianate office building that housed the Savings and Loan Society. The older man, who looked to be in his thirties, was quite extraordinarily dressed even for San Francisco. His commanding figure bore a long linen "duster," on his head was a broad-brimmed sombrero, and on his feet beaded moccasins. His companion, in his midtwenties, looked the very incarnation of the young poet, with his blond curly hair thinning at the temples and dark eyes that seemed prone to melancholy. The one guiding the other, they entered the center portal and ascended the stairs to a set of rooms on the second story. The older man, with the mustache and long curly hair sweeping his shoulders, was Cincinnatus Hiner "Joaquin" Miller, a would-be poet from Oregon just arrived in San Francisco. His guide was the San Francisco poet Charles Warren Stoddard, who had been to meet Miller's boat at the wharf. Their destination was the editorial rooms of the *Overland Monthly*.

Miller's first words on meeting Stoddard had been "Well, let us go and talk with the poets!" As indicated by his poem "The Bards of San Francisco Bay," Miller pictured himself as "a skilless

us go and talk with the poets!" As indicated by his poem "The Bards of San Francisco Bay," Miller pictured himself as "a skilless northern Nazarene" and now he was finally come "to join the youth / Of some sweet town in quest of truth." Stoddard tried in vain to convince him that the poets of San Francisco did not quite correspond to his guest's poetic vision; they "feasted at no common board; flocked not; discoursed with no beaded rills; neither did their skilled hands sweep any strings whatsoever." The best Stoddard could do was to bring him to what had become the Mecca and Medina of the literary West, the offices of the *Overland*.

One was indeed in luck if on a given afternoon one found the editor of the magazine in his editorial rooms. To the despair of his new publisher, John H. Carmany, during the summer months he preferred to conduct the business of the magazine largely from his "retreat" in San Rafael, making necessary a frequent and cumbersome exchange of letters, manuscripts, and proofs through the mails. More than thirty years later, Joaquin Miller would recall his first meeting with the editor of the *Overland Monthly*. He was a spare, slim young man in a summer dress of the neatest and nattiest cut, Miller recalled, who took the new arrival cordially into his confidence at once. Miller liked his low voice and his quiet, earnest, and unaffected manner from the first and thought him the cleanest man he had ever met. "He was always as clean, modest, and graceful of speech as a girl," Miller wrote in the *New York Times* in May 1902, when Harte was three weeks in the grave.

On Miller's visit to the "Clay Street sanctum," he found an elegant, neat, and pleasant set of rooms with attractive murals on the walls done by an artist friend of Harte's called Munger. Apart from Harte and his protégé Stoddard, it is highly likely that Miller would have met three women in the office, engaged in a lively conversation while they were supposed to be proofreading, vainly trying to concentrate on their manuscripts. In addition to being editorial assistants, all three were contributors to the magazine. Senior among them was a tall, strikingly beautiful woman of almost Spanish appearance with long, dark, curly hair. Ina Coolbrith was twenty-nine that summer. Since the *Overland*'s inception she had been one of its chief poetic contributors; in fact, the first volume contained only one poem that was not by her or Charles Warren Stoddard. This apparent favoritism had been remarked in the local press, and Harte, Coolbrith, and Stoddard were now known as the "Overland Trinity." The three were close, and Ina would later say the two men were like brothers to her during these years. When they were not in the Clay Street office, they could often be found enjoying tea and talk in Ina's apartment on Russian Hill. Bret Harte did not then quite realize his genius, Coolbrith recalled a few years before her death in 1928, and "Charlie was the more obsessed with his poetical desires." She "used to tease him with his 'moonstruck vacuity' and 'ethereal unreality.'" To her eyes Stoddard was "the ideal poet in appearance, beautiful, beautiful as Shelley." Harte was "more manly and distinguished in appearance, though not tall or robust."

Stoddard had been Harte's protegé for several years. Sending one of his poems to H. W. Bellows, the prominent Unitarian clergyman and editor of the *Christian Examiner,* Harte wrote in the accompanying letter that though Stoddard was yet young, he "exhibits indications of poetic excellence in my opinion, beyond any other writer on the coast." Harte found him full of poetic sensibility and a good deal like Keats in disposition and fancy, "perhaps as much out of place in this very material country as Pegasus in a quartz mill." During the last few years, the peripatetic and troubled Charles Warren Stoddard had converted to Catholicism, worked as a clerk and bookkeeper for the dying *Californian,* and made his acting debut as the priggish Arthur Apsley in Boucicault's *The Willow Copse.* Encouraged by Harte and assisted by him in selecting and editing, Stoddard had published a volume of poetry in 1866, which was not generally well received; the best review in the East or the West being Harte's mention in the *Springfield Republican* for October 12, 1867. In a letter of advice on March 16, 1868, Harte assured him that "Whatever you do—short of arson or chinese highway robbery, which are inartistic and ungentlemanly,—I am, my dear boy, always yours, Fr. Bret Harte."

When Stoddard went off to Hawaii for the second time in October 1868 and gave no report of himself, Ina Coolbrith wrote to him that she was "exceedingly pained": "I have never given more—or as much expression to my friendship as yourself—and yet I am compelled to believe that the real depth and sincerity of it—was confined to my own heart." She added that "Harte is not as formidable as I imagined him; we get on very nicely." "Harte says," she concluded, "one end of our triangle is too far removed from the other two, and ought to be drawn nearer."

Harte wrote to Stoddard himself during his eight-month absence, closing his letter of March 22, 1869, with the words: "You do not want my advice; I should give you more than I should take myself. But you have my love already, my boy, and whether you stay with the bananas or return to beans, I am always / Yours F.B.H." Stoddard had gone to Hawaii, as he would later write to Walt Whitman, "to get in amongst people who are not afraid of instincts" and, as his frank sketch "A South Sea Idyl" (published in the *Overland* in September 1869) illustrated, he had finally been able to give full expression to his attraction to members of his own sex.

The second of the three women Stoddard and Miller might have encountered in the *Overland* office on that day in July 1870 was Josephine Clifford, known in the circle as "Jo." With her thin, straight hair and plain, masculine face, she was a marked contrast to Ina's exotic beauty. The daughter of a German nobleman who had emigrated to the United States in the late 1840s, Jo had come to California from New Mexico in 1867, fleeing an abusive husband, who was wanted on a murder charge. When Jo had heard of the founding of the new magazine, she had decided to try to write for it. Harte had not only encouraged her to write but invited her to visit the editorial rooms. Whenever she stopped by he found her something to do, either looking over manuscripts or copying them. Soon she was a permanent feature. Her first piece, entitled "Down Among the Dead Letters," had appeared in December 1869.

Harte had been equally encouraging to a young woman from New York, who by the summer of 1870 had also become an informal member of the *Overland*'s staff in the capacity of proofreader. Hattie L. Dolson was a capable young woman with "advanced ideas" in whom Harte placed unreserved confidence. She soon began to advise him on literary matters and on personal ones as well. Under the nom de plume of "Hilda Rosevelt," her short story "The Farmsley House" was to be published in the *Overland* for July 1870, making her one of the few contributors to write fiction for the magazine apart from the editor himself.

It seems the three women were united in their dislike of the dominant female presence in Harte's life, his wife, Anna. They could only stand by in amazement as she swept into the office demanding that her husband accompany her on sundry shopping expeditions. Jo, who lived near Harte's mother across the bay, was a rapt audience to Mrs. Williams's descriptions of the Hartes' marital relations. "How my heart aches for the poor boy," Harte's mother would say to Jo:

> They expect him to write something for the magazine every month. But how can he write? Through the day, in his office, he is always interrupted—he is never alone, and when he comes home at night, she (meaning his wife) just wears the life out of him. He waits so pathetically till she and the children have gone to bed before he attempts to do any writing, but he gets no peace even then. It is: "Frank come to bed, the light disturbs me;" "Frank, go to bed now, or you'll disturb me when you put the light out;" "Frank, if you don't put the light out now, I'll get up again and sit down by you."

In Jo Clifford's recollection, Anna Harte never seemed a lovable woman: "There was a morose, stubborn expression on her face which invited neither cordiality nor sympathy; and when she put her foot down her husband 'had to toe the mark.' " Dolson had openly confronted him with his marital situation, saying that it was absurd in him to give in to his wife in everything, to the detriment of his own interests and against his own better judgment. Harte replied sagely: "I don't care about making points; when it comes to anything of importance you will find that I get my own way." The women continued to doubt it.

The Hartes had lost their third child, a son, in late October 1867, eleven days after his birth, and the nervous tension to which Anna was prone was no doubt worsened by this experience and may explain her seemingly excessive demands on her husband's time and attention. Harte had given up his position at the mint in mid-August 1869, and they had taken up more or less permanent residence across the bay, in the village of San Rafael.

In the summer of 1870, Harte was nearing thirty-four and had been editor of one of America's leading periodicals for two years.

The *Overland Monthly* was the brainchild of Anton Roman, the Montgomery Street bookseller and publisher who started selling books in Shasta County as far back as 1851, extended his business to Trinity and Siskiyou Counties, and then opened his first bookstore in San Francisco in the fall of 1857. As a publisher Roman received manuscripts that were not suitable for book publication but were too valuable to be lost, and he became convinced that starting a magazine that could publish such contributions would be a viable venture. He had discussed his idea with his literary friends and colleagues: Harte, Samuel Williams, and William C. Bartlett at the *Bulletin,* Noah Brooks at the *Alta Californian,* George B. Merrill, and Benjamin P. Avery. The hardest to convince had been Harte, especially when Roman let it be known that he wanted him as editor. Harte had felt he lacked experience at magazine editing, and he was worried that there would not be enough contributions coming in and that there was not a large enough readership to make it financially feasible. On the thirtieth anniversary of the magazine in 1898, Roman would recall that he had convinced Harte by showing him a map and indicating San Francisco's central position between two hemispheres. He could also show Harte an already assured advertising income of nine hundred dollars a month on yearly contracts.

The first issue appeared in July 1868. From a distance, one might have mistaken it for the *Atlantic Monthly*—it had the same buff-colored cover and quarto format—but the *Overland Monthly* carried the legend "Devoted to the Development of the Country" over the logo of a bear stepping warily over a railroad track. Between the covers there were poems, sketches, and essays, a section called "Etc.," and reviews of "Current Literature" right at the back. The "Etc." section had no parallel in the *Atlantic.* It was the editor's pulpit, but as Harte explained in the first issue, he would use the first person rather than the editorial plural, for "in this dept. of the overland there is nothing oracular—nothing but the expression of an individual, generally inexact, rarely positive, and certainly never authoritative." He also explained the motivation behind the title (a new magazine that was to represent the West must indicate the route as well as the termini) and the thinking behind the logo (the meeting of nature and culture in the form of the bear and the encroaching railroad, which each day was coming closer to the Pacific Coast).

As "the only reliable and characteristic exponent of the Pacific Slope," the *Overland Monthly* had captured the attention not only of the eastern seaboard but of English readers as well. Tom Hood, the noted comic writer and editor of *Fun,* had made frequent mention of the magazine in the columns of his paper. Of the January issue of 1869, he wrote that Harte's latest story, "The Outcasts of Poker Flat," was "worthy of Hawthorne" and "as has always been the case with this magazine, every paper in it is thoroughly readable." Another eager reader was Charles Dickens, who sent two numbers of the magazine to his close friend John Forster with a letter saying he found in Harte's stories "such subtle strokes of character as he had not anywhere else in late years discovered." Forster had "rarely known him more honestly moved." Only a few months after this, Dickens passed away, and as Harte hurriedly penned what would become Dickens's most famous poetic eulogy, "Dickens in Camp," a letter from the dead man was on its way to San Francisco inviting Harte to contribute to *All the Year Round.*

The success of the *Overland Monthly* could largely be ascribed to the hard work and dedication of its editor. Though it had originally been intended that he should have the editorial assistance of his friends Noah Brooks and William C. Bartlett, it soon became clear that the *Overland* would be Harte's baby. With the definite ideas he had about both its form and content, he would be better off running it himself. Harte had three qualities that made him a good editor: an acute awareness of what would interest his readers, a knack for drumming up copy from reluctant contributors, and, not least of all, the ability to encourage young writers.

Harte's treatment of Joaquin Miller is typical of his attitude toward young (and not so young) hopefuls. About a year before his arrival in San Francisco, Miller had sent Harte a couple of poems together with a copy of his volume of verse entitled *Joaquin et al.* Though Harte was not able to use either of the poems, he wrote Miller an encouraging letter, trying to outline what he saw as his poetic strengths and weaknesses. "I see nothing in you worse than faults of excess," he wrote, "which you can easily check by selecting less emotional themes for your muse." "You are on your way to become a poet," he added, "and will, by and by, learn how much strength as well as beauty lies in repose." He would be glad to receive further contributions from him in the future. Harte, who was more doubtful of Miller's talent than his letter indicates, never did publish any of his poetic effusions, but he did print a sketch of Miller's entitled "Rough Times in Idaho" a couple of months after Miller had left California. Among the others who got their start as prose artists in the pages of the *Overland* were Charles Warren Stoddard, who published his South-Sea idyls in the magazine. They would prove his most lasting achievement. Stoddard later wrote that "to his [Harte's] criticism and encouragement I feel that I owe all that is best in my literary efforts." Another who trusted implicitly in Harte's literary judgement was Ambrose Bierce. The *Overland* would publish a series of his earliest sketches, starting in January 1871, under the collective title "The Grizzly Papers."

The *Overland Monthly* had not become the exclusively literary magazine that the publisher had feared it might become with Harte as editor. Though Harte was given a free rein, Roman was helpful in drumming up material; in his own estimate, he had brought in two-thirds of the matter that appeared in the first two volumes. Harte's journalist friends, such as Benjamin P. Avery, George B. Merrill, Sam Williams, and William C. Bartlett, all chipped in as they had promised, but scholars and scientists also got behind the venture. The noted geologist, head of the U.S. Geological Survey, and Harte's soon-to-be-friend, Clarence King, would publish his sketch "The Falls of the Shoshone" in October 1870, and in the third issue of the magazine, Harte had published Henry George's first article, "What the Railway Will Bring Us," which anticipated the thesis of George's classic text *Progress and Poverty* (1879). Mark Twain, who had left San Francisco for good in June 1868, had one piece in each of the *Overland*'s first four issues. They were all "reminiscent of foreign travel."

There can be no question that despite the high quality of the prose in the *Overland Monthly*—both fictional and essayistic—it was Harte's short stories that were the magazine's major attraction. The *Overland*'s rival on the East Coast, the *Atlantic Monthly*, wrote that "Readers who were amazed by the excellent quality of the whole magazine were tempted to cry out most of all over 'The Luck of Roaring Camp,' and the subsequent papers by the same hand, and to triumph in a man who gave them something new in fiction." As mentioned in the *Atlantic* notice, Harte had his breakthrough with "The Luck of Roaring Camp," which appeared in the second issue, in August 1868. It was followed by other stories at regular intervals: "The Outcasts of Poker Flat" in January 1869, "Miggles" in June, "Tennessee's Partner" in October, and "The Idyl of Red Gulch" in December.

The initial impact of these brief and seemingly unsophisticated narratives is today hard to realize. It was such that immediately after the publication of the first story, James T. Fields, editor of the illustrious *Atlantic Monthly,* wrote to Harte soliciting contributions. Harte was forced to decline because of his duties both at the *Overland* and at the mint but added that as the magazine was still an experiment, he might be able to do more should it fail and "the bear get the better of the locomotive." A year later, Fields, Osgood and Company, the country's leading publishing company, wanted to publish a volume of Harte's California sketches. By this time Harte felt he had enough material to put together a distinctive book, and in January 1870 he signed a contract for its publication. The volume, entitled *The Luck of Roaring Camp and Other Sketches,* appeared on the shelves in late April that same year. At its core were the five stories Harte had recently written for the *Overland.* To this he added six stories from the *Golden Era,* including "The Man of No Account," "Mliss," and "Notes by Flood and Field," and four of his "Bohemian Papers" from the same periodical.

Harte's third book was well received. The *Chicago Times,* one of the first major newspapers to review it, wrote that "the sketches have attracted more attention and won more applause than any other contemporaneous efforts of a similar nature in American literature" and continued: "Newspaper correspondents have filled columns, and authors have made up books upon that which Mr. Harte presents to us in a few pages, and we must confess that he has given us the first clear idea of that wonderful California life of 18 or 20 years ago." The *Alta Californian* found the volume contained "very correct photography of our local life": "it may be counted as a very fortunate thing that such an honest historian and appreciative artist has been raised up to catch the inspiration of the times and give to literature the grotesqueness, sentiment and wildness, which is peculiar to California and its earliest development." A more critical note was found in the *Nation*: "It is a fault of Mr. Harte's that his pathos very often runs into sentimentality, and that he apparently needs all his sense of the humorous and all his turn for analyzing and satirizing his own feelings to prevent a lapse into the falseness and mawkishness of sentimentalism." Yet the reviewer also found that "Hawthorne might have done 'The Right Eye of the Commander' and be pleased to do it." According to the *Buffalo Express*: "Nothing so thoroughly picturesque or so thoroughly native in subject and spirit has appeared yet in American literature, nor has a finer genius displayed itself than that to which we owe these California sketches." In faraway England, the publication of Harte's book did not go unnoticed. The *Spectator* reviewed it in December 1870, pointing out one of the distinctive features of Harte's style: "Mr. Harte knows when and how to stop. His habit is to break his stories off short directly the culminating point of interest is reached, often leaving a good deal of sequel to be added by the reader's imagination."

The *Overland* stories were the result of fourteen years of observation of life in California, of hours spent listening to the tales of mining life and the imprint these impressions made on a vividly imaginative mind, fed from an early age on Greek mythology, Cervantes, Jean Froissart, Dumas, Dickens, Washington Irving, and the popular women writers of the "feminine fifties." That Harte should have turned to his store of first- and secondhand experience of pioneer life—which he had all but ignored since writing "A Lonely Ride" in late 1862—was in his own reckoning owing to a desire to treat the fresh subjects that lay ready to his hand in California and to give the new magazine a certain amount of "local coloring." This desire was probably not entirely spontaneous. If we are to believe Anton Roman, he had no small role in trying to impress upon Harte the fictional possibilities inherent in the gold rush. In his own telling, Roman secured for Harte whatever he could of sketches, tales, and incidents in print and picture form showing the life of the miners in the early pioneer days in California. Yet, contrary to Roman's claims, we know that Harte had been depicting California scenes since the early 1860s, in stories such as "The Man of No Account," "Mliss," "Notes by Flood and Field," and "High-Water Mark." One of the most interesting of these early stories is one he published in the *Golden Era* as early as November 18, 1860, entitled "A Night at Wingdam." Written in the first person, indicating an autobiographical germ, it is the story of a traveler's midnight encounter with a pioneer woman, proprietor of a rustic hotel in "the Arcadian hamlet of 'Wingdam.' " Through the narrator's interview with this "little delicate-looking woman," we get a vivid impression of the hardships of a pioneer woman's life. Even at this early stage Harte sees the situation in Greek terms, picturing the young wife as Parthenia and her hulking husband as the Ingomar of Greek legend. This view of the gold miners would culminate in Harte's lecture "The Argonauts of '49" a dozen years later.

In his stories for the *Overland Monthly*—he would write a total of nine between 1868 and 1870—Bret Harte introduced characters, scenes, and situations the likes of which American readers had never seen before. In this handful of stories he conjured up a rough-and-ready pioneer society, a new world of men and women (but mostly of men), and created the cast of characters that would people the "Bret Harte Country" for more than thirty years. Here we find the gentleman gambler in his earliest incarnation in the form of John Oakhurst of "The Outcasts of Poker Flat" and Jack Hamlin, the epic seducer of "Brown of Calaveras" and more than a dozen later stories. In "The Outcasts" we first encounter the whore with a heart of gold in the figure of Mother Tipton. The illustrious lawyer and consummate southern gentleman of the old school, precursor of Colonel Sellers and the like, Colonel Culpepper Starbottle first makes a cameo appearance in "Brown of Calaveras" and "The Iliad of Sandy Bar." In "The Idyl of Red Gulch" Harte first creates the figure of the rural schoolmistress, here called Miss Mary. The immortal wisecracking stagecoach driver Yuba Bill is first encountered in "Miggles."

From an aesthetic standpoint, the stories Harte wrote for the *Overland Monthly* were the best he would ever write. "To my mind," wrote Theodore Watts-Dunton, noted *Athenaeum* critic and loyal supporter of Swinburne, "there is nothing so new, fresh and piquant in the fiction of my time as Bret Harte's pictures of the mixed race we call Anglo-Saxon finding itself right outside all the old sanctions, exercising nevertheless its own peculiar instinct for law-abidingness—of a kind." G. K. Chesterton credited him somewhat romantically with discovering "the intense sensibility of the primitive man." A reviewer for the *Spectator* pointed out one of the characteristics of Harte's style, which would have the greatest influence on the development of the American short story: "Mr. Harte possesses, almost in perfection, the science, as we may call it, of suggestiveness; he trusts daringly to his readers' intelligence, thereby not only sparing himself and them weary pages of explanation, but augmenting tenfold the verisimilitude of that which is not explained." Harte cut his narratives down to the bone; every part of a Harte story must be functional in the sense that it must contribute to the flow of the action. This is clearly illustrated by the opening lines of the stories. "The Luck" begins simply: "There was commotion in Roaring Camp." "We were eight, including the driver" is the sparse beginning of "Miggles." "Tennessee's Partner" begins with "I do not think we ever knew his real name." "The Idyl of Red Gulch" commences plainspokenly: "Sandy was drunk."

Harte created this unique character gallery of gamblers, whores, miners, stagecoach drivers, and highway robbers during a period in American history unparalleled in its prudishness, hypocrisy, and false piety. His characters swore, drank, and committed acts of gross indecency, and through their very existence in the pages of the *Overland* and later of the *Atlantic*, they expanded the reach of American fiction and the range of characters and situations it was possible to bring before a respectable American audience. The bindings of his first slim volume of stories covered some quite explosive material. The collection opened with the story of an Indian prostitute giving birth to a half-breed baby in a mining camp with no female assistance. This was followed by the narrative of a whorehouse madame and a gambler being sent into exile and succumbing in the wilderness. In "Miggles," a woman of ill repute is openly cohabiting with a man who is not her husband, and it is quite apparent that they once had "known" each other in the biblical sense. "The Idyl of Red

Gulch" opens with the meeting between a prim and proper schoolmistress and a dissolute miner sprawled drunkenly under an azalea. In "Mliss," as we have noted, a minor runs off with her schoolteacher.

More than any other author, Bret Harte was responsible for the representation of the gold rush and for putting California on the literary map of the world. The challenge he faced was how to represent a lawless and uncivilized phase of American history in a way that not only would capture the imagination of the middle-class, magazine-buying public but would also be socially accept-able. His solution was to import romantic situations and plot structures into a hitherto unmapped fictional landscape. The combination was one of great rhetorical power. His aim, as he described in his preface to *The Luck of Roaring Camp and Other Sketches,* was "to illustrate an era of which Californian history has preserved the incidents more often than the character of the actors . . . an era replete with a certain heroic Greek poetry, of which perhaps none were more unconscious than the heroes themselves." As Patrick Morrow has astutely pointed out, "Harte saw California in mythic and archetypal terms and wrote parables which showed the Eastern reading public that picturesque West-ern scenes really were a part of universal experience and truth." Living in a city that to him was the epitome of crass commercial-ism and grasping materialism, Harte created a world of chivalry, honor, and loyalty on the foundations of a real period in the early history of California.

The first of Harte's Californian short stories to achieve nation-wide and worldwide circulation was "The Luck of Roaring Camp," published in the *Overland Monthly* in August 1868. One modern reader has described the story as "a parable where Christ-like Tommy Luck converts several picturesque miners to a facsimile of Victorian civilization—before raw, savage, anarchistic wilderness wipes them all out." As Patrick Morrow correctly ob-serves, in "The Luck of Roaring Camp" Harte incorporates ele-ments from one of the most familiar and beloved stories in western culture—the birth of Christ. With this starting point, the story sets out to describe the effect of the introduction of a child into an all-male community. The major part of the narrative is taken up with the relation of how the men raise this child, son of an Indian prostitute and an unknown father.

The modern reader may wonder at how the author dared to confront a postbellum audience both with prostitution and miscegenation. Harte, of course, ran a calculated risk. Yet in the early years of the Gilded Age, no author would prove more adept at walking the tightrope between novelty and convention, between piquancy and propriety, than Bret Harte. As it turned out, the time was ripe for an expansion of the field imaginary of American fiction. Even the Iron Madonna might under certain conditions press a fictive fallen sister to her chilly bosom, not to mention her sister's child. The success of Harte's experiment can be no better demonstrated than by quotations from two representative reviews of Harte's first collection of short stories, which included "The Luck of Roaring Camp" and others equally bold. The *Chicago Times* wrote of Harte on May 4, 1870, that "He has taken even the lowest phases of this life, and, with a human sympathy and artistic directness that do him equal credit, he has proved that the best of poetry can be made of rude slang, and that the purest human motives and affectations can be found in the most repulsive exteriors." On the other side of the Atlantic, the *Spectator* wrote on December 31 that same year: "No reader, however innocent, however sensitive, need fear any harm from this book."

The timing was good, and Harte's textual strategy was even better. One of Harte's brilliant sleights of hand was to link his metaphorical acquisition of the story of Christ's birth with a strikingly exact simulation of the child-rearing practices of middle-class white women of his day. These practices were epitomized and largely influenced by Catharine E. Beecher's *Treatise on Domestic Economy,* which was first published in 1841 and republished nearly every year until 1856, and by the expanded version, *The American Women's Home,* which Beecher wrote with her sister Harriet Beecher Stowe and published in 1869. It too went into many printings and was published as a "text-book for the use of young ladies in schools, seminaries, and colleges" in 1870, under the title *Principles of Domestic Science.*

By 1870, Catharine Beecher had spent a large part of her life and numerous pages of print trying to prove that "the family

state . . . is the aptest earthly illustration of the heavenly kingdom, and in it woman is its chief minister." In August 1868, a
little short story of some three thousand words made the diametrically opposed, provocative, and evocative claim that a mining
camp—the most male-dominated, coarse, inveterately sinful and
unchristian environment in America—could be the aptest
earthly illustration of the heavenly kingdom, and an illegitimate
child of mixed race its chief minister. For as the expressman in
the story notes with wonder: " 'They've a street up there in
'Roaring,' that would lay over any street in Red Dog. They've got
vines and flowers round their houses, and they wash themselves
twice a day. But they're mighty rough on strangers, and they
worship an Ingin baby.' "

In one sense, what is literally "up for grabs" in "The Luck of
Roaring Camp" and subtextually in *The American Woman's Home*
is the child; the contested practice is child rearing. On a broader
level, both Harte's short story and Beecher's treatise are expressions of a battle between the sexes, a battle for control over the
home, for the power to define what a "home" is and what is the
proper definition of gender roles. In this context, Harte's story
can only be seen as a countermove to the attempt to establish a
female hegemony in the home. Writing at a time fraught with
tensions between the sexes, Harte took on the cult of domesticity
on its own terms and showed that its rhetoric might be made to
accommodate a diametrically different picture of the American
home and the American family.

Described by Jane Tompkins as "a blueprint for colonizing the
world in the name of the 'family state' under the leadership of
Christian women," *The American Woman's Home* was Catharine
Beecher's final and most detailed attempt to define the woman's
sphere and to professionalize American housekeeping. In the
opening chapter she writes: "Woman's profession embraces the
care and nursing of the body in the critical periods of infancy
and sickness, the training of the human mind in the most im-
pressible period of childhood, the instruction and control of servants, and most of the government and economies of the family
state." Of the role of men, she writes: "To man is appointed out-
door labor—to till the earth, dig the mines, toil in the foundries,
traverse the ocean, transport merchandise, labor in the manufac-

tories, construct houses, conduct civil, municipal, and state affairs, and all the heavy work." Furthermore, "the great stimulus
to all these toils, implanted in the heart of every true man, is the
desire for a home of his own, and the hopes of paternity."
Harte's story illustrates Beecher's points about men's labor and
desires to the full, but what the story claims with even greater
eloquence is that these labors do not make men unfit to take an
active part in raising children.

Bret Harte's miners are such good "mothers" that we might
suspect them of reading up on Beecher's *Treatise on Domestic Economy* on the sly. The point-for-point parallels between Harte's text
and Beecher's are so exact that it would be difficult to imagine a
closer homology between the "theory" of the treatise and the
"practice" of fictional representation. We do not know if Harte
ever read any of Beecher's works, nor does it matter. The extent
to which the questions he addresses must have been "in the air,"
so to speak, are no more dramatically illustrated than by the fact
that *The American Woman's Home* was published a year *after* Harte's
short story. In that sense, the fictive text was the "background"
of the factual one as much as vice versa. Though large parts of
Beecher's 1869 text are taken from *The Treatise on Domestic Economy,* there are important revisions in the final version relating
particularly to gender roles. "The Luck of Roaring Camp" reveals the remarkable extent to which Harte had absorbed the
language of domesticity, from whatever source, and as my discussion will show, the extent to which he was able to manipulate it
to his own ends.

Harte begins his story by conjuring up the womanly ideal. He
speaks of the dying "Cherokee Sal" being sadly bereft of "the
ministration of her own sex," "sympathizing womanhood," and
"her sex's intuitive tenderness and care." The assumption, soon
to be undermined, is that it is woman's work to care for the sick
and the dying; only the female of the species has the innate sym-
pathies that this type of work requires. Even at this early point,
though, the picture is not black and white. Despite "the half-
contemptuous faces of her masculine associates . . . ," notes the
narrator, "a few of the spectators were, I think, touched by her
sufferings." Stumpy, "the putative head of two families," who

has had "experience in them things," goes in to see what he can do, and manages to save the child if not the mother.

Having deftly done away with the only woman in the community, Harte has the miners replace her with the only other female inhabitant of Roaring Camp, an ass. The implication is that even as a provider of nourishment for the baby, the mother is not strictly speaking necessary. As Catharine Beecher also notes, milk from a new-milch cow mixed with one-third water and a little white sugar would do as well. When it is suggested that the child be sent to Red Dog, which represents civilization in the story and where "female attention could be procured," this "unlucky suggestion" meets with "fierce and unanimous opposition." Nor will the miners suffer the introduction of a female nurse in their midst. It is decided that Stumpy and the ass will rear the child. "There was something original, independent, and heroic about the plan that pleased the camp."

The child thrives. The narrator hypothesizes that "Perhaps the invigorating climate of the mountain camp was compensation for material deficiencies" and waxes eloquently: "Nature took the foundling to her broader breast. In that rare atmosphere of the Sierra foot-hills,—that air pungent with balsamic odor, that ethereal cordial at once bracing and exhilirating,—he may have found food and nourishment, or a subtle chemistry that transmuted asses' milk to lime and phosphorus." Stumpy inclines to the belief that the baby's well-being is due to plenty of fresh air and good nursing; " 'Me and that ass,' he would say, 'has been father and mother to him!' "

In *The American Woman's Home* no less than two chapters are devoted to the need for fresh air and how to get it. "The first and most indispensable requisite for health is pure air, both by day and night," Beecher writes, also informing her readers that "[t]he human race in its infancy was placed in a mild and genial clime, where each separate family dwelt in tents, and breathed, both day and night, the pure air of heaven." Her rhetoric here is strikingly like that of the narrator of "The Luck"; her "mild and genial clime" could very well be "that rare atmosphere of the Sierra foot-hills."

The child thrives and the regeneration of the camp begins. The first necessity is to make Stumpy's cabin into a proper

"Christian house." The cabin is kept scrupulously clean and whitewashed, and it is boarded, clothed, and papered. In their collective parenthood, the miners become good consumers, sparing no expense on " 'lace, you know, and filigree-work and frills,—d——m the cost!" A rosewood cradle is imported, which "kills" the rest of the furniture, necessitating a complete refurbishment. To compete as a social center, "Tuttle's grocery" acquires a carpet and mirrors. The mirrors show the miners how dirty they are and "produce stricter habits of personal cleanliness." Stumpy imposes "a kind of quarantine upon those who aspired to the honor and privilege of holding 'The Luck.' " It is a cruel mortification to one of the miners, Kentuck, when he is debarred from holding the baby because he is not clean enough. Stumpy is nevertheless adamant in following Beecher's admonition that "Both the health and comfort of a family depend, to a great extent, on cleanliness of the person and the family surroundings." Kentuck cleans up, appearing regularly every afternoon "in a clean shirt, and face still shining from his ablutions." He and the other miners clearly demonstrate Beecher's point that "If men will give as much care to their skin as they give to currying a horse, they will gain both health and wealth." As the narrator observes: "They were 'flush times,'—and the Luck was with them."

"Nor were moral and social sanitary laws neglected," the narrator further states. " 'Tommy,' who was supposed to spend his whole existence in a persistent attempt to repose, must not be disturbed by noise," and Roaring Camp roars no more. Profanity is given up, as "There is no more important duty devolving upon a mother, than the cultivation of habits of modesty and propriety in young children. All indecorous words or deportment should be carefully restrained; and delicacy and reserve studiously cherished." Music is still allowed, "being supposed to have a soothing, tranquilizing quality," and being known to be a "very elevating and delightful recreation for the young." The baby gets plenty of fresh air and exercise in his open-air nursery, where "Nature was his nurse and playfellow. For him she would let slip between the leaves golden shafts of sunlight that fell just within his grasp; she would send wandering breezes to visit him with the balm of bay and resinous gums." The baby is placed in the shade of a tree, as direct sunlight would endanger his eyes. Spending most of the day on his blanket spread over pine-boughs, little Tommy is "always tractable and quiet." The child has clearly not been allowed "to form such habits that it will not be quiet unless tended and amused. A healthy child should be accustomed to lie or sit in its cradle much of the time." It is even recorded that "once, having crept beyond his 'corral,' . . . he dropped over the bank on his head in the soft earth, and remained with his mot-tled legs in the air in that position for at least five minutes with unflinching gravity. He was extricated without a murmur." All in all, Tommy appears to be "securely happy," in perfect accord with Beecher's observation that "A child who is trained to lie or sit and amuse itself, is happier than one who is carried and tended a great deal, and thus rendered restless and uneasy when not so indulged."

As these numerous examples indicate, in "The Luck of Roar-ing Camp" Harte brings the cult of domesticity to the Sierra foothills. What makes the text so novel is not only that Bret Harte erects the "American Woman's Home" in the wilderness but that he does it *without* the American woman. The men of Roaring Camp become everything she could wish for—they are docile, sensitive, caring, and not least of all, clean, they stop fighting and swearing, they even develop an aesthetic sense—yet it is a child and not a woman who brings about their regeneration. This can-not be seen as anything but a direct challenge to the woman's self-appointed role as the "minister of the family state" and the savior of "the Homeless, the Helpless, and the Vicious" (the lat-ter is part of the title of Beecher's penultimate chapter).

As to Beecher's claims for a woman's superior fitness as "the chief educator of our race, and the prime minister of the family state," "The Luck of Roaring Camp" proved with convincing clarity that "it ain't necessarily so." Neither was marriage neces-sary to establishing a "Christian house," that is, "a house con-trived for the express purpose of enabling every member of a family to labor with the hands for the common good, and by modes at once healthful, economical, and tasteful." Stumpy's rural cabin is a Christian house *avant la lettre* and probably looks not far different from the illustration on the title page of Bee-cher's book. In one of her last chapters, Beecher suggests that the same building may serve as a home, a church, and a school-house. In Harte's story, it is the great outdoors that takes on this triple function. Tommy is christened in the open air "as seriously as he would have been under a Christian roof, and cried and was comforted in as orthodox fashion." Roaring Camp as a whole is a Christian house with the heavens as its roof. Here is the "out-door labor for all" that the family state demands and plentiful "exercise in the pure air, under the magnetic and healthful rays of the sun."

From the most unpromising of starting points, Harte creates an all-male utopia. In a central image from the story, "Man-o'-War Jack" is depicted rocking the baby in his arms as he croons forth a naval ditty to soothe him to sleep. The men "lie at full length under the trees, in the soft summer twilight, smoking their pipes and drinking in the melodious utterances. An indis-tinct idea that this was pastoral happiness pervaded the camp. 'This 'ere kind o' think,' said the Cockney Simmons, meditatively reclining on his elbow, 'is evingly.' " Roaring Camp has been depicted from the beginning as "a city of refuge," though what it is a refuge *from* is not directly stated. We may now discern that it is a refuge from American womanhood in general and from marriage in particular. In the background of the story lurks the specter of beset manhood, so vividly delineated by Leslie Fiedler and, in the context of theories of American literature, by Nina Baym. "The Luck of Roaring Camp" features not just one but a hundred men that more or less fit Fiedler's description of the "typical male protagonist of our fiction": "a man on the run, harried into the forest and out to sea, down the river or into combat—anywhere to avoid 'civilization,' which is to say, the con-frontation of a man and woman which leads to the fall of sex, marriage, and responsibility."

Misogyny is not veiled in the text, it is explicit; the men are described as being "fiercely sceptical in regard to [the female sex's] general virtue and usefulness." In this they may have something in common with their eastern brethren, as Catharine Beecher notes with dismay the "increasing agitation of the pub-lic mind, evolving many theories and some crude speculations as to woman's rights and duties." It was not manifest to all that women had "a great social and moral power in their keeping"

and clearly not to the author of "The Luck of Roaring Camp."
His strategy was to beat his contestants at their own game. In
subtlety it was worthy of the "Heathen Chinee," the hero of
Harte's famous poem "Plain Language from Truthful James." By
putting middle-class domestic ideals to work in a camp full of
roughs, Bret Harte made himself and his story unassailable. Who
could object to the regeneration of sinful manhood? Who could
pillory a child, however dubious its origins, for being the cause
of this regeneration? Beecher herself reminds us in her chapter
entitled "The Christian Home" that Jesus Christ "chose for his
birthplace the most despised village, for his parents the lowest in
rank," and Tommy Luck (and his author) does just the same in
midcentury America. What parents could be lower? What village
more despised? What precedent more illustrious?

Harriet Beecher Stowe's contribution to *An American Woman's
Home* was four new chapters on home decorating and gardening
that had not been part of the original *Treatise*. These chapters
reveal an interior decorating aesthetic that sounds like a recipe
for bringing the California wilderness to Nook Farm. Whether in
the shape of pretty rustic frames, brackets, hanging baskets, or
planted in "Ward cases" (tabletop conservatories), pine is the
wood of preference in 1869 and pine cones very much de ri-
gueur. Ivy is the thing to decorate a room with, just like the won-
drous "vines and flowers" round the houses of Roaring Camp.
Among the inexpensive yet beautiful cabinet pictures recommended by Stowe is Bierstadt's "Sunset in the Yo Semite Valley."
Yet, as the gold miners show, it is not necessary to buy works of
art to beautify the home, and poverty is no excuse for negligence: "If you live in the country, or can get into the country,
and have your eyes opened and your wits about you, your house
need not be condemned to an absolute bareness. Not so long as
the woods are full of beautiful ferns and mosses, while every
swamp shakes and nods with tremulous grasses, need you feel
yourself an utterly disinherited child of nature, and deprived of
its artistic use." As the narrator of "The Luck" comments: "The
men had suddenly awakened to the fact that there were beauty
and significance in these trifles, which they had so long trodden
carelessly beneath their feet." In this realization, the men of
Roaring Camp are way ahead of Stowe. As early as 1851 they

are busy decorating the baby's bower "with flowers and sweet-smelling shrubs." Their "wild honeysuckles, azaleas, or the painted blossoms of Las Mariposas" are far more exotic and beautiful than Stowe's mundane forest ferns, trailing arbutus, mayflowers, eyebright, and violets.

The miners, of course, do not have to pay twelve dollars for a chromo of the Yosemite. They and their child can have the real thing completely free, and we may well imagine that "Surrounded by such suggestions of the beautiful," Tommy is being "constantly trained to correctness of taste and refinement of thought" at least as well as any eastern child. What need has he of a "Ward case" to "learn to enjoy the beautiful, silent miracles of nature"? How sorry seem the "grottoes from bits of shells, and minerals, and rocks," when compared with "A flake of glittering mica, a fragment of variegated quartz. . . . [P]laythings such as never child out of fairy-land had before." "The Luck" does not have to be content with only having "a fragment of the green woods brought in." He does not need plate glass between him and nature. Or does he?

At the end of the story, Little Tommy Luck, not yet a year old, is drowned in a flash flood. Mother Nature's spring cleaning wipes the "Virgin Sierras" free of impurities, literally throwing the baby out with the bathwater. It is not insignificant that it is the only "female" influence in the child's life (besides the ass) that finally kills him. Mother Nature, who had taken the foundling "to her broader breast" and been his "nurse and playfellow," drowns him through an act of wanton negligence, while Kentuck, one of Tommy's many foster fathers, gives his life trying to save him. Ironically, despite the efforts of one hundred motherly men to raise the child according to the most modern and enlightened principles, Harte's story reenacts a sad truth in the America of the late 1860s: "*one fourth* of all who are born die before reaching the fifth year."

Toward the end of her life, Catharine Beecher found it increasingly difficult to see the family as an institution that would bridge the ever-widening gulf between the sexes. As Kathryn Kish Sklar has noted, by 1869 the family seemed to her "to embody rather than to meliorate the tensions between . . . men and women." An important difference between *The Treatise on Domes-*

tic Economy and *The American Woman's Home* was that in the latter book, Beecher began to outline alternatives to the traditional family. She "appended to the usual domestic forms an entirely female domesticity, in which a woman 'who earns her own livelihood, can institute the family state' by adopting children." Despite these new developments, *The American Woman's Home* was an end point for Catharine Beecher; she was "too deeply immersed" in the ruling ethic of domesticity "to break away completely from domestic forms." Not so Bret Harte. For him "The Luck of Roaring Camp" was only the beginning. He went on to build an entire literary career on exalting the strength and beauty of male bonds, particularly as represented by the institution of "partnership" between men in the mines. In such stories as "Tennessee's Partner" (1869) and "Uncle Jim and Uncle Billy" (1897), partnership represented an idyllic contrast and a viable, lifelong alternative to marriage.

"Which I wish to remark, / And my language is plain, / That for ways that are dark / And for tricks that are vain, / The heathen Chinee is peculiar, / Which the same I would rise to explain." During the fall and winter of 1870, these lines and those of the eight verses that followed were on many Americans' lips. The poem entitled "Plain Language from Truthful James" had originally appeared in the September issue of the *Overland Monthly*, and the table of contents published in the last issue of the year would reveal what everyone already knew: that it had been written by the *Overland*'s editor, Fr. Bret Harte.

Harte had not abandoned poetry since he began writing fiction again. His first piece for the new magazine was a poem, "San Francisco (From the Sea)"; it began: "Serene, indifferent of Fate, / Though sittest at the Western Gate; / Upon thy height, so lately won, / Still slant the banners of the sun." It was followed by other equally earnest efforts, such as "The Angelus," "The Arsenical Spring of San Joaquin," and the lengthy "Friar Pedro's Ride," redolent of old Spanish California, and nature poems, such as "Madroño," "Coyote," "Grizzly," and "The Mountain Heart's-Ease." "Fate," a poem often reprinted, was about the earthquake of October 21, 1868. But far more popular and original than these conventional poetic efforts were his seriocomic "dialect poems" from the same literary landscape as his short stories. "The Society Upon the Stanislaus," which appeared in the *San Francisco News Letter* in September of 1868 was a satiric description of the proceedings of the "Academy of Natural Science at Smith's Crossing." "In the Tunnel" and "Jim" were understated dramatic monologues about two men's love for their respective partners, "Flynn of Virginia" and Jim Wild. In "Her Letter" we first encounter the figure of the young daughter of a nouveau riche miner, here writing from New York to her beau three thousand miles away in California. The "belle of the season" and heiress to "the best-paying lead in the State" concludes with a sigh that she wishes her father had not struck "pay gravel" and a reminder to Joe that "my heart's somewhere there in the ditches, / And you've struck it,—on Poverty Flat."

"Plain Language from Truthful James" was a thinly veiled attack on anti-Chinese sentiment in California in the form a satirical portrayal of a seemingly ingenuous character, Ah Sin, fooling a couple of card sharps at their own "fixed" game of euchre. One of the losing miners finally exclaims, " 'We are ruined by Chinese cheap labor,' " the remark epitomizing the ruling attitude among the white population of California at the time. In the words of one contemporary San Francisco resident: "Chinese cheap labor was popularly blamed for everything; for the price of chickens; for the prevalence of scarlet fever; for the small attendance at church; for the baldness of sundry literary men." Beginning in the early 1860s, thousands of Chinese laborers had been brought to the state by a firm known as the Six Companies. The laborers commonly worked as laundrymen and cooks but also as housepainters, carpenters, and plasterers. "We will be ruined by Chinese cheap labor" was in fact a favorite phrase of the boss truckman Dennis Kearney, the "Sandlots Orator," when he spoke about the dangers Chinese immigration represented.

"The Heathen Chinee," as the poem would be popularly known, was not Harte's first treatment of Chinese Americans in California. Among the three sketches from the *Golden Era* included in *The Luck of Roaring Camp and Other Sketches* and thus given national circulation was "John Chinaman" from April 1863, where Harte gave a sympathetic description of Chinese theater, dress, appearance, and general demeanor and concluded with the remark that "From the persecutions of the young and old of a certain class, his life was a torment." Harte created his first Chinese character in fiction, maybe *the* first Chinese character in American fiction, in "The Iliad of Sandy Bar," published in the *Overland* for November 1870. From then on Chinese Americans characters would often be part of his stories, frequently in minor roles, but also on center stage, as in the story "Wan Lee, the Pagan," about a little boy who is stoned to death during a racist riot.

Harte's satirical poem was copied everywhere, in literary, religious, and scientific journals alike. The *Alta Californian* wrote that with the exception of a few Civil War poems, "no poem has appeared within the last twenty years . . . that has so hit the fancy of the great world of readers." An article in the English periodical the *Spectator* entitled "The Political Influence of Humor in America" claimed that "Bret Harte's 'Heathen Chinee' has distinctly modified the popular appreciation of the Chinamen, and helped to beat down the previously threatening dislike felt to them." The *North American Review* commended Harte for the "admirable good sense" shown in such poems as the "Heathen Chinee," "which, with a deadly thrust of humor, gave the *coup de grace* to the barbarian cant on the Chinese question." Harte himself would come to regret he had ever written the poem. In a letter to his publisher and friend James T. Fields, enclosing a copy of the poem for Mrs. Fields's autograph book, he wrote that he would have liked to withhold it "on account of all this 'damnable iteration' and inordinate quotation wh. have divested it of all meaning to me, and make me loathe it so that I can not even copy it legibly."

By the time "Plain Language from Truthful James" appeared, Bret Harte had taken on a new dignified position. Despite his unpopularity in some quarters, there were powerful San Franciscans bent on keeping the youthful editor of the *Overland* on the Pacific Coast. To this effect he was appointed professor of recent literature and curator of the library and museum of the University of California at Berkeley on August 16, 1870. His salary was fixed at three hundred dollars a month. Stating that the position would interfere with his profession and a contemplated visit to the Atlantic States, Harte resigned a month and a half later. The time had come to make a move.

What probably clinched the matter with regard to Harte's removal to the East was a proposal from the Boston publishers of his sketches, Fields, Osgood and Company, in June 1870. They offered him five thousand dollars a year to connect himself with their periodicals, foremost among them the *Atlantic Monthly*. This proposition, as Harte interpreted it, was contingent on his satisfying them as to how much he could produce for the money. "This I did not then and do not now propose to do," he responded in September, "believing that you ought to be aware by this time what are my abilities and usefulness." Nor was he willing "at any price and under any circumstances to agree to furnish any specified amount of 'copy'—or to undertake any specific performance, except that which I now perform in the *Overland*." As *Putnam's* and *Galaxy* had both made him direct propositions for editorial work, he wrote, he did not deem it necessary to wait for an offer from Fields, Osgood and Company. But he did wait and finally got what he wanted. By mid-October 1870, he could write to the editor of *Galaxy* that a publishing house in Boston had offered him five thousand dollars per year to retain him for their periodicals without specifying the amount of copy he was to deliver. Despite a lucrative offer from Carmany if he stayed on, Harte resigned his position at the *Overland*, effective from the new year. Just in time for Christmas, Fields, Osgood and Company published Harte's *Poems*, which included "The Heathen Chinee." The first six editions sold out within five days of being announced, and the volume would go into more than twenty printings.

It was "with such a blaze of glory about his head as never will fall to the lot of any other writer" that Bret Harte left the state in which he had spent exactly half his life. When he, Anna, and the boys—seven-year-old Wodie and five-year-old Frankie—boarded the parlor car of the *Overland Express* on February 2, 1871, they turned their backs on California forever.

CHAPTER 6

Age of Innocence

(1871–1875)

> Beyond the small and slippery pyramid which composed Mrs.
> Archer's world lay the almost unmapped quarter inhabited by artists,
> musicians and "people who wrote." These scattered fragments of
> humanity had never shown any desire to be amalgamated with the
> social structure. In spite of odd ways they were said to be, for the most
> part, quite respectable; but they preferred to keep to themselves. . . .
> Mrs. Archer and her group felt a certain timidity concerning these
> persons. They were odd, they were uncertain, they had things one
> didn't know about in the background of their lives and minds.
>
> Edith Wharton, *The Age of Innocence*

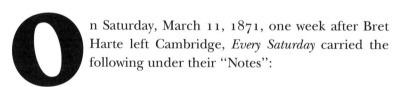n Saturday, March 11, 1871, one week after Bret
Harte left Cambridge, *Every Saturday* carried the
following under their "Notes":

The recent transit across the continent of Mr. Bret Harte has been
a remarkable illustration of the deference and almost homage which
our age pays to literary genius. This young man, all unknown two
years ago, and who has bounded into fame by the aid of half a dozen
poems and about the same number of short magazine stories, has
had his progress from city to city heralded by the telegraph and the
journals, as if he were a Chinese embassy, instead of the author of
the "Heathen Chinee"; or, as if he were General Von Moltke, rather
than the writer of "The Luck of Roaring Camp."

The *London Daily News* devoted a column and a paragraph ten
days later to the new "Transatlantic Genius" and his triumphant
return to the East, quoting liberally from "The Heathen Chinee"
and Boston newspapers. Harte's journey east was an event that
would be remembered and memorialized thirty, even fifty years

later. Mark Twain, who would follow Bret Harte's career longer
and more closely than any of his friends, wrote with grudging
admiration in the early years of the twentieth century that Harte
"crossed the continent through such a prodigious blaze of national interest and excitement that one might have supposed he
was the Viceroy of India on a progress, or Halley's comet come
again after seventy-five years of lamented absence." Lilian Woodman Aldrich recalled in 1920 that "the newspapers heralded his
progress from city to city in the manner befitting a prince of
royal lineage." On that Saturday in March 1871, _Every Saturday_
went on to say of Harte's quick renown, which it felt paralleled
the Dickens furor when Pickwick was created: "It is nothing to
be ashamed of; but it imposes upon the writer who is made subject of it the severe test of keeping up to the high-water mark of
his own achievement, which must be rather trying to a modest
man."

Maybe not at the height of his modesty after the glorious week
in Cambridge, Harte wrote to Ambrose Bierce that he had had
no conception of the commercial value of his work. On March 4
he had accepted James R. Osgood's offer of ten thousand dollars
"for the exclusive publication of my poems and sketches (not to
be less than twelve in number) in your periodicals for the space
of one year commencing March 1, 1871." Samuel Bowles, who
had been the first person to introduce Harte to an eastern audience five years before, through his newspaper the _Springfield Republican,_ wrote to his daughter in near reverential tones: "Bret
Harte is brighter and nicer than I thought, and was very frank
and kindly with me, and promises to come up with his wife and
make us a visit. Indeed, he planted a hope that he might settle
down in Springfield for the summer. He is very happy over his
flattering prospects."

Bowles was not the only one to be charmed by Harte's presence. Back in Cambridge, he had made a vivid impression on
several of his new acquaintances. Annie Fields confided to her
diary: "He is a dramatic, lovable creature with his blue silk
pocket-handkerchief and red dressing slippers and his quick feelings. I could hate the man who could help loving him—or the
woman either." Howells wrote to his father the day after the
Hartes had gone: "It has been a very pleasant visit to us—one of

the pleasantest that we've ever had made us." Over thirty years later, he recalled the early 1870s in a letter to Thomas Bailey Aldrich and remarked: "Those were gay years, and bless God, we *knew* they were at the time!" Aldrich wrote the week after Harte's death that it brought him the sadness it brought to Howells, and the memories. "Wasn't he entertaining company!" he added. "I'm afraid, as I look back, that I was most entertained by things in him that were least commendable. It was a careless, blithe spirit. I wonder where it is now."

Bret Harte's hold on the memories and affections of his American contemporaries was strong. In 1905, Jeannette Gilder remembered him as "all the most exacting hero-worshipper could have asked." Anna Dickinson, who would cross paths with him throughout the 1870s, wrote to her mother after their second meeting, in Chicago in 1871, that he was "satisfying." "One thinks all sorts of things about men & women who have accomplished wonders of some kind," she added, "& then are disappointed at sight. Not so here."

But Bret Harte would fail to impress his peers in other ways. With hindsight we can see that his week in Cambridge, Massachusetts, represented the pinnacle not of his fame, for he would be famous all the rest of his days, nor of his popularity, for he would never lack for readers, nor of his worldwide renown, for that lay still ahead of him, but of his literary reputation among his peers, his own generation of American writers. In their eyes, though he had forty-six volumes yet to write, Bret Harte would never equal or surpass what he had already done, and done before he even came among them. On Harte's death, more than thirty years after their initial meeting, Aldrich wrote to Howells that he had dropped reading him when he found he had not added anything to those first eight or ten fine stories of his— "What a hit they made!" Howells himself said of his dead friend that he "wrote Bret Harte over and over as long as he lived" and continued: "Probably he would have done something else if he could; he did not keep on doing the wild mining-camp thing because it was the easiest, but because it was for him the only possible thing. Very likely he might have preferred not doing anything." With a wife and a growing family to support and the expectations of an entire nation to fulfill, "not doing anything" was not in the cards.

As Harte's fame increased and with it the public demands on him, his shyness became an increasing burden to him. Josephine Clifford well remembered his dread of appearing in public, and he himself readily admitted it, wishing people would realize that he was not a "representative American," that he liked to dodge dinners and speeches. Though occasions that would put him in the spotlight had been difficult to avoid in San Francisco in latter years, they were well nigh impossible to get out of in the East. New England expected its great poets to be visible, to be seen literally giving their poetry to the populace. Poets and their readings garnished all public events of note. No sooner had he arrived in the East than invitations to write occasional poetry came from all quarters. He said no to Dartmouth, only to be faced with a similar invitation from Harvard. This one was harder to dodge, coming as it did from the Phi Beta Kappa Fraternity of which he had been made an honorary member, through the efforts of Edward Everett Hale, the previous fall and being delivered in the person of its president, James Russell Lowell. Harte finally accepted "the honor of delivering the poem," on the condition that Lowell predate his acceptance so that Dartmouth would not feel slighted. Also, he wanted Lowell to indicate something for him to say: What did the graduates want?

What Harte came up with and read before a large audience at the Harvard commencement on June 29, 1871, was "The Lost Beauty," which had originally been published in the *Golden Era* on December 28, 1862. Harte probably chose the poem simply because it was the longest he had written that had not been published in volume form nor copied in an eastern newspaper and would thus be completely new to his audience. In Howells's words, it was "a jingle so trivial, so out of keeping, so inadequate that his enemies, if he ever truly had any, must have suffered from it almost as much as his friends." Another who was present on this august occasion was Lilian Woodman Aldrich, wife of *Every Saturday*'s editor. In her eighties, Aldrich felt called upon to write her memoirs and therein air the accumulated dirty laundry of several decades of Boston and Cambridge life. Among the impugned parties, in addition to Mark Twain and Harriet Beecher Stowe, was Bret Harte. As far as the Phi Beta Kappa poem was concerned, she was in agreement with Howells in thinking that Harte "did not recognize the dignity of the occasion." And she went further: "He made his appearance in gaudy raiment and wearing green gloves. His poem was as inappropriate as his dress. Clothes and the man were equally disappointing to Harvard. The poet fully realized the situation, and fled in dismay." Whether he realized the situation immediately or not—chances are he did, though Howells was under the impression that "he took the whole disastrous business lightly, gayly, leniently, kindly"—the newspapers soon made him painfully aware of his "unfortunate experience at Cambridge."

When he should have been fashioning stirring commemorative poems to sustain his literary reputation, if not fill his purse, Bret Harte's time was taken up—as always—with family concerns. That he had more money to spend than ever before did not spur him on to greater literary efforts but rather channeled his energies into finding a suitable place for his family to live. In April, he moved his wife and children into Lenox House, a mansion turned into a small hotel, just up the street from his sister's place on Fifth Avenue. It was, in his words, "exceedingly neat, surprisingly comfortable, eminently respectable." But they could not stay in a hotel forever. He used his convalescence from scarlet fever (he found it "rather provoking to come three thousand miles to the home of one's boyhood to relapse into infantile diseases") to examine some country houses in the vicinity, with a view to leasing one for the summer. A month later, after having "overrun" New Jersey and ventured into Connecticut and upstate New York, he wrote despairingly to Howells: "Where are the farms of my youth? Where are the farm yards—meadows, barns, orchards?" There was nothing now between a shanty and a villa. Needless to say, he settled for the villa.

The summer of 1871 found the Hartes at fashionable Newport, not yet "that breeding place—that stud farm, so to speak—of aristocracy" it would be in the 1880s and 1890s but rather the Newport of Edith Wharton's *The Age of Innocence.* The Hartes sojourned briefly at Hannah Dame's literary boardinghouse on Broad Street but eventually settled at Edgar Cottage on Harrison Avenue. On the Point by Brenton Cove, overlooking

Newport Harbor, it was really not a cottage at all but a good-sized house that rented for four thousand dollars for the summer season. To make this humble abode run smoothly, Harte hired an Irish cook and a maid.

Their sojourn in Newport came to an end when Anna fell ill in September. She went to Mount Vernon to recoup, as the seaside did not agree with her, and before joining her there, Harte found time for a visit to James T. Fields and his wife, Annie, at their place in Manchester, Massachusetts. He entertained them with descriptions of California, mostly negative, and of Newport, mostly positive. He was delighted with its fragrant lawns and told them a ghost story relating to the house he was renting, which he was working up into a poem. Annie Fields wrote in her diary that she found him a very sensitive and nervous man. "He struggles against himself all the time," she observed, adding that he was most kindly and tender. "His wife has been very ill and has given him cause for terrible anxiety. This accounts for much left undone."

That his wife's health continued to worry him is evinced by a conversation he had with Ralph Waldo Emerson and his wife, Lidian, at Concord in mid-October. The day after he was gone, his host wrote the following to his daughter Ellen: "Yesterday Bret Harte departed . . . at 11 o'clock, to take the train from Lexington,—an easy, kindly, well-behaved man, who interested your mother by his account of his wife, who is a despairing invalid." Harte and Emerson had also discussed the latter's "Essay on Civilization," Harte claiming that in California it had been the gamblers and prostitutes that had brought culture to the state in the early days, in the form of music and New York fashions. Emerson answered that in his essay he had spoken from Pilgrim experience "& knew on good grounds the resistless culture that religion effects." Harte was not impressed.

That Harte was aware he was lagging behind in his writing is evident from a letter he wrote to his friend Dr. J. G. Holland, the editor of *Scribner's Monthly,* on September 20, when he and Anna had just returned to Newport from Mount Vernon: "My wife's continued ill-health . . . has so preoccupied my heart and time that I have barely been able to furnish my quota of copy to my publishers." He had returned to the pages of the *Atlantic Monthly* for the first time in almost eight years in July 1871 with "The Poet of Sierra Flat." One of the first of Harte's stories to feature cross-dressing, it told the story of the miner Morgan McCorkle, who pays the editor of the *Sierra Flat Record* fifty dollars to publish the poems of his young friend Milton Chubbuck, convinced that he is "a borned poet." Milton, who becomes a celebrity and object of fun, is drawn to the male impersonator and artist known as California Pet. On the evening the practical joker Boston has determined that Milton is to be driven out by the town's collective ridicule, California Pet comes to his defense and the two of them make their escape together. In the final line of the story it is revealed that the "Poet of Sierra Flat" was a woman.

This satirical short story was followed by "A Grayport Legend (1797)" and "A Newport Romance," both capitalizing on old Newport myths and legends in the manner of Harte's Spanish-American poems. Harte thought the latter poem "poor stuff." Both poems were included in his latest volume, *East and West Poems,* published by James R. Osgood and Company in time for Christmas. In the same volume was also found "The Stage-Driver's Story," published in the *New York Times* for October. "The Romance of Madroño Hollow," a story of love and revenge starring Harte's by now familiar Colonel Starbottle and the latter's nephew Culpepper, appeared with "A Grayport Legend" in the September issue of the *Atlantic,* and the year ended with, "Princess Bob and Her Friends," a sentimental Pygmalion story about Jessamy Portfire, the daughter of a local fort commander, who takes it upon herself to civilize the Indian girl Princess Bob, with disastrous result. Neither of the latter two stories can have done much to enhance Harte's literary reputation.

By the end of 1871, ten months into his contract with Osgood, Harte had furnished only seven pieces of the stipulated twelve: a poem, "Chicago," and "Lothaw" for *Every Saturday,* and two poems and three stories for the *Atlantic Monthly.* Despite being the most highly paid author in America, he was in debt. Anna, despite her near-invalid status, was pregnant with the couple's fourth child, counting the infant they had lost.

From the time of their leaving Newport in the fall of 1871 and for the next year and a half, the Hartes would make their home in New York City. They leased a relatively modest four-story townhouse at 217 East Forty-ninth Street. It was a quiet, tree-lined street of equally unassuming townhouses, slivers of cream or brown plaster with narrow, rounded windows and the requisite stoops, that looked very much one like the other. The house was just the right size for the family, and in a city full of cavernous mansions of five and six stories, they were lucky to get it.

Bret Harte's failure to fulfill the role of a public poet in the best New England tradition and his unease in the Boston-Cambridge environment after his experiences of the spring of 1871 may have been partly responsible for his decision to make his home in New York. After he had been on a visit to Boston in January 1872, Annie Fields noted in her diary that she found it "curious to see his feeling with regard to society." She continued: "For purely literary society, with its affectations and contempts, he has no sympathy. He has at length chosen New York as his residence, and among the Schuylers, Sherwoods, and their friends he appears to find what he enjoys. There is evidently a gêne about people and life here, and provincialisms which he found would hurt him." In later years, he would indirectly touch on the subject when trying to convince his daughter of the importance of learning foreign languages: "Think how awkward it would be to you in New York," he wrote, "if you didn't understand the language of Boston and Washington." He then added tellingly in parenthesis: "Papa doesn't understand the language of Boston yet, but Papa is peculiar." We may gather there was more of Boston he could not understand than the dialect.

In New York, Harte found plenty of congenial company. Though Boston would remain the cultural center of America till the end of the decade, New York was younger and more dynamic. For the artist, it was hardly as bad as Newland Archer dryly observed in *The Age of Innocence*: "I don't know that the arts have a milieu here, any of them; they're more like a very thinly settled outskirt." The Hartes could pick and choose among many different sets and appeared to be welcome everywhere, from the first families to the shadowy world of New York bohemia, that "unmapped quarter inhabited by artists, musicians and 'people who wrote,' " that Mrs. Archer felt so uncertain about. Harte's favorite people to mix with were not the hoity-toity, Boston-Cambridge literati and old New England families, as Mrs. Fields so correctly observed, but the pressmen, journalists, magazine editors, and literary critics of the more cosmopolitan and catholic New York. The city was crawling with them—the most brilliant in the country—and within his first year in the East, Harte had met and befriended both the coming men and those who had already "arrived."

Of the friends Harte made during his first years in the East, his closest and most enduring friendship was formed with the author of *Pike County Ballads and Other Pieces,* a collection of poems of small-town life in Ohio, inspired by Harte's work. Thirty-two when he first met Harte, John Hay had been a secretary to Lincoln during the Civil War, had spent five years as a diplomat in Europe, and in 1870 had been drafted onto the staff of the *New York Tribune,* where his first poems were published. Hay was a fellow contributor to the *Atlantic* and a fellow member of the Century Club, and he knew many of the same people as Harte: Parke Godwin, Whitelaw Reid, Bayard Taylor, Clarence King, Richard Watson Gilder, to name but a few. He had been a friend of Mark Twain since 1867, Twain admiring his willingness to shock the genteel with unorthodox and slightly risqué language. In this respect, the creator of Jim Bludso and Little Britches had outdone even his own literary precursor. Hay thus had much to recommend him to Bret Harte when the two met for the first time at a dinner party in New York in late March 1871. It was the beginning of a friendship that would last till the end of their lives.

No sooner had Harte installed his family in their new house than he had to go off on a business trip to Boston. He wrote to Anna on January 10, 1872, that he had had a talk with his publisher Osgood that morning and thought their trouble could be "speedily arranged." "Their trouble" was clearly the fact that Harte was not going to be able to fulfill his contract by the time it ran out on February 28. He had written a poem, "Grandmother Tenterden," which had just appeared in the January issue of the *Atlantic,* and he brought with him a new story, "How Santa Claus Came to Simpson's Bar," which would be published in March, but that still left him short three contributions. The upshot of the whole discussion was that Harte would continue to contribute until his quota was filled, but his contract would not be renewed. Annie Fields, ever the shrewd observer of human nature and the Boston literary scene, wrote in her diary on January 12, after Harte had been there to breakfast: "Bret Harte has a queer absent-minded way of spending his time, letting the hours slip by as if he had not altogether learned their value yet. It is a miracle to us how he lives, for he writes very little. Thus far I suppose he has had money from J.R.O.[sgood] & Co., but I fancy they have done with giving out money save for a *quid pro quo*."

If Bret Harte was worried at this point about becoming a freelance writer again, there is no record of it. He returned to New York, where he continued to be a fixture of the Century and the aristocratic Knickerbocker Club. William Dean Howells came to town for five days in May. Harte had seen little of him, since he became editor of the *Atlantic* in June the year before and there had been some unpleasantness over Harte's poem "Concepcion de Arguëllo" for the May issue. Harte had sent Howells the poem in March and asked for any suggestions he might have. When Howells questioned the accuracy of parts of the poem, Harte responded sharply that he might be careless in composition at times "but never with regard to facts, outlines, details or color." He reminded Howells that he had read everything relating to the early colonial history of the Western Coast and that he was for three years "Keeper of the Archives" of the state of California in the surveyor-general's office. Howells took offense at the "tone" of Harte's letter. Harte, not one to stay mad for long, wrote a conciliatory letter back, saying that he wished Howells could come to New York and dine with him and some mutual friends. Howells came, and their common publisher, James R. Osgood, gave a dinner at Delmonico's. They also saw each other at the Knickerbocker and made some calls together on ladies of their acquaintance. Harte said he was working on a new story, but it was not forthcoming. He sent Howells a poem, "Half an Hour Before Supper," in June, writing that it was "one of half a dozen I hope to write, when the seed that is in me shall germinate." But his chief concern by this time was a germination of an entirely different order. On May 31, 1872, Harte had become a father for the fourth time.

The Hartes' first daughter was christened Jessamy but would be known throughout her childhood as Tottie. Both before and after her birth Harte found precious little time for literary work, as the crises piled up on the home front. Writing to decline an invitation to a festival in June, he gives us a small glimpse of the situation at 217 East Forty-ninth Street: "This morning, my wife's nurse—who with the baby satellite, is the center of a solar system about which we all revolve—leaves us unexpectedly, and chaos is come again."

The great heat of that summer so prostrated the baby that the family was "obliged to fly" on July 3 to Morristown, New Jersey. Morristown was a quiet little village with a proud revolutionary history and a salubrious climate, which had become quite popular in latter years as a retreat from the torrid heat of a New York summer. Harte's brother-in-law, Fred Knaufft, was the proprietor of a comfortable family hotel there, Grand View House, on the corner of Sussex Avenue and Ketch Road, two and a half miles west of Morristown. Writing to say they could not yet come to visit the Godwins at their summer place on Long Island, Harte described himself as "a walker of hospitals in quest of a wet-nurse," the doctor saying that such would be necessary to ensure the baby's recovery.

On August 11, 1872, Bret and Anna had been married ten years. Their financial outlook after more than a year in the East—a move that had promised to bring them such rich rewards—was no brighter than it had been when they were first married. Rather the opposite. For the first time since his marriage, Harte had no steady income of any kind and no prospect of getting any in the near future. Anna was in the anomalous situation of being married to one of the most popular and famous writers in the country, yet not knowing where their next dollar was coming from. In this situation, she and Bret Harte were a bad combination, as Anna appears to have had as poor a money sense as her husband. When Harte commented years later in a story that "the only combination in business that was uncertain—was man and woman," he was speaking from personal experience.

Like other women of her class, Anna did not do any work in the house, which was staffed with a cook and a maid at all times, and a nurse after Jessamy was born. Her apparent lack of participation in the running of the household can no doubt be largely

ascribed to the poor condition of her health. She suffered from
long bouts of nervous depression and melancholia, exacerbated
by their tenuous financial position. Harte, who was ever the in-
dulgent and solicitous husband, always wanted her to have the
best. This is not to suggest that he did not spend money on himself. Mark Twain has written one of the most vivid descriptions
we have of the way Bret Harte appeared in the middle years of his
life, which also sheds some light on one reason for the Hartes'
pecuniary difficulties: "He was always conspicuously a little more
intensely fashionable than the fashionablest of the rest of the
community. He had good taste in clothes. With all his conspicu-
ousness there was never anything really loud nor offensive about
them. They always had a single smart little accent, effectively located, and that accent would have distinguished Harte from any
other of the ultrafashionables." Twain added that: "Harte's
dainty self-complacencies extended to his carriage and gait. His
carriage was graceful and easy, his gait was of the mincing sort
but was the right gait for him, for an unaffected one would not
have harmonized with the rest of the man and the clothes."

Twain is borne out in his description by contemporary photographs, which show a dandified man, in elegantly cut, boldly
striped woolen suits or velvet, piped jackets, his hair so fancifully
curled that one suspects something other than nature had a
hand in it. Ethel Parton would never forget as a child getting an
unsolicited peck on the cheek from Bret Harte on one of her
walks in New York with her grandparents Fanny Fern and James
Parton. "He wore drooping moustaches, a velvet waistcoat, a
shiny looped watch chain, and looked very much like one of his
own gamblers," she recalled in 1936. The records show that
many of Harte's debts were in fact to tailors.

By 1872, the couple was heading into an evil cycle. With his
head full of domestic and financial worries, Harte had neither
the time nor the concentration to write, and he had to write if
they were to live. His total literary output in the second half of
the year was a single poem. They were living beyond their means,
and each day saw them further and further in debt. The press
was buzzing with rumors of his projected activities. So much so
that Harte felt it necessary to set the record straight in a letter to
Osgood's partner, John Spencer Clark: "My dear Clark, I am not

boarding with Mark Twain at Hartford. . . . I am not giving readings at Newburgh—nor have I been daily seen on Bellevue Avenue at Newport; I am not contemplating an early return to California nor am I preparing for a three years visit to Europe. I am not engaged regularly with Daly at the 5th Ave. Theatre nor am I to be hereafter a regular contributor to Scribners (unless I wish) but am until my contract is completed, always yours & J.R.O.[sgood]'s—Bret Harte."

The offer from *Scribner's* was a real one. Holland had been soliciting contributions from Harte for two years, but his exclusive contract with the *Atlantic Monthly* had prevented him from contributing. In January 1873, he published his first piece in *Scribner's Monthly*. "After the Accident (Mouth of the Shaft)" is another of his dramatic monologues in dialect. It is in the voice of a Welsh immigrant woman waiting to see if her husband has survived a mining disaster. That Harte was aware of the iniquities taking place in the mines we see from an editorial he wrote for the *Overland* at the time of the collapse of the Crown Point Shaft in Gold Hill, Nevada, four years before: "The sudden death from which we pray to be delivered is terrible. But sudden death to Dives, who owns half a mine—whose children are comfortably provided for—means but little; sudden death to Dives' humblest workman means starvation and suffering to his widow; suffering, and ofttimes sin and crime, to his children." The poem for *Scribner's* was unsigned. In August, September, and October of 1873, under his full name, *Scribner's* featured "An Episode of Fiddletown," a novella in Harte's most melodramatic and tortuous vain. For its sixteen pages, the magazine paid one thousand dollars.

Writing a piece now and then for *Scribner's,* one of the few magazines that could afford Harte's prices, was not going to keep the home fires burning. The solution Harte came up with to augment his income was one he had considered when he first came East. He would go on the lecture circuit. Mark Twain had been lecturing for years, and there appeared to be money in it. Famous lecturers such as his friend Anna Dickinson, Henry Ward Beecher, and Petroleum V. Nasby were said to get $200–250 in the towns and $400 in the cities. Harte was at least as famous as them, and if he wrote a successful lecture, it could be a steady source of income for years to come.

He began to write what was to become "The Argonauts of '49." The lecture was a survey of the early history of California from the arrival of Junipero Serra in 1769 to the middle years of the nineteenth century, concentrating, of course, on the story of the "Argonauts of '49," "an episode in American life as quaint as that of the Greek adventures; a kind of crusade without a cross, an exodus without a prophet." "It is not a pretty story," Harte continued in his opening, "perhaps it is not even instructive; it is a life of which perhaps the best that can be said is that it exists no longer." Interwoven with the edifying history lesson were personal anecdotes and observations on the curious character of daily life in the mines so that both aspects of Boileau's dictum—to please and instruct—were taken care of. A eulogy over a vanished world and way of life, "The Argonauts of '49," appealed both to tears and laughter in much the same way as did Harte's fiction. On the platform, Harte would appear as the unrivaled expert on the California gold rush and a part of the world he himself had done more than anyone else to put on the map.

After testing out his lecture on audiences in Baltimore and Albany, Harte was ready for Boston. His lecture in the Tremont Temple on December 13, 1872, was a resounding success. Two days later, James T. Fields wrote that Harte could have no idea how great a hit it had been: "I have met, since that auspicious evening, many men and women who heard it, and they are all of one opinion—that you cannot be beaten! . . . I never heard warmer encomiums from every mother's son and daughter of them. They fairly boiled over with delight as they recalled your numerous felicitous passages." Little did they know—the "tip-toppers" among Harte's listeners, the "artists, clergymen—chaps with brains . . . in every walk of life" who crowded his benches and applauded his wisdom and humor—that Harte was making his lecture debut in a major American city with a bailiff in the next room waiting to collect an outstanding debt. William Dean Howells knew, though, and Lilian Woodman Aldrich suspected that when Harte had showed up at their doorstep "late on a stormy December night" a few evenings before the lecture, he was trying to escape the clutches of the same sheriff waiting for him at his hotel. The Aldriches loaned him a room for the night, and "The next morning, still arrayed in his evening clothes, he went unembarrassed and airily hotelwards."

Fortunately, the lecture in New York's Steinway Hall on December 16, was no less of a success. The *New York Times* ran a detailed summary the next day under the heading: "Bret Harte's Lecture at Steinway Hall Last Evening—A Sparkling Treat to a Large Assemblage—Ninety Minutes of Immoderate Mirth and Laughter." No better index of the lecturer's success can be found than the numerous times the word "laughter" in square brackets indicated that Bret Harte had made a humorous impression. As 1872 drew to a close, it looked as if the wolf might be kept from the door a little longer.

Omaha, Nebraska, Sunday, October 26, 1873
As Harte had ridden into Omaha that morning, the streets had been dumb with snow, and winter—savage and pale—had looked into the windows of the train. Sitting in the pretty furnished parlor of the Grand Central Hotel, with the cars of the Union Pacific starting on their long overland trip but a few blocks away, he was reminded of his own eastward journey. In the past week, he had lectured five nights in a row in places miles distant from each other. Each day was a mad rush to arrive on time. Miraculously, he had not missed a single engagement since he left New York on October 12, exactly two weeks before. This evening there had been no lecture, it being the Sabbath, and it was a blessing to have a day of rest. Last Sunday, he had been very good and gone to church. When the contralto began to sing the *Te Deum*—"We believe that Thou shalt come"—to the same minor chant that he used to admire, he thought of Anna. They had been her best sentences.

The twilight hour was always the bluest time for him. He tried to comfort himself with the thought that he was halfway on the grand sweep of the West that had taken him to Chicago; St. Louis; four towns in Kansas; St. Joseph, Missouri; and now Omaha. He had reached the westernmost point of his tour; every day would bring him closer to home. But where was that? It seemed they had not had a proper one since they left the Forty-ninth Street house nearly a year ago. He had been reminded of it when he stayed with the Hodges in St. Louis. His bedroom there was hung with the same chintz as used to adorn their old house. He had left Anna and the children at a hotel in New York for the first two months of the year, while he went off to lecture in Michigan and Canada. She had almost been a hostage there, not being able to leave till he had been able to cable her money to pay the bill. The tour of Canada had been a mixed blessing. He had been very optimistic after Toronto, despite the drama of his late arrival, but Montreal and Ottawa had been a disappointment—financially, at any rate. They had had no choice but to move into Eliza's new boardinghouse at 45 Fifth Avenue. The summer was spent at Grand View House in Morristown, as the year before.

The plan was that Anna was to find a house for them in the country while he was away, but he had heard nothing for weeks—he had not even known where she was—and then it came, a letter, to say that she was still at the "moated-grange." The summer season at Liza's was long since over, and when he thought of Anna living in that deserted house with his empty room beside hers, he felt like giving up his trip and going home at once. He had written her right away and insisted that she find a house for them, even if it cost $125 a month. He was weary of boarding and living with others. They had to do it for the boys' sake, if not for their own.

To cheer her, he had tried to emphasize how well the tour was going and that he himself was in good spirits most of the time. "I always enter a new place with distrust," he wrote, "and leave it with hope." The reviews had been mixed at best. The newspapers were probably right in saying that he was no orator, that he had no fire, dramatic earnestness, or expression, but when they intimated that he was running on his good looks, he had to confess, he got hopelessly furious.

Despite the newspapers' sour grapes, the western tour was a great success. He had had the honor of inaugurating the first lecture series ever given in St. Louis, he had larger and more appreciative audiences than he had ever known, and he had been greatly touched with the very honest and sincere liking that people seemed to have for him. They appeared to have read everything he had written. Imagine a rough fellow in a bearskin robe and blue shirt coming up to him and repeating "Concepcion de Arguëllo"! Even in Atchison, which he had heard was pretty rough, the audience was thoroughly refined and appreciative and very glad to see him. Had they only been able to imagine the savage, half-sick, utterly disgusted man who glared at them over his desk that night and damned them inwardly in his heart!

The train had broken down at four o'clock that afternoon, leaving him no choice but to make his own way. He had gotten a saddle horse—there was no vehicle to be had—strapped his lecture and blanket to his back, given his valise to a little yellow boy, who looked like a dirty terra-cotta figure, and ordered him to follow on another horse. He had gotten to Atchison one hour before the lecture was to start. It was not the first close call. The whole year had seemed like a constant struggle against the elements. He had braved floods and snowstorms, hired special trains and sundry other conveyances to get him to his engagements on time. All his plans for writing in the cars had come to naught, as his thoughts were occupied with nothing but worries about not arriving on time for his engagement. He had not been able to make much headway with the new lecture he was working on. The year's literary output for 1873 was a long story and two poems for *Scribner's.*

As soon as he returned from his lecture tour on November 12, 1873, Harte set about finding a house. Though neither he nor Anna were particularly fond of Morristown—he would later describe it as a "bigoted, self-righteous, hypocritical place"—they found it easiest to stay there, moving from the Grand View into a fine period house on Elm Street, close to the center of town. In mid-November, Harte wrote to Jeannette Gilder, the journalist sister of Richard Watson Gilder, saying he hoped she would soon come to visit them in their snug little house, "chiefly remarkable," he added in the facetious manner that was so typical of him, "as being the only house in Morristown that George Washington did not occupy as his headquarters during that dreadfully historical winter. I believe Mrs. Washington objected because it did not have stationary washtubs, and George said it was too far from the depôt. But they do say here the original proprietor had a few cherry trees on the property and that he did not entirely trust G. W."

Harte had written a new lecture entitled "The Progress of American Humor." After a trial run at the Methodist church in Morristown to benefit the library and lyceum, and a brief tour of upstate New York, Harte was ready for the big city itself. The large audience that was present in Association Hall on January 26, 1874, was first told that Harte thought it was doubtful that there was any such thing as American humor "as a nationally distinctive, intellectual quality." American humorists were not so much purely American as they were modern; they stood in legitimate succession to their early English brethren. What was called the humor of a geographical section was only the form and method of today. The Yankee dialect, the earliest expression of American humor, was first embodied in the figure of Sam Slick of Slickville, created by Judge Haliburton, a Canadian and not an American. Continuing with a survey of humor in America, Harte mentioned Lowell, who at best "reproduced a type of life of a small section of the great American Union." He commended Stephen Foster, who wrote "Old Folks at Home," as "a young man who, more than any other American, seemed to have caught the characteristic quality of negro pathos and humor." To prevent his discourse from becoming entirely academic, Harte injected one or two choice anecdotes, but they were to the point. He gave tribute to Artemus Ward, though he feared there was a want of purpose in him. "Today," Harte concluded, "among our latest American humorists, such as Josh Billings, 'The Danbury Newsman' and Orpheus C. Kerr, Mark Twain stands alone as the most original humorist that America has yet produced."

Even if 1874 looked as if it were going to be largely taken up with lecture engagements, Harte would need to augment his income by the efforts of his pen. He found the time and the concentration to write a couple of new poems, which were published in the *New York Times*. A large part of Harte's material for the *Atlantic* had been reprinted in the *Times,* but "The Ghost That Jim Saw" was the first poem Harte had sold to them directly. It was followed by a story, "The Rose of Tuolumne," in April, the poem "Don Diego of the South" in May, and the short story "A Passage in the Life of Mr. John Oakhurst" in June. For this rather risqué narrative of an adulterous wife, starring John Oakhurst of "Outcasts" fame as one of her two lovers, Harte received $500.

Even with new outlets for his work, Bret Harte and his family were still living the writer's version of hand-to-mouth, that is to say, from poem to poem, from story to story, and from lecture to lecture. Harte desperately needed a source of steady income. Lecturing had not proven to be as financially rewarding as he had hoped, $150 a lecture being all he could hope to get in these panic years. There were no editorial positions in the offing; one needed capital to land one of those, things being as hard as they were. The one remaining solution seemed to be to write a novel.

As it happened, *Scribner's* had been wanting him to write a serial story for them for some time. This in combination with a proposal from Mark Twain, who was on the board of the American Publishing Company in Hartford, to publish a subscription novel with them could only lead to one thing. In June 1874, Bret Harte sat down to write his first novel. He was off to an extremely slow and laborious start. As exacting and perfectionistic when he was writing a story that was to be six hundred pages as when he was writing one of six, he spent a month on the first few chapters, writing about 350 pages to make the 49 he finally sent his publisher, Elisha Bliss. "How am I to live?" he queried.

By late August, the Hartes' financial situation had become even more precarious. Anna was lying ill in Morristown, Harte was in New York trying to get some work done, and there was no money. He had been to see Bliss, but his publisher was short of funds and could only give him a check for $200. Bliss said he thought he would have been further along in the novel by then, and Harte agreed that at the rate he was going it would not be finished for a year. Their impecunious position did not prevent him from hiring a new cook. Sending her to Anna with a letter and two good references, he wrote: "She doesn't profess to be more than a plain cook, but seems to have Mrs. Nast's predilection for washing and scrubbing." He was desperately weak, he added, and wanted to go away to Long Branch for a holiday. Hiring a "waitress" would have to wait until after he came back.

To get money, he had to write something for immediate sale. While at Long Branch, he wrote "The Fool of Five Forks," a story of a faithful old miner pining for his sweetheart in the East and eventually saving her husband's life in the cave-in of a mine shaft, while sacrificing his own. It was picturesque, it contained a sprinkling of Harte's familiar characters in minor roles, and it was about the length of "John Oakhurst" and "The Rose of Tuolumne." He sent it to *Scribner's,* who had paid $500 for a shorter story in January. They only offered him $350 for it. Thinking it was worth at least $500, Harte sent a telegram to his old friend Howells at the *Atlantic,* asking if he could get the magazine's new proprietor, Henry O. Houghton, to take it for that price. Howells's answer arrived the next day. They could not possibly take the story sight unseen and pay such an "extraordinary price"; had Harte been writing exclusively for the *Atlantic Monthly,* it would of course have been another matter. Howells begged him to be prompt in responding to letters and to send back immediately the proof of his poem "Ramon" for the October issue. He needed an answer to whether Harte would sign a new exclusive contract with them: "It is a main object with us to know *before the 7th of September* whether or not you engage yourself with us or not."

Harte needed to sell his story, but after his experiences the last time he had a contract with the *Atlantic,* he was not eager to be tied to a magazine again. Thus he sent the manuscript, accompanied by a noncommittal, nonchalant note: "I want to leave town to-morrow, (3rd Sept.), at 5 p.m. to be gone for a few days vacation and I need the money. Try, like a good feller, to bring them to answer to-morrow by telegraph at my expense." Harte was, of course, not going on any vacation, he was desperate to get back to his sick wife and children, but he needed to play it cool. To Anna he wrote in quite a different mood on Saturday, September 5, still not having received an offer from the *Atlantic:* "I shall have to take whatever price I can get. But I shall not return until I get something." Maybe sensing that Harte's need was greater than he let on, Houghton offered him only $150 for the story. Harte was livid and wrote to Howells that he had never received so small an offer for any story since his arrival in the East. He felt justly exasperated, he added, as he had said no to other offers to make the story the basis of a deal with the *Atlantic Monthly*. He had never before been required to send a manuscript for examination: "My stories have always been contracted for, accepted and the prices fixed before I had put pen to paper."

It does not seem likely that Harte had ever intended to enter into another exclusive contract with the *Atlantic*. Apart from his reluctance to write to a deadline, he had taken a strong dislike to Henry Houghton, which this episode can only have served to exacerbate. Houghton had only been willing to pay $125 for "Ramon," when Harte thought it was worth at least $200, and Harte bitterly regretted selling it to him. Relations with Howells had also been chilly since the publication of "For the King" in May. As with "Concepcion de Arguëllo" two years prior, Howells had permitted himself to suggest a number of alterations. Harte responded in high dudgeon that he preferred that his infelicities should be left for himself to defend and that Howells print the poem as Harte sent it rather than suggesting corrections. It vexed him sorely to hear Howells "voice the 'blameless priggism' of a certain kind of criticism." Howells made good the loss of Harte's contributions by securing Mark Twain for a series of sketches for the following year that would become *Old Times on the Mississippi*. Bret Harte would never publish in the *Atlantic* again.

During the next month and a half, Harte worked furiously on his novel, to be able to draw the $250 from Bliss he was getting for each installment of 100 pages. By October 5, 1874, he had written a total of 300 pages or 45,000 words. Half a month behind in paying his rent, he wrote to Bliss for more money and could finally return to his family in Morristown. In addition to his growing brood—Anna was pregnant with their fifth child—Harte also had to support his aged mother and stepfather, who came east in the early 1870s. To Bliss he confided on September 16, 1874, that his mother was dangerously ill with Bright's disease and it was feared she would not live long. Anna had been confined to her bed for over a month. The Hartes, young and old, were now living at "The Willows," the 88-acre estate of Joseph Warren Revere, naval officer, adventurer in California and Mexico, and grandson of Paul Revere. Chatham master builder

Ashbel Bruin had built the house for the Revere family in 1854. The striking Gothic Revival structure, with its unusual two-story veranda, steeply pitched roofs, and pointed arches, stood high on a willow-clad hill to the west of Morristown. Ill health had forced Revere to move into town a couple of years before, and that winter he leased the house to the Hartes for $150 a month. It featured a grand hallway and dining room with trompe l'oeil murals and Minton tiles, a parlor and a study, four large bedrooms upstairs, a kitchen wing, and servants' quarters.

Harte did not stay long in his beautiful new home. On October 25, still not having received any money from Bliss, he set off for Louisville, Kentucky, the first stop on a three-week lecture tour of the South that would also take him to Indiana, Tennessee, Georgia, and Alabama. The trip would make a strong impression on him. Writing long, impassioned letters home to Anna, he regretted that she was not there to share his strange and stirring experiences: "I want you to see something that I have seen here—I want *you* to share the strange experience I have had. I think you would be affected very much as I have been." From Milledgeville, Georgia, he wrote, on November 4: "I have had occasion to change my views of the South very materially, and from what I have seen I am quite satisfied that the North is profoundly ignorant of the real sentiments and condition of the people. They affect me very deeply and sadly." After a lengthy discussion of his experiences in the South, he wrote: "You wonder, dear Nan, to hear me talk so strongly of a political question—knowing how little interest I have in it usually. But I never before had such a fateful problem brought before my eyes—I never before stood by the bedside of a ruined and slowly dying people. If I were a statesman, I should devote my life to save them. I can think of no loftier ambition for any man—any Northern man, I mean; for they are helpless: any Northern man who was large enough to see that it is not only the ex-slave to be saved, but the ex-master." Seeming a bit embarrassed by this idealistic outburst, he commented ruefully in a letter the next day that he was afraid he had bored her with a lot of political talk and that he still remembered that he was in debt and had a heap of practical work to do yet before he "rode ahead redressing political grievances."

In January of 1875, Harte felt compelled to write a letter to the editor of the *Boston Transcript,* denying a report in his newspaper that "Bret Harte, is said to have obtained, through influential friends, a $3,000 position in the New York Custom-house, as a relief from pecuniary embarrassment." "I think you will do me the justice to admit," he wrote, "that I am not in the habit of troubling the press with corrections. . . . but it really seems to me that justice to myself, my friends, my profession, and, finally, perhaps, the present Administration, demands that I should correct this false and perfectly gratuitous report."

Despite his assurances in the *Transcript,* that "I have always found my profession sufficiently lucrative . . . and quite as honorable and manly as any," the burden of Harte's debts at the close of 1874 was heavier than ever. Money sent back to Anna from his lecturing engagements would often be accompanied by instructions to, for example: "Pay Rosen and Cooper and Tivell, equally, installments as far as you can without leaving yourself without money." Things got even more serious over the new year, when one of Harte's creditors, Lord and Taylor of Boston, appeared loath to accept a compromise and threatened to go to court. If they won the case, they could seize the profits from the sales of Harte's books in the state of Massachusetts. By spring they had decided to take legal action, and Harte waited anxiously for the court's decision. "How comes on the Jarndyce v. Jarndyce decision?" he asked Osgood on May 26, 1875. "Are they going to settle my ability to live in the State of Massachusetts and do business before vacation?" Harte wanted to publish a collection of his latest short stories to be called *Tales of the Argonauts and Other Sketches* before publishing his novel but did not dare to do it with the court case hanging over him. "I shall not trouble myself to provide pabulum for those cormorants," he wrote to Osgood. "Apart from their hoggishness—I don't think it is just to the few of my creditors who have been patient and obliging. I will give up all further publishing in the state of Mass. rather than submit to this Yankee gouging."

Harte was winding up his novel by the end of May. It would simply be entitled *Gabriel Conroy,* after its hero. Harte reasoned that "the shorter the title, the better the chances for its quotation and longevity." *Gabriel Conroy* would be published first as a serial novel in *Scribner's Monthly*. For the American serial rights, *Scribner's* paid no less than $6,500. Harte was to receive a 7$^{1}/_{2}$ percent royalty from Bliss on sales of the book in America, and 10 percent on the English sales, in serial numbers and in book form. The final pages of the novel were handed over to Bliss to be set into type on June 9, 1875, nearly a year to the day since Harte started writing it.

On September 30, 1875, Bret Harte wrote an exuberant letter from Cohasset, Massachusetts, to his friend Frank Holcomb Mason in Cleveland, whom he had not been in touch with for some months. He had done a heap of work in the last year, he wrote, finally completing his novel ("no slouch, but a 600 page—printed page—story, and dd good if I say it!") and writing a play of 100 pages: "As to the latter's merit, I can't say—the actors like it."

The Hartes had been at Cohasset since the middle of July. When they left Morristown in May 1875—for good this time—they nearly moved to a house in Hartford, but Tottie fell ill and "an absolute change to sea air and sea sounds" was necessary. On the recommendation of Osgood and the actor Lawrence Barrett, who always summered there, they finally settled on the seaside village of Cohasset, fifteen miles southeast of Boston. The move from the Pequot House hotel in New London, Connecticut, where they were staying for the first part of the summer, was accompanied by the usual practical difficulties, but this time Harte was fortunate in having the help of Barrett, who was already in Cohasset and had found them a house. Writing to Barrett on July 11, Harte regretted that his wife would not be able to come to Cohasset to supervise the arrangements. "Mrs. H. places an abiding confidence in your wife's judgement. Tell her to go on in her noble work. The eyes of posterity are upon her. Her mission, divinely appointed, is to furnish houses for B. H.," he wrote, adding: "I must go—with the thermometer at 90 to N.Y. to do the necessary packing. Pity me." Three days later came another letter. Harte was back in New London, awaiting the arrival of the cook from New York. "I am to know positively tomorrow if her Serene Culinary Highness will consent to try, with the advice of her physician, the Eastern shores of Massachusetts for a couple of months. If she concludes not to come—or what is more probable, fails me at the last moment—we shall perforce try to get a cook in Boston. Does your completely furnished house include a cook? Has your magic any limitation?"

The Hartes' household now numbered four children. In addition to Griswold, who was twelve, Francis King, who was ten, and Jessamy, who was three, there was now little Ethel Bret Harte, born in Morristown on March 9, 1875. There was also a Cochin China hen, Benventuro. Staying with them at Cohasset was Colonel Williams, who had become a widower that spring. Elizabeth Ostrander Harte Williams succumbed to the debilitating effects of her disease on April 4, 1875, and was buried two days later from Grace Chapel in Manhattan. Apart from this, nothing had changed; the children were still giving their parents cause for worry with their illnesses, and the household still suffered discomfort, dissatisfaction, and disorganization, as illustrated by the letter Harte wrote to Barrett toward the end of their stay: "There has been a slight improvement in our hospital. . . . The patients are convalescing—and only one new case is reported, my stepfather, who rashly visited us. . . . The Southwest wind which always blew in the dog-days has left us in the first chilly autumn days. The wind is East now, and the house as unbearable from cold as it was from heat. We are out of water! Another skunk has fallen in the well! 'Bring me no more reports!' " Despite these trials, Harte was happy enough to be there. He told Annie Fields, whom he brought the manuscripts of his play and novel to read, that it reminded him of Yarmouth as Dickens depicted it in *David Copperfield*. Anna was of a different opinion. Harte could inform Barrett that she "has been very patient and long-suffering, but even she has expressed her opinion that she did not like Cohasset." After all the trouble he had gone to, it is doubtful whether Barrett appreciated this frank appraisal of his summer paradise.

Among the actors that kept them company that summer was Stuart Robson, best known for his success as Hector in Boucicault's *Led Astray*. On March 18 that year, Harte had signed a memorandum of agreement with Robson to write and furnish him with an original play to be completed on or before August 1, 1875. For the sole right to act and perform this play, Robson was to pay Harte one thousand dollars on April 1, one thousand dollars at the surrender of the manuscript, one thousand dollars on August 1, and fifty dollars for each New York representation, performances to take place during the 1875–76 season.

By the deadline for the delivery of the manuscript, Harte was not finished. The third act of the play was not completely done until a month later, and not till September 10 was Harte ready to read the fourth and final act to Robson. As it was first handed to its commissioner, it would take about $4^{1}/_{4}$ hours to perform. Harte was forced to cut seventeen pages of it. "It is more than assault and battery—it is mayhem!" he wrote to Barrett, who was then on tour in California. "And I am afraid it is too long now. Nothing more can be worked upon its defenseless body but dramacide! Still if you were here—I should boldly hand you over the scissors."

A year after the crisis of September 1874, the outlook was brighter. *Tales of the Argonauts* was to be published soon. Harte had written his first full-length play, with a realistic chance of seeing it performed in the course of the coming year. *Gabriel Conroy* would begin to run serially in the November issue of *Scribner's Monthly* and be published in volume form by the American Publishing Company in the spring. He had felt confident enough in his future to decline an invitation to return as editor of the *Overland Monthly*. As Bret Harte embarked upon his fortieth year, it looked as if his future might be the potentially more profitable one of a novelist and playwright.

CHAPTER 7

"How am I to live?"

(1875–1878)

"Luck," continued the gambler, reflectively, "is a mighty queer thing. All you know about it for certain is that it's bound to change. And it's finding out when it's going to change that makes you."

John Oakhurst in Bret Harte's "The Outcasts of Poker Flat"

One announced one's self as an adventurer and an office-seeker, a person of deplorably bad judgement, and the charges were true. The chances of ending in the gutter were, at best, even.

Henry Adams on those who went to Washington in search of a presidential appointment in the 1870s, *The Education of Henry Adams*

Hartford, Connecticut, December 1876

A t 351 Farmington Avenue in Hartford, Mark Twain was reading a letter from Bret Harte written in New York on December 16, 1876. Harte could report that he had met with Charles T. Parsloe, who was to be partner in their new dramatic venture and to play the lead role, and that he and Parsloe would come up to Hartford early the following week to sign the contract. Harte had read for Parsloe those parts of the first and second act that indicated his role; "As nearly as I could judge," Harte wrote, "he was pleased." Of the contract, its nature and what would be Parsloe's share of the profits, Harte wrote that he had said nothing. He was only too glad to leave all that business to Twain. Harte asked to be remembered to Mrs. Clemens and Mrs. Langdon. He asked Twain to tell his wife that she must forgive Harte for his heterodoxy; until she did, he would wear sackcloth (fashionably cut) and he would also have put ashes on his head, if it were not for the fact that Nature had anticipated him. His message to Mrs. Langdon was that he forgave her for liking her son-in-law so much and her general disposition to weakly defer to Twain's "horrible egotism and stubbornness."

There had been several visits from Bret Harte that fall, ever since he came to Hartford in early October to suggest that he and Twain write a play together. Twain was to contribute Scotty Briggs from the "Buck Fanshaw's Funeral" story in *Roughing It* and Harte was to put in the Chinese character that had stolen the show in *Two Men of Sandy Bar* that fall. At the end of November, Harte had come to Hartford and ended up staying two weeks. They had made wonderful progress on the play, Twain recalled, starting work in the billiard room the morning after his arrival. He had named his characters and described them and Harte had named his. Then Harte began to sketch the scenario, act by act and scene by scene. He worked rapidly and seemed to be troubled by no hesitations or indecision; what he accomplished in an hour or two, Twain thought, would have cost his host several weeks of painful and difficult labor and would have been valueless when he got through. Twain had himself spent six days in October, working eight or nine hours a day to build his plot and it had very nearly killed him. Now it looked as if it would be mainly Harte's plot that they would be using. It was an extremely complex affair of mistaken identity, intrigue, and romance in the California mines, centered around Harte's "Heathen Chinee" Ah Sin, who gave the play its name, young Henry York, and the nouveau riche Plunkett family from Harte's story "Monte Flat Pastoral." Harte wrote that he was still "fussing over the manuscript," writing himself up and making Twain's part not quite so "prononcé." He found, he wrote, that Mrs. H.'s opinion of the Plunketts agreed with Mrs. Clemens's and that they would have to modify Miss Plunkett at least, deferring to their wives' ideas of "what a woman ought to be."

On reading this, Twain could not help thinking that Harte had not shown much deference toward his hostess during his recent visit. All that fortnight at their house he had made himself liberally entertaining at breakfast, at luncheon, at dinner, and in the billiard room with smart and bright sarcasms leveled at everything in the place. For his wife's sake, Twain had endured this in silence, but he felt that the time was not far distant when he would have to give Harte a piece of his mind. He would begin:

Your wife is all that is fine and lovable and lovely, and I exhaust all praise when I say that she is Mrs. Clemens's peer—but in all ways you are a shabby husband to her and you often speak sarcastically, not to say sneeringly, of her, just as you are constantly doing in the case of other women; but your privilege ends there; you must spare Mrs. Clemens. It does not become you to sneer at all; you are not charged anything here for the bed you sleep in, yet you have been very smartly and wittily sarcastic about it, whereas you ought to have been more reserved in that matter, remembering that you have not owned a bed of your own for ten years; you have made sarcastic remarks about the furniture of the bedroom and about the tableware and about the servants and about the carriage and the sleigh and the coachman's livery—in fact about every detail of the house and half of its occupants; you have spoken of all these matters contemptuously, in your unwholesome desire to be witty, but this does not become you; you are barred from these criticisms by your situation and circumstances; you have talent and a reputation which would enable you to support your family most respectably and independently if you were not a born bummer and tramp; you are a loafer and an idler and you go clothed in rags, with not a whole shred on you except your inflamed red tie, and it isn't paid for; nine-tenths of your income is borrowed money—money which, in fact, is stolen, since you never intended to repay any of it; you sponge upon your hard-working widowed sister for bread and shelter in the mechanics' boardinghouse which she keeps; latterly you have not ventured to show your face in the neighborhood because of the creditors who are on watch for you. Where have you lived? Nobody knows. Your own people do not know. But I know. You have lived in the Jersey woods and marshes and have supported yourself as do the other tramps; you have confessed it without a blush; you sneer at everything in the house but you ought to be more tender, remembering that everything in it was honestly come by and has been paid for.

Twain recalled a brief visit during the first week of November. Harte had come down the day before the presidential election. His host had been as excited and inflamed as had been the rest of the voting world and was surprised when Harte said he was going to remain with them until the day after the election. He had suggested Harte go back to New York so as not to lose his vote, to which he responded that he did not care about voting, he had come away purposely in order that he might avoid voting.

Through influential friends he had been promised a consulate both by Mr. Tilden and by Mr. Hayes and he could thus not afford to vote for either in case the other found out and considered himself privileged to cancel his pledge. Harte's lack of involvement in the tumultuous political events only strengthened his host's impression that he had no more feeling for his country than an oyster for his bed, in fact less so. But then the higher passions were left out of Bret Harte, Twain thought; what he knew about them he got from books.

As the elderly Mark Twain recalled the events of the winter of 1876, he clearly revelled in the way in which he had spoken his mind to Harte after the latter's two-week visit to Hartford. He dated the delivery of his diatribe to the last day of Harte's stay: December 9, 1876. Yet if Twain actually delivered the speech of indictment he gives us in his *Autobiography,* and it seems unlikely, it was not in early December 1876. Bret Harte's pride and sense of honor would have made it impossible for him to have anything more to do with Twain if such words had passed between them. Yet we have Harte's letter of December 16, addressed to "My dear Mark" and signed "Always, dear old fellow, yours B.H." Harte is solicitous about the state of his friend's bowels and asks Twain to implore his youngest daughter, Clara, to add Harte to "the Holy Family."

There was also at least one more visit to Hartford that we know of. It took place just before Christmas in 1876, thus not long after the letter mentioned above. As Twain recalled it, Harte had arrived at dinnertime on a Friday, saying he needed peace and quiet to finish a Christmas story for the *New York Sun.* They had chatted long into the night, Harte helping himself to large amounts of whiskey punch and seeming completely to have forgotten his story. When Twain finally called it a day at one o'clock, Harte had taken an unopened whiskey bottle to his room and had worked steadily all through the night. At five or six in the morning, the butler had provided him with a quart bottle at his request. When Twain met him again at nine, he showed signs neither of fatigue nor inebriation and his story for the *Sun* was completed.

Though we must make some allowance for Twain's tendency

to exaggerate, when we combine this episode with sources on the state of Harte's finances at this time, it becomes a vivid illustration of Twain's observation that Harte "could never persuade himself to do a stroke of work until his credit was gone, and all his money, and the wolf was at his door; then he could sit down and work harder—until temporary relief was secured—than any man I have ever seen."

From the time Harte started writing his novel in earnest, in the fall of 1874, he had been living on advances from his publisher Elisha Bliss. By the time of the completion of *Gabriel Conroy* in June 1875, they had reached a total of $3,600, including interest. Apart from his novel, which began to run serially in *Scribner's* in November 1875, he published nothing else in prose or verse during 1875. The year 1876 was little better: he published one novella, the centennial story "Thankful Blossom," and a single poem, "What the Bullet Sang," in *Harper's Weekly*. The increasingly unwelcome visitor to Hartford during the fall and winter of 1876 was a man in debt both to his host (who had loaned him $750) and, if we are to believe Mark Twain, several other people.

One possible creditor was the noted New York lawyer Samuel Barlow. Starting in the mid-1870s Barlow's estate "Elsinore" at Glen Cove on Long Island had been a welcome refuge for Harte and his family. It may have been Barlow who introduced Harte to his Long Island neighbor, the editor of the *New York Sun,* Charles Anderson Dana. With the help of backers, Dana had bought the *Sun* in 1867, making it, in Henry Adams's words, "a very successful as well as very amusing paper," and through it he pioneered the syndication of newspaper fiction in the late 1870s. One of his instruments in carrying out this project was the still widely popular Bret Harte, whom he would advance money in return for sketches and short stories. Starting with "Thankful Blossom" in December 1876, Dana would for the next ten years have nearly exclusive rights to the serial publication of Harte's fiction in America and would publish more of Harte's stories than any other editor. Harte and Dana became friends and the writer would welcome the chance to exchange the stifling heat of New York for the comforts of Dana's beautiful estate, Dosoris, on a fifty-acre island in the Long Island sound, two to three miles from Glen Cove.

Trips to Long Island would take Harte away not only from the sticky New York summer and his creditors but also from the quotidian chaos of 45 Fifth Avenue. By the fall of 1875, upon returning from the summer spent in Cohasset, Harte had seen himself forced to move back in with his older sister, Eliza Knaufft, and her family. It must have seemed ironic to Harte that more than twenty years after leaving the uncongenial atmosphere of Eliza and Fred Knaufft's home to go to California, there he was right back where he started. Twain's memory served him well, when he recalled that Eliza ran a boardinghouse in New York, but when we consider its location on New York's ultrafashionable Fifth Avenue, it seems unlikely that it was a mechanic's boardinghouse. Nor was Eliza a widow at this point. Be that as it may, the bustling and overcrowded atmosphere of the Knauffts' home in the mid-1870s was probably no more conducive to artistic inspiration and creation than had been their homes on Broadway and at Irving Place in the early 1850s. Eliza, who was now in her midforties, and Fred, who was sixty-five, had had nine children together since they married in 1851. Three had died in infancy, leaving Nina, Fred Jr., Dora, Ernest, Wilhelmina, and Sarah, in addition to the Hartes' four.

When Harte needed peace of mind to work or to tend to his correspondence, he would go down to the offices of E. P. Dutton and Company at 713 Broadway, corner of Washington Place, where his friends Dutton and Charles A. Clapp had allocated him a desk in a quiet corner. He was also wont to drop by the offices of the *Sun* in old Tammany Hall on Park Row to read his proofs, collect his checks, or merely chat. Edward P. Mitchell, a writer in his early twenties at this time, remembered Bret Harte nearly fifty years later as a "dapper, debonair, medium-sized person of easy manners, good looking without striking personality, scrupulously attired, as if he deemed correct neck-ties a needed apology for his years in the rough-and-tumble West, affable in the extreme." "Yet there was something indefinable," he recalled, "which made one wonder. I have heard others who knew him better . . . speculate concerning that elusive 'out' [defect]— that something which could not possibly suggest itself, in the case of Mark Twain or of Eugene Field."

At the end of March 1876, Harte encountered Anna Dickinson in New York. She wrote to her mother that she thought he looked "not well" and continued perceptively: "Poor fellow, he ought to have lived in the day when rich men were the patrons of genius.—If he could be put into a great library & fed & clothed, & have all his worldly wants supplied, & be allowed to write & work unrestricted & unhampered he would do what is in him to do but will never now come out of him." Half a year after its completion, *Two Men of Sandy Bar* had still not been brought before the public. Harte wrote to Twain about the play in January: "To think that Stuart Robson has it in his pocket while he is quietly drawing a good salary from his manager for not playing it, and that its appearance at all depends entirely upon a manager and an actor who can afford to do without it—is exasperating." *Gabriel Conroy* was running serially in *Scribner's,* but Harte was not publishing anything anywhere else and had no other source of income. Though he had already been advanced between three and four thousand, he wanted Twain to use his influence with Elisha Bliss to Harte's advantage and get him to advance him a further thousand dollars on his copyright. With regard to money, Bliss was, in Charles Dudley Warner's words, "more difficult to open than an Egyptian tomb," and Bret Harte did not get a further advance. In the spring of 1876, he agreed to sell his rights to *Two Men of Sandy Bar* to Robson for a further three thousand dollars, making the play "the personal chattel of Mr. Robson" and absolving Harte of any responsibility for or pecuniary interest in its production.

Soon after Anna Dickinson met Harte, he made a trip to Cleveland to visit his friend Frank Holcomb Mason and his wife, Jennie. From thence he went to Washington, where he wrote to his sister Eliza on April 2, 1876, that he thought he had laid the foundations for success in the plans they had spoken of. "I've made many friends," he added, "and kept some old ones." Harte had gone to Washington armed with letters of introduction from Mason to Congressman James A. Garfield of Ohio and Senator James G. Blaine of Maine, both Republicans. On the Sunday he wrote Eliza, he had dined with the Garfields and taken tea with the Blaines. The reference in his letter to certain "plans" is the first intimation of a possible diplomatic appointment for Bret Harte.

New York, New York, late February 1877

As he issued from a large townhouse on the right-hand side of Fifth Avenue between Eleventh and Twelfth Streets, Harte reflected that, as usual, the beautiful breadth of this fashionable thoroughfare was deserted. It was six o'clock; he was an early riser, but in an area where early rising was confined exclusively to domestics, he could not help but feel that he was desecrating traditional customs. This reflection and other impressions from the wee hours of the city that had been his home for most of the last six years he had just incorporated in a sketch for the *Sun* entitled "Morning on the Avenue, Notes by an Early Riser." His finances were at a low ebb again, and during the last few days he had been busy working for his bread and butter. After finishing "Morning on the Avenue," he planned on writing a similarly autobiographical piece, this time a reminiscence of a tramp he had met during his summer at Newport. He often met and had a keen interest in people from the lower walks of life.

This frosty winter morning, when the ice storm of the preceding night had made the sidewalks glistening and impassable, he journeyed down the middle of Twelfth Street with a mechanic so sooty as to absolutely leave a legible track in the snowy pathway. The mechanic was a fireman attending the engine in a noted manufactory, and during their brief conversation he told him many facts regarding his profession, which, Harte reflected, interested him more than the after-dinner speeches of the distinguished gentlemen he had heard the preceding night. The man introduced Harte to a restaurant where chicory, thinly disguised as coffee, was served with bread at five cents a cup and honorably insisted on being the host, paying ten cents for their mutual entertainment. It was quite a change from the morning cup of coffee he usually enjoyed in the café of ultrafashionable Delmonico's.

Uppermost in his mind on this particular morning in late February 1877 was a letter he had just received from Mark Twain. He had deliberately waited in answering it, as he had heard nothing from John T. Ford about the production of *Ah Sin* and, more important, because had he written the day after hearing from Twain he doubted whether they would have had any further business together. Pleading poverty, Twain had refused to lend his friend money, but only the other day Parsloe had shown Harte a letter from Twain in which the latter offered to spend five or six hundred dollars to send Parsloe to California to study the Chinese character. The suggestion was simply preposterous. If there was one thing they were sure about regarding their play, by actual experience, by general report, by universal criticism, by the consent and acknowledgment of the public, it was that Parsloe was a perfect Chinaman! Harte also felt keenly the insult implied by the fact that on a mere whim and idiotic impulse, Twain had offered Parsloe the very sum he had refused to advance his collaborator, which would have given him some much needed peace from the importunities of his creditors.

Part of the reason for Harte's impecunious position was that so far Elisha Bliss had managed to sell only two thousand copies of *Gabriel Conroy*. No publisher of any of Harte's works, at any day or time, had ever done as badly as he. It was no excuse to repeat, as Twain had done in his letter, the formula "that the book was delayed by Harte, that his reputation had suffered by it, that he had lost his popularity, etc., etc." The only test was what other publishers were doing now, and since then, with Harte's other books. Inside of a month after beginning sales of *Thankful Blossom* at 65 cents a copy, Osgood had credited Harte with one half the amount of copyright that Bliss showed for his sales in five months of *Gabriel Conroy*, a book that sold for $3.50. In brief, Osgood had sold more copies of *Thankful Blossom* in a month than Bliss had sold of *Gabriel Conroy* in five months, and looking over his copyright accounts, Harte had found that he had never in his literary experience sold less than four or five thousand copies in the first three months of publication. Either Bliss had to confess that he ran his concern solely in Twain's interest, and that he used the names of other authors to keep that fact from the public, or else he was a fool. There was something very wrong somewhere, and, as Harte's friend, Twain should have looked into Bliss's books and Bliss's methods before recommending that he publish with him. Though he didn't like to do it, he felt he would be forced to remind Twain that he had agreed to pretend to Bliss that the contract for the book came about through Twain's influence and that, as a result, a disputed question of one or two thousand dollars was settled in Twain's favor.

No, Harte reflected, as he entered Washington Park, he did not think it advisable for Twain and himself to write another play together. Twain had made him an offer of "$25 per week and board," but he thought that if he accepted it, Twain would come to despise him for it. The plan seemed a travesty of his own suggestion a few years previously that he and Twain establish themselves in an empty farmhouse somewhere, a mile or two away from their families, where they could do their work. When he had asked Twain for a loan he had not had the slightest idea of him speculating on his poverty and, as a shrewd man, a careful man, a provident man, Twain would have to admit that in Harte's circumstances the writing of plays with Twain was not profitable. Even if Harte went to Hartford on a salary of $25 per week, he could not, after Twain's letter, break bread or eat salt with him; his board at the cheapest hotel would cost him at least $7.50 per week, leaving him with $17.50 to support his wife and four children. It would be better to struggle on in New York at $100 per week and not write any more plays with Mark Twain.

On Thursday, March 1, 1877, Bret Harte sat down at his desk at Dutton's in Broadway and wrote a long accusatory letter in which he blamed Twain for not protecting his interests vis-à-vis the publisher of *Gabriel Conroy,* Elisha Bliss, and refused to enter into any further dramatic collaboration with his old friend at Hartford. From this point on they were no longer on speaking terms, and, as far as the world knows, they never saw each other again during the quarter of a century that remained to them. They had had quarrels before. Harte had been incensed that, after all his help in revising *The Innocents Abroad,* he had not received a complimentary copy, and as a result they had briefly been "off" in the early 1870s. This present parting of the ways was final and had been building up for some time.

Mark Twain's strong and unbending animosity toward Bret Harte, which began to manifest itself in the mid-1870s, can be explained by two contradictory impulses: envy and disgust. Twain regarded Harte as his chief professional rival. He once wrote to his brother that "I must and will keep shady and quiet till Bret Harte simmers down a little and then I mean to go up head again and *stay* there." Yet he began to feel more ambivalent about

Harte's writings as the seventies progressed. This is made clear by Twain's response upon reading *A Drift from Two Shores* (1878), the last collection of stories Harte would publish while still living in the United States. "The struggle after the pathetic is more pathetic than the pathos itself," Twain wrote to William Dean Howells; "if he were to write about an Orphan Princess who lost a Peanut he would feel obliged to try to make somebody snuffle over it." Yet Twain had to admit in all fairness that after reading the volume a second time he "saw a most decided brightness on every page of it—& here & there evidences of genius." In his public attacks on Harte's work, which began in print in his "Contributor's Club" article for the *Atlantic* in June 1880, Twain would often charge him with a lack of realism, especially in his use of Pike County dialect. "[N]o human being living or dead," Twain wrote in 1880, "ever had experience of the dialect which he puts into his people's mouths."

That Bret Harte was still a force to be reckoned with in the world of American letters was shown in January 1877, when the *North American Review,* which "stood at the head of American literary periodicals," carried a lengthy essay on Harte by Ehrman Syme Nadal. Nadal was not overly enthusiastic about Harte's poetry, considering his dialect poems "and those not in dialect which preserve their spirit" to be the only ones of value, but found reason to say that Bret Harte "is a writer of marked genius, and has produced works which are as certain as any of his time and country to be read in the future." Harte's literary gifts, as Nadal described them, were "a vivid imagination, color, dramatic dialogue, power to attract and power to entertain, a good sense of nature, a lively and daring humor, and considerable keenness of perception." His power of dialogue was surpassed by no living writer, wrote Nadal.

During his first six years in the East, Harte had not produced anything to rival his poems and stories for the *Overland.* His novel was more or less a total failure, and his plays fared no better, but there was evidence that toward the end of his ill-starred eastern sojourn he was beginning to pick up. It was Mark Twain's conviction that the novella *Thankful Blossom* (1876), a historical romance set in Revolutionary Morristown, belonged "at the very top of Harte's literature," and he was not alone in his positive opinion. Whitelaw Reid wrote to John Hay in January 1877, just after Osgood had issued the story as a book, that it was "a delicious bit of work—slight & sketchy, but with some touches not unworthy of Henry Esmond." "The fellow has really made an advance," Reid concluded, "just when we thought he was breaking down." During the spring of 1878, Harte wrote "Two Saints of the Foot-hills," a highly amusing satire on western small-town life—by modern standards, quite the best thing he had written since he came east. His account of the fire at the Patent Office on September 24, 1877, published in the *Sun* a week later, was a satirical tour de force, revealing contemporary Washington in all its bureaucratic absurdity. Paradoxically, Harte wrote these humorous pieces during the most trying time in his life.

Bret Harte's continued prestige can also be gauged by the universal measure for anything during the Gilded Age: money. He continued to be able to demand more money per printed word than nearly any other writer, whether it was from newspapers or magazines. As we have seen, for his longer stories, such as "The Rose of Tuolumne" or "A Passage in the Life of Mr. John Oakhurst," he would receive $500–600. His dealings with the *New York Times* were simple, as he generously explained to Mark Twain, who wanted to get into the same market. Harte simply named his price and handed over the unseen manuscript. From Dana at the *Sun,* he would regularly get $150 for one of his two-to-three-column sketches of about four thousand words. As Harte also wrote to Twain, he felt they owed it to their profession to keep up the prices. Yet he found that other writers did not quite see it that way, and he had been cut dead in the street by a fellow poet a day or two after it was reported that the *Atlantic* had bought a poem of his for $400. Harte was accused by several publishers of spoiling the market together with Mark Twain.

In trying to comprehend Twain's hatred toward Bret Harte it is important to keep in mind that Harte was one of the few men in the East who could remember Twain when he was an obscure journalist in California. As Twain readily admitted, Harte had been his mentor during the mid-1860s, and, partly because of that, we find evidence of a slight condescension in Harte's attitude towards his friend, which Twain would have found more and more irritating as the decade progressed. Howells tells us in several places of the infamous luncheon given for the up-and-coming Boston literati by Ralph Keeler. This was Mark Twain's first introduction to the Mecca of literary America and the demigods that peopled it, and we can only imagine his dismay when in the midst of the revels Harte slapped him on the back and exclaimed to the whole company, "Why, fellows, this is the dream of Mark's life!" When in August 1874, Harte heard that Twain had dramatized *The Gilded Age,* he wrote to him magnanimously and with evident surprise: "I never thought of you in that way. I dare say you will get before the footlights before I do—but the stage is large and there is audience for us both. Wherefore go on, my dear boy, and conquer. No one will applaud louder than myself—among the *claque.*" Throughout his life, Harte continued to regard Mark Twain as no more and no less than a talented humorist.

Bret Harte was everything that Mark Twain was not. He was charmingly facetious and strikingly elegant. He was solidly grounded in the classics and completely au courant with the current writing, be it in America, England, or France. And he was well liked. In a small commemoratory volume entitled *My Mark Twain* (1910), William Dean Howells wrote candidly and revealingly: "I cannot say just why Clemens seemed not to hit the favor of our community of scribes and scholars [in Boston-Cambridge], as Bret Harte had done, when he came on from California, and swept them before him, disrupting their dinners and delaying their lunches with impunity; but it is certain he did not, and I had better say so."

While Twain was giving his autobiographical dictations in February 1907, where Harte would be the target of more vitriol than any other person Twain had ever known, he had a visit from Howells. Howells said that he thought Bret Harte was one of the most delightful persons he had ever met and one of the wittiest. To this Twain responded grumpily that the character of Harte's wit was spoiled, "it consisted solely of sneers and sarcasms; when there was nothing to sneer at, Harte did not flash and sparkle and was not more entertaining than the rest of us." That Twain felt himself the target of Harte's pointed remarks is amply evidenced in the pages of the *Autobiography.* If Twain was justified in his indignation is harder to say. Harte—in Twain's version a most dissatisfied guest who did not show the requisite respect for his hostess—clearly admired Livy Clemens. On the birth of the Clemenses' daughter Susy in 1872, just before the Hartes' own daughter Jessamy, he concluded a letter to his friend with a sigh: "You ought to be very happy with that sweet wife of yours and I suppose you are. It is not every man that can cap a hard, thorny, restless youth with so graceful a crown." We have evidence from other sources that Twain was extremely touchy about his palatial new home and its appointments. On the day after Thanksgiving 1876, Harriet Beecher Stowe's half-sister, Isabella Beecher Hooker, took a friend along to see the Clemenses' home and was unfortunate enough to make a joke about her host "not caring for a pretty lamp shade after he found it so very cheap." Twain was not amused. Incidentally, Bret Harte was also there, and when passing through the billiard room afterward, Hooker had seen Twain and Harte together "& there were bottles of spirits near." Isabella Hooker confided to her diary that "I felt a new distrust of such companionship [for Twain, that is] & ever since the thought has haunted me that perhaps I have something to do there by way of warning."

So much for envy. The other side of the matter was that by the mid-1870s, as the incident I have just related indicates, Bret Harte was in danger of moving socially beyond the pale. As the noted businessman Henry Huttleston Rogers would preach to Mark Twain in the 1880s, when Twain found himself deep in debt, "Business has its laws and customs and they are justified; but a literary man's reputation is his life; he can afford to be money poor but he cannot afford to be character poor; you must earn the per cent and pay it." Harte was deep in debt and, as far as anyone could see, was not making any strenuous efforts to repay the money he had borrowed. His reputation, both literary and personal, had also suffered through a scandal that exploded in the fall of 1876 in connection with the long-awaited production of the play *Two Men of Sandy Bar*.

Though he had sold the play outright for six thousand dollars to the veteran comic actor Stuart Robson, who was to star in the role of Colonel Starbottle, Harte attended rehearsals at the Union Square Theatre in New York prior to the premiere there on Monday, August 28, 1876. The play and the company had

had a trial run at the Adelphi Theatre in Chicago in mid-July, and there the manager, Leonard Grover, had come to the conclusion that "to give 'Sandy Bar' any considerable dramatic importance would require three or four of the characters to be wholly rewritten, which might make a very bad play of what, at present, the public seem to consider very good nonsense." The New York critics had even crasser things to say. According to the *New York Times,* Robson was "an object of public pity. . . . He has paid an enormous sum for a piece of writing that has not a scintilla of wit nor the slightest degree of literary merit"; the play "may be set down as the worst failure witnessed on the boards of our theatres for years." The *New York Herald* said of the assembled audience that it was "as brilliant as if Mr. Shakespeare had just produced one of his best comedies." When the reviewer wrote further that he had never seen a worse play than this, he desired to be understood with the special qualification that he had never known such a celebrated writer to produce such a worthless work. The play was like "one of Beadle's dime novels struck by lightning"—"Heaven forbid that we should attempt to give an idea of the plot."

The plot was indeed incredible. The *New York Times* devoted no less than an entire column of very small print in a futile attempt to do justice to its intricacies. Harte had taken one strand of the action from "Mr. Thompson's Prodigal," maybe the poorest of his stories for the *Overland Monthly,* and thrown in some of his favorite recurring characters for good measure, including the pompous, bumbling Virginian lawyer Colonel Starbottle, the gambler John Oakhurst, and the Chinese laundryman Hop Sing (the latter made the decided hit of the play). Grover was right in describing the result as "essentially undramatic" and simply "a series of Bret Harte's characterizations." Harte had meant his play to be about "the domination of a stronger man over a weaker one," as he wrote to Robert Barnwell Roosevelt, but he had to admit that one of its cardinal weaknesses was that he had endeavored to show this through narrative instead of action.

When all the papers had had their say, it turned out that only A. C. Wheeler of the *New York World* had had anything good to say about *Two Men of Sandy Bar.* Harte, who was staying at Demarest, New Jersey, and had not yet seen the finished production,

wrote to thank Wheeler personally for showing his fellow journalists that "the function of a critic are not incompatible with the
instincts of a gentleman." On that very same day, September 3,
1876, Harte published in the *New York Herald* a letter he had
received from Stuart Robson, in which Robson claimed that the
New York critics had condemned the play because they had not
been paid to praise it. As it turned out, ironically enough, after
weeks of demands for Harte and Robson to "Give the Names!"
of the critics who wanted their palms greased, it turned out to be
an employee of the *World* who had approached Robson's manager for a bribe.

By publishing Robson's letter, Harte had mainly hoped to
quiet the rumors that the actor felt he had been swindled and to
express his belief, as he wrote to Twain, that he still didn't think
it a bad play: "It seems to me a little like the three parts of a
charade with the answer left out, but it's pretty and picturesque
and Robson is satisfied." Harte's strategy backfired. Rather than
showing that there were at least two sides to the question of the
play's merits, the result was a roar of outrage from the journalistic establishment, who united in condemning Harte for "approving Mr. Robson's blunder." The scandal raged on during the
entire month of September. On September 17, 1876, the *World*
concluded that "As the case now stands, it is not the repute of
the dramatic critics of New York which is in question, but the
good faith of the authors of this tempest in a teapot." This was
written despite the fact that the editor knew the accused was one
of his own employees and, at least ostensibly, had dismissed the
man. Harte could not let this pass in silence and published a
letter in the *New York Daily Graphic* four days later, making the
facts clear. "If, after all this clamor," Harte wrote, "the first name
that I offer to the press is thus withheld, I might well hesitate to
intrust further names and proofs to such a tribunal." He gave a
detailed version of his side of the story in an interview with the
Washington Capital on October 1, which would be the last word
in the case, but it was a sordid affair indeed. Howells wrote to
Twain when the storm had passed that he thought Harte had
"acted crazily about the criticism of his play, but he's been
shamefully decried and abused." "Of course," he added, "no

man knows till he's tried how absurdly he'll act, but I wish Harte had not been tried."

The following summer, in dire need of money, Harte embarked on a long story about the struggles to gain possession of a California quicksilver claim. "I have nothing to invent," he wrote jubilantly to his wife from Washington, "only romantically and dramatically cast a really wonderful *true* story." Harte's standing in respectable society, particularly in Boston, was not improved by his irreverent burlesque in the story of "Charles Sumner and other public buildings of Boston." Sumner had been dead for four years when *The Story of a Mine* was published in volume form in February 1878, and "for weeks after," Harte wrote to John Hay, "whenever my name was mentioned good Bostonians got upon their hind legs and pawed the air like their own heraldic supports. . . . Whenever a stranger alludes to me there is a dead silence, a slight cough from the host, a remark upon the intellectual quality of Wagner's music, the foot of the luckless speaker is silently pressed under the table by his neighbor, there is another silence—and the ladies retire. What is said then—never has transpired. Nobody but Bostonians are permitted to be present." The *Atlantic Monthly,* which considered Harte's latest book "one more advertisement of his wasted powers," also found that "The caricature of Charles Sumner is in the worst taste,—recognizable, and therefore unpardonable."

During these years, Mark Twain had a front-row seat to the social debacles of his old-time friend, and as Hamlin Hill has pointed out, Twain's "savagery" must have been motivated in large part by fear: "If Harte could descend thus far in six short years, the meaning was obvious: so could any Western humorist." Yet the factor that contributed more than anything to the souring of relations between Mark Twain and Bret Harte was not, as has often been supposed, their collaboration on *Ah Sin.* As we have seen, as long as the two were on speaking terms, it progressed well and Twain was full of admiration for Harte's skill and industry and wanted to write more plays with him. But work on the play coincided with a rising conflict about Mark Twain's role in getting Harte to publish his first novel with the American Publishing Company, of which Twain was the principal author and a major stockholder. As it became clearer and clearer that

Gabriel Conroy would become an economic liability for all involved, Twain came under fire both from Harte, who blamed him for using the contract to further his own ends and for not protecting Harte's interests, and from the publisher Elisha Bliss, who was facing a loss amounting to several thousand dollars.

The novel finally appeared in September 1876, exactly four years after it had originally been contracted for, and received largely negative reviews on both sides of the Atlantic. The poet and critic Andrew Lang wrote in the *Academy* that "The plot is always falling to pieces, as if it had outgrown its strength, and recovering itself by a spasmodic jerk," yet he found the novel "far better worth reading than most well-constructed and sedate romances." The *Athenaeum* objected to the fact that "The reader is called on to sympathize with the trials and lament the deaths of the characters before he has had time to become acquainted with them" and found "the way in which they disappear and reappear under other names is most bewildering." The London *Times* wrote that they had always suspected that Bret Harte's genius was better suited to desultory successes than to sustained efforts, and *Gabriel Conroy* confirmed them in that idea. In the terse argot of the California miner, they wrote, "'taint nothing short of an everlastin' failure." Reading *Gabriel Conroy* today is a curious encounter with a tradition of intricately plotted, literally incredible romance that has entirely died out in our own century. Harte's story centers on the trials and tribulations of the simple-souled hero Gabriel Conroy and his two sisters Grace and Olly and involves a web of mistaken identities, conflicting claims both to identity and property, natural disasters, and coincidences that defy summary. In his longest work, Harte pulled out all the stops, including an array of his characteristic scenes, settings, and stock characters that range from San Francisco to the Sierras to San Antonio and from Colonel Starbottle to Jack Hamlin to Spanish-American donnas such as Maria Sepulvida and Donna Dolores Salvatierra.

Despite the fact that they were joined together by each having a third interest in a play that was not going to be performed anywhere without their mutual cooperation, it appears that Twain and Harte managed to avoid each other entirely during the rehearsal period. In early April, Harte was in Washington to negotiate with John T. Ford, who had theaters in Baltimore, Washington, and Philadelphia. Between April 25 and May 1, 1877, Twain intermittently attended rehearsals in Baltimore before returning home because of an attack of bronchitis and because he found he was not absolutely needed. Harte did not arrive on the scene until the premiere at the National Theatre in Washington on May 7, 1877. Twain was not present. *Ah Sin* played for a week, and then the production moved as planned to Baltimore.

The drama of Harte's final year in the United States is enacted in the surviving letters:

Mark Twain to William Dean Howells, June 21, 1877
Three or four times lately I have read items to the effect that Bret Harte is trying to get a Consulship. To-day's item says he *is* to have one. Now if I knew the President, I would venture to write him. . . . You *do* know him; & I think your citizenship lays the duty upon you of doing what you can to prevent the disgrace of literature & the country which would be the infallible result of the appointment of Bret Harte to any responsible post. . . . I have befriended this creature for seven years. I am even capable of doing it still—while he stays at home. But I don't want to see him sent to foreign parts to carry on his depradations.

   (William Dean Howells had written President Rutherford B. Hayes's campaign biography, and his wife, Elinor Mead Howells, was Hayes's cousin.)

Mark Twain to William Dean Howells, late June, 1877
Never mind about Harte—I mean never mind about being bothered with the letter. I had to have an outlet to my feelings—I saw none but through you—but of course the thing would be disagreeable to you. I must try to get somebody to plead with the President who is in the political line of business & won't mind it.

William Dean Howells to Mark Twain, June 30, 1877
I have just simmered down to-day after nearly two weeks of arduous journeying and junketing. . . . Mrs. Howells kept your two letters about B[ret]. H[arte]. for me. I think *now* there is no danger of the national calamity you feared, and I don't believe there ever was much.

Birchard A. Hayes to Elinor Howells, July 9, 1877
A few days ago Webb received a letter from Laura Mitchell enclosing

two letters from Mark Twain to Mr. Howells on the appointment of Bret Harte to some consulship. Father has read the letters and directs me to tell you there is no danger of his appointment.

(Birchard and Webb were both sons of President Hayes. Laura Mitchell was Hayes's favorite niece and a cousin of Elinor Howells.)

Bret Harte had gone to Washington, D.C., for the opening of *Ah Sin* at the National Theatre on May 7, 1877, and remained there until early August. During the summer he continued to hope for a diplomatic post and was offered the position of joint editor of the new Washington newspaper, the *Capital*.

Harte to Anna Harte, June 24, 1877
I've not seen Evarts [William Maxwell Evarts, Hayes's secretary of state] since I wrote you last. Then it seemed to me from his very cautious and diplomatic speech, that I ought to have *political influence. I can get it if I choose.* Shall I choose? Jones, the great millionaire and Senator from Nevada, told me that he *demanded* of the President as part of his patronage an office for me. The member from New Mexico not only offered his own personal influence but to pledge all the Territorial delegates for me. I can easily secure the whole California delegation. But what effect this may have upon the "Facing-both-ways" administration I don't know—nor do I care! . . . I have "some new hope for each new day"—I can not return until I have *achieved something.*

Harte to Anna Harte, July 8, 1877
My dear Nan,
. . . For the first time in many years I have for the last few days been confined to my bed. The Doctor says it is Gastric Catarrh—which is the polite name for dysentery. . . . As regards Appointments, I know nothing. Whatever is done now, must come to me without solicitation . . . Kiss the chicks for me. God bless you, patient Nan, says Limick.

Harte to Anna Harte, July 10, 1877
I am better—but only very slowly recovering. . . . For the first time in my life I have attended to my diet. I've lived the last few days on beef-tea and broth—eschewing all vegetables, liquors or stimulants. I had to be half killed before I could show any self-control.

Harte to Anna Harte, July 27, 1877
[Donn] Piatt's latest offer is three thousand dollars a year and one

half the paper. . . . I think I'll close. . . . Do you know that I should have to live here?—and that it is very unhealthy in summer for children. . . . The question is a little too large to be dismissed or settled at once. It is in every way a new departure for me.

Olivia Clemens to her husband, July 29, 1877
Youth I want to caution you about one thing, don't say harsh things about Mr. Harte, don't talk against Mr. Harte to people, it is so much better that you be reticent about him, don't let anybody trap you into talking freely of him—We are so desperately happy, our paths lie in such pleasant places, and he is so miserable, we can easily afford to be magnanimous toward him—but I am afraid that my desire to have you in the quiet is not from generosity to him, but from my selfish desires toward you. I don't want you in the position of having talked against him—be careful my darling.

The following is the conclusion of the speech Mark Twain gave after the opening night performance of *Ah Sin* at Daly's Fifth Avenue Theatre in New York on July 31, 1877. Bret Harte was still in Washington and Twain had spent three weeks doing extensive revisions on his own:

When our play was finished, we found it was so long, and so broad, and so deep—in places—that it would have taken a week to play it. I thought that was all right; we could put "To be continued" on the curtain, and run it straight along. But the manager said no; it would get us into trouble with the general public, and into trouble with the general government, because the Constitution forbids the infliction of cruel and unusual punishment; so he [Augustin Daly] cut out, and cut out, and the more he cut out the better the play got. I never saw a play that was so much improved by being cut down; and I believe it would have been one of the very best plays in the world if his strength had held out so that he could cut out the whole of it.

Twain wrote to William Dean Howells on August 3: " 'Ah Sin' went a-booming at the Fifth Ave. The reception of Col. Sellers [the play version of *The Gilded Age*] was calm compared to it."

Harte returned to New York in August. Back in town he finally had an opportunity to see the production of the *Ah Sin* at the Fifth Avenue Theatre. He wrote to Donn Piatt on August 20th: "My lawyers are drawing up the agreement between us based upon your proposition. . . . I think you and I can make a team of it. If we *can,* there is money, and reputation, and self-respect in our venture. . . . My play is a sort of success. At least it's valuable enough for Parsloe to try and buy my third, which I don't intend to sell him." Bret Harte returned to Washington on September 11, 1877. Anna Harte had taken up residence in a hotel at Sea Cliff, Long Island, where she and the children would remain until the fall of 1878. On October 18, Harte wrote to his wife: "[T]he money I've expected from the *Capital* for my story is seized by its creditors. That *hope* and the expectations that I had from the paper and Piatt in the future amount to nothing. I have found that it is bankrupt. Can you wonder Nan that I have kept this from you?" By mid-October, Twain could report to William Dean Howells: " 'Ah Sin' is a most abject & incurable failure! It will leave the stage permanently within a week, & then I shall be a cheerful being again. I'm sorry for poor Parsloe, but for nobody else concerned."

On November 8, 1877, Harte joined Anna at Sea Cliff House, Long Island, where he would remain until late March 1878. He then returned to Washington, D.C., to make a final bid for a consular appointment.

Harte to Anna Harte, March 26, 1878
Nan! Nan! Nan!
. . . When I telegraphed to you that "I had succeeded" I meant that the President, the Secy. of State, and Carl Schurz, the Secy. of the Interior, had all recognized my claims and had assured me personally of their intention of sending me to the Netherlands, Switzerland, or perhaps *a little higher up in the diplomatic scale.* . . . I could not help sending you that joyful telegram, and feeling, as dear Carl Schurz said to me, that I was "all right". . . . Whatever I receive from the Department of State I have come *by my own individual efforts,* I have not had to wet the sole of my shoe in the political mire—Even the Masons, with their "cousinry" really have not done anything for me,—and in the beginning I saw at once that I must stand alone. I am so full of my experience that I cannot write and wait until I can see you. Then I will talk for half a day. In my whole life I have never had such an experience, or one so fateful of good or ill. . . . I am perhaps making the turning point of my life.

(Jennie Birchard Mason, wife of Harte's friend Frank Holcomb Mason, had discovered when calling on the Hayeses at the White

House that her father was a second cousin of President Hayes's mother.)

Rutherford B. Hayes to William Dean Howells, April 5, 1878
Can you give me for personal and private use your views of appointment of Bret Harte consul at Nice? Have I not heard sinister things about him from Mark Twain?

William Dean Howells to Rutherford B. Hayes, April 9, 1878
Personally, I have great affection for the man, and personally I know nothing to his disadvantage. . . . He is notorious for borrowing and was notorious for drinking. This is report. He never borrowed of me, nor drank more than I, (in my presence) and yesterday I saw his doctor who says his habits are good now; and I have heard the same thing from others. From what I hear he is really making an effort to reform. It would be a godsend to him, if he could get such a place; for he is poor, and he writes with difficulty and very little.

Harte to Anna Harte, April 19, 1878
I had an interview with Mr. Seward [Frederick William Seward, Ass. Secretary of State] yesterday. . . . [He] said kindly . . . "Mr. Harte, wouldn't you like to take the map and look at some of the places talked of for you. . . . Here is 'Crefeld,' near Düsseldorf, in Germany, on the Rhine, not much to do and it's worth about two thousand dollars now and may be raised to three or four thousand. What do you think of it? It is vacant now, and has the advantage that you could take it at once." Of course, I was wise enough not to commit myself—although you can imagine that, with all my disappointments, this seemed like a glimpse of Paradise. . . . I heard that enemies were trying to poison Mr. Evarts's ear with reports of my debts, extravagancies, etc. . . . In this extremity I remembered that I had held a pretty responsible position in the Mint, honorably, for seven years. . . . So it's all right, Nan—there!

"[T]here is a prospect of the East and Europe in the distance," Bret Harte had written to his wife in San Francisco in the fall of 1870. Now, eight years later, he was finally going to Europe, but he was going alone. On May 11, 1878, he wrote to the State Department to accept the appointment as United States Commercial Agent in Crefeld, Germany. Six weeks later, among the many people who came to bid him farewell at Hoboken Pier were his two sons, Griswold and Francis King Harte. Wodie, also known as "The Malignant," was fifteen; Frankie, nicknamed

"Peeker," was thirteen. Harte had parted with Anna and the girls at the Sea Cliff Hotel on Long Island. Tottie had turned six the month before, and Ethel, also known as "Miss Badness," was only three.

Aboard the ship, as it lay off Staten Island, there was time to scribble a few hasty last words in pencil: "My dear Nan, The missing baggage hasn't turned up yet, but I'm in hopes that it will before long. It would be a joke if—no it wouldn't be a joke at all. But I send this line back by the pilot to beg you not to worry about it. The boys will tell you how they left me. God bless you Nan, keep up a brave heart, and be patient and pray for Limick." We do not know what were Harte's last words to his sons, yet we can imagine the tenor of his parting from a letter he wrote to Wodie while he was on a lecture tour in 1873. "I have been far away on a very long journey," he wrote then, "but I have been very fortunate and have met with no delay or accident. But if anything had happened to me and I never came back any more to Mamma or my little boys, you, Wodie, would have to take my place. When Papa dies, you Wodie and Frankie are the only ones that will bear his name, and Papa wants you to be so good and clever, and honorable and manly, that you will always make and keep that name sweet and fresh before men." They were prophetic words. Harte would never see his native land nor his eldest son and eldest daughter again.

On June 27, 1878, accompanied by his publisher and friend, James R. Osgood, Bret Harte sailed for Europe aboard the *Suevia* of Hamburg.

PART II

The Cherished Exile

It is one of the great unwritten books—the revelation of what lay behind that self-indulgent and laborious, that miserable and flattering, that lonely and cherished, exile.

Wallace Stegner, introduction to Bret Harte's
The Outcasts of Poker Flat and Other Tales

CHAPTER 8

The Vanishing Consul

(1878–1885)

"We know too much about people in these days; we hear too much.
Our ears, our minds, our mouths, are stuffed with personalities.
Don't mind anything any one tells you about any one else. Judge
every one and everything for yourself."
                Ralph Touchett in Henry James's *The Portrait of a Lady*

O n October 16, 1878, Bret Harte sat down and com-
posed nine densely written pages to his wife, Anna.
It was not the first letter he had sent her since his
arrival in Crefeld three months before; there had
been at least a dozen letters mingling hope and despair since he
had begun his new life in a place where he knew no one and did
not speak a word of the language. Harte had come to his posting
from Paris, "nearly four hundred miles through an utterly foreign country, on one or two little French and German phrases
and a very small stock of assurance." In London, where he had
spent six days, he had hardly seen anyone; it "only seemed to me
a sluggish nightmare . . ." he wrote, "and Paris a confused sort
of hysterical experience." Nor did Crefeld meet with the approval of its sole American resident. In his letter of mid-October,
Harte described in excruciating detail the discomforts and im-
practicalities of German life in general and life in Crefeld in
particular. He had previously described the small provincial town
to which he had been exiled as "about the most uninteresting
place you ever saw," "a cramped Philadelphia without its neatness, with all its whitened glare." Now he added vivid but far
from complimentary descriptions of German cooking, furniture,

ventilation, hygiene, and heating, and of the German language. His conclusion was that he did not think his wife would be comfortable coming to live in Crefeld. "I want you to be comfortable, Nan, and have no worry about money, and live where you think it best." As for himself, he should try to keep off homelessness "by moving around actively."

During this period, Crefeld was (with Lyons in France) the chief European town for the manufacture of silks and velvets. Thus the commercial agency's chief task was to check, record, and sign invoices for shipments of goods to the United States. It was the fees from this activity that provided the salary of the commercial agent and his "vice-consul." In the latter position, Harte installed Rudolph Schneider, who was to receive all the consular fees above $2,500 per year, up to $3,500. The estimated fees were about $3,000 a year. In the short story "Unser Karl," written in 1897, long after Harte had left Crefeld forever, he gives us a humorous description of the atmosphere of the commercial agency during business hours. It was the consul's chief duty, Harte recalled, "to uphold the flag of his own country by the examination and certification of divers invoices" sent to his office by textile manufacturers. When Harte was not signing and recording invoices, he might divert himself with such engaging tasks as constructing tables "showing the Rainfall, Snowfall and Thunderstorms" occurring in his district during the course of the year, finding out "as full and exact information as possible, respecting the cost of manufacturing and the market price of hatbands," or writing quarterly reports.

While he was in England during the autumn of 1878, Harte had written to Schneider to arrange quarters for him when he returned. During his first weeks in Crefeld, he had stayed at the Hotel Wildenmann, "a very old and very uncomfortable building," but was then invited to stay at the home of Schneider's brother-in-law, Wilhelm Jentges, one of Crefeld's wealthiest men. According to a letter to his son Frank, living in Jentges's palatial residence was "a gorgeous picnic all the time, and not like home one bit." Pleasant as this was, it was not a lasting solution to his housing problem. When he returned to Germany from England, he had decided that he would live in Düsseldorf and moved into a "quiet bachelor den" at 134 Drüsberger strasse in the Breidenbacher Hof.

Each morning Harte would commute from Düsseldorf to 86 Neue Linnerstrasse in Crefeld, a trip he found "very preoccupying." This address not only served as the commercial agency but was primarily the home of Rudolph Schneider, his wife, Clara, and their children. Neue Linnerstrasse became a home away from home for Harte, and the Schneiders became his surrogate family. This is apparent from the many letters that passed across the channel after Harte had left Germany. In sharp contrast to the largely disgruntled and dissatisfied reports he sent his wife during his Crefeld years are the constant reminders of happier days in his letters to the Schneiders, with whom he kept in touch until his death. They give us some idea of Harte's quotidian existence during the two years he spent in Germany, as in the letter he wrote to Clara Schneider in late August 1882, where he dearly remembered trying to translate the better pieces in the *Fliegende Blätter* with them during the half hour in the morning before official duties started. "Nothing . . . ," he wrote, "can compensate me for our charming intermissions from the severity of business by dinner up stairs with the children, and the coffee and cigars & *petite verre* Schneider and myself were obliged to take to recuperate ourselves with." He fondly remembered his little back office overlooking the garden and the dinners he was always inviting himself to, when he "played" he was "company" and sat in the parlor while his hostess played piano. "I miss our old gossiping chats," he wrote to Clara, "and the sympathy that was already ready for me when I used to come over growling and dyspeptic from Düsseldorf in the morning." He begrudged Mr. Potter, his successor in Crefeld, having Düsseldorf added to his district: "*I* ought to have had it in my time; think how nice it would have been for you and your husband to have taken a pretty little house, near the Hof Garten *for us all*!" This last wish is revealing, as it shows that Harte clearly envisioned himself as part of the family. It is a pattern that we shall see repeated several times: Bret Harte as the avuncular adopted member of a family whose solicitation and care he can enjoy without the responsibilities of a provider. As he wrote to the Schneiders eight years after leaving Crefeld, he was still "Uncle Bret Harte" to them.

It was not long after he had settled into his new lodgings that Harte was joined in Düsseldorf by Callie Cooper, one of the two daughters of Harte's cousin on his mother's side, Georgiana Cooper (née Thacher). During his time in Washington, Harte had frequently stayed at the Georgetown home of Georgiana and her husband, David Mack Cooper, who worked as an engraver in the Treasury Department. It was one of Cooper's great-great-grandmothers that lent her name to Harte's revolutionary heroine Thankful Blossom. Callie was coming to Düsseldorf to study painting. During the year of her stay, Callie was a good friend to her older cousin. She studied German with Marie Wilhelmi, a schoolgirl who had also taken on the task of trying to teach Bret Harte something of the language, and became friendly with the Schneiders, as well as drawing Harte into the circle of expatriate Americans in Düsseldorf. One such was Belle Flower, who lived at 123 Drüsberger strasse and who could report to Callie when she had returned to the United States in mid-October 1879 that "the gentleman across the way" had seemed "very dull and out of sorts" after her departure and had gone to Paris "as he felt miserable."

When Germany became too oppressive or lonely, Harte escaped. Of the twenty-three months he was commercial agent in Crefeld, Harte spent about eight months in other European cities. His travel route frequently took him to Paris and from there to London. In Paris he had family, of a kind. His niece Gertrude Griswold was studying singing at the Conservatoire and lived with her mother, Anna's sister-in-law Medora Griswold, at 27 Rue Baudin. Anna's brother had been a prosperous New York shipowner and importer who had suffered financial reverses and died from the blow. By the late 1870s, his widow, Dora, was a semi-invalid and his seventeen-year-old daughter, Gertie, who was musical like many of the Griswolds, had decided to try to live on her extraordinary voice, despite suffering from diphtheria. She looked, wrote Harte to Anna on first seeing her in Europe, "like an intelligent and self-absorbed ghost." "Dora is the same Dora you know. But Gertie I think has changed—very much for the better. She is a strong *woman*—very mature and full of intelligence and character. She is wrapped up in her Art. I do not know if she will *succeed,* but I have an uneasy feeling that unless she

Harte's grandfather, Bernard Hart.

The house to the left, at 487 Hudson St. in New York, is reputed to have been one of Harte's childhood homes.

Harte at seventeen, shortly before going to California.

Jim Gillis's cabin (above) at Jackass Hill, popularly known as the "Mark Twain cabin" after its most famous guest. Harte may have stayed there briefly in 1857.

Harte in San Francisco in 1861 (right).

The octagonal house (below) on San Francisco's Rincon Hill where Harte lived with his sister Maggie in the early 1860s.
Courtesy of the Bancroft Library.

Jessie Benton Frémont.
Courtesy of the Bancroft Library.

Thomas Starr King.
Courtesy of the Bancroft Library.

Anna Griswold.

Mark Twain in 1868.
Courtesy, The Mark Twain Project,
The Bancroft Library.

Ina Donna Coolbrith.
Courtesy of the Bancroft Library.

Charles Warren Stoddard.
Courtesy of the Bancroft Library.

Harte in 1870.
Courtesy of the Bancroft Library.

William Dean Howells's home in Berkeley St., Cambridge, Mass., where Harte and his family stayed soon after their triumphant return to the East in 1871.

Harte in 1884, while American Consul to Glascow.
Courtesy of the Bancroft Library.

Harte in the early 1870s.
Courtesy of John Bret-Harte.

Arthur Collins.
Courtesy of The Royal Archives
© Her Majesty Queen Elizabeth II.

Grace, Duchess of St. Albans, as she appeared in
Munsey's Magazine *in 1894.*

One of the illustrations for Harte's story "In the Tules," which appeared in the Strand in 1895.

74 Lancaster Gate. Harte's home in London from 1895 till his death.

Arford House, May, 1896. Harte is seated on the veranda.
Courtesy of John Bret-Harte.

Harte in 1896.

Bret Harte

*Clockwise (above) from upper left:
Harte, Madame Van de Velde,
Madame's married daughter
Beatrice Norris, and Harte's
daughter-in-law Aline Harte.
Taken in the late 1890s.*
Courtesy of John Bret-Harte.

*Clockwise (right) from upper left:
Harte, Aline Harte, Anna Bret
Harte, Ethel Bret Harte. Probably
taken in front of Francis King
Harte's house "Warren Heights"
at Reading in late July 1899.*

One of the last portraits of Bret Harte.

*Harte's grave in the churchyard of
St. Peter's parish church, Frimley, Surrey,
as it looked in August 1992.*

makes a great success, her life will be hopelessly wrecked." There was something "very pathetic" about her; "Indeed their life—in four little rooms in the fourth story of a French lodging house is something pathetic of itself." Harte wrote to John Hay of his niece that "although she belongs to my wife's family she is charming." When they were not both living in London, Harte and Gertie kept up a lively correspondence.

Far the greater part of his time away from his official duties Harte spent in England. Though his first arrival in London directly from America in mid-July had not created much of a stir, his one-month visit from mid-August 1878 was a decided hit. Harte had two English friends from his New York days who were ideally suited to introducing him to English society, both literary and aristocratic. One was the historian and journalist James Anthony Froude, the other was the politician and man of letters Richard Monckton Milnes, knighted for his services to the nation in 1863 as the First Baron Houghton. Harte first met Froude when the latter came to lecture in America in the winter of 1872. He first met Lord Houghton at a breakfast given for him in New York in September 1875. Both men were considerably older than Harte. Lord Houghton was born in 1809 and educated at Trinity College, Cambridge. He was the friend of Tennyson, A. H. Hallam, Thackeray, the Brownings, Walter Savage Landor, and Heinrich Heine and had "discovered" Swinburne. He was himself a published poet and had edited the *Life and Letters of Keats* in 1848. Ironically, he may best be remembered today for his large collection of pornography and erotica. His country seat Fryston Hall at Ferrybridge in Yorkshire was known as "Aphrodisiopolis."

Froude was hardly more conventional a man. Born in 1818, he was educated at Westminster and Oriel College, Oxford. He had been "an early casualty of the Oxford movement" led by J. H. Newman and lost his faith when Newman left the Church of England in 1845. Four years later he wrote a scandalous novel, *The Nemesis of Faith,* in which he revealed his religious doubts and sexual frustrations, and was obliged to resign his fellowship at Exeter College. His life from then on had been full of controversy. He maintained himself by journalism and edited *Fraser's Magazine* from 1860 to 1874. An intimate of Thomas Carlyle, he would cause one of the greatest biographical scandals of the nineteenth century by his editing (or rather lack of editing) of Carlyle's *Reminiscences* (1881) and by publishing the *Letters and Memorials* of Carlyle's wife, Jane Welsh Carlyle, which revealed that the national hero was impotent.

Yet the Carlyle scandals lay still ahead of Froude when in mid-August 1878 Harte visited him at the picturesque country house in Devonshire. Froude had leased the Molt for the summer from a relation, the Earl of Devon. Froude was sixty, had lost his second wife in 1874, and lived with his three children and widowed sister-in-law. The visit made quite an impression on his American friend, who wrote of it at length both to his wife and to his niece Gertie. In the letter to Anna he exclaimed that Froude, "dear old noble fellow," was "splendid":

> I love him more than I ever did in America. He is great, honest, manly—democratic in the best sense of the word—scorning all syco-phancy and manners, yet accepting all that is round him . . . There are only a few literary men like him here, but they are kings. I could not have had a better introduction to them than through Froude, who knows them all, who is Tennyson's best friend, and who is anxious to make my *entrée* among them a success. I had forgotten that Canon [Charles] Kingsley, whom you liked so much, was Froude's brother-in-law until Froude reminded me of it. So it is like being among friends here.

The eldest daughter, but for her pronunciation, would be in style and intellect a perfect copy of an educated Boston girl, he wrote to his niece: "She knows all kind of dreadful things . . . and talks about them as freely as a man." Her sister was only ten years old, but remarking something Harte had said to her father one day, she said to her sister that "she feared Mr. Bret Harte was inclined to be skeptical." Gertie could "[i]magine how I regard this terrible infant." The sister-in-law was the widow of a bishop and "looks like Queen Elizabeth and asks me civil questions about America in a voice like Mrs. Siddons." He wasn't sure if there was a Mrs. Froude and didn't dare ask.

During the next few years, when he was in London Harte would be invited to Lord Houghton's notorious breakfasts and would also meet him through the Rabelais Club, of which they were both members. Froude he would see more often, staying at his London home at 5 Onslow Gardens when visiting from Germany and later seeing much of him socially when Harte himself moved to London. It was maybe not surprising that as unconventional a writer as Bret Harte should find these iconoclasts congenial company and vice versa, but Harte soon found favor with a much larger segment of English "high society." As one observer wrote after Harte's death, "No visitor to this country who was merely a man of letters ever had so much the run of English social life as Bret Harte." "No one is made more cordially welcome in literary society, and, indeed, in society of any kind when he chooses to favour it with his presence," wrote the novelist Justin McCarthy in his *Reminiscences* in 1899.

Upon returning to London from the Molt, Harte was invited to Lord Byron's legendary home, Newstead Abbey, now owned by Colonel William Frederick Webb and his wife, Geraldine. Strangely enough, Harte thought he owed his invitation to his old San Francisco acquaintance Joaquin Miller. Miller had been the only familiar face he had seen in London when he first arrived in Europe, and he had taken Harte to see Dickens's grave in Westminster Abbey. Miller, who had been creating a sensation in London with his chaps and his sombrero, had been back and forth across the Atlantic several times since he and Harte parted in San Francisco eight years before. In mid-August, Lord Houghton had sent him off to Newstead with some trepidation, and Miller promised to observe all he had said "about *Rules*" and thanked him heartily for his advice.

Harte's and Miller's host was a retired officer, famous African traveler, hunter, explorer, and friend of Dr. Livingstone, "as brave and good as he is tall and strong." He and his wife took instantly to their new celebrity guest from America. "I have been told," Harte wrote to his wife while he was there, "that this beautiful house must be considered my 'English home'—to come here whenever I want, do as I like—and always feel that my English 'first cousins' would be glad to see me." Harte had never been so pleasantly convinced of the truth of all he had heard about English hospitality and he would make at least two more visits to Newstead Abbey during the coming years. He would use Newstead as the model for Oldenhurst in his romance "A Phyllis of the Sierras" (1887), Harte's rendering of the story—common both in life and literature of the time—in which the American heiress marries the lord of the manor.

On September 4, 1878, Harte wrote to Schneider from Newstead that his health had so improved that he was strongly tempted to stay longer. There was another temptation, which he also mentioned, in the form of an invitation from a newfound friend, the Duchess of St. Albans. Grace St. Albans was the Webbs' neighbor and lived at Bestwood Lodge with her husband, the Tenth Duke of St. Albans, a widower she had married in 1874. The letter to Schneider is the first mention of a woman Harte would always place on quite a particular pedestal. To Anna he wrote that she was "[a] sweet, bright, sympathetic, graceful lady to whom I took a great fancy." "I met her once or twice in my wanderings with the Webbs out toward 'Annesley' and Hucknall," he continued, "and have a very picturesque recollection of her coming through the graveyard at Hucknall Church, where Byron is buried, with a train of some of the prettiest women in England behind her—but herself the nicest of them all."

When Harte first met her, Grace St. Albans was only thirty years old. She was the younger daughter of "that brilliant and volatile wit and politician" Ralph Bernal Osborne of Newton Anner. A friend would say of her that her "chief quality was a genuine enthusiasm for life and her fellow-creatures. She loved to give sympathy and could not understand the lack of it in others." The duchess also had a keen sense of humor. Described in her obituary as an "intensely patriotic Irishwoman," she "regarded Gladstonian Home rule with abhorrence." It was this that chiefly prevented her from accepting a position as Queen Victoria's Mistress of the Robes in 1886; as an Irishwoman she could not accept an appointment under Gladstone's government. Queen Victoria, who had received similar refusals, wrote to the Prince of Wales that she honored the duchess for what she had done and added in high dudgeon: "*I know* it is NOT meant out of *want of respect for me*, but of a *sense* of *patriotism which ought always to be above party*. Still it is atrocious of Mr. Gladstone, or Lord Granville even more, to expose *me* to having only half a Household."

Harte, who always valued frankness over delicacy, continued

to write rapturous accounts of the duchess to his wife. "I'm glad
to hear from all who know her that my first impressions are correct, and that she is one of the brightest and most noble-souled
women in the peerage," he wrote in November, when he was
back in England and staying at Bestwood Lodge. Early on in their
acquaintance, the duchess had confessed to him that she had set
her heart on taking their prize guest away from the Webbs and
installing him at Bestwood, a highly ornate mock-Gothic pile de-
signed for her husband by S. S. Teulon in the 1860s. Harte had
graciously declined then, so as not to offend his hosts, but promised to return later in the season. It would not be the last time
hostesses would fight over him, though in this case he found an
equitable solution.

We do not know Anna's reaction to all this, only that when
Harte sent her a photograph of the duchess that he thought
did her justice, Anna responded that she reminded her of an
acquaintance of theirs. This was not at all what her husband
wanted to hear, and he sent off yet another photo: "You'll see
she doesn't look a *bit like Mrs. Salter,* and indeed is not. She is
really a very true, noble gentlewoman." The Duchess of St. Albans was indeed one of the highest ranking women in the realm,
irrespective of her personal noble qualities. Bret Harte also got
on very well with the duke. Descended from Charles II and Nell
Gwynn, William Amelius Aubrey de Vere Beauclerk had succeeded to the title of the second oldest dukedom in the land in
1849 at the tender age of nine. "We are very good friends—,"
Harte wrote to Anna from Bestwood, "and he is a great study to
me—and I don't know why, but I feel sometimes awfully sorry
for him. I would rather be my own dyspeptic, miserable self than
he, and the lord of this princely house and its solemn woods."

Harte would continue to send Anna bulletins of his social successes, as when he went on his first English lecture tour in early
1879. "I am asked out everywhere—and have all kinds of atten-
tions shown me—," he wrote, adding characteristically, "but I
have lost my taste for that sort of thing long ago." To his old
lawyer friend Samuel Barlow he wrote a year and a half later that
the English treated him very well as "Americans are very much
to the fore just now." Despite his inherent dislike of polite society
per se, he was perfectly aware of the advantages to befriending

someone like Grace St. Albans. In connection with his anxiousness to make her the promised visit to Bestwood, he wrote to Anna that "it would be quite a matter of *policy* in my coming lectures, to have friends among the best people."

Froude may have been the one who recommended that he go on the lecture circuit again. We know he advised his friend to ask for at least fifty pounds from the people in Hull who had expressed an interest. It was while he was at Bestwood that Harte began to make arrangements for the lecture tour. He was quite right in guessing that "with this nation of snobs" it would not hurt him "to be a friend of a Duke and an inmate of his house." When the Lord Mayor of Nottingham dined at Bestwood while Harte was there, the duke had drawn him aside and told him that Harte might be induced to lecture that winter. Whereat the mayor took Harte aside and offered him sixty pounds for a single lecture.

Harte kicked off his tour at the Crystal Palace in Sydenham on January 28, 1879. He had had a sort of dress rehearsal before Christmas in the Kursaal at Wiesbaden, where about four hundred English people had come to hear him speak. As usual, he had had his "old nervous dread" of the lecture and it took him a week to recover from it. The Crystal Palace lecture, which he thought went off very nicely, was followed in February by lectures in Hull, Southport, Hastings, and Nottingham. By February 8, he wrote to Schneider of the tour that "It's been a wretched blunder all through. Nothing has gone right, except the *Press,* and the *people.*" Harte decided to put off any further engagements and return to Crefeld immediately. After three weeks in England and five lectures, he had cleared only two hundred dollars above expenses. He spent the money on a new stock of clothes, as his wardrobe was in a "shocking state."

In late March 1879, Harte returned when he was offered eighty-five pounds (nearly $450) to lecture in Manchester. He took his cousin Callie with him for company. She was suffering from bad headaches and, as he wrote to her mother, "she needs some change from the monotony of her life here." The Manchester lecture was "a most decided hit"; the audience even cheered him when he stopped to drink a glass of water and applauded everything he said. Pecuniarily it was not quite so rewarding; there were only one hundred people present, and Harte received only half his fee from the manager, who said he had still to collect the rest. During the first week of April, Harte lectured at Halifax, Brighton, and Birmingham. Callie, who had gone with him to Manchester, decided to remain in London during the latter part of Harte's circuit and went to stay with the Trübners at their home in St. John's Wood rather than be left alone at the vast Langham Hotel.

Nicholas Trübner was a German-born publisher, a good friend of James R. Osgood, and through him a friend of Harte's since his earliest days in Europe. He also acted as Harte's London agent, and Harte was delighted with the way in which Trübner engineered a deal with Chatto and Windus in early 1880 for them to publish Harte's complete works. Trübner's wife, Cornélie, was the daughter of the Belgian consul in London, Octave Delepierre, and a woman with marked social ambitions. Despite the fact that she had her dying father in the house, the Trübners gave a dinner for Bret Harte and his cousin with their neighbor, the artist William Powell Frith of *Derby Day* fame, among the guests. "[N]o one could get up a dinner like Trübner," wrote Harvard historian John Fiske, who enjoyed his hospitality only a few months after Harte and Callie; "a sip of his wine gave one a new conception of the heights to which civilization can attain." On previous trips to London, Harte had often stayed with the Trübners at 29 Upper Hamilton Terrace, and he would continue to do so until 1881, when something happened to put an end to their friendship forever.

In early August 1879, Harte went off with Callie to Switzerland to try to regain his health, and they spent most of the time with the American consul in Zurich, Samuel Byers, at an old chateau at Bocken, ten miles outside the city and overlooking Lake Zurich. Consul Byers was evidently so taken with his notable guest that he kept notes of Harte's sayings and doings, which he worked into a two-part article for the *Overland Monthly* after Harte's death. They provide us with vivid insights into various of Harte's salient character traits and idiosyncrasies. These include his humility (he refused to let his fellow Americans at Bocken drink a toast to his health); his conversational powers (their dinners on the terrace at Bocken were "things to be catalogued in life's diary as forever worth the recalling"); his fastidiousness and "exquisite" sense of dress (he brought suits enough with him to Switzerland "for a respectable-sized gentleman's furnishing shop"); and his largesse bordering on profligacy (he nearly made the party lose their train in Zurich by running after the porter to give him two more francs when he had already paid him double wage).

In his fascinating portrait of Bret Harte in middle age (Harte left Byers and Bocken on his forty-third birthday, but said not a word about it), Consul Byers tempers his admiring stance and adds to the credibility of his narrative through his many balanced observations. Harte "was not always the ray of beaming sunshine people thought him," Byers observes, and he "had his moods of moroseness and grim dissatisfaction with all about him." At these times Callie Cooper did everything she could to cheer him up. One such time must have been when they went on an outing to Obstalden, an Alpine hamlet several thousand feet above the Wallensee, where they ended up having to sleep in a hayloft due to the lack of beds. "Mr. Harte in his stunning new clothes in the hayloft was simply mad enough to have out-done the proverbial wet hen in pure fussing." When he finally quieted down, it was with the sardonic remark that "One night of 'perfect Alpine simplicity' . . . was enough for him." To Schneider he wrote that though Obstalden was three thousand feet above the sea "it smelt and looked as dirty as if it had been in a cellar."

This is a typical reaction from Harte to the European sights he encountered. Nothing seemed to find favor with him. He was, in fact, unabashedly patriotic and, as his soon-to-be friend and traveling companion the novelist William Black observed, an "inveterate comparison-monger." The Paris exposition in 1878 was not as good as the one in Philadelphia; the Avenue de l'Opéra— "one of the great sights of Paris"—"was not as fine nor as noble as the Madison Square before the Fifth Avenue Hotel"; the Paris Opera itself was "a great ugly, pretentious building—gilded to a vulgar extent—and absolutely stifling for want of ventilation"; "the California mountains and Coast ranges" were "vastly superior" to the famous Alps; the Rhine was inferior to the Hudson; Switzerland was inferior to California and even to the Catskills; the yodel "was like the caterwauling of fifty cats, with an obligato from a donkey"; the Swiss were "the biggest frauds" he had ever met; the list goes on. The Tower of London, Holyrood Palace in Edinburgh, and Versailles all failed to impress him. The cave at Staffa in Scotland, he observed to a friend, "was really the only 'sight' in Europe that quite filled all my expectations. But alas! that magnificent, cathedral-like cave was presently filled with a howling party of sandwich-eating tourists, splashing in the water and climbing up the rocks."

In mid-March 1879, Harte had first seriously began to consider asking the State Department for a change of location. "Germany is no place for me—," he wrote to Anna, "I feel it more and more every day." He would write quietly to one or two Washington friends, he said, to see if it could be arranged. By good luck, he feared, more than through his management, consular business had been record high that year, and he felt that his record was good. One of the friends he wrote to was Charles Dana, saying that the climate was killing him in Crefeld. His health had indeed been consistently poor since he arrived in Europe. In late 1878, he had had a recurrence of his old troubles with his eyes from too much writing; his digestion was in a continual uproar, and if that wasn't bad enough, he had his first attack of rheumatism just before Christmas in 1878. In the spring of 1879, he was attacked by neuralgia—sharp nervous pains in his teeth and jaw—a thing he had previously been spared. To Anna he wrote that he slept exactly four hours no matter when he went to bed. His attacks of neuralgia and rheumatism were bad throughout the spring and summer. He blamed his ill health on the German climate and considered it the strongest reason for asking for a transfer: "I can get any number of certificates from the best German physicians here that this part of the country is injurious to my temperament and condition."

Yet he waited with his request for a transfer. He realized that when he wrote he had to have outside friends to champion his cause. At present he could not think of anyone with influence enough in Washington to assist him. It was not until later in the year, on October 7, that Harte finally sent his formal application for a transfer to Secretary of State William Evarts. He asked for a two-month leave of absence, which was immediately granted, and an exchange of station if his health did not improve in that time.

When he heard nothing further from the department in three months, he wrote to John Hay, who had been appointed assistant secretary of state in November 1879. Quite of his own accord, Harte's New York lawyer friend Sam Barlow had promised to help him, as had Clarence King, and now Harte asked Hay to do what he could.

That ill health was not the only reason for Harte's request for a transfer and that he too felt acutely the "lowering" effect of his life in Crefeld is made clear by the letter he wrote in answer to one from Hay dated January 30, 1880. Hay had encouraged him to write "frankly and fully," and Harte did not need to be asked twice. The letter is a vivid exposition of the anomaly of his position in Crefeld. "[A]s a residence for a nervous impressionable literary man, practically, socially and intellectually, no place could be more outrageously absurd than Crefeld." Did Hay—did anyone in Washington—have the remotest idea what Crefeld was like? He could imagine a town of about the size of Paterson, New Jersey, without its contiguity to a great city, without a horse railroad or a single improvement. Harte had had to remove to Düsseldorf because there were no decent lodgings to be found. All this, annoying as it was, could be borne, if it were not for the "ridiculous contrast and anomaly" with his "real standing socially and intellectually in Germany": "you cannot have—I did not have before—the least idea of my tremendous popularity as a writer here. My books are everywhere, my name is as well known as their own writers."

Harte was not exaggerating. When he arrived in Crefeld in 1878 he was already "one of the all-time bestselling American writers in Germany." By 1885, fourteen separate German editions of *Gabriel Conroy* had appeared. Until the turn of the century, Harte exceeded Mark Twain in the number of editions of his works published in Germany (109 separate editions of prose and poetry by 1912). So much more absurd, then, did it seem to the Germans that he had been relegated to such an obscure post. In Harte's words, people could not understand why the government would send a man to Crefeld whom they wished to honor, and there were even rumors about that he "was in a sort of *degrading exile for holding political opinions adverse to the government!*" His English friends got over the anomaly of his official position by simply refusing to believe he held so relatively low a rank. Benjamin Disraeli's foreign secretary till 1878, the Earl of Derby, had sent Harte an official invitation addressed to "His Excellency the American Envoy to Rhenish Prussia."

By 1880, Harte's position as an expatriate American in England was also unique. While he and Callie were in England during the spring of 1879, he was invited to the annual dinner at the Royal Academy, "the great swell dinner of the season." On April 25, when he was back in Crefeld, he received a letter from the president of the Academy, Sir Frederick Leighton, who invited him to respond to the "Toast to Literature" at the dinner. In honor of Harte's literary position, the Academy had for the first time deviated from the standard practice of asking a British author. Harte's delay in replying to the invitation put Sir Frederick Leighton "in a vexed dilemma," as he could not ask anyone else until Harte had answered. Leighton enlisted the help of the expatriate American artist George Boughton, who wrote to Trübner that Leighton "so admires Bret Harte and we all do for that matter, that he wants *him* if possible. It will be a very Grand Occasion. The Prince of Wales and no end of Big Wigs will be there—and I feel it a tremendous honour to our side that Harte is looked up to as the best man to reply. Do 'prod' him up to it. Join my humble prayer to yours or send him *this* even—I shall n e v e r NEVER forgive you Bret Harte if you don't reply at once like a good fellow and *say you will* speak!" Harte dallied and finally declined at the last moment, using Schneider's illness and the need to attend to his consular duties as a convenient excuse. Besides dreading holding a speech before so many prominent people, he was not sure it would pay, even if it would be "a good advertisement." Froude held a speech in Harte's place. It was not the first time a friend had had to step in for him.

The following year, Harte was again invited to the dinner. This time he hoped James Russell Lowell, being the newly appointed minister to the Court of St. James and the older man, would be asked to respond to the toast. Yet Harte was again asked to speak. This time he did, and when it was all over, he reported to Anna in his matter-of-fact way: "I made a neat little speech—not bad and not very good—the Prince of Wales asked to be introduced to me (he's more like an American than an Englishman), a lot of swells were 'glad to make my acquaintance,' etc., etc., and that was about all. It was a good deal of trouble for very little result." He would, no doubt, have been glad to see that his speech was reported in the *New York Tribune,* which concluded that "To his great literary reputation is now added a social popularity which comes from personal acquaintance." His society friends thronged to hear him lecture in Steinway Hall on June 21, 1880. The hall was "crowded with fashionable folk in *full dress,*" and the occasion was, in fact, "more like a small reception than an honest lecture," Harte reported to Schneider: "what between rustling silks and laces *inside* and rattling carriages and bawling footmen outside—it was a most extraordinary and amusing affair. . . . It wanted only the handing around of ices and tea, to have made it perfect." That same year—the year of the "American 'boom' " in Britain—there were even serious plans under way to start a new magazine called *Bret Harte's Monthly* with Harte as editor, but the idea was finally abandoned when *Harper's* announced plans for an English edition.

By the time of the Royal Academy dinner on May 1, 1880, Harte had been appointed American consul to Glasgow by President Hayes. According to Clarence King, who had also " 'pitched into Evarts,' " John Hay had " 'never lost an opportunity' " to work in Harte's best interest, and Harte was grateful. He agreed with Hay that Glasgow was "in every way better than Crefeld" and thanked him "very, *very* much." Glasgow had the advantage of being a full consulate, it was near Edinburgh and not too far from London and was worth three to four thousand dollars a year.

On June 17, 1880, Harte left Crefeld. After five weeks of "living in his trunks" in Paris and London, he was finally able to take over the Glasgow consulate on July 24. His predecessor, Samuel F. Cooper, "an awful old fogy," hung on until Harte had got all his papers from Washington and left the offices of the consulate in a state similar to "Mr. Micawber's office at the time of his unsuccessful coal brokerage." Harte "ran away" to Paris as soon as he could, after arranging to retain the services of the present vice-consul, "a hard-headed Scotch lawyer" named William Gibson. He went specifically to hear his niece give a concert on July 29. Gertie Griswold had just won the first prize for singing at the Conservatoire—the first ever won by an English-speaking girl—and was "thought to be 'the coming American Prima donna.'" After a few days in Paris, Harte returned to Glasgow and the Queen's Hotel, "anxious to get the consulate running smoothly."

Bret Harte got a warm reception in Glasgow. "The Scotch folk have been very kind and hospitable," he wrote to Clara Schneider; the Lord Provost had put a yacht at his disposal, and he had been invited to more "shootings" and visits than he could well attend. As in Crefeld, he had trouble finding suitable lodgings and decided to commute from Innellan, "a lovely little watering-place on the Clyde, an hour and a half from Glasgow." In a letter to a friend, he gave a vivid description of the resort, where he would live during his first fall in Scotland: "*this* is not the staring, over-dressed, negro-minstrel haunted, children-shovelling beach of Brighton, nor the fashionable, full-toiletted sands of Trouville or Etretat. It is a craggy shelf of tangled seaweed and rocks, blown over by foam and breeze; the gentlemen bathe from small boats in the offing, quite au naturel, and honest but awfully plain Scotch lassies apparently are baptized in long grey and black gowns and then stride home without stockings." He added that "[a]s I am trying to get up a good reputation here I stay at my post pretty regularly." To Schneider, he reported the same day that he was staying "close to the consulate," as he needed to "get the hang of the business." He was working hard, he wrote to Gertie, so that he might later join her "at 'Borribola Gha' or thereabouts"; "Borribola Gha" was his and Gertie's name for Newstead Abbey.

His decision not to go to Newstead Abbey but rather to accept an invitation to join a shooting party at Cumbernauld House in Scotland turned out to be a fateful one. On Monday, September 13, 1880, he suffered an accident. The gamekeeper had overloaded his gun and it recoiled, the hammer striking his mouth and cutting his lip in three places. When he returned to the house a lady fainted at the sight of him, thinking he had been shot. Harte referred to the accident as "trifling," but the wound required stitches and prevented him from talking, laughing, and, what was worst of all, smoking for several weeks. Only fear of the incident getting into the press in an exaggerated form made him write to his wife about it three days later, when he had gone into hiding at Innellan. Everyone at Cumbernauld House had been sworn to secrecy. Harte spent two weeks "invisible" at the coast and then went down to Newstead to recruit. Despite these precautions, the item got into the press in no less than three garbled versions. One had the famous American writer thrown from his horse in the hunting field, another had him "shot by a brother sportsman and seriously wounded," and yet a third reported that he and his fellow author William Black had been knocked overboard from a yacht and nearly drowned.

The accident had resulted in a great loss of blood, and by early October he was still "far from strong." By mid-October Harte was "helplessly ill," "scarcely able to sign my name to official documents, going to my office in a cab, and often being able to stay there only an hour at a time." The doctors said his condition was owing to the loss of blood, "shock," and his need to acclimatize himself to Glasgow. After he had been there a week, he had written to Anna that "the vapours from chemical factories and the thick mists make a compound that is simply diabolical. I cough night and day—for night and day are almost the same here—and suffer from neuralgia between whiles. . . . My transfer from Crefeld here on account of my health resolves itself into a ghastly farce." Harte did not begin to recover until the middle of December 1880.

There were three women who had an important influence on the course of Bret Harte's life and especially on his life as a writer. The first, as we have seen, was Jessie Frémont. The second was, of course, his wife, Anna. The third we have yet to meet. As Harte's foremost friend, companion, and advisor, her position would be unrivaled till the end of his days.

Hydeline Rodolphine Emma de Seigneux was born in Switzerland on January 12, 1833, the daughter of Emma de Hallwyl and Charles-François-Fréderic de Seigneux. She had traveled to America in her youth, and after her father's death, her mother's remarriage to the Sardinian diplomat Edouard Count de Launay, brought Mademoiselle de Seigneux to the great courts of Europe. They were stationed in Madrid in the late 1840s; in 1855, Count de Launay was appointed minister of the Piedmont to Berlin, a position he would hold till his death nearly forty years later (from 1860 as the minister of united Italy).

It was probably in Berlin that Mademoiselle de Seigneux met her future husband, Arthur Van de Velde, who was attaché and later second secretary at the Belgian legation for three years from late 1859 till 1862. She gave birth to her first child in 1864, when she was thirty-one, and when she and Bret Harte met for the first time in London in late 1878, she was the mother of no less than eight children. Her last child, Marcel, was born in 1879, when she was forty-six. Arthur Van de Velde had been attached to the Belgian legation in London since 1862, and he and his family lived in St. John's Wood, across the street from Harte's friends the Trübners.

It seems likely that it was Nicholas and Cornélie Trübner who brought Harte together with the Belgian diplomat and his wife, probably when he was staying with them at 29 Upper Hamilton Terrace in early November 1878. During the years Harte lived in Germany, their meetings were not frequent, but by the time of his removal to Glasgow, Bret Harte and Madame Van de Velde were in correspondence. The openhearted and bantering tone of the first extant letter we have from Harte to his new friend indicates the congeniality of this oddly assorted couple. Harte encouraged Madame to write him again, as he liked her letters. During the quarter century of their friendship, he never referred to her as anything other than "Madame."

On February 18, 1881, while he was staying at the Trübners' in London, he noted in his diary that he had dined for the first time at the Van de Veldes'. In the diary, which briefly records his social engagements each day, we find during 1881 frequent mentions of the Van de Veldes, who together with the Trübners and the young painter Frank Miles, formed a party that frequently dined together and went to the theater and the opera. On August 3, feeling very poorly, he accepted an invitation from the Van de Veldes to enjoy the hospitality of their summer residence in Bournemouth. He was still at Stirling House on September 19, when he heard that President Garfield had died. He returned to London the next day, picked up his trunks at Bailey's and moved them to 15 Upper Hamilton Terrace, the Van de Veldes' London home. Little did he know then that they would remain there for the next twelve years. After seeing the American minister, his old Cambridge acquaintance James Russell Lowell, Harte left for Glasgow on September 21.

Harte was back at 15 Upper Hamilton Terrace when on November 11, 1881, he first made mention of the Van de Veldes to his wife. Suffering terribly from rheumatism and dyspepsia, he had not been able to write to her for a long time. He wrote that he had "stayed with some kind foreign friends . . . —Count Van de Velde and his family—for over a month at Bournemouth" and returned to Glasgow "in company with one of my hosts, who thought me unfit to travel alone." He did not specify that his companion was *Madame* Van de Velde, with whom he toured Scotland till the end of October. His circumspection may have been owing to a nasty incident that had occurred on their return. No sooner were he and Madame back in London than Harte felt himself subjected to "mischief and innuendos." Upon investigation, he found them to originate with Cornélie Trübner. On November 4, he wrote her to demand an explanation. He found her answer "unsatisfactory" and informed her that their acquaintance was at an end. Mrs. Trübner was clearly incensed at Madame Van de Velde for annexing her prize guest; the unconventionality of Harte and Madame traveling alone in Scotland for several weeks gave her a welcome outlet for her spleen. It was not until a whole year later that Harte wrote of the incident to Anna, saying that he had only been obliged to give up one friend, Mr. Trübner: "His wife got to quarrelling with my other friends, because she and her husband could not 'run me' and keep me as their peculiar property in Society. I'm sorry—because I liked the husband."

Harte had returned to his post alone on December 19, 1881. Three days later he felt so unwell that he fired off a telegram to 15 Upper Hamilton Terrace to the effect that he was returning at once. He arrived on 7:45 a.m. and found the whole household up to receive him. It was Christmas Eve, there were presents to unpack and he had to say it felt like home. On the last day of the year he noted significantly in his diary: "Feel better again and able to write." Harte had finally found the "patron" Anna Dickinson had felt he needed. More important, after three and a half years in a "vagabond condition" in Europe, Bret Harte had finally found a home.

15 Upper Hamilton Terrace, Saturday, June 10, 1882
At the beginning of a day that promised mainly to be taken up with the arrival of his niece Gertie in London and meeting with Boucicault about his dramatization of "The Luck," Harte first had to tend to his correspondence. He was writing to thank J. Usher for giving him a letter from Longfellow on the occasion of the Celebration of the Centenary of Sir Walter Scott in 1871, and closed his letter with the words: "any line written by the 'wizened hand' that now 'lies cold' has a loving significance." It was in 1871 that he had first met Longfellow. On his desk was a copy of *Good Words* with a commemorative essay he had written on the poet, now two and a half months in his grave, in which he had recalled a certain evening eleven years before, when he had been the guest of honor at a dinner hosted by James Russell Lowell.

At midnight, Harte remembered, he and Longfellow had been the last to take leave of their host under the elms by his porch. He recalled gazing out at the moonlight night and being reminded of a line from a poem: "God makes such nights." He would have spoken it aloud if it were not for the fact that Lowell had written it. He was gripped by a sudden desire to walk the two miles back to the Howellses' house, and Longfellow had playfully offered to be his guide home through the "midnight perils" that might threaten a stranger in Cambridge. They dismissed the carriage and began to walk. Longfellow, half-earnest, half-jesting, kept up the role of guide, philosopher, and friend and began an amiable review of the company they had just left. His voice was a very deep baritone without a trace of harshness. In the sharp moonlight of the snow-covered road, a dark mantle-like cloak hiding his evening dress and a slouched felt hat covering his full, silver-like curls, he seemed the most impressive image Harte had ever seen. The experience was an echo of one he had had a short time before, when he had penetrated Niagara at sunrise on a Sunday morning after a heavy snowfall and found that masterpiece unvisited and his own footprints the only track to the dizzy edge of Prospect Rock. Thankfully, Longfellow was as sublimely unconscious of Harte's exuberance as had been the waterfall.

They passed the bridge where the older poet had once stood at midnight, and saw, as he had seen, the moon "like a golden goblet falling and sinking in the sea." They passed a plain Puritan church, whose uncompromising severity of style was so like the meetinghouse in Lexington Longfellow once had conjured up. Finally, they reached Longfellow's home, Craigie House, one of the few colonial mansions still left intact in Cambridge and at one time headquarters of General Washington.

They had parted at the gate. What Harte had not recorded in his essay was that Longfellow was so beautiful then that his companion could only think of the whiteness of the moon. He had told Annie Fields years before that had he stayed a moment longer, he feared he should have put his arms around him and made a fool of himself then and there. Instead he abruptly said good night and went on his way.

By Christmas of 1881, Bret Harte had embarked on a double life. On the one hand he was the American consul to Glasgow, the chief official representative of the United States government in Scotland. On the other, he was the literary celebrity and author, whose sayings and doings were the subject of remark and report on both sides of the Atlantic. These two roles were in potential conflict, and Harte's need to sustain both of them would constitute the most delicate balancing act of his life.

The year 1881 was one of illness but also of much pleasure and leisure, and it had shown Harte to the full the manner of life he might lead in England. The time spent in the Van de Veldes' lap of luxury, whether at Stirling House in Bournemouth or 15 Upper Hamilton Terrace, must have convinced him that he would never be happy alone in Glasgow again. When there he felt that he was "living by gaslight in a damp cellar with an occasional whiff from a drain, from a coal-heap, from a mouldy potato-bin, and from dirty washtubs." He shuddered to think of the loneliness and dreariness of his first lodgings and did not think much better of the rooms he had in the fall of 1882 at the half-empty McGregor's Hotel in St. Vincent Street: "some one's 'folly,' " a building too fine for its locality in which he was able to rent two rooms at a moderate sum. The only advantage, he wrote to Anna, was that he could "offer some English or German friend a room for a night out of the dreary waste of unoccupied suites of apartments."

In fact, Harte was rarely in Glasgow, and on the few occasions when he visited the city, he always had with him one or more members of the Van de Velde family. He wrote to Anna on April 22, 1881, that he was finding the consular work difficult—a seaport consulate was all new to him—and it was only the support of American friends such as John Hay that kept him at his post. As a matter of fact, despite the difficult and unprecedented cases that had come up, Harte was not at his post at all at the time of writing this letter and had not been since the middle of March; he would not return to Glasgow till September and then he was only passing through. In 1881, he spent a total of three weeks and four days in Glasgow; in all 1882, he spent no more than two weeks there. His absences in 1882 brought a reaction from Washington. The assistant secretary of state wrote to ask about the rumors that he had been absent "a very large proportion of each quarter." Harte wrote back that "As I do not keep a diary, I cannot . . . give the Department the exact dates of these absences"—a downright lie. Harte did keep a diary, which makes it possible to know exactly where he was during these years. During the five years of his appointment to Glasgow, he spent no more than one fifth of his time at his post.

His extreme absenteeism was possible because he could safely leave the consulate in the hands of his vice-consul, William Gibson. As he noted in defense of his absences, the Glasgow merchants preferred to do their purely clerical business with the vice-consul, "one of the best and most efficient lawyers in Glasgow." There was only one other American resident in Glasgow, and he was after Harte's place. "No Americans come to Glasgow to *complain*," he added. "In fact, it is the utter desolation and loneliness which often makes me run down to London to see the face of a fellow country-man." Ever since he came to Europe, he had been "dying for a breath of Western slang." On hearing that an old New York friend was in London, Harte wrote to him from Crefeld, where he was waiting for his successor to arrive: "I am so longing for a good talk with a live New Yorker—so longing and homesick, dear old fellow, for *your* smile and hand-shake—that if it were not that I should be obliged to return here again I should post off to that Friday dinner at once!"

Harte wrote to Anna in February 1882 that he felt he was "rather a good Consul": "All I believe they can say about me is that I don't go much into society, and that I escape the fogs of Glasgow whenever I can. But even when I am away, all my letters and documents pass under my eye, and I telegraph often twice a day." As he was nearing the end of his consular years, he returned to the same theme, writing somewhat defensively that "For the last five years I have never been a day without communication with the Consulate and even when I am in London for a holiday, or for work (I find it difficult to write in Glasgow), I always write daily and personally superintend—though at a distance—my consular work."

The greatest challenge to Harte's ingenuity during these years was how to hide from the public and the press the extent to which he was absent from his post. This he did by consistently dating his America-bound letters from Glasgow, regardless of where he was actually writing them. This meant that he had to mail them to Gibson in Glasgow and have him send them on to ensure that they had the correct postmark. This practice even extended to Harte's letters to his wife.

In the spring of 1885, we find a good example of how Harte's life during these years was ruled by fear of the press. That year he felt he again had to decline an invitation from Count de Launay to his annual Court Ball in Berlin in honor of the German emperor. Harte was to have gone with Madame, who was assisting her mother as hostess, on April 13; there was also to be a separate party at the embassy in his honor, and Bismarck's son had invited him to come and stay at the German chancellor's home. "[I]t would have been an affair of only two days," he wrote to Anna, "but—you can imagine what would have been said in America!" And yet, he had not taken a leave of absence since his appointment to Glasgow, he claimed.

When Harte left America, it was a relief he wrote to Anna, "not to see the daily papers, or hear the ugly things said about my poverty, my debts, and my 'failing honours.' " Upon his first arrival in Europe, the French and English papers had copied "all the ugly things" that had been said about him, but then things had quieted down. In late March 1880, at about the same time it became apparent that he was being transferred to Glasgow, the *Röhmische Zeitung* published an article that said Bret Harte " 'was sick of Germany and was going to resign.' It then added that it was 'well known' that the 'genial poet' was beset with an ungovernable passion for 'fire-water' (*feuerwasser*—brandy) brought on by his early habits in California: that his Government had sent him to Germany hoping to cure him of it . . . , but that, alas, it was all in vain." Harte, confined to his bed in Düsseldorf because of an inflammation of the throat, referred to the article as "abominable and filthy slander" in a letter to Schneider, and at once wrote to demand a retraction or he would instigate proceedings against the paper. Harte's doctor Van Köhlwalter wrote an indignant letter to the paper, stating that from Harte's nature, habits, and symptoms, he "not only was not, but never could have been, a drunkard," and the Berlin paper retracted its statements. When Harte reported the incident to his wife, he commented that "anybody who really knew me—or saw me in company or at dinners—knows that I drink sparingly (I think I told you that I could not take any stimulants here), so that to them the story was absurd."

Because of his acute dyspepsia, Harte may in fact have cut back on his consumption of alcohol. When Anna ordered him to try the German wines to improve his health, he answered that "almost every form of wine or alcohol disagrees with me." Yet we know that he partook of a "petite verre" with Schneider, and Consul Byers, who had to share a bedroom with Harte at Bocken because of the lack of rooms, could report that because he suffered from dyspepsia and neuralgia, Harte kept a bottle of "prescription" by his bedside "for temporary relief." "[N]o one ever saw Bret Harte the worse for his 'prescription,' " Byers wrote. "It did not even make him jolly." From what we know of Harte's drinking habits in the late 1870s, it is not unlikely that his "prescription" was indeed whiskey.

One of the first things Madame Van de Velde did when Harte became a more or less permanent feature of her household was to send him off to her doctor. In early November 1881, he told Harte he had to give up "stimulants," and his patient duly noted this in his diary. Harte got the same advice from a doctor he saw in Bournemouth the following year. On April 13, 1883, he wrote triumphantly in his diary: "Give up whiskey for good and all!" It appears that he was able to stick to his resolve. In February 1884, Harte wrote to his wife that he was "quite a blue-ribbon man" and in the interest of his health had "not touched any alcohol of any kind for a year." A year later he described himself as "almost a teetotaller." Yet when William Black wrote to him on May 25, 1884, inviting him to Brighton, he regretted that because his house had burned down he could only offer him "a lodging-house bunk by way of a bedroom," but he hastened to add that "the whisky is of the same quality as heretofore." Maybe he was not aware that his friend had reformed.

What Harte had not told his German friends about the *Zeitung* story was that the "*slander came from America!*" In speculating on who could have put out the slanderous report copied by the German newspaper and reports of a similar nature, it is tempting to recall what Mark Twain wrote to William Dean Howells in June 1878, when he had first heard of Harte being sent to Germany: "Harte is a liar, a thief, a swindler, a snob, a *sot*, a sponge, a coward, a Jeremy Diddler" [my italics]. Twain felt snubbed by the president ignoring his testimony and thought sending "this nasty creature to puke upon the American name in a foreign land" was too much. Significantly, Twain demanded to know what German town Harte was "to filthify with his presence" and threatened to write the authorities there that he was "a persistent borrower who never pays."

We will never know if it was Twain who originated the report that was copied by the *Röhmische Zeitung*, but it does not seem unlikely, taking into account his intense dislike of his former friend and our certain knowledge that throughout his life he let no opportunity to impugn Harte's reputation pass him by. In Heidelberg (at the time of the letter to Howells quoted above), he shocked journalist Frank Harris, who had mentioned that he liked Harte, by inveighing against him. Harris never liked Twain after that and actively avoided him. When Henry James made a similar mistake by asking Twain if he knew Bret Harte, he responded that "Yes, I know the son of a bitch." Time did not diminish his choler. On a trip to Australia in 1895, he raised a storm of protest by saying that Harte was a "sham and shoddy." We have already had ample evidence of the vitriol in his *Autobiography*; while he was composing it, he entertained visitors such as Thomas Wentworth Higginson with unflattering stories about Bret Harte. In contrast, Harte appears never to have given his lost friend so much as a passing thought after they parted forever in 1877. When he happened to mention him, it was en passant, in an entirely innocuous way or with admiration for his writings.

It is not likely that Mark Twain was the source of all the bad press Bret Harte was subject to in America during his later life. In a letter to Hay in 1880, Harte wondered who could be "the paragraph fiend" who continually pursued him, and in 1885, he wrote to his wife that "[t]he attitude of the press in my own country shows me very plainly that there is not personal sympathy whatever for me there." Much of the press antagonism against Harte probably had its origin in the scandal surrounding the production of *Two Men of Sandy Bar* in 1876. That scandal marked Bret Harte's definitive fall from grace with the American press, and once he had made a bad impression it was hard to right it again.

In the spring of 1885, Bret Harte was anxiously waiting to see if he would be retained in office. Grover Cleveland had been elected president and, "unless by some extraordinary intervention," Harte did not expect to be kept in place by a Democratic administration. Thus it was no surprise to him when the ax fell on July 18, 1885. As so often before, Harte first received word through the newspapers. Under "Latest Intelligence. The United States," the *Times* printed a notice to the effect that "The President has appointed Mr. Francis Underwood, of Massachusetts, American Consul at Glasgow." Typically, Harte was in London when he read the news. Accompanied by Madame and her daughters Beatrice and Marguerite, he had gone to Scotland for a month in June, partly to investigate the affair of his chief clerk Peter Forgie, who had been dismissed for embezzling consular funds. The party had returned to town on July 7. Harte did not write Anna the news until August 3—he expected she would read it herself in the American newspapers—and kept up the farce of pretending to be in Glasgow waiting for his successor till the middle of August. On August 20, the official day Underwood was to take over, Harte was in fact in the country with the Van de Veldes. He never returned to Glasgow at all, but only wrote to give up his rooms at the Grand Hotel and warehoused his effects.

Harte had been expecting to be replaced but "was quite unprepared for the excuse that I was removed for 'inattention to duty' ". The "gratuitous insult" galled him. In the opinion of his vice-consul, who had served under four of Harte's predecessors, "the office had never been as purely administered" as under Harte. He regretted that "this is the kind of thing the Government cannot know, so, except for the knowledge that my V.-C. respects me—I am none the better for it." What the government did know was the story they heard from eager office seekers, such as F. Marion Tower, who wrote to Secretary of War William C. Endicott in the spring of 1885: "[I]t has come under my personal experience in what a loose and shiftless manner the duties of the Glasgow consulship have of late years been treated. Other business men in Glasgow have continually remarked upon it to me as an American and I have had occasion to call personally on the consul six or eight times during the last 2 or 3 years without ever being able to find him."

Harte, of course, was an easy target. In one sense, it was a bit of a miracle that he had been retained as long as he had—five full years in Glasgow and before that two in Crefeld. He kept the wheels turning, even from a distance, but his lengthy absences did not look good. When the Republicans returned to power with the election of Benjamin Harrison in 1888, Harte, ever the optimist, wrote immediately to John Hay asking what he thought were his chances for a new appointment. "I believe my record in the State Department is a good one . . . ," he wrote, "and I have reason to think that the affairs of my Consulates in Crefeld and in Glasgow were so well administered that the fact of my being absent, could have been only known by actual personal inquiry." Hay approached Secretary of State James G. Blaine in late 1889 and received the following reply: "I have been and still am anxious to serve Harte especially as it would be gratifying to you. Harte has injured himself in these prosaic days by making himself (so says the Consular Bureau) the worst consul thus far recorded—only I want to appoint him for his grace and gain in other fields! . . . When I think of the pleasure Harte has given me I am eager to appoint him & don't care how badly he neglects his official duties!" Yet by 1890, Hay was still not "sanguine of success" in getting his friend a new consular appointment. Bret Harte never held a government post again.

CHAPTER 9

Lord of Romance
(1885–1892)

I see no limit to the future in art of a country which has already given us Emerson, that master of moods, and those two lords of romance, Poe and Bret Harte.

Oscar Wilde to A. P. T. Elder, 1885

In the issue of *Belgravia* for August 1881, an essay appeared entitled "Francis Bret Harte." The four-page article concluded with the following rhetorical flourish: "The public of both continents is now impatiently awaiting a new volume from the gifted pen that has given the world so rich an intellectual feast. The golden vein cannot be exhausted, the muse must not be silent, for it is more especially to the aristocracy of talent and genius that the motto applies, 'Noblesse oblige.' " The author of the essay was probably in a better position than anyone to bring about the desired result. It was Madame Van de Velde, or "M. S. Van de Velde" as was her nom de plume. By the end of the year, Harte had begun to write again under her very roof, after a hiatus of one and a half years. During his two years in Crefeld, he had written and published a total of nine stories, which appeared simultaneously in the *New York Sun* and *Belgravia,* a well-produced English literary monthly that published poems, stories, and serialized novels by names such as Charles Reade, Wilkie Collins, Mark Twain, Ouida, Swinburne, and Thomas Hardy. The last of these stories, "A Gentleman of La Porte," appeared on July 4, 1880. Because of the increasing pressure of his new consular duties in Glasgow and his ill health during 1880–81, Harte did not publish a story again until "Found at Blazing Star"—an intricate murder mystery with the typically passive Hartean hero and forceful heroine— appeared in early March 1882. "I have at least one satisfaction," he wrote to his wife on February 10, 1882. "During the last ten years I have done scarcely anything in the way of literary work. I began to fear that I had lost the power. It is with heartfelt gratitude that I find I can at least *seem* to do it." In unbroken succession, Bret Harte would write well over a hundred stories during the next two decades. Nearly all these stories were written in one or another of Madame Van de Velde's homes.

Harte wrote to Anna in 1882: "I suppose I am most at ease with my friends the Van de Veldes in London." The Van de Veldes had adopted him into their family, he added, "Heaven knows how or why," as simply as if they had known him for years. Harte was naively unconscious that there could be advantages to having a "writer in residence," especially if you were a lady with literary ambitions and a precarious social position. Correspondence in Arthur Van de Velde's file in the archives of the Belgian Ministry of Foreign Affairs shows that there were skeletons in the closet at 15 Upper Hamilton Terrace.

In November 1889, we find two of the Van de Velde daughters in Berlin, where their presence is threatening to create a diplomatic scandal, albeit on a small scale. On November 15, Baron Greindl, the Belgian minister to Berlin, writes confidentially to his foreign minister in Brussels. He has had a visit from Monsieur d'Usedom, the "introducteur des ambassadeurs," who wanted to know if the Van de Veldes were indeed married and what was the status of the two young girls handing out calling cards under the name of Van de Velde. Baron Greindl had told him that the Van de Veldes *were* married but that the girls had to be regarded as the legal children of Madame Van de Velde's first husband. Baron Greindl wanted to know what he should do if the Countess de Launay asked him to present the girls at court? It was clear she regarded her grandchildren as Belgian and had already come to present them to Madame Greindl at the legation. The reply he received from Brussels was that there was no record of the Van de Veldes ever having been married or of Madame having obtained a divorce from her first husband, who was still living in 1886. The conclusion regarding the children was that if they *were* Arthur Van de Velde's, they were born out of wedlock. Thus the two girls were not legally Belgian and should not be presented at court by the Belgian minister.

The birth certificates of the nine Van de Velde children, all born in London between 1864 and 1879, list Arthur Van de Velde as the father and a certain "Marie de Sauges" as the mother. Madame Van de Velde was baptized Hydeline Rodolphine Emma but signed herself "*M. S.* Van de Velde." Does M. S. stand for Marie de Sauges? Very likely. In a letter to an editor Harte refers to " 'M. de S.'—Madame Van de Velde's letters," making the inference explicit. We can only wonder why Madame changed her name. Maybe it was her way of putting the past behind her. The only other piece of factual information we have on this piquant state of affairs is in the records of the Seigneux family, which show that Madame Van de Velde *had* been married previous to her union with Arthur Van de Velde and that she was indeed divorced. Her first husband was a second cousin of the Seigneux family called Ludolph Bacon. We can be fairly certain that the Van de Veldes met in Berlin while Arthur Van de Velde was stationed there between 1860 and 1862. Madame was probably already married at this point. In November 1862, Van de Velde was transferred to London, and regardless of when Madame followed him there, they had their first child together on January 14, 1864. Most likely the couple cohabited until 1879, when Madame was finally able to obtain a divorce and they could be legally married. It was possibly the fear of scandal in connection with the divorce and the revelation that he had had eight children with a women that was not his wife that forced Monsieur Van de Velde to resign his diplomatic post on February 16, 1879. Five months later the couple had their ninth and final child. The official reason for Van de Velde's early retirement (he was only forty-two) was that "he could not with his large family take an important appointment offered him at Mexico." He wanted his children to be educated in England.

How much did Bret Harte know about all of this? Probably not much, at least not in the mid-1880s. On April 19, 1886, he wrote to his wife: "She [Madame Van de Velde] and her family have always been very kind to me and my position in their family [crossed out] household has been . . . homelike—but there are many things I don't understand that occur frequently and which I prefer not to question under[?] their hospitable roof." At any rate, this new information about Harte's host family throws light on the question of why Madame would press the American author so ardently to her capacious bosom. When Van de Velde retired from public life in 1879 with the rank of councillor of legation, he applied for the purely honorary title of "ministre résident." His application was granted more as a sign of the respect held for him in the Belgian Foreign Ministry than for what his former diplomatic duties had involved. Despite their wealth and culture, in high society terms, the Van de Veldes were, strictly speaking, nobodies. Though they appear to have been able to keep the murky origins of their liaison under wraps—at least for a time—their social position was indeed precarious. Madame Van de Velde was a woman with keen intellectual interests and an artistic bent, but in the late 1870s her chance of ever being published or of establishing a literary "salon" in St. John's Wood seemed infinitely remote. Enter Bret Harte, author celebrity and the darling of the British aristocracy. In brief, Madame Van de Velde saw an opportunity to enter the gilded portals of the social elite riding on Harte's eminently fashionable coattails, and Arthur Van de Velde—by all accounts a most amiable man, who had already proven his devotion to his wife by sacrificing his career to be with her—clearly had no objections. As we have seen, Harte himself was ripe for the picking, and making him part of the Van de Velde family was really a matter of a few months in the fall of 1881.

On the opening page of the second volume of Madame's *Cosmopolitan Recollections* (1889), we find the following passage: "It has been the good fortune of some celebrities—princes, statesmen, poets, artists, inventors, or savants—to have near them through life a devoted and loyal woman, demanding nothing in return for her steadfast affection but the privilege of being silently useful; obliterating her own personality, but ever at hand; accepting her effacement in the hours of success and joy; upheld by the secret consciousness that her sympathy will be sought in the time of sorrow and need, and that she can minister to a troubled mind." Based on what we know about Harte and Madame

Van de Velde's friendship, we realize that this is a thinly veiled self-portrait. In 1883, Harte wrote the following letter to Madame:

My dear friend,

When I beg you to accept the enclosed portfolio I do not for a moment ever expect it to supplant the memory of the old one which is endeared to me by the recollection of the hours you have spent over it in deciphering my exasperating manuscripts and making them intelligible to the printer, or in giving them another chance for immortality by clothing them in the language of your own native land. I am only trying to symbolize in this little gift something of my gratitude to you as amanuensis, translator, critic, and above all—friend.

I am not King of France or I should quote to my Prime Minister the words of Louis to Richelieu: "Lord Cardinal, you must take up again the portfolio you have laid down. In all my empire there is none worthy to follow you."

Always, dear friend,
yours most gratefully,
Bret Harte

The letter shows the extent to which Madame Van de Velde acted as Harte's unpaid secretary and, in addition to being his translator, hostess, and friend, was truly his "guardian angel." The most self-denying task Madame set herself was the painstaking drudgery of transcribing Harte's diaries for the years 1881–88 into a single morocco-bound volume. She gave ample return for the benefits she drew from her relationship with the famous author, and there is no reason to revise the belief, prevalent even in Harte's day, that to her and her family's "kind care . . . does the world owe the later stories which have served to rehabilitate periodically a fame that might have been lost."

In his widely circulated guide to aspiring authors, *The Pen and the Book* (1899), Walter Besant estimated that there were only sixty to seventy authors on both sides of the Atlantic "whose incomes reach the four figures" (that is, of course, in pounds). The census of 1891 showed 5,800 authors, editors, and journalists resident in England and Wales alone, and Besant estimated that when the part-timers were included the real number of people writing one thing or another was closer to twenty thousand. During his years abroad, Harte's income places him squarely in the select company of the four-digit earners. During the twenty years when Harte was fully active as an author in England, he earned at least $175,000, that is not taking into account his consular salary from 1878 to 1885 (which came to $20,000) and income from his one produced play, *Sue* (1896/98). This sum averages out to $8,750 or £1,750 a year. In England, a literary journalist was fortunate if he earned $1,500 a year during this period. In present-day dollars $175,000 would be about $2,500,000.

In the spring of 1882, as he was about to embark on the twenty most productive and remunerative years of his literary career, Bret Harte wrote to his wife:

> I am only too thankful to be able to still keep the ear of the public in my old way. For, in spite of all the envious sneers and wicked prophecies that follow me, I find I still hold my old audience and that the publishers are quite ready for me when I have anything ready for them. It is quite wonderful also what a large and growing audience I have all over the Continent; anything I write is instantly translated. I should be, indeed, content if it were not that play-writing is so vastly more profitable, and that, with all my popularity as a *romancier,* I fear I could not more than make a scanty living.

Had Harte written the letter at the end of the year, his dire predictions about the "scanty living" of a popular romancer might have been somewhat different. He sold the short romance "Flip" for a total of $2,350 or $152 per one thousand words. In addition, he got $1,025 for the volume rights. Together with the two other romances of similar length he wrote in 1882, his total income from his literary labors that year was $6,210. At his regular rate of six hundred words per day, these three stories were the work of a little over two months.

Every word Harte wrote was published, usually on both sides of the Atlantic simultaneously and in several European languages. Most of his stories were sold before he even put pen to paper and at the prices he named. For every word he wrote between 1878 and 1902, Harte could expect to earn eleven cents on average, that is sixty-six dollars for the six hundred words he wrote on an average day. By 1895, as Harte's agent A. P. Watt wrote to the editor of *Scribner's Magazine,* his average rate for the serial rights to a story was $50 per thousand words in England, $25 per thousand words in the United States, and $70 per thousand words for both serial rights combined. This was at a time when the regular rate paid by the better American magazines was between half a cent and a little over a cent per word or $5–12 per thousand words. During the 1880s, one cent per word was standard even for highly valued contributors, and two cents was rare. *Harper's Weekly* paid well, giving their regular contributors $10 per thousand words. They paid Bret Harte $26 per thousand words for "Maruja" (1885), $18 per thousand words for "The Crusade of the Excelsior" (1887), $20 per thousand words for "The Heritage of Dedlow Marsh" (1889), and $25 per thousand words for "The Bell-Ringer of Angel's" (1893). *Cosmopolitan* wrote to Theodore Dreiser in 1898 that their rate was one cent per word, yet they gave Harte 2.4 cents per word for one of his last short stories, "Mr. MacGlowrie's Widow" (1902).

Though Harte initially published everything he wrote in periodicals of one kind or another, he continued to collect his stories and publish them in volume form at regular intervals. As the *Dial* noted in 1885: "When Mr. Bret Harte has completed three of his short stories, he puts them into a dainty little volume." The number of stories in each volume would vary, but the regularity of their appearance did not. In August 1897, the trade journal the *Book Buyer* could announce that a new romance by Bret Harte called *Three Partners* was about to appear. The announcement of a new book by Harte was familiar reading, they wrote, but less generally known was the fact "that his popularity, as manifested in sales, remains unbroken. For each new book that he writes there is the same sure demand as for the last." This statement is supported by the production ledgers of Chatto and Windus, the company that published most of Harte's books in England between 1878 and 1902. Though the ledgers give the number of books *printed* and not the exact number sold, they give us a good indication of how many books Harte was selling in England in the latter part of his career. *The Heiress of Red Dog and Other Tales,* the first volume published by Chatto and Windus, containing stories and poems written during the last years of the 1870s, sold 3,200 copies between its appearance in mid-March 1879 and July 4. By August 8 that year, the initial print run of 4,000 copies had been sold out and the publisher printed 2,000 further copies. The book was reprinted in 2,000 copies again in 1882 and in 1,500 copies exactly ten years later. Harte appears to have had a 15 percent royalty on the book and received a total of $365 for it. His next book, *The Twins of Table Mountain* (1879), a thin volume containing only the title story, had an initial print run of 5,500 copies. This time Harte sold the English volume rights for a lump sum, $375, and that appears to be the way he continued to dispose of the volume rights to his books. Despite the publisher's assertion that the book "is not selling nearly so well as we expected," they printed a further 3,000 copies of it only a month after its initial release. *Jeff Briggs's Love Story* (1880) was equally successful. *Flip and Other Stories* (1882) sold upward of 13,500 copies during its first year, *Maruja* (1885)—which was not well received by the reviewers—nearly 6,000 copies. Harte's many later volumes for Chatto and Windus were usually printed in 5,000–6,000 copies and the bestseller *A Waif of the Plains* (1890) in a total of 17,000 copies. As these numbers show, the sale of Harte's books in England was steady and high. Nigel Cross tells us that the print run of the average novel rarely exceeded 2,000 copies and more often than not it was set at 1,000 copies or less. Walter Besant estimated that if a novel sold six hundred copies, it would in fact have paid its expenses with a small margin left over.

The sale of Harte's books in both England and America was clearly high enough to bring his publishers the required profit, but it seems fairly certain that none of his many later volumes gained the circulation of *The Luck of Roaring Camp and Other Sketches* (1870). This is not to say that he was getting fewer readers. As a story writer rather than a novelist, Harte's main readership was a magazine and newspaper readership. This public grew spectacularly toward the end of the century with an increase in literacy and leisure and a corresponding increase in the number of periodicals and their affordability. "Think!" Walter Besant exclaimed in 1899. "One-hundred-and-twenty millions of possible readers at the present day, against 50,000 in the year 1830—only sixty years ago!" In America, where according to some witnesses he was "played out," Harte probably reached more readers than ever before with his story "The Indiscretion of Elsbeth" (1896) for the *Ladies' Home Journal,* which was one of four circulation leaders from 1890 and had reached a record circulation of 600,000 by 1891. Another of Harte's outlets, the *Saturday Evening Post,* had a circulation of 250,000 to 300,000 in the late 1890s and close to half a million in 1902. More than half a million buyers could read his "How I Went to the Mines" in the *Youth's Companion* in 1899. The *New York World* had a circulation of 375,000 in 1891, when Harte published several stories there. In England, an issue of the *Strand* containing one of his stories might sell half a million copies and at least 300,000. By comparison, the *Atlantic* only had a circulation of 35,000 in the early 1870s.

In the size of his audience and the prices he could obtain for his stories, if not in their quality, Bret Harte had come a long way since the late 1860s. For the 3,400 words of "Tennessee's Partner" he was paid $23 in 1869—a little over half a cent per word—and the story appeared in a magazine with a circulation of 10,000. Thirty-two years later, "The Adventures of John Longbowe," a story of exactly the same length brought in at least $210—over six cents per word—and appeared in a magazine with a circulation of more than 300,000.

It has been the opinion of nearly everyone who has studied the many narratives Harte produced during his years abroad that he never wrote anything to compare with his short stories for the *Overland Monthly.* Despite Donald Glover's attempts to upgrade the evaluation of Harte's later work, there can be no question that from the point of view of originality, Harte never equaled his stories of the late 1860s. But before we dismiss this large body of later texts as a set of inferior, diluted copies of the *Overland* tales, we need to realize that they represent a distinctive phase of Harte's career in which his goals, his possibilities, and his audience were different from the period from 1868 to 1871, when he was editor of a literary magazine, when he was exclusively a short story writer, and when he was not yet world famous.

During the last quarter of a century of his long writing career, Harte became a leading exponent of one of the two major genres of prose fiction in the late nineteenth century: the romance. The genre in defining opposition to the romance was, of course, the novel, both in the minds of late Victorian authors and readers and in the generic system of a theorist such as Northrop Frye. As Frye writes in his *Anatomy of Criticism,* "The essential difference between novel and romance lies in the conception of characterization. The romance does not attempt to create 'real people' so much as stylized figures which expand into psychological archetypes." Other distinguishing features of the genre have been pointed out by Gillian Beer. In her monograph *Romance,* she points out that "[t]he romance, however lofty its literary and moral qualities, is written primarily to entertain . . . It absorbs the reader into experience which is otherwise unattainable . . . It oversteps the limits by which life is normally bounded." She writes further that the romance "is usually acutely fashionable, cast in the exact mould of an age's sensibility. Although it draws on basic human impulses, it often registers with extraordinary refinement the peculiar forms and vacillations of a period. As a result it is frequently as ephemeral as fashion and, though completely beguiling to its own time, unreadable to later generations."

When we consider these characteristics of the romance, we begin to understand both why Harte's romances were so popular with his contemporaries and why they have found so little favor with modern readers, academic or otherwise. What we see as the shortcomings of Harte's later fiction turn out to be exactly those features that make his stories good romances: "flat," archetypal characterization; an emphasis on the entertainment value of the story; "a serene intermingling of the unexpected and the everyday," and "a complex and prolonged succession of incidents usually without a single climax." The work of Frye and Beer is a useful reminder of the futility of judging the romance by the standards of the realistic novel, as has so often been done in twentieth-century criticism of Harte's works.

In addition to this generic perspective, a historical perspective will bring Harte's later writing career more sharply into focus. In *English Criticism of the Novel, 1865–1900,* Kenneth Graham gives us a thorough and illuminating account of the almost forgotten "warfare" between the new school of realism and the rival school of romance during the last two decades of the nineteenth century. "The challenge of the new realists in the early eighties," Graham writes, "brought the romance quite dramatically into the foreground of the controversy, almost as a rediscovered genre." More recently, Nancy Glazener has shown that the "romantic revival" was a transatlantic phenomenon.

Among the more voluble voices ranged on the side of romance were Robert Louis Stevenson, the critic Andrew Lang, and Rider Haggard, author of *King Solomon's Mines* (1886). In 1882, Stevenson wrote an early manifesto on behalf of romance in the first issue of *Longman's Magazine,* which was to publish several of his own and Harte's romances. Stevenson wrote candidly that "It is one thing to write about the inn at Barford, or to describe scenery with the word-painters; it is quite another to seize on the heart of the suggestion and make a country famous with a legend." To "make a country famous with a legend" was of course what Harte had done and would continue to do all his life. The year Harte published "The Crusade of the Excelsior," 1887 became a "year of recognition for the new romance" with manifestos by George Saintsbury, Rider Haggard, and Andrew Lang. Lang published his essay "Realism and Romance" in the *Contemporary Review* and described the current debate as "the old dispute about the two sides of the shield":

> On one side, we are told that accurate minute descriptions of life as it is lived, with all its most sordid forms carefully elaborated, is the essence of literature; on the other, we find people maintaining that analysis is *ausgespielt* (as Mr. Bret Harte's critical shoeblack says), and that the great heart of the people demands tales of swashing blows, of distressed maidens rescued, of "murders grim and great," of magicians and princesses, and wanderings in fairy lands forlorn. Why should we not have all sorts, and why should the friends of one kind of diversion quarrel with the lovers of another kind?

The revival of romance, according to Graham, was largely based on a yearning for escape from the harsh realities of Victorian life. "As I live," wrote Robert Louis Stevenson in a letter, "I feel more and more that literature should be cheerful and brave-spirited, even if it cannot be made beautiful and pious and heroic. We wish it to be a green place." Harte echoed this feeling in 1890 when he asked a friend to recommend something for him to read. "It must be amusing," he wrote. "I am getting too old to find any pleasure in being made sad." But it was not just older readers and writers who found the romance a welcome refuge from the pressures of their quotidian existence. Hall Caine, author of *The Manxman* (1894) and various other popular romances, was only thirty-seven when he became the romancers' new standard-bearer through his essay for the *Contemporary Review,* "The New Watchwords of Fiction" (1890). In this "high-water mark of romance theory," Caine pronounced that fact was "only an aid towards the display of passion": "true concern must be with the mysteries of human nature in its highest development—that is, in the regions of heroism."

Despite the reference in Lang's article to his "critical shoe-black," Harte kept a low profile in the ongoing debate. With the exception of an appreciation of Longfellow and of Lowell on their deaths in 1882 and 1891 respectively, his critical faculty had been lying dormant more or less since his days as editor of the *Overland Monthly.* Then, in 1897, he was induced to write an essay for *Munsey's Magazine* called "My Favorite Novelist and His Best Book." In 1888 he had expressed his "private doubts as to the relevancy . . . of such information to literature"; nearly ten years later he may have felt it was time to stand up and be counted. His essay was a glowing appraisal of Alexandre Dumas's *The Count of Monte Cristo,* a book Harte had loved since he was a child. It is interesting that Harte chose for his defense of the romance the exact same book that Stevenson had chosen in his essay fifteen years before. In contrast, by 1897 the new romance was on the wane and Harte's defensive attitude becomes increasingly clear toward the end of his essay. After a detailed analysis of the particular strengths and weaknesses of Dumas's book, Harte suddenly interjects in the final paragraph:

> But "Monte Cristo" is *romance,* and, as I am told, of a very anti-quated type. I am informed by writers (not *readers*) that this is all wrong; that the world wants to know itself in all its sordid, material aspects . . . that "the proper study of mankind is man" as he is, and not as he might be; and that it is very reprehensible to deceive him with fairy-tales, or to satisfy a longing that was in him when the first bard sang to him, or, in the gloom of his cave dwelling, when the first story-teller interested him in accounts of improbable beasts and men—with illustrations on bone. But I venture to believe that when Jones comes home from the city and takes up a book, he does not

greatly care to read a faithful chronicle of his own doings; nor has Mrs. Jones freshened herself for his coming by seeking a transcript of her own uneventful day in the pages of her favorite novel. But if they have been lifted temporarily out of their commonplace surroundings and limited horizon by some specious tale of heroism, endeavour, wrongs redressed, and faith rewarded, and are inclined to look a little more hopefully to Jones's chance of promotion, or to Mrs. Jones's aunt's prospective legacy—why blame them or their novelist?

It seems ironic that Harte published his defense of the genre in the year he wrote his last book-length romance, *Three Partners*. In the struggle between the romance and the realistic novel, it was of course the latter that emerged victorious. The voice of the future was heard in an essay entitled "The Decline of Romance" in the *Westminster Review* in 1894. "A marked feature of contemporary literature" wrote D. F. Hannigan, "is the growing antipathy to the unreal, and the desire to depict life as it is, without illusion and without exaggeration. Romance is, so to speak, at its last gasp. The attempts made by certain writers to revive it are characterised by a kind of ghastly grotesqueness. . . . The day is gone by when the novelist can be regarded as a mere caterer for the amusement of sentimental old maids or indolent fogeys. We are sick of lying and cant and platitude. We want facts, not romantic dreams."

With an understanding of the polarization of taste in the 1880s and 1890s, it becomes easier to understand the contemporary critical response to Harte's writings. Reviews of Harte's books during his last two decades were largely positive, varying from the benign to the adulatory. In the *London Academy*'s regular column "New Novels," for example, E. Purcell reviewed Harte's latest volume *By Shore and Sedge* on July 18, 1885, saying: "We keep Mr. Bret Harte's book to the last, for true genius should not be confounded among Grub Street incompetence. We need say little about what everyone will read." William Morton Payne of the *Chicago Dial*, wrote of the same book, which contained "The Ship of '49," "An Apostle of the Tules," and "Sarah Walker," "These stories are further gleanings in the romantic field of western life which the author so assiduously cultivated, and whose resources seem to be still unlimited, for Mr.

Harte does not repeat himself, although he writes so much upon the same general subject, and these stories are quite up to the level of his many earlier ones." Payne, ever a staunch supporter of Harte's work, found it "a relief" in 1888 "to turn from the lay figures so ingeniously devised by Mr. Howells and other popular novelists, to the men and women of Mr. Harte's far West—far, but familiar to us through the mediation of his genial observation and description." Eighteen years later, when Harte was dead, Payne wrote about his last collection of stories: "We could say nothing of these stories that has not been said many times before. They are like their countless predecessors, and yet their charm is unfailing, and they may be read with a zest from which the edge is hardly worn, however familiar we may be with the scores, if not hundreds, that have delighted us in earlier years." The *Times Literary Supplement* made the comment on the seven stories contained in *Trent's Trust and Other Stories* (1903) that "One might almost range them in order of merit according to their brevity, for in these shorter tales Bret Harte knew exactly what to say, how to say it, and when to stop." As in the 1870s, it is characteristic that his reviewers were most inclined to be munificent when Harte stayed within the above-mentioned "romantic field of western life." When he attempted a different type of story in "The Indiscretion of Elsbeth" (1896), the *London Athenaeum* found him to be "a not very successful imitator of 'Anthony Hope' " and added the comment that "in his stories of the wild West he is on ground where he has not been beaten." Bret Harte became, in a sense, a victim of his own success. He became typecast, like some highly successful actors the audience only believes and wants to see in one kind of role.

There was probably no single topic on which Bret Harte expended more epistolary ink than the question of how, when, and where he might be reunited with his family. The net result of these intense, prolonged, transatlantic negotiations was that for twenty years Harte did not see his wife and three of their four children. The reasons for this lengthy and ultimately permanent separation are manifold and complex. During the seven years Harte held a diplomatic post, he feared the press focus on his absenteeism that might result from even a brief visit to America.

Harte also feared that his American creditors would come after him as soon as he set foot on native soil. Though he had paid back his debt to Charles Anderson Dana within six months of coming to Europe by sending him sketches and stories for the *New York Sun,* he still had debts outstanding. It was only his distance from his creditors that prevented him from being "harried perpetually." In addition, the uncertainty of retaining his posting after the presidential election of 1880, and again after the assassination of President Garfield and the advent of the Arthur administration in 1881, made Harte reluctant to bring his family to Europe. He also pointed out that he had no regular home in England.

After he lost his consular position in 1885, Harte explained to his wife that the lack of international copyright would make it financially disastrous for him to live permanently in the United States. By the mid-1880s, the larger part of his income was earned in England, where he was paid about double what he received at home. This income was only guaranteed by his continued residence in England. From 1891, Harte also used ill health as a factor preventing him from traveling. Worries about money and the pressure of work were constant excuses.

None of these excuses, save the copyright situation, can stand up to rigorous scrutiny. We know Harte was earning more money in the 1880s and 1890s than he had ever earned before and was even able to save some of it. His wife and children would certainly have been welcome to stay with the Van de Veldes and other of his friends had they made a trip to Europe. No one would have thought it strange that Harte made a visit to his wife and family after such a long separation, and his agent, A. P. Watt, could perfectly well have handled the business side of things while Harte was away. One is forced to come to the conclusion that Bret Harte was not eager to be reunited with his family. Harte's married life had been turbulent and unsettled. The disruption of his new way of life brought about by the more or less disastrous visit of his youngest son Frank during the fall of 1884 would not have served to incite his family feeling.

To find the real reason for Harte's reluctance to be reunited with his family anytime, anywhere, anyhow, we must look behind the practical difficulties and into the realm of psychology. Behind Harte's excuses we may discern a deep fear of poverty. From the moment he first began his new life in Europe, the single most important consideration in his life was that he never again experience the degradation and desperation of his last year in America. To avoid even the possibility of a return to the hand-to-mouth existence, the ever-increasing debts, and the indignity of 1877, he was willing to be ruthless. To Anna he wrote in 1886, with uncustomary candor: "It is simply a question of money, and I scarcely dare to confess to you how, as I grow older, and my best days are behind me, that assumes a paramount importance. I could not, and would not under any circumstances, again go through what I did in New York the last two years and particularly the last winter I passed there." His letter of November 28, 1887, contains an equally revealing analysis of the determinants of the situation as he saw them:

> God knows I should not be an exile here if it were not for fear of the poverty and struggling that I am getting too old to fight against, single-handed, and which would ruin even the power of work in me. I do not believe I could do the amount of actual labour I perform now if I were, on two thirds of my present income, competing in New York with other writers, at the mercy of publishers who knew of my precarious income and availed themselves of it. The half of my success here—in fact, the whole reason why I am able to keep up my prices—is because my publishers think I am independent, and as a distinguished foreigner I have a peculiar position which my agent makes the most of in dealing with them. These are the selfish considerations that are keeping me here, in spite of estranging years that are ageing *both of us,* apart from each other, and adding an unnatural loneliness to our lives.

Experience had showed him that if he lived in London with the Van de Veldes, if he took on all the work Watt provided for him, and if he kept his family on the other side of the Atlantic, he could make ends meet.

As Bret Harte grew older, he developed an almost manic need for control over a situation that was fundamentally uncontrollable. He had no independent income to fall back on and, after losing his consular position, no steady salary. He could never know how much he would earn each year. Each new day might bring him face to face with the same decreasing payment for his work in England that he had experienced in America. That would mean ruin and humiliation. With hindsight we can see that that day never came. For the last twenty years of his life, Harte was a mainstay of the best magazines in England, and the demand for his work never let up. But Harte himself had no way of knowing that such would be the case. So he did what he could to minimize the risks and promised the moon—tomorrow. "*I* haven't lost heart yet—if *you* have—" he wrote to Anna, "I haven't yet given up the hope of being with you all again." When he wrote this, they had been apart for nearly a decade.

From 1878 onward, Bret Harte effectively returned to bachelorhood. The closest thing he had to family in actual physical proximity was Gertie Griswold, who in pursuit of her operatic career stayed for long periods in London. Harte was a most attentive and solicitous uncle, even though Gertie was properly Anna's niece. He dropped everything to go to Paris for her unexpected debut at the Grand Opera in June 1881. Whenever Gertie came to England, Harte secured lodgings for her (she preferred not to stay at a hotel) and showed her every possible attention. Just before Christmas 1883, he reported to Anna that he had "*almost* secured for Gerty the principal rôle in Gilbert and Sullivan's new opera of the 'Princess' . . . but Gerty did not quite come up to their requirements as an actress." "[F]rom all I hear and all they tell me," he continued, "I fear that Gerty *has not made a success* on the Continent and that England—or America perhaps eventually—is their *dernier ressort*." There were also financial problems, as the ill health of Gertie's mother made it necessary for them to "move around with a larger ménage than was economical." Harte demanded attention from Gertie in return for his solicitation, as he so often did from those he cared about. The following was not an untypical response to one of her prolonged silences. He was sorry to hear she had been ill, he wrote, "even though it may be a just punishment for your neglect of your noble and beautiful uncle, and that Christian and perfect example he set you and your mother—often at considerable pains and expense to himself—during your last stay in London." There was always a painful grain of truth to Harte's jesting.

With his real family three thousand miles away, it is interesting to observe how for the remainder of his life, Harte repeatedly inveigled himself into other households in the role of the avuncular "friend of the family." The Van de Veldes are only the most striking example. Before them there had been the Schneiders. In 1883, Harte met a young couple in Glasgow who would come to play a similar role in his life as had the German family. Alexander Stuart Boyd was a Scottish artist; his wife, Mary, would become a travel writer during the 1890s. They were resident in Glasgow until 1892. Harte dined with them on his visits there before his removal from office in 1885, and the Boyds were the guests of the Van de Veldes in London on several occasions. Boyd illustrated several of Harte's stories starting in 1885, and when he and his family moved to St. John's Wood, the proximity to Harte made for even greater intimacy. The Boyds had a son, Stuart, in June 1887. Harte's letter of congratulation is full of his customary caustic humor: "I hasten to congratulate you and your wife, while there is yet time, and before the artful stranger, introduced into your peaceful home, shall have revealed himself in all the plenitude of his despotic power! . . . I extend my heartfelt sympathy and compliments to Madame."

Harte's tone in his letters to the Boyds is always playful and frequently childish, as in the following to Mr. Boyd, referring to some promise his wife has not kept: "Don't let's play with her anymore! I know a nicerer girl in the next street, round the corner, who don't go with her kind of boys, and I'll introduce you." One would like to have known what the Boyds made of this pose in a man of fifty—even more, how they reacted to Harte's temper tantrum when they decided to take their vacation somewhere more suited to their son than to Harte, who was to have gone with them. When Mrs. Boyd ventured to write him of some mishap during their holidays, Harte shot back: "Don't expect me to feel the least sympathy or concern in your doings at the seaside! I have washed my hands of that ghastly fraud and deliberate deception. But I hope that Stuart paddles, and that the 'sly sea crabs' bite him; that he regularly overeats himself with unripe fruit . . . and that you will both try to make me believe that you *went away* and *hurried back* entirely on *my* account." Hyperbole aside, it is impossible not to discern the petulance at the core of this outburst. Harte was a charming but demanding friend. "Am I not thoughtful, and a treasure to any respectable and growing family?" he asked in 1892. He needed to be needed by someone, and for whatever reason, he settled on the Boyds.

Harte's many letters to his wife during the 1880s and early 1890s are a poor indicator of the real quality of his life. That he was affected by a certain amount of homelessness and loneliness is hardly surprising, but during these years he was never for a moment alone unless he himself chose to be. His diary is full of social engagements: excursions, countless theater outings, afternoon calls almost every day, weekend visits to friends in the country, concerts, exhibits. The range of Harte's friends and acquaintances is no less varied, though limited socially to the upper-middle and upper classes. As his English biographer noted after his death: "It has not fallen to his lot, as it has to mine, to mix much, and intimately, with the middle and working classes of this country."

The numerous social engagements and outings recorded in his diary from the 1880s are an important and necessary counterweight to the impression one might get from his letters that his later life was one of unremitting drudgery. Even if we consider one of his most productive years, it is hard to see that Harte's complaints in letters to his wife and Clara Schneider need make serious demands on our sympathy. In 1885 Harte wrote about 103,000 words, which was nearly four times as much as in 1884 and more than he had ever written in a year since *Gabriel Conroy*. At a rate of about 600 words per day, it still means he was only writing 172 days out of the year, slightly less than half the year. In 1886, the year he began "The Crusade of the Excelsior," the longest work of his later career, his total output was only about 90,000 words. He claimed for the first time in his life to be writing nearly a thousand words a day, which makes for only ninety days spent writing—three months of the year. In 1892, when Harte was working on the 50,000-word romance "Susy," he complained to Clara Schneider that he was "chained to the oar" like a galley slave. Yet he wrote about 100,000 words in 1892, which averages out to five and a half months' work writing 600 words per day. We know from another letter to Clara Schneider that, to Harte's way of thinking, spending six hours a day at work was excessive.

One of the factors that greatly facilitated his later life as a writer was that Harte got himself an agent, who freed him entirely from the business side of authorship and ensured that he was making maximum profits from the efforts of his pen. By the end of the nineteenth century the life of an author had become complicated. There was a myriad of literary rights to protect and exploit. An author resident in England had to ensure simultaneous publication in America, so as not to lose the American copyright. The pitfalls were as plentiful as the possibilities, and it was no wonder that Walter Besant wrote in 1899 that "The Literary Agent has now become almost indispensable for the author of every kind." "Authors as a rule," he commented laconically, "know nothing." A. P. Watt began to represent Bret Harte in 1882. He was a godsend to Harte in his role as go-between in dealing with publishers and editors. Harte wrote to his wife in 1886, after Watt had secured a third contract with the *Illustrated London News,* this time for "The Crusade of the Excelsior": "I have a very good agent here, who looks after my interest, and to whom I pay a percentage, and who relieves me from all the horrible torments of being obliged to offer my manuscripts personally to publishers, as I used to do in America. It takes away half the pains of authorship. I generally know before I trust pen to paper that my work will be disposed of and the amount it will bring." Watt took a flat rate of 10 percent on the sale of all literary property.

The seven years from 1885 to 1892 may very well have been the happiest years of Harte's life. As we have seen, in his early fifties Harte had attained a social position and a style of life that most writers could only dream of. By force of his literary reputation and ever-lengthening residence, he was one of the most prominent expatriate Americans in London. However much he might complain about the dirt and the gloomy London winters, he was living in the greatest city in the world. He had nearly all the things he most valued: a good income, fine clothes and jewelry, a highly comfortable home life, a few close friends and a large circle of interesting acquaintances—and self-respect.

During the 1880s Harte met everyone who was anyone in literary London. Of his earliest friends among English men of letters, he kept in touch with James Anthony Froude, dining frequently at 5 Onslow Gardens, Froude's London home. Harte also kept in touch with Lord Houghton until his death in 1885 at age seventy-six. In 1880, they were both founder members of the Rabelais Club. "[W]e know nothing whatever about Rabelais," Harte wrote to John Hay, who was about to become a member, "and . . . except drinking our one toast to the 'Memory of the Master,' it is considered bad form to speak of him. Nor do we, with the exception of Silenus Houghton, tell naughty stories." Among the fellow members of this "anti-club" were the noted jurist Sir Frederick Pollock, Walter Besant, Thomas Hardy, Henry James, and the artist and novelist George Du Maurier.

Harte met Henry James Jr., as he referred to him, for the first time in nine years at the inaugural Rabelais dinner in early January 1880. Just two months before, Harte had written in response to a question from the Duchess of St. Albans that yes, he had met James in Boston "some years ago," but he did not think he would recognize him. Since their first meeting he had read a collection of James's short fiction. Harte found the fate of Daisy Miller "absurdly illogical" but considered "An International Episode" to be "very good, as far as regards the American sketching." "Nothing could be more truthful than that picture of Newport life," Harte wrote to the duchess, "but here again Mr. James sees only something odd in the spectacle of that New York husband, working to keep up the Newport court of his queenly wife, and loyally accepting his own separate existence. Mr. James does not see the pathos of this figure, nor how perfectly characteristic it is of our woman-worshipping race, no more than the Englishman did." As he was himself sending his entire consular salary to his wife in America, Harte was clearly in sympathy with Mr. Watergate. "My impression of the man, however," he wrote to the duchess, "is that he is an American who has lived long enough abroad to be critical of his countrymen and countrywomen, and to be nervous, in a nice ladylike way, at the spectacle of their unconventionality. I think he hardly sees below the surface, nor understands what that unconventionality means. Seeing and feeling superficially, he never has any plot or design or moral in his work." He qualified his criticism by saying that "A literary man can hardly estimate a contemporary fairly, and I may be quite wrong in my ideas of Henry James." To his wife he wrote after meeting James again that "he looks, acts, and thinks like an Englishman, and writes like an Englishman, I am sorry to say, excellent as his style is."

Harte's first impression on meeting Thomas Hardy was that he was "A singularly unpretending-looking man, and indeed resembling anything but an author in manner or speech." Three years later Hardy would invite him to lecture to the Dorchester Lecture Society, and when Harte declined, as he had done to every invitation to lecture for the past three years, he got an "absurdly offended letter" in return. Throughout his life, his respect for Hardy's art was undiminished. In a letter to a friend not a month before meeting the English author for the first time at the Rabelais dinner, he wrote that he did not despair of her liking Hardy and wished he had another volume to send her. *The Woodlanders* was the book he was reading when he died.

Harte's contemporaneous first meetings with Hardy and George Eliot elicited a ten-page letter to his niece Gertie, which he unfortunately "thought better of sending." Yet we have a lengthy description of the sixty-year-old Marian Evans in a letter he wrote to Anna after he had called on her with Nicholas Trübner on January 4, 1880, at her home near Regent's Park. He writes:

> I was very pleasantly disappointed in her appearance, having heard so much of the plainness of her features. And I found them only strong, intellectual, and *noble*—indeed, I have seldom seen a grander face! . . . It is at times not unlike Starr King's—excepting King's beautiful eyes. Mrs. Lewes's eyes are grey and sympathetic, but neither large nor beautiful. Her face lights up when she smiles and shows her large white teeth, and all thought of heaviness vanishes. She reminds you continually of a man—a bright, gentle, lovable, philosophical man—without being a bit *masculine*. . . . She said many fine things to me about my work, and asked me to come again to see her, which was a better compliment, as she has since Lewes's death received no one.

He would return to the "Priory" several times. Four months after Harte's initial visit, George Eliot married John Cross, and just before Christmas she died.

Regrettably, Harte's impressions of Robert Browning and Oscar Wilde have not survived, if he ever recorded them. He met Browning several times in the first half of the 1880s. They exchanged books, and Harte was among the many literary notables to crowd into Westminister Abbey for Browning's funeral on New Year's Eve 1889. Harte once told Consul Byers that he thought Browning's "Bringing the Good News to Aix" the finest poem in the English language, and while staying at Bocken in 1879, he recited it "with effect and feeling." Oscar Wilde he met for the first time at an "at home" at the Lawrence Barretts on July 3, 1884. This was some years before Wilde began to write his major works. As Kipling would do some years later, Wilde had seen California through Harte's eyes on his lecture trip there in late March and early April 1882. Wilde had a keen appreciation for Harte's writings, and in his review of "Cressy" (1888), which he found one of Harte's "most brilliant and masterly productions," he compared him favorably to Hawthorne (the title character was one of Harte's unique rustic ingenues, who wreaks havoc in the little community of Indian Spring). Wilde is known to have dined at Upper Hamilton Terrace on July 7, 1887, and six days later to have entertained Harte and the Van de Veldes at an "at home," which also featured Buffalo Bill Cody, Lady Wilde, Lady Neville, and Lady Monckton.

During the latter part of the 1880s, Harte continued to have close links to the upper classes and the aristocracy. The Duchess of St. Albans was still a good friend and one of the few he mentioned in the minimalistic account of his social life he gave Anna in late 1882. In the first part of August 1885, Harte was finally able to visit the duchess at her ancestral home of Newton Anner in Ireland "in fulfilment of an old promise." "[M]uch depressed in spirits, with a severe cold," he licked his wounds after losing his consular post and considered the outlook for the future. Harte was entertained many times at the duchess's home in London, but after attending the annual ball just after Christmas in 1883, he never appears to have returned to Bestwood Lodge in Nottinghamshire. Nor do we have any mention of further visits to the St. Albanses' neighbors, the Webbs at Newstead Abbey.

There was only so much Bret Harte to go around. A partial explanation for the neglect of the Webbs may be found in the endless list of titled folk parading through the pages of the eighties diary: Lady Bouch, Sir John Clarke, Lady Goldsmid, Lord Alfred Paget, Lady Airlie, Lady Ogelvie, Sir Henry Parks, Lady Stanley, Lord Dunraven, Lord Granville, Lady Londonderry, Lady Bing, Earl and Lady Cowper, Lady Shrewsbury, Lord Abinger, Lord and Lady Pembroke, Lord Baring, Baron Ferdinand de Rothschild, the list goes on. When rumors reached Anna that he was so "greatly lionized" in England that he had no time to himself, Harte was quick to counter the charge: "This to all who know my quiet life here—is exquisitely absurd! A half-dozen nice people—or, as they call them here, 'smart people'—have always been very polite to me. As they all happen to be 'titled' folk, it is quite enough for the average American that I am a 'lion' in consequence and in fashionable society." Anyone reading Harte's diary can hardly fail to come to the same conclusion as the "average American."

One wonders what Harte the American patriot, Harte the democrat, Harte the champion of the oppressed, Harte the self-made man really thought of the nobs he was mingling with. In September 1889, he sat down to write Anna a lengthy letter on that very subject. "The spectacle one ever has," he began, "of a privileged class with nothing to think about but their own amusement, who apportion their lives with a certain kind of ridiculous formality to the regular habit of hunting, shooting, and race-going, who even arrange the meetings of Parliament so that the duty of governing the country shall not disturb their sacred institutions—is a little too dd comfortable—to be even *manly*." He continued on the all-important role of "games" in the public schools: "Once a year all England—I mean all fashionable society—flock to see their schoolboys—*not rehearse their studies,* oh, no!—but *play their games!* The Eton and Harrow cricket matches thrill the fashionable parents as no examination of studies ever could or would do . . . ; to be the mother or father or sister of a great cricketer or football player is a prouder distinction than to be related to a prize scholar." Yet Harte reserved his real scorn for "Americans who worship this sort of thing—and send their children here to have an English education!" It was maybe the one thing that most irritated him in his later life, this American pandering to English prejudices. Harte was "heartsick and consumed with shame to observe how despicably and shamelessly 'English' we are becoming in American society. . . . I really believe that the American reverence for the aristocracy and their habits is greater than it is among those to the manner born, and it is most humiliating to think that at a time when the best of England is seriously skeptical of the old and conservative, or honestly striving toward the new and democratic, American flunkeyism, in borrowed plumes, and ill-fitting cut-off clothes, swaggers into the road before it." One grave offender was James Russell Lowell, who as American minister in the first half of the 1880s "made himself vastly popular here by doing the Boston-English style, and judicious trucking." Harte was not sorry he was recalled.

Living in London in the 1880s, Bret Harte had a front-row seat as the signs of social upheaval multiplied. Though he lived in the most prosperous district in the city, he could not help but feel the unrest that threatened to erupt into violence at any moment and the attendant fear among the propertied classes. Harte was safely at home in St. John's Wood on the afternoon of February 8, 1886, when a meeting of the unemployed called by the Fair Trade League in Trafalgar Square was interrupted by the leaders of the Social Democratic Federation. The SDF led part of the crowd out of the square with the intention of dispersing in Hyde Park, but tempers flared up in Pall Mall when the demonstrators were provoked by clubmen, and stones were thrown at the Carlton Club. The march turned into a riot: "all forms of property were assailed, all signs of wealth and privilege were attacked. In St. James's Street all the club windows down one side of the street were broken, and in Piccadilly looting began." In Hyde Park carriages were overturned and their wealthy occupants robbed of money and jewelry. Shops in South Audley Street were looted. For the next two days the West End remained "in a state of near-panic," which came to a head on February 10, when the rumor spread that "10,000 men were on the march from Deptford to London, destroying as they came." Though the rumors turned out to be unfounded, these events "bore witness to the reality of the fear of an uprising of the casual poor, but also showed that this was not entirely without justification. While the mob from Deptford was a product of frenzied imagination, the crowds of unemployed who gathered to join it, were not."

Interestingly, one of the leaders of the Social Democratic Front was Harte's friend Henry Mayers Hyndman. Born of a wealthy family in 1842, Hyndman dedicated his life and fortune to the socialist cause and founded the SDF's forerunner, the Democratic Foundation in 1880, "the first important socialist body in England." Hyndman had met Harte on a visit to San Francisco in 1870, and in his memoirs he prided himself on being the one to bring the first copy of Harte's "Heathen Chinee" to England. Hyndman was of the group of leaders put on trial for the West End riots in 1886. He was acquitted.

Harte may have received a firsthand account of the riotous events of February 8 from Hyndman, as well as had the opportunity to hear the socialist point of view from its most eloquent spokesman. He was not unsympathetic to the cause of the "poor starving devils of unemployed labourers" and at age fifty-five had written to his wife that "with my usual fickleness, instead of becoming conservative with the years, I'm only getting more radical." He wrote the following of the Trafalgar Square riot, on February 15, 1886:

> For once I have seen the English upper classes shaken in their firm belief in their own superiority and eternal power. I have seen them brought face to face, though through plate-glass windows, with the howling, starving mob they and their fathers have trodden upon and despised for all these years, and they have grown pale, as the plate glass shattered around them. For once their sacred police could do nothing! For once they saw these terribly famished creatures, whom they had patronized in workhouses, petted in hospitals, and kept at a distance generally with good-humoured tolerance, absolutely breaking their bonds and clamouring for Heaven knows what! You will read all these accounts in the papers—but you will never understand it until you see these people as I have seen them—of both classes!—and learn how hopeless is the ditch that has been dug between them by centuries of class government. God knows whose bodies will fill this ditch that better things may walk over! If the poor devils themselves—I don't think they care much. As one of their speakers said—a kind of English Danton—"I suppose they will kill us—but it's better than sheer starving."

To John Hay, he summed up the political situation in late 1887: "[T]here is nothing going on here in London, except the usual one-idead stupidity of the governing classes, and the feeble revolutions of Trafalgar Square, which like the English thunderstorms, thicken, without clearing the air. The upper classes go on with their pleasure just the same—conscious only of the vices of the lower class." To Anna he wrote on September 15, 1887: "I am an earnest Republican—and I think a *just* one; but I can understand how a man feels when he is a Communist and a Socialist—and what makes him one! I like these people [his upper class friends] very well—but Heaven help them when the day of reckoning comes!"

15 Upper Hamilton Terrace, Saturday, February 6, 1892
Staring out into the gathering gloom, Harte thought how much he would have liked to be gone from this place—London had well earned the title of "City of Dreadful Night." The oldest Londoners remembered nothing like it. Everywhere one heard of friends—whole households—stricken down. It was partly the fear of falling ill, as so many had, among entire strangers and with his family three thousand miles away that had made him give up his intention of going away. He had been poorly with a succession of colds that had put him behind in his work, yet he ought not to complain, for he was in the midst of much more serious illness, resulting from the dreadful influenza and the poison that seemed to be in the air everywhere. There was no place exempt from the scourge—although probably there might be spots where the weather was less depressing. In London, it had been fittingly dark and gloomy; days when one existed only by artificial light and the streets at noon were like midnight.

For the last six weeks he had been living in an atmosphere of illness, doctors, and night and day nurses, with all the anxiety that comes from watching and waiting and seeing others anxious. Monsieur Van de Velde, a middle-aged man, whose strength and youthfulness he had always envied, was taken down with all the dreadful complications of the epidemic—particularly the helpless nervous exhaustion that also seemed to have infected the rest of the household. Harte felt he could not desert the ship with half the ship's company on the sick list, so he had given up his plans to go away with Maurice, the eldest son of his hosts. Christmas had been spent writing a short story, "The Home-

Coming of Jim Wilkes," for Joseph Hatton's *Sunlight* annual. George B. Burgin, a writer for Jerome K. Jerome's new magazine, the *Idler,* had called on New Year's Day with a Mr. Hutchinson. They wanted to do a biographical notice about him, but he had said he hardly thought it necessary. So much of that had already been done! His story, "The Conspiracy of Mrs. Bunker," had appeared in their first issue, out this month, and he was going to write several more stories for them, including a contribution to the series "My First Book." Madame Van de Velde had turned fifty-nine on January 9. A week ago, he and Maurice had been to visit Mary Boyd in her new home, the "Hut," close by in St. John's Wood.

A telegram had just come from Madame's daughter Marguerite in Berlin. She was nursing her ailing step-grandfather, Count de Launay, and begged her mother to come and help her in the count's extremity. Madame would have to tell her what she had been keeping from the poor child—that she could not leave the bedside of the dying father!

Arthur Van de Velde died in the early hours of Sunday, February 7, 1892. He was in his fifty-sixth year, exactly the same age as his longtime houseguest Bret Harte. Harte wrote to Anna that "It was a sad breaking-up of the household which his kindness and almost brotherly friendship did so much to make a possible home for me here so long among strangers." For Madame, her husband's death was in Harte's words "a terrible blow," she was already in mourning for her mother, who had died the preceding summer. As fate would have it, Madame's stepfather survived her husband by only a few hours. On February 10, the High Mass and Requiem service for Arthur Van de Velde was held at the Church of Our Lady in St. John's Wood at the time appointed for the ceremonious funeral of Count de Launay at Berlin. Monsieur Van de Velde was laid to rest in St. Mary's Cemetery, Kensal Green.

CHAPTER 10

The Scent of Heliotrope

(1892–1898)

"[T]ell me, which is your favourite scent?"

"*Heliotrope blanc.*"

Without giving me an answer, he pulled out his handkerchief and gave it to me to smell.

"All our tastes are exactly the same, are they not?" And saying this, he looked at me with such a passionate and voluptuous longing, that the carnal hunger depicted in his eyes made me feel faint.

"You see, I always wear a bunch of white heliotrope."

> Conversation between the male lovers in *Teleny,*
> an erotic novel from 1893, believed to have been
> authored by Oscar Wilde and some of his friends

Even the briefest visit was accompanied by luggage sufficient for a State occasion. There was at least one trunk, and several gladstone bags, with smaller satellites known as satchels. . . . The most remarkable and to him most precious piece of luggage was a portable heliotrope plant which he allowed nobody to touch and always carried himself. . . . This plant stood always on his bedside table, or desk, or in summer before the open window. Its fragrance filled the room and very soon found its way throughout the entire house.

> Geoffrey Bret Harte, recalling his
> grandfather's visits in his memoirs

109 Lancaster Gate, Saturday, March 30, 1895

In between revising the first act of the play, he had to write to Anna. Apart from the letter accompanying the monthly draft in late January, he had not written to her in months; not even on January 9, when she turned sixty, or on February 27, when their second grandson was born. All his time had been taken up with working on the new play and making trips to see his collaborator Pemberton in Birmingham. He had been waiting until the last moment to send her this month's draft, in the miserable hope that Frank would pay back the twenty pounds he had borrowed. He had told his son that he did not have any more money and that he would only be able to send Anna thirty pounds if he paid him back, and yet Frank had not repaid him. This morning he had had to borrow the money to make up the draft.

He could not see, he wrote to Anna, why he should be blind to faults in Frank, which he himself had never had. He had never lived on any woman—mother, wife, or mistress—but had been content to do any honest work that would support him. He could not see that Frank had suffered, as Anna had written in her last letter; in fact, during his whole misplaced career on the stage he had had advantages that even the greatest actors had never had. He had caused a scandal by marrying a woman with five thousand dollars a year and was now content to live on her and his father and mother. And all this without having any irresistible vices such as gambling or drinking but rather being inordinately conceited and satisfied with his own sagacity. He did not know how or when it all would end. He only knew that his hope in Frank—and the feeling he had after Frank's marriage that at least one of the children had completely settled, although not exactly as he would have wished—was gone!

In mid-January 1895, Harte had received a letter from T. Edgar Pemberton proposing a dramatization of Harte's story "The Judgment of Bolinas Plain," which had appeared in the Christmas issue of the newly started *Pall Mall Magazine*. Harte was skeptical—he had made several failed attempts at dramatizing his stories in the early 1880s—but he was glad to hear from his friend again and wrote him back that they might discuss the idea. Maybe they could make something of it together. Harte had first met the Birmingham industrialist in April 1879, when he lectured in Pemberton's native city on the latter's instigation and stayed as a guest in his home. They had gotten out of touch in the intervening years, during which Pemberton had written several successful plays, biographies of theatrical figures such as E. A. Sothern and T. W. Robertson, and had gained "a distinct reputation as dramatic critic on the *Birmingham Post*." He managed to convince Harte that he understood the business of playwriting thoroughly, and Harte reported to Mary Boyd on his return from Birmingham that his business there looked much more promising than expected. By May 1896, Harte could tell his wife that Pemberton had completed a contract with an American manager for the production of their play, which was to be called simply *Sue,* after its heroine.

Charles Frohman brought out the play at Hoyt's Theatre in New York on September 15, 1896. None of the authors were present. Frohman cabled immediately: "Well received, acting fair, press praises." Harte, ever suspicious, wrote to Pemberton that the wording of Frohman's telegram did not strike him as being a confirmation of *Sue's* success. He received further news of the play from Anna and from his friends in America. His old naval friend John Tobin wrote that the play was "a success," that Annie Russell was "lovely" in it, and that he had had a talk and "second drinks" with the stage manager, who was "wildly enthusiastic about it." Yet Harte had to admit to Pemberton that Tobin was "a dear good fellow—but I don't think a great critic— though he would swear and fight if necessary to prove that everything I did was perfect." Anna called it a "perfect play" and said further that "there is not a line in the whole play that does not *tell* with the audience and its pathos reaches every heart."

When the play had been running for nearly a month, Harte wrote to his wife that he was "still very uncertain about the actual success of the piece." It had received mixed reviews and yet the lead actors appeared to have made a hit. "You understand," he wrote cynically, "I don't care for *criticism*; I am quite content if the papers abuse the play so long as the audience like it, and the thing pays. For the rest, I know it is a *wholesome* play, and my conscience is clear." *Sue* featured a sexually frustrated rural housewife married to a man many years her senior. She harbors a fugitive acrobat in the barn and the pair end up running off together. Early on in their collaboration, Pemberton had expressed some apprehension about the acrobat's nudity in the scene where he and Sue have a tryst in the hayloft. Harte assured Pemberton that the acrobat, Jim Wynd, would be outfitted in "the spangles and tights of his profession." He added that "we need all the *colour* we can get to lift the incidents and scenery out of their grim and grey monotony."

By November 1896, *Sue* had been taken on tour and by early February the following year, it was "flickering out" in the provinces. After having seen the play at the Museum Theatre in Boston, Horatio Alger wrote to a friend that "The plot is faulty. Some of the minor characters are quite picturesque, especially those who take part in the lynching court scene. I don't think, however, the piece can on the whole be regarded as a success."

An interest in the theater ran in the family. Harte's youngest son, Frank, pursued a career as an actor during the 1880s. By the fall of 1888, he had had the run of the acting companies of several star actors, including Lawrence Barrett and Edwin Booth, but had given up acting in plays for writing them, with equal lack of success. He arrived on his father's doorstep almost out of the blue just before Christmas in 1888 and stayed two weeks at Upper Hamilton Terrace. Harte wrote to Clara Schneider that his twenty-three-year-old son now had mustachios, was ever so much older and wiser than him, and "I dare say finds his father an old fogy." On becoming reacquainted with his younger son, Harte found that "He lives in a world of the feeblest expediences and makeshifts, and thinks they are wise. He has no idea of a long aim in anything. He mistakes his indulgences for experience." He wrote to Anna that he could see that she was terribly troubled about their son, even while, womanlike, she had helped to make him think lightly of those troubles. "Frank is like all spoiled men and women—most impatient of those that have spoiled them." His father hoped and prayed that as he was still young he might change yet. "A spoiled child of thirty is a monstrosity even the gods won't permit, much less womankind." He found that Frank had evidently been greatly influenced by women and believed that even an unhappy marriage would save him.

From his mouth to God's ears. In 1891 Frank was married, to Aline Bouton Smith, a rich widow three years his senior with two sons. There was a scandal involved, as Frank had borrowed money from the woman prior to their marriage. In September 1890, Harte wrote to his sister Eliza that Frank "seems to be the victim of a woman who has sacrificed everything to him, *but* her income of $6,000 a year—for which she holds him in debt $10,000! This may be 'infatuation' as Anna calls it—on his part.

I don't see it!" Infatuation or not, the couple were finally married and would remain so for twenty-five years. By 1892, Frank was living in Paris. Just before Christmas of 1893, he and his wife, their son, Richard, and Frank's stepsons, Sidney and Charles Bouton Smith, arrived in England intending to make their home there.

During most of the eight years that remained to Bret Harte, the proximity of his son and daughter-in-law was a boon to him. They settled in great style at Weybridge in Surrey at a house called Hurst Guiting, and whenever he had some spare time, Harte would visit them for the weekend or just "to dine and sleep." He got on famously with Aline, who idolized her famous father-in-law. "He was to her a genius," her son recalled, "an almost fabulous being at whose feet the world had once lain and still rightfully belonged; a man of wit and infinite charm, handsome, dignified, immaculately groomed, impeccably dressed, moving in an aura of fame amongst the most distinguished people of his age." During his lifetime and even after his death, her son never heard her refer to him other than as "Mr. Bret Harte"; "in the very manner she pronounced the words," he recalled, "she imparted to them a magic touch, as though what she had really said was 'His Excellency, the Ambassador.' " Harte took a considerably less formal tone with his daughter-in-law, calling her "the chocolate girl" in reference to her "healthy taste" for chocolates.

In the fall of 1894, Frank took another house, equally grand. Harduémont at Weybridge was owned by the Van de Veldes' Dutch friend Count Van den Steen. Harte wrote to his son that the rent was cheap, and he wouldn't mind paying half the gardener's wages, but was Frank sure he wanted to stay at Weybridge for another nine months? Frank was sure, and it was at Harduémont that his second son, Geoffrey, was born in February the following year. After a brief period in London in 1895–96, the family settled at Caversham near Reading. There Frank eventually built a large brick house on the bank of the Thames, called Warren Heights.

All Frank's country homes were on the river, and, as he and his father shared a passion for boating, there were many all-day picnics in which the entire family participated. Aline would pack a wicker hamper with everything they needed for afternoon tea, the two men would row up the river, find a tranquil nook in which to moor the boat, and they would laze away the hours until evening. Madame Van de Velde would sometimes come along on these outings and would return the hospitality by inviting Frank and Aline to stay with her at her country house.

Madame had determined to leave Upper Hamilton Terrace upon her husband's death and to take a larger house in town that would have room for the fine furniture, tapestries, and paintings she had inherited from her mother and stepfather. The process of house hunting and moving took some time, and it was not until early August 1893 that she was settled at her new address: 109 Lancaster Gate. Her new home was an enormous, six-story, late-Victorian townhouse at the end of a long row looking out on the Bayswater Road and Hyde Park—just where Henry James places the residence of Kate Croy's formidable Aunt Maude in *The Wings of the Dove*. Harte had written to Anna in April 1892 and in January the following year that he would remain with the family only until they moved to a new house; yet in 1895 he was still living with the widow Van de Velde.

During his final decade, Madame Van de Velde continued to be the mainstay of Bret Harte's life—and vice versa. Throughout the 1890s and into the new century, they would have increasing need of each other's support as domestic squabbles and the infirmities of old age assailed them from all sides. The idyllic St. John's Wood days were over. Harte wrote to Gertrude Griswold in May 1895 that "the *household* has never been the same since his [Arthur Van de Velde's] death, and since the children—(the children who used to come with me in the carriage when I called on you in Baker St.!) have grown up, gone away or married! It is almost a foreign household to me now, with these changes and their new relatives, and there only lingers the memory of the old London house I came to—and where you met me years ago! I am away from it often, so are the family."

Madame continued to rule her household with an iron hand. Her nine children appear to have been largely a disappointment to her, and this would have created yet another bond between her and Harte. Beatrice, Madame's third eldest daughter and the only one to inherit her mother's beauty, had married Major

Richard Norris, a longtime friend of the family fourteen years her senior, in 1894. This union brought on a family war, which caused Madame great worry. In the mid-1890s, she still had four daughters between twenty-one and thirty-one and four sons between sixteen and thirty to see settled in life. There was an escalating conflict with her saintly eldest daughter, Berthe, who was increasingly dissatisfied with her mother's extravagant lifestyle, threw all her time and energy into charitable work, and would eventually give away two-thirds of her annual income. Madame's second youngest son, René, was seriously ill, and though he married and fathered two children, he died before he was thirty. We know Madame's daughters found her "severe and unfeeling" and that they in particular resented the affection she lavished on Bret Harte. Long after his and Madame's death, he was remembered in the family as "a great bore."

It was probably the disharmony at 109 Lancaster Gate that finally precipitated a change in Harte's living arrangements in early 1896. After spending Christmas with friends at Fair Oaks, he returned to new lodgings at 74 Lancaster Gate. His modest suite of rooms on the second floor of a Bayswater boardinghouse were just down the road from Madame's palatial residence. Though they no longer lived together in town, Harte would continue to make lengthy visits to Madame in the country when she resumed her old habit of taking a country house. The first of these rural pied-à-terres was Arford House, at Headley in Hampshire. Harte called it "a little cottage"; though it was not as massive as the estates of former days, it was a finely proportioned Georgian house from 1820, in two stories, with a beautiful arched veranda along the garden front.

For two and a half years, from 1896 to 1898, Madame and her semipermanent houseguest enjoyed this country retreat. Harte was able to work well in "the monkish seclusion" of his semidetached greenhouse study, and when he needed a break, he would lay aside his pen and "ramble through the loveliest and quietest lanes in all England." As he and Madame faced their first winter there in 1896, he wrote exuberantly to his fellow boarder at 74 Lancaster Gate, Mrs. Kingham:

> But really! It *is* lovely here! Almost as charming as in the flush of summer! Madame V. de V. was always afraid that the little house and

garden would not stand the ordeal of winter, but I think she is quite satisfied with it now. With the verandah "glassed in," the chrysanthemums in single file on either side, the house itself is as snug and comfortable and as *warm* as in summer! The sloping garden breaks the force of the wind and in the morning the house lies in a sort of "sunny," Sleepy Hollow. The outlook over the meadow and common is still as green as June, and there is very little mud in the road—and even that is a lovely "Vandyke brown!"

The Kinghams were among Harte's friends who were invited to Arford. Frank and Aline were also frequent guests. The ease and intimacy with which Harte's son and daughter-in-law socialized with Madame is a sign that any impropriety was out of the question. That Harte and Madame's relationship was platonic is further evidenced by the tone of a letter Harte wrote to his daughter-in-law on September 20, 1896:

> Poor Madame V. de V. is all alone at Arford House, and I felt awfully sorry to leave her. With her anxiousness about René—and her loneliness she has a terrible life. I am going back there again after I have seen Pemberton and made another visit, and I think she is having Miss Miles on the 23rd and one or two of her children to fill up the time afterwards, but I wish you would invite her to come and stay with you for a few days *later on* or at any time. She might not be able to come, but I know it will make her feel less lonely to know that she was invited by you and had some friends where she could go when she wanted a change. Don't say I told you this.

He signed himself "your pious father-in-law B.H." After 1885, when he no longer had to worry about being reported to be away from his post, Harte was open in the letters to his wife in America, making no secret of his frequent stays with Madame Van de Velde and how he was able to receive visits from his son and his friends through her kindness.

Harte made new friends even toward the end of his life. One with whom he would keep up a close correspondence was Lord Houghton's literary-minded younger daughter Florence Henniker. She was born Florence Ellen Hungerford Milnes in December 1855 and named after her godmother, Florence Nightingale, whom her father had wooed without success. In 1882, she had married the Honorable Arthur Henry Henniker-

Major, the "somewhat impecunious" younger son of the fourth
Lord Henniker of Thornham Hall in Suffolk. Harte first met her
four and a half years after her father's death, in January 1890, at
the home of a mutual friend at Ripon. By the end of the month
they were in correspondence, and by September that year he was
giving her detailed advice on how to improve her romance, *Mary
Garnett*. He helped her as best he could with getting her work
published in America, and she dedicated her third novel, *Foiled,*
to him in 1893. The Honorable Mrs. Henniker was also a friend
of Kipling and of Thomas Hardy. Hardy fell in love with her and
took her as a model for Sue *Florence* Mary Bridehead, the heroine
of *Jude the Obscure* (1895). Yet Harte was the star of her "salon"
when he chose to grace it with his presence.

At the large dinner given by William Waldorf Astor on May 3,
1894, to launch the *Pall Mall Magazine,* Harte was seated between
Frederick Sleigh Roberts, the hero of the Second Afghan War,
and Rudyard Kipling. Harte reported to Mary Boyd the next day
that the general had interested him more than "our mighty intellect" Kipling. Mark Twain thought Kipling's talk "might be
likened to footprints, so strong and definite was the impression
which it left behind," and Henry Adams, who crossed the Atlantic with him, has related how Kipling "dashed over the passenger
his exuberant fountain of gaiety and wit—as though playing a
garden hose on a thirsty and faded begonia." Yet Harte was not
impressed. Maybe Kipling was overwhelmed by meeting in the
flesh the man who had conjured up California for him so vividly.
Harte would sometimes make criticisms of Kipling's latest writings to his friend Florence Henniker. On her instigation he read
Plain Tales from the Hills (1888). "I like the freshness of *choice of
subject*," he wrote to his friend, "and the apparent *truthfulness* of
character sketching but I was repelled by a certain smart *attitude*
which struck me always as being in excess of the *actual smartness
of the work done,* or of any smartness *that the character of the work
required*." Harte would parody Kipling in "Stories Three," published in the *Saturday Evening Post* in June 1900. Divided into
three parts—"For Simla Reasons," "A Private's Honor," and
"Jungle Folk"—the parody was part of his second series of "Condensed Novels," which he started writing thirty years after his
initial success with the form.

It was through Florence Henniker that Harte met several of his aristocratic friends of later years. One of these was Florence's brother Robert, heir both to his father's baronetcy and, through his mother, Annabel, to the Earldom of Crewe. Harte had long expressed a desire to make his acquaintance, but this apparently did not come about until 1895. At Christmastime that year, Harte was finally able to pay a visit to Fryston Hall in Yorkshire, where he had never been in Lord Houghton's day. One of the advantages of Harte's noble connections was that they brought with them invitations to stay at some of the most beautiful country houses in England. This was especially the case with another titled couple, friends also of Florence Henniker, Lord and Lady Compton. Lord Compton, later Lord Northampton, was the owner of Compton Wynyates, which Harte visited for the first time in early June 1894. The house captured Harte's imagination. "[A] small edition of Hampton Court," it was "most wonderful" and far beyond what he had expected. To Clara Schneider he wrote in 1898 that it was "an ideal house" where he often went to visit an old friend. In June 1895, Harte made his first visit to Cliveden, the magnificent home of his old New York acquaintance, now self-exile William Waldorf Astor. He wrote to Pemberton on his return that "either from being walked off my legs through the woods on Sunday morning or blistered on a steam launch on the river in the afternoon, I somehow managed to develop as fine a cold as I could in mid-winter! ... And this was the 'quiet Sunday' that Mr. Astor promised me!" This experience did not prevent him from visiting again.

Not far from Compton Wynyates, in the vale of Evesham, at the foot of the Cotswold hills, lay the idyllic village of Broadway. Harte made several visits there to Pemberton's "Pye Corner" during the last seven years of his life, as he and his friend collaborated on three further dramatizations of Harte's stories: *Clarence* (based on the novel of that name); *Rushbrook* ("The Mæcenas of the Pacific Slope"); and *Held Up* ("Snow-Bound at Eagle's"). None of them reached the boards during Harte's lifetime, but on June 10, 1898, Harte and Pemberton had the satisfaction of attending the opening night of the London production of *Sue* at the Garrick Theatre, with American actors and Annie Russell still in the title role. The play ran for a month, but the financial returns were "very disappointing." Toward the end of 1898, Harte summed up their experiences with *Sue* in a letter to Pemberton: "We are, if we consult the notices and critiques of 'Sue,' the authors of a highly successful and much talked of play—even a distinctly 'novel' one—yet we couldn't draw a paying audience for that one, nor can we get an order for another from actor or manager—or know what was the matter with the last. Verily a dramatist's life is not a happy one!"

Though we can rule out the possibility of a romantic liaison between Harte and Madame, we are still left with the problem of accounting for Harte's sexual history during the last quarter-century of his life. There is no clear evidence in the form of letters or diary entries to show that Harte formed romantic attachments or that he was anything but celibate during the last two and a half decades of his life. In this connection, there may be cause to recall what Mark Twain said about his friend and enemy: "I think he was incapable of emotion, for I think he had nothing to feel with. I think his heart was merely a pump and had no other function. I am almost moved to say I know it had no other function." The best corroboration of this statement would seem to be Harte's treatment of his wife and children. In his letters, he shows a marked ability to let the mind rule the heart. The extant correspondence with Anna is remarkable for being devoid of expressions of devotion of other than a lukewarm and platonic nature. He is solicitous with the ease of one who is three thousand miles away. He is concerned, but where is the longing and the yearning?

After having read the many letters from Harte to Anna published by their grandson, Wallace Stegner thought it was "probable that intimate passages have been edited out of Harte's letters to his wife." "Certainly," he added, "what remains is so cool, so oddly confiding and courteous and responsible, yet so transparently determined that circumstances will not permit a reunion, that one itches to know more." Having read all 380 extant letters from Harte to Anna from the years of their separation (there is no reason to believe many have been lost), I can state that 1) Geoffrey Bret Harte did not omit "intimate passages" from the letters he published; and 2) the unpublished letters are no different in their tone from the published ones, with the exception of a few angry outbursts in the letters from Harte's final years.

Considering this, it seems ironic that Harte's stories had long and often contained a sexual emphasis. In writing to Mary Boyd in 1889, he had to admit that "your dear good Mamma is right in her criticism, when she alludes to the redundancy of 'passion,' and the tensity of 'satisfaction' she gets from my books!" He enclosed a copy of his latest, *The Heritage of Dedlow Marsh*, with the words: "I think I may avow, with my hand on my heart, that I have at last written a volume which any young married woman can thoughtfully put into the hands of her innocent Mother! It is possible that it may be still unsatisfactory in conclusion, though greatly diminished in fervour. The fact is my characters *will not* do as they ought to do, at the end. I may give them the advantages of a perfect (my own) example; I may clearly point out to them what the virtuous reader expects! but they won't have it." In his *Education*, written during the early years of this century, "[Henry] Adams began to ponder, asking himself whether he knew of any American artist who had ever insisted on the power of sex, as every classic had always done; but he could think only of Walt Whitman; Bret Harte, as far as the magazines would let him venture; and one or two painters, for the flesh-tones." In a story from late 1894, Harte referred to the sexual as "the strongest and most magic of all human passions."

It is interesting to note that in Harte's stories "the power of sex" (be it a question of gender or sexuality) is overpoweringly attributed to the female of the species. As Henry Seidel Canby wrote of Harte's heroines in 1909: "The virginal dew is dried from the cheeks of his untamed women." Jeffrey F. Thomas has shown in a more recent article how "[o]ne of the most common character types in Harte's tales is the ruthless woman who wreaks havoc through the force of her sexual desires." He gives many examples, including Elsie Decker in "A Passage in the Life of Mr. John Oakhurst" (1874), Joan Blandford in "The Argonauts of North Liberty" (1888), Safie McGee in "The Bell-Ringer of Angel's" (1893), and Cota Ramierez in "What Happened at the Fonda" (1899). The Hartean hero, on the other hand, is frequently a shy, retiring young creature such as Gabriel Conroy, a man about whom one might readily use Gabriel's own defensive words: " 'mebbe he don't take to wimmen and marriage nat'ral, and it's jest his way.' " Cass Beard, the passive, sweet-smelling hero of "Found at Blazing Star" is another classic example. He is advised by the decisive heroine Miss Mortimer that he "really ought to get up a little more muscle"; he has "no more than a girl," she remarks.

As we glance across Harte's social landscape in the late 1870s, '80s, and '90s, we discern a large number of ladies. Letters to these ladies survive, and they are all written in a charming, avuncular tone that is entirely devoid of sexual excitement, romantic worship, or even flirtation. Harte befriended and socialized with women who were unavailable, surrounding himself with aged dowagers, young married women, and resolute spinsters. Being himself a married man, he was out of bounds for any respectable woman.

Harte's relationships with Jessie Frémont, his wife, Anna, and Madame Van de Velde show the extent to which he valued the counsel of women and was dependent on it. Yet, it is clear that Harte also felt a curious and slightly patronizing detachment from women, as indicated by the way he described his close friend Madame Van de Velde. When Charles Anderson Dana chose not to publish one of Madame's letters to the *New York Sun*, Harte wrote the following of his protégée: "You know best; I only do not want you to fret, or make nervous by overcurbing, such a thorough-place goer as she is. She will learn the[?] country and all the walls and fences and ditches like a thoroughbred as she is, if you only will give her her head. And Heaven forfend! she should ever read these lines or know this elegant comparison." In connection with the escalating rivalry between Anna Harte and Madame with regard to Harte's Christmas presents, he wrote to his wife in 1886: "As a general thing my experience teaches me that granddames are very much like other dames—and that no mere position insures liberality, genuinety, truthfulness, unselfishness, or sense of humor. I've seen housemaids as refined in instinct as Countesses and tradesmen's wives as uncertain as both."

Bret Harte had a recurring fictional theme that was even more marked than, and in contrast to, his depictions of the battle between the sexes. It has long been recognized that the depiction of relationships between men is the dominant topos of Harte's fiction throughout his forty-year writing career. These relationships have variously been referred to by reviewers and critics as "blood-brotherhood" and "friendship," and the biblical expression "brotherly love" has also been used. Madame Van de Velde, who knew his work better than anyone, noted in the long essay she wrote after his death that "By temperament or from deliberate purpose, Bret Harte has eliminated from his work the all-pervading factor of modern fiction—passion." Here she is using "passion" to indicate romantic heterosexual love, and goes on to qualify her statement: "Love, legitimate or otherwise, plays a subservient part in his stories, and is always inferior to friendship, devotion and fidelity." Henry Merwin, one of Harte's early biographers, notes with surprising candor in 1911: "In Bret Harte's stories woman is subordinated to man, and love is subordinated to friendship. This is a strange reversal of modern notions, but it was the reflection of his California experience,—reinforced, possibly, by some predilection of his own." "In modern times," Merwin continues, "the place which the friend held in classic times is taken by the wife; but in California, owing to the absence of women and the exigencies of mining, friendship for a brief and brilliant period, never probably to recur, became once more an heroic passion." Patrick Morrow noted in 1979 that "the brotherly love theme fascinated Harte," and in a recent essay Peter Stoneley writes that Bret Harte "seems to have founded a tradition."

Bret Harte chose to interpret and mythologize the West in Greek terms. This was no doubt a result of his having been familiar with Greek culture from an early age, being the son of a tutor of Greek. References in his writings show his familiarity both with the Greek tradition of heroic friendship, represented by Damon and Pythias, and the Christian tradition, symbolized by David and Jonathan. He would also, no doubt, have known the widely read novels of the talented but short-lived author Theodore Winthrop. His *Cecil Dreeme* and *John Brent* (both 1861) thematized the romantic friendship between men, and the latter was one of the first novels set in California.

During the 1870s, Bret Harte traveled throughout the United States and in England giving a lecture entitled "The Argonauts of '49" in which a large part was taken up with describing the manner of life of the gold miners in California. After pointing out that "They were splendidly loyal in their friendships," Harte goes on to say:

> The heroic possibilities of a Damon and a Pythias were always present; there were men who had fulfilled all those conditions, and better still without a knowledge or belief that they were classical, with no mythology to lean their backs against and hardly a conscious appreciation of a later faith that is symbolized by sacrifice. In these unions there were the same odd combinations often seen in the marital relations: a tall and a short man, a delicate sickly youth and a middle aged man of powerful frame, a grave reticent nature and a spontaneous exuberant one. Yet in spite of these incongruities there was always the same blind unreasoning fidelity to each other.

In his lecture, Harte concluded the section on the gold miners by saying that they were "above all, faithful to their partners and loved them with a love passing women." This is an allusion to what David says of Jonathan in 2 Samuel 1.26: "I am distressed for you, my brother Jonathan; / very pleasant have you been to me; / your love to me was wonderful, / passing the love of women." It is highly interesting that this mention of the love "passing the love of women" was not included in the expanded version of Harte's lecture published as an introduction to Houghton Mifflin's *The Writings of Bret Harte*. This standard edition was published starting in 1896, the year after Oscar Wilde's trials for homosexual practices, which in Eric Trudgill's words: "took the bloom off society's pre-Freudian innocence." There were now stricter limits to how far one could go in "advertising" romantic bonds between men, and Harte was evidently aware of it.

"Tennessee's Partner" (1869) is only the most famous of Harte's many stories about "friendship" among the Argonauts. He would continue to write these stories throughout his life; "Captain Jim's Friend" (1888) and "Uncle Jim and Uncle Billy" (1897) being most clearly in the mold of his classic story from 1869. In the former story, the eponymous hero sacrifices everything to help his worthless friend Lacy Bassett. His devotion is so great that when Lacy shoots him, Captain Jim expends his final effort to clear him of all complicity by saying that he shot in self-defense. Lacy observes: "He's a queer man—is Captain Jim." "Uncle Jim and Uncle Billy" is "Tennessee's Partner" nearly thirty years later and with a happy ending. The gold miners of the title are goaded into separating by their friend Dick Bullen, who accuses them of being "stuck here like children 'playing house.' " After many adventures, including the belief by one partner that the other has got himself mixed up with a woman, they are finally reunited in San Francisco. They decide to buy a ranch and live happily ever after.

The culmination of a line of development starting with "Notes by Flood and Field" in 1862 was "In the Tules," the most blatantly homoerotic story Harte ever wrote. While "Tennessee's Partner" was largely a seriocomic story despite the pathos of its ending, "In the Tules" was a deadly serious romance without a trace of humor. Described by one critic as being "as intense as a poem and as inward as a prayer," the story opens with the rugged young Pike County, Missourian Martin Morse settling on the banks of the Sacramento River. There he nightly observes with wonder the passing of the steamboat. One evening he spots a black shape in the river, which turns out to be a man, whom he saves from drowning. The man, "Captain Jack," pays him to fetch a horse, and the next day he is gone. Shortly afterwards, Morse discovers the corpse of a middle-aged man on the riverbank and receives two fine horses from an anonymous donor. Suspecting that his gentlemanly friend has sent them, he determines to set out to find his benefactor. On the steamboat to Stockton, he overhears a conversation that makes it clear that Captain Jack is the gambler Jack Despard, who fell overboard on the very same steamboat with the sheriff Seth Hall and has not been seen since. Realizing now why Despard has been avoiding him, Morse returns to his home and falls ill. Out of the blue, a doctor and nurse arrive from Sacramento, and Morse recovers only to be nearly drowned by the great flood of '54. He is saved just in time by Despard, who leaves him in Stockton. Destitute, Morse joins a pack train as a muleteer and makes his fortune in the mountains. He comes across Despard about to be lynched and is shot while trying to save him. Despard is hanged, and they are buried in the same grave.

Harte's romance was published in the *Strand* in 1895 and widely reprinted. Though we have no historical evidence concerning his intentions in writing the story, it seems too much of a coincidence that he should choose to write a story that to such a great extent thematizes the love between men at the very moment when this love was being put on trial and subjected to unprecedented opprobrium and lethal attack. Oscar Wilde's three trials took place in April and May of 1895. Harte wrote "In the Tules" during the spring or summer of that same year; the story was sold on September 14, 1895, and appeared in the December issue of the *Strand*. Living in London and having known Wilde since the early 1880s, Harte cannot but have been keenly aware of the widely publicized scandal.

Literature is one thing, life is another. The question is, of course, the extent to which the predominance of this theme of "brotherly love" in Harte's fiction does represent "some predilection of his own." After a brief discussion of "The Luck," "The Outcasts," and "Tennessee's Partner" ("the story of a love passing the love of woman, true unto death and beyond death") in her 1881 article, Madame Van de Velde remarks: "Reading those tales, one cannot help wondering what the man who wrote them must have known himself of friendship and of pity."

Among the old friends for whom he held a strong love and admiration, pride of place must be given to John Hay. Evidently the feeling was mutual, as in 1881 Hay wrote to him the following on the eve of his departure from the State Department: "I want, before my sands run out, to say How to you once more and to assure you of my eternal love and esteem. . . . I do not know what Heaven meant by creating so few men like [Clarence] King and you. The scarcity of you is an injury not only to us but to yourselves. There are not enough of you to go round, and the world pulls and hauls at you till you are completely spoiled." Harte quoted the passage in a letter to his wife and kept the original for reading when he was in low spirits. Harte was overjoyed whenever Hay came to visit in England and equally so when Hay was appointed ambassador to the Court of St. James in 1897.

Another man Harte admired, though probably only from afar, so to speak, was Rudolph Schneider. In the eyes of his boss

Schneider was "quite the snell [sic], German-English 'macho' ";
Harte would refer to him as "my Schneider" and was voluminous
in his praise of his vice-consul's performance. After his departure
from Crefeld, Harte corresponded mostly with Clara Schneider
but expressed the repeated hope that her husband would find
time to write. Harte went to great lengths to try to engineer a
reunion after their separation in 1880 and was very disappointed
that Rudolph Schneider did not come to visit him at Tynemouth
when he was in England later that year. It would in fact be more
than thirteen years till they met again. By the time of their reunion at 109 Lancaster Gate in October 1893, the bloom had
apparently gone somewhat off the rose. Harte did not take the
trouble to go to Crefeld on his continental trip two years later,
though he visited Cologne and had written rapturously to Clara
Schneider in 1894: "I am afraid I am forgetting the flight of time
and all the changes since the old days. However I believe it is
best to forget these changes, and keep our youth, and if we do
meet, it will be exactly as then—we will believe we are not a day
older (I know I am not a bit wiser), and you and I and your
husband will enjoy ourselves just as foolishly as we did in the
brave days of the Consulate." At this point it was fourteen years
since he had seen Clara Schneider, and he was never to see her
or her husband again.

When considering the existing evidence relating to Harte's
relationships with men, the best index of intimacy is his epistolary mode of address. Despite friendships of thirty and nearly
twenty-five years with John Hay and Rudolph Schneider, he was
never on a first-name basis with either of them. His surviving
letters show that there were only four men outside his family
whom Harte addressed by their Christian names. They were the
two "Charleys"—Charles Warren Stoddard and Charles Watrous—Mark Twain, and his closest male companion during the
last seventeen years of his life, Arthur Collins.

Charles Warren Stoddard was an active homosexual who
throughout his life had a number of romantic and sexual relationships with men. Mark Twain, it has recently been suggested,
"engaged in a series of romances with men" between 1862 and
1865. We might wonder about the intensity of Twain's animosity
toward Harte and about the true motivation for his many verbal

assaults, which a combination of fear, envy, and disgust does not seem fully to explain. We might ask, as does Andrew J. Hoffman in connection with the breakup of two of Twain's other friendships, "Is it possible to have two close relationships end with such passion if the relationships themselves had not been passionate?" He answers in the affirmative but adds the suggestive remark: "[I]t is more likely that these relationships assume romantic forms, at least in their endings, because they were romances." As Peter Stoneley has pointed out, Twain "relates much of his contempt to Harte's alleged effeminacy," yet "There is an odd sense in which all of Twain's accusations are reversible; that, in destroying Harte, he was also compiling a catalogue of self-referents." What exactly did Harte know about Twain's "hard, thorny, restless youth?"

Harte met Arthur Collins at the home of Lord Alfred Paget on January 26, 1885. Colonel Collins was nine years younger than Harte, being born in 1845, the son of Reverend Ferdinando Collins of Betterton, Berks. Educated at Marlborough, he had joined the army and seen active service in South Africa in 1879. Since 1880 he had been comptroller and equerry to Queen Victoria's daughter, Princess Louisa, Marchioness of Lorne, and from 1892, Gentleman Usher to the Queen herself. Collins had long been an admirer of Harte's work and used to read and reread his stories to his soldiers in Ceylon. Harte's diary from the 1880s shows that the two men saw much of each other—at the Beefsteak Club, which Harte joined in mid-1886 at Collins's instigation, and later at Brooks's and in their respective homes. Harte was among the select group of men, including George "Kicky" Du Maurier, Arthur Sullivan, the conductor Alfred Cellier, Arthur Blunt, and the actor John Hare, who celebrated Collins's birthday on June 26 each year. The two men shared a love of the stage, and in his "Personal Appreciation" written after Harte's death, Collins recalled their many trips to the theater. "We met constantly," he recalled, "and I much valued his affectionate and true regard." Harte's friend and biographer Pemberton, who notes that Harte was "never prone to very close friendships," remarks that Collins was "one of his most intimate friends. . . . He was ever an appreciative theatre goer, and on such occasions he loved to have Colonel Collins for his comrade." Pemberton adds: "He always wanted sympathy, and in him he had a friend who understood him."

As the example quoted at the end of this chapter shows, the surviving letters from Harte to Arthur Collins display an uncustomary familiarity of tone. When, in the summer of 1895, Harte finally took his first vacation outside the British Isles in fourteen years, it was to accompany Collins and a "young friend of his" to Aix-la-Chapelle, where the colonel was to undergo "the 'cure.'" He said nothing of this to Anna; in fact, despite their intimacy (or maybe because of it), it had taken five years before he so much as mentioned his friend in passing in a letter to his wife. He did not give his name even then but described him as "a very charming 'Warrington' sort of fellow" and as "one of my London friends." Warrington was, of course, the trusty companion of the eponymous hero of Thackeray's *Pendennis* (1850), most significant in this connection for being described by the narrator as a "woman-hater" and by Pendennis as a "professed misogynist."

There is no way of knowing whether Harte had a physical relationship with Collins or any of his other men friends. Such relationships in Victorian England were, of course, illegal and were often based on great differences of age or class or both, as is no better illustrated than by the case of Oscar Wilde. Of Colonel Collins's sexual nature we know that he was drawn to young boys. In 1898, for example, he became interested in the painter-prodigy Brian Hatton, to whom he remained a devoted friend and mentor till the latter's death in World War I. Collins liked to be photographed with his gardener boy Willie Weston in front of his country home Cow Leaze at Hayling Island. His scrapbook contains several poems he has clipped out, with titles such as "The Child Eternal," "Ad Filiolum Meum," "Young Never-Grow-Old, with your heart of gold . . . ," "Death and the Boy," and "To the Little Boy. From His Father." Collins's obituary notes his concern for the welfare of the District Messenger Boys, while his will mentions a "bronze statuette of a nude boy" given to him by the artist Goscombe John.

As for Bret Harte, we have no clear evidence that he ever let his homoerotic impulses "go outside the pages of a book," nor that he ever allowed himself to love again—be it a man or a woman.

THE

SCENT

OF

HELIOTROPE

242

74 Lancaster Gate, December 14, 1898

My dear Frank,

I am greatly surprised by your letter, as your mother never intimated to me her intention of coming to England, nor have you ever told me that you were sending for her or intended to send for her. In her last letter to me, while acknowledging the receipt of the $250.00—which in my straightened circumstances that month I had to borrow—she hoped that I would still be able to send her that *full* amount monthly, for the rest of the year, as she could not reduce her expenses at once. But she said nothing whatever of her coming, nor of your proposal to her.

Of course I can only hope and wish that the arrangements you have thus made may prove perfectly satisfactory to you all, and that in being able to share your house with your mother and sister you may have all the pleasure you have looked forward to.

Your affectionate father

B.H.

P.S. I sent this morning a line to Madame Van de Velde, as you wished, informing her of what you found yourself able to do, and had done.

74 Lancaster Gate, December 15, 1898

Dear Arthur,

Yes. Saturday "suits" and looks auspicious. I have had the cook examine the entrails of a fowl, and find the omens propitious! Let it be Saturday, then.

You will give me "bread and pulse" at Brookes,' and I will lead you to Arcadian stalls at the Alhambra or Empire. For heaven's sake let us go somewhere where we can laugh in the right place!

I have not yet dared to face my Christmas shopping, but I'll pick up your offering at the Club and send you mine. It is so difficult to find something sufficiently idiotic and useless, to keep up our fond, foolish custom with.

Yours always,

Bret Harte

CHAPTER 11

No Time for Dying
(1898–1902)

Sick or not, in spirits or out of spirits, I must work, and I do not see any rest ahead.
> Bret Harte to Anna Harte, February 19, 1890

I think our chance for being remembered in the future is the luck we have had in keeping the affections of our friends.
> Bret Harte to A. P. Watt, Christmas Eve, 1901

On August 2, 1920, Dr. Howe was called to 58 Rutland Gardens, Hove, to write out a death certificate for an elderly woman, who had died that day. Mrs. M. R. Carloss, who had been present at her death, informed him that her full name was Anna Bret Harte, and that she was the widow of an American author. Carloss thought she was eighty-five years old. The doctor noted as cause of death: "1. Senility; 2. Gangrene, 3 months, Exhaustion, 7 days." His duties completed, he left the body to be prepared for burial in an unmarked grave in the poorest section of Hove Cemetery.

As he went on his way, the doctor may have wondered what strange fate had brought this old American lady to die in a sleepy English seaside village, among strangers, without a friend or relation near. We who know a little more about her, who can picture her filling the First Unitarian Church of San Francisco with her voice, encouraging her husband to insist on the publication of the "The Luck of Roaring Camp," or waiting in a boardinghouse in New Jersey for him to send for her, while her hair got grayer and her lips thinner—we may wonder all the more at the sad vagaries and the dramatic contrasts of her life. Anna Harte was married for nearly forty years, yet she only shared a roof with her husband for sixteen of them. She raised two sons and two daughters single-handedly. A semi-invalid for nearly sixty years, she nevertheless survived her husband by eighteen years and saw all three of her sons buried. She lived to see her older daughter put in an insane asylum and her younger daughter an object of public charity. After her husband's death, Anna herself had been entirely dependent on the bounty of her daughter-in-law. Some of her sadness and her hopelessness comes across in the following letter, written on a visit to Paris when she was sixty-six. It is the only personal letter we have from her hand:

11 Rue Lord Byron, Paris, April 8, [1901]

Dear Mrs. Rudge,

Should the weather permit, it will give us much pleasure to take tea with you tomorrow afternoon, though we do not look confidently for anything very "warm or sunny." Such days live in our memory, and we look forward to them again, in the dim future.

My son and his wife desire their kindest remembrances to Mr. Rudge, the children, and yourself, and with love to all, I am,

Very sincerely yours,
Anna Bret Harte

Of Anna and her life in America, we know only what we can read between the lines of her husband's letters. Not one of her letters to him survives. After they parted at Sea Cliff, Long Island, in the summer of 1878, Anna and the children stayed on there at least until mid-October. The late 1870s and first half of the 1880s was a restless period when the amputated family moved often. When the boys were sent to commercial college in early 1879, they were living at an address at West Washington Place in New York, not far from Washington Square, but they did not stay there long. Harte's sister, Eliza Knaufft, still ran Grand View House in Morristown, and Anna and the children spent a large part of the early 1880s there. Anna also lived with Eliza and her large family at Caldwell, New Jersey, in the first part of 1883 and at 332 Lexington Avenue, New York, during the winter of 1883–84. The idea was that Harte would take the second floor of Eliza's New York house for his family when he returned to America. By April 1884, both the Knauffts and the Hartes had removed to Plainfield, New Jersey, and Plainfield would be where Anna would spend most of the next fifteen years, until she too left America forever.

Anna Harte's widowhood began long, long before Bret Harte's death in 1902. She was a grass widow for more than twenty years. For twenty years she waited for the call that never came. In the opinion of her daughter Ethel, Anna would have joined her husband in England before she did "had he made the genuine or complimentary gesture which she felt her dignity as his wife demanded." When she *did* receive a summons, it was not from her husband but from her son.

Francis King Harte had built a house in Caversham in 1898. As long as both his sisters were living with his mother, it was difficult to make room for all of them, but in early 1898 the eldest, Jessamy, was married to Colorado industrialist Henry Milford Steele. Without Harte's knowledge, mother and son then planned a Christmastime reunion, which, when it came about, took the father of the family totally by surprise. Harte might have suspected that something was up, as Anna had practically stopped writing to him. He himself hardly wrote to her; from 1898 (prior to Anna's arrival), we only have two letters to his wife. Ostensibly it was because he was waiting to see if the English production of *Sue* would be a financial success, but by the fall of 1898, he had to admit that "Alas! I have been once more cruelly disappointed": "I need not tell you that for six weeks I had hoped to delight and astonish you with news of a good fortune that would spare me all the trials and troubles I have had lately over my literary work—and how deeply disappointed I have been!" The father of the bride did not even have a heart to write to his daughter. "Even now," he wrote to Anna, in August 1898, "I can only congratulate her upon finding a husband who can take the place of her father and his precarious fortunes. It is hard to face this fact, which for the last six months I have been trying to avoid."

The Hartes' incredible transatlantic marriage was over when Anna finally set foot on English soil on December 19, 1898, twenty years, five months, and eleven days after her husband's first arrival there in 1878. Though they were no longer so far apart, their marriage by correspondence would continue and they would never live together again. Harte was not on the dock to greet Anna when she arrived, nor did he go to Caversham to celebrate Christmas with the reunited family. He contented himself with sending Frank Anna's check for January, and when he received word that she had arrived, he wrote her a short note to say that he would come up for a day or two as soon as he could. It appears that he fulfilled his promise at the very end of December, on the way to visit the Pembertons in Birmingham.

We have no record of the long-awaited meeting between husband and wife and between the father and the grown daughter he had not seen since she was three. All we have is a letter to Frank, written a few days later, where Harte promises to come again soon. "I will come to luncheon, if you like," he writes; "I am afraid I could not achieve a dinner as it would involve a late journey and I am obliged to work at night now. I have been very busy, but I am glad enough to be so if it will bring me more quickly the money I am very much in need of." As for Frank's new house, Warren Heights, which he had just seen for the first time, he was afraid that he had thought more of the inevitable expense than the glories of its "Sheraton and Chippendale" furniture. Harte was indeed hard at work—he published ten short stories in 1899 and twelve in 1900—and the promised second visit was frequently postponed. It did not take place until late July 1899, right before Anna went to Eastbourne with Frank and the family. It is likely from this visit that we have the group portrait of Bret Harte, Aline Harte, Anna Harte, and Ethel Bret Harte in front of the brick wall of Warren Heights. This photograph forms an uncanny parallel to the contemporaneous one of Harte, Aline, Madame, and her daughter.

Harte's youngest grandson, Geoffrey, recalled that prior to his grandfather's visits there was always "preparation." His grandmother Anna, who had a "fiery temper," "had to be carefully couched in self control and in the avoidance of any dangerous topic of conversation." "When the actual visits took place," Geoffrey writes in his unpublished memoirs, "they must have been about as relaxing as sitting on a powder keg watching the fuse slowly burning, and waiting for the bang which would blow them all sky high. The entire family was on tenter-hooks and the sigh of relief which all members breathed when the ordeal was over was heartfelt." All in all, between Anna's arrival and Harte's death, a period of more than three years, we know of a total of only six meetings between them. These visits were always at Frank's home; there is no record of Anna ever visiting Harte's bachelor quarters in London or of him introducing her to any of his English friends. Apart from the note he wrote to Madame Van de Velde on Frank's request, there is not a single mention of Anna's presence in England in any of the many letters to the Boyds or the Pembertons or the Schneiders or any of his other friends. For all practical intents and purposes, Bret Harte carried on living his life exactly the same way he had been doing when Anna was on the other side of the ocean.

This meant that the person with whom he still spent most of his time was Madame Van de Velde. After she lost the lease on Arford House in the spring of 1898, she rented Averley Towers in Farnham, Surrey, for a season, before settling into what would become her and Bret Harte's final home away from home. It was called the Red House and was located in Camberley in Surrey, about an hour from London by train from Waterloo Station. As stated the prospectus of a resort development there in 1898, Camberley, "Amidst the Pine Woods of the Surrey Hills," was "The Arcachon of England" and "one of the healthiest and most salubrious districts in all England." According to the same prospectus, Camberley was "rapidly and deservedly becoming the most popular of select health resorts and residential districts within reach of town." Among its royal residents, it could boast the Duke of Connaught at Bagshot Park, the widowed Empress Eugénie at Farnborough Mount, and the Crown Prince of Siam. Harte made his first visit to Madame Van de Velde's "new country home" in early March 1899. He spent Easter there rather than visit Anna at Caversham and the Pembertons at Broadway as he had planned. As had been the case with his dear Arford House, he clearly found that he could work well at Camberley, and he returned time and time again for lengthy visits during the years that remained to him.

Geoffrey Bret Harte's unpublished memoir vouchsafes us a rare glimpse of "that other awe-inspiring personage" of his childhood, Madame Van de Velde:

> Referred to in the intimate family circle as Madame V. de V. or simply as Madame, this indomitable woman merited the prestige

that surrounded her. She and her husband who had died some years earlier, had been among my grandfather's closest friends. A woman of wit and of singular charm, an accomplished linguist, a brilliant hostess, she was also possessed of tremendous energy and determination. . . .

No. 109 was one of those enormous houses long since converted into flats or else pulled down to make place for other buildings less ornate but more modern. . . . At the age of six I was readily impressed both by the setting and its center figure. Because I was a little boy, I was given a stool to sit on at the feet of this olympian person, which as far as I was concerned was the equivalent to being seated at the foot of the throne. My first visit was also my first lesson in wordly comportment; on how to balance a cup of tea and a plate on which slithered a hot buttered muffin, and to eat the muffin at the same time; an ordeal I should not have survived had not my hostess, with brusque kindness and commonsense, swooped down, sliced up the offending muffin and ordered a little table to be placed beside me.

That Madame was an exalted personage was proved to me beyond question not so much by the splendour over which she presided as by the way she treated my grandfather. She laughed and talked and contradicted him with perfect composure as though they were equals, without trace of that deference, almost reverence that surrounded him on his visits to us. And he seemed to enjoy it!

Geoffrey was not the only little boy to be impressed by Madame Van de Velde. Her grandson, Claude Van Zeller, would give her a large place in the two volumes of his published memoirs. She died when he was eight, but throughout his life he retained very distinct memories of her and of the atmosphere of 109 Lancaster Gate. His earliest memory was of leaving the table at breakfast one morning and going down to the kitchen to ask the cook to make a brioche for one of his aunts. By doing this he had broken the unwritten rule that no one should leave the breakfast table until Madame had given the signal for everyone to withdraw to the morning room. He was quickly whisked back upstairs.

To her grandson Claude, Madame "typified . . . a state of life": "A noble and agreeable state of life. She stood for authority, tradition, stability." He recalled her heavily ringed fingers and how she would wear her thick hair, for which she had been famous in her youth, in a chignon covered in the finest possible net. She frowned upon emotion of any sort, he remembered, and throughout her life she had been found "alarming." This was to her a source of pride and amusement. She adopted an iciness of manner and accentuated the aloofness of her nature. In her own estimation, there were only two people who were not afraid of her: a certain porter at the Italian embassy in Berlin and her grandson Claude. Claude could never recall having heard his grandmother laugh. A cousin of the family whom he asked about this remembered that once, coming back from a funeral, Madame had "emitted a series of low grunts which may have been laughter" after observing in her deep mellow voice that she preferred cemeteries abroad: "They look more lived in." In imitating Madame's laugh, the cousin "dropped her mouth as low as it would go on her face, and made the noise 'her . . . her . . . her.' " In retrospect, Claude found he could speak more confidently of his grandmother's dislikes than of her likes. The former included: "motor cars, the Liberal Party, the smell of camphor, scenes of any sort, continental hotels, and criticism of Bret Harte."

Of his old friends, Harte continued to see much of the Boyds, the Pembertons, and Arthur Collins. He formed a few new friendships and frequently visited Lord Northampton and his invalid wife at Compton Wynyates and Castle Ashby, but he was out of the high-society limelight for good. He no longer had the energy or the time for it, and it had never been important to him to know people just for the sake of knowing them. As he wrote to Miss Chappell in early 1899, when thanking her for a reminder of a theater engagement: "Unfortunately I am not so certain about my ability to accept your kind invitation to sup afterwards, for I am, as you know, an early-homing and much-dieted man!" Miss Chappell, the niece of the musical antiquary William Chappell, was one of his latter-day spinster friends, as was Miss Spenceley, whom he described in a letter to Frank in 1901 as "a kind friend, though a recent one." Harte may have met Miss Chappell through Colonel Collins and Miss Spenceley through Madame Van de Velde. Starting in 1898, he developed an entirely epistolary friendship with one of his devoted readers, Miss Minnie Jackson.

Their common love of books was the basis for his friendships with Chappell and Jackson, as it was with Mary Boyd and Florence Henniker. Bret Harte was a voracious reader all his life, and in middle and old age he continued to keep abreast of current developments in fiction, reading everything from Hardy's latest novel to Marie Corelli's latest romance. When Mary Boyd sent him Corelli's *The Gateless Barrier,* in which "the heroine ghost is materialized by degrees," he agreed with his friend that " 'that way madness lies.' " He was more tolerant of Lady Augusta Gregory's flirting with the supernatural in *Celtic Twilight.* Writing to the author that he had been reading her "delightful book" during his only "really intelligent and lucid interval—in bed, at night!" he added, in allusion to the author's ghostly apparitions, "Let us hope that we may all live such a life in this world—that we shall be able to reappear in it hereafter, always to the 'most respectable people,' and in the best society!"

Harte's opinion of his old friend William Dean Howells's latest effort, *The Traveller from Altruria* (1894), was less complimentary. In the novel, its author was "very imperfectly disguised as a banker, a manufacturer, a professor, a clergyman, a lady," and the foreigner of the title. The characters seemed to Harte "colourless and even flavourless." "There isn't a sensation of any kind in the book, nor an out-and-out laugh in its pages," he commented to Mary Boyd: "You feel that it would be vulgar, and this is perhaps the crowning satire on American fashionable literature—because quite unconscious. And the most delicious touch, equally unconscious, is when Howells speaks of *himself,* 'the novelist,' as a writer of *romance!* "

In 1889, Harte was full of admiration for his friend Froude's romance, *The Two Chiefs of Dunboy*: "It thoroughly directed my mind from everything else, held all my intent and at times thrilled me with that delightful little tumult of the blood—which is the applause of the whole listening body! If you were an old romance reader you would understand what I mean, and know that *this* is the best test for a really good story!" To Harte, Wilde's scandalous *Dorian Gray,* which he was reading in early October 1890, was simply a not very adept romance, and he could not see why people saw such terrible things in it. "It amused me greatly," he wrote to Henniker, "as an instance of how a man may be witty and cynical without the slightest trace of humour."

Besides reading, Harte's favorite hobby starting in 1896 was amateur photography. He got himself an inexpensive camera and even began to develop his own prints in an improvised dark room at Arford House. In August 1897, he could report to Mary Boyd that he did not have "a stick of clothing or an exposed finger that isn't stained." He promised Anna he would send her some of his photographs of Arford "when I am a little more proficient in the art. Alas! I have only a cheap instrument and am very bungling." The only one of Harte's own efforts that survives is a picture of Miss Spenceley taken at the Red House in the fall of 1899.

Harte shared his interest in photography with his son Frank and with Pemberton's daughter May. To the latter he wrote the following comment on one of her photographs: "It may be a foolish, human weakness, but I *should* have liked (as the photos are small) to have had *one* plate *all to myself*!" Pemberton's foot had intruded on one of them. He added the query: "Do you keep a lot of small plates with *his* foot in the corner—a sort of perpetual reminder, a kind of *ex pede Herculem,* you know? I don't mind, but it must be very discomposing and ominous to the average young man whom you may take!" It was also to May that he reported in February 1900 that because of the heavy fall of snow at Camberley, he was getting his exercise shoveling out the garden paths. Evidently proud of his efforts, he wrote to Pemberton that the odd-job man attributed his easy handling of the spade to his early life as a gold digger. If we are to believe Mary Boyd, exercise was not something Bret Harte was generally fond of, and his liking for golf "proved merely a fleeting fancy." He nevertheless listed golf as one of his hobbies in "Who's Who."

In 1899, thirty-eight-year-old Hamlin Garland made his first trip to London. William Dean Howells had provided him with three letters of introduction: one to Thomas Hardy, one to Mark Twain, and one to Bret Harte. Garland was one of the few members of the rising generation of American writers who ever met Bret Harte, as Harte had left America long before they began their careers. While taking tea one afternoon at the home of the writer Joseph Hatton, his "attention was drawn to a man whose appearance was almost precisely that of the typical English club-man of the American stage. He was tall, and his hair parted in the middle was white. He wore grey-striped trousers, a cutaway coat over a fancy vest, and above his polished shoes glowed laven-der spats. In his hand he carried a pair of yellow gloves." "Who is that?" Garland had asked of his companion, Israel Zangwill. He was amazed when Zangwill replied that it was his "noble com-patriot, Francis Bret Harte." Could that dandy, that be-mono-cled, be-spatted old beau be the author of "The Luck of Roaring Camp" and "Two Men of Sandy Bar"?

Not many days later, he received a note from Bret Harte, dated May 3, 1899:

> Dear Mr. Garland
>
> I would call at your hotel if my work did not confine me so closely to the house for the next few days. But if *you* could drop in *here* on Friday (5th) at about 1/2 past 4, to tea, *I* should be delighted!
>
> It was a rare pleasure to get a line from Howells and to find him, once more, the very charming flesh-and-blood creature I knew of old, and not only the distinguished author who of late years I merely know from his books.
>
> Yours very sincerely,
Bret Harte

On the appointed day, Garland duly presented himself at Harte's "bachelor apartments" at 74 Lancaster Gate. They seemed to him on entering to be "very ladylike, spic and span, and very dainty in coloring, with chairs of the gilded, spindle-legged peril-ous sort which women adore." When Harte came in to greet him, "he was almost as aristocratic as the room." "His whole appearance," Garland continues, in an account written thirty years later, "was that of an elderly fop whose life had been one of self-indulgent ease. His eyes were clouded with yellow, and beneath them the skin was puffed and wrinkled." Harte wanted to hear all about Howells and Aldrich "and all the rest of the boys." When asked when he would return to America, Harte an-swered that he feared he never would. Twice Garland rose to go, twice Harte made him resume his seat. He wanted to hear more about the West, as he seldom met anyone who knew western America. When Garland finally departed, Harte accompanied him downstairs and onto the street. For the third time, Garland clasped his hand and said good-bye. Did Garland think as he walked away that he had just met the man who published Henry George's first article in the pages of the *Overland Monthly?* We know that he thought Harte "a leader (in point of power as well as of time) in the local-color school of fiction," which Garland was then advocating "as the most vital development of fiction."

As it happened, at the time of Garland's visit Bret Harte had just completed his well-known essay on "The Rise of the 'Short Story.' " In the essay, he sketched a theory of the development of the short story form in America, which linked it closely to the rise of American humor. While he was not willing to admit to begetting the genre in toto, he felt he might have contributed to making the American short story more characteristic of American life, habits, and thought. He concluded his analysis and what was indirectly a closing statement about his life's work, with the following words:

> [T]he secret of the American short story was the treatment of characteristic American life, with absolute knowledge of its peculiarities and sympathy with its methods; with no fastidious ignoring of its habitual expression, or the inchoate poetry that may be found even hidden in its slang; with no moral determination except that which may be the legitimate outcome of the story itself; with no more elimination than may be necessary for the artistic conception, and never from the fear of the "fetish" of conventionalism. Of such is the American short story of to-day—the germ of American literature to come.

Hamlin Garland would have been able to read the essay in the issue of the *Cornhill Magazine* for July 1899. After his visit to Harte in early May, he noted briefly in his diary: "He was affable and polite but looked old and burnt out, his eyes clouded, his skin red and flabby. He has lived hard and fast, that is evident." After parting with his host in the street that afternoon, something had moved him to turn and glance backward. Bret Harte was still "standing on the doorstep, his hand on the railing, the sunlight on his bent head, making his hair gleam like silver." It was the last time Garland ever saw him.

Garland's account, written when he himself was in the autumn of his life and published in 1930 in *Roadside Meetings,* is filled with pathos. He writes that he was "saddened by this decay of a brilliant and powerful novelist." He portrays Harte as a tragic exile wishing he had never left California, "a burned out London sport," "old and feeble and about to die," "poor and the subject of gossip," rumored to be "living on the bounty of a patron." How much of this is colored by what he would later hear from Mark Twain is revealed in Garland's "literary chronicle," *Companions on the Trail* (1931).

Like so many others, Hamlin Garland was witness to one of Twain's rantings and ravings against his former friend. The occasion was a lunch for Henry Harland given by William Dean Howells in New York on January 6, 1904. "Mark got started almost immediately on Bret Harte, whom he heartily despised, and told some very pungent stories of Harte's early life." This in turn led Howells to relate the old story of the bailiff on the platform when Harte first lectured in Boston. Twain was the only one who did not laugh at the anecdote, cursing Harte as a "whelp" and a "blackguard." Harland, who had been living many years in England, could relate that "at the time of his death he was very poor and living with a woman not his wife." "I can believe it," said Mark Twain, adding that Harte had deserted his wife and children many years ago and had lived an irresponsible life in London ever since, "working over the tailings of his California mine, till all his readers fell away from him." Though "knowing Mark," Garland discounted the charges, he did not discount the last one, writing in his "American Expatriates" sketch that when Harte died, his books were no longer in demand. Such was Bret Harte's reputation among his fellow writers in America in the late 1890s and early years of the twentieth century.

However much Harte might be in need of sympathy and understanding from his countrymen, it was not because of a falling off in his popularity. The demand for his stories was steady, so steady that he spent the last years of his life literally writing himself into the grave. He kept on telling tales of mining towns, rural villages, and Spanish missions, peopled with the same archetypes and stock characters—dispossesed Spanish grandees, lazy Mexican peons and conniving vaqueros, sensual señoritas, devoted mining partners, adulterous heroines, and puritanical displaced New Englanders—that he had been conjuring up for forty years.

Harte's stories got shorter toward the end of his life, but he wrote more of them, so that his income, however precarious, remained stable. Nevertheless, from the time of the loss of his consulate in 1885, he appears to have been constantly hard-pressed for money. This was not because he was not *earning* it, but rather because, like his wife, and excepting the $5,000 he was able to put aside at one point, he was not able to *save* a penny of the thousands of dollars he earned each year. If we consider the last twenty full years of his life, we know he earned in the vicinity of $185,500. Of this, $10,500 represents his consular salary from 1882 to 1885 and $175,000 his income from his literary labors. Of the latter amount, he paid Watt a commission of 10 percent, amounting to $17,500. He sent his wife and children $3,000 a year (plus around $150 a year for summer and Christmas extras) from 1882 to 1898 and $1,800 from 1898 to 1902, making a total of about $58,000. Subtracting his payments to Watt and to Anna, this still leaves Bret Harte with $110,000, an average of $5,500 a year for twenty years. It will probably remain a mystery how one man, living practically rent-free for the first fourteen of these years, managed to get through all this money, but get through it he did. By 1897, he was forced to begin having Watt advance him money against the future income from his stories. His "balance" with Watt was £519.14 ($2,600) in Watt's favor by May 30, 1899, and he had signed over the present and future rights to twenty of his stories and sketches to ensure the recovery of the money. The advances from Watt kept him afloat while he waited for the frequently tardy payments from publishers. Harte could not press for payment, as that would have made him seem anxious and revealed the reality behind his image of economic independence.

Despite not having to maintain his own establishment until 1896, it naturally cost money to keep up with the upper echelons of English society. Besides renting country houses with the Van de Veldes and entertaining his friends at restaurants such as Verey's on Regent Street, we can well imagine that Harte's vast wardrobe and fine jewelry cost a pretty penny and that in sum his travel expenses, his hotel vacations at Royal Leamington Spa and various seaside resorts, his club memberships, his books, his gifts, all took a bite out of his income. During the last ten years of his life, if not longer, we know he had his own horse and carriage (a brougham) and a coachman, Lambert, to go with it—no mean expense in that day and age. As for his savings from the 1880s, they were most likely spent in the 1890s rather than having been lost in risky investments. At as late a date as 1898, we find him sending Christmas greetings to Mr. Smelmann, with whom he invested the money back in 1885.

The aging expatriate that Garland met in 1899 was an ailing man. When Garland left his host standing in the sunlight on that May afternoon, Bret Harte had exactly three years left to live—May 5 would be the day of his death. The record of his three final years is bleak. He was slowly dying of cancer of the throat, and no one, not himself, not his family, not his friends, not even his doctors realized it. At a time of life and in a condition of health that should have ordained plentiful rest and a little recreation, Bret Harte had to keep on working to support himself and his family. During the last full year of his life, he published no less than fourteen short stories and his final romance, "Trent's Trust." In 1902, two poems and six stories from his hand appeared, some of them posthumously.

In mid-September 1901, Harte returned from a brief holiday to find a "wretched batch of lying, begging letters" from his older son Griswold to Anna, which Anna she had sent her husband in explanation of her once again sending her son part of her monthly allowance. It turned out that Griswold was going to be a father and intended to marry the mother of his child. That required money. Harte was furious, finding Griswold's letters utterly unconvincing: "Fraud and Incompetancy [sic] are written all over them in letters large enough for the most self-blinded and doting mother to read! I cannot believe that even *you* were deceived by them. If you believed in them, and that it was your mission to sacrifice yourself and others for Wodie, you would never have left America, where, with the money I sent you, you could have easily taken Wodie into your home and looked after him—instead of now expecting the father of *over sixty years,* in his old age to support a son of *nearly forty!* You would not have wished to add a dubious grandchild to my decreasing income and increasing years, whom you could have made part of your household *there* with very little extra expense." Anna was now proposing to support them "without personal supervision and without surety of its being a necessity." Even the letters laughed in her face at the suggestion, Harte wrote.

Having gotten up his wind, he went on to say that a man who was able to earn $10 a week or over £2, "a sum on which many gentlemen in this country are obliged to support themselves," was not the subject of charity:

> It was for *him* to say—not *you*—*how* his child should be looked after—and for *him* to do it! You have not even the power to take the child, and keep it—even if you had the money.
>
> If you were a rich woman and able to support yourself—or had a husband who was not obliged to work increasingly, without help from any of his family, even in his old age, you might indulge in such folly. If you had saved anything out of the $60,000 I have sent you in the last twenty years, you might do it. But you are still in debt after spending that money. And this mismanagement—or wilfull blindness as to my income and its insecurity—you recognize in Wodie as a reason for your supporting him!

Harte wrote that he had been warning her the last seven or eight years of his decreasing income and ill health. A month's illness would stop her income; "three months incapacity for work would be more apt to make *me* a subject for charity and the hospital than it would Wodie!" "When you came to England, without my knowledge or consent, I was told by Frank that you expected in that way to reduce your expenses by living with him, and *that*, I conceived to have been his reason for advising you to such a rash and expensive step and being himself responsible for it. But that expectation has not been realized." He now gathered from Frank's letters that his plan of making a home for her in his home was for some strange reason or other no longer possible. To make matters worse, Frank was proposing to move to London and to put his mother in lodgings somewhere near him, when in Harte's opinion they could all live comfortably in the country on Frank's own income and what he gave Anna, as thousands of well-bred people did. They could have that leisure that he himself could not. If it weren't for kindness of friends whom he visited, he could scarcely keep up his lodgings in London for his work when he was there. But, Harte sighed, he had told her all this before and was "heart-sick with repeating it": "It is only when you now calmly propose 'a fund' for the maintenance of a man like Wodie and his child that I do it."

Griswold Harte married Jennie Astoria Chapin in Brooklyn on September 24, 1901. Griswold was thirty-eight, Jennie thirty. It is uncertain if their child was already born at this point; most likely she was not, as they were married by the parish priest. Since the mid-1880s, Griswold had been scraping by as a journalist. He had been the business manager of *Town Topics,* a penny society journal, for a brief while in 1885–86, followed by a stint as the editor and part proprietor of the *Green County Advertiser,* based in Cairo, New York. When that venture failed, his father wrote that he must not lose heart and try again. Harte wished he knew how he could help him and thought it better if he would stick to something that was permanent, even if it barely supported him or had only the prospect of support, than to get into any more speculative ventures. In 1887, he wrote to Anna that it was an extra Christmas gift that his son had had a chance to write something for the *New York World*: "Heaven grant that it may be a permanency!" With his usual frankness, he wrote to Anna that he did not think Wodie would ever make a great newspaper writer, but he might make a successful journalist and be able to run a paper. This was in 1889. During the 1890s we have no evidence of how Griswold was getting on until the dénouement of September 1901.

None of the increasing inner turmoil of his mind and body can be read in the pictures of Bret Harte taken toward the end of his life. The retouched black and white photographs only show a well-groomed, dignified elderly man, perpetually dressed at the height of fashion down to the flower in his buttonhole. They do not show the redness of his skin in his final years, "suggesting permanent sunburn from the blaze of the California sunshine," or, for that matter, what one of Pemberton's daughters also remembered twenty years after Harte's death: that he had light blue eyes and very small feet. They do not capture what Gertrude Atherton observed, that he "walked with short mincing steps, as if his patent leather shoes were to small for him," or the differing impression of S. R. Elliott that there "was something in his movements, and especially in his walk, that recalled the unconscious grace of some wild animal." "Many a time," wrote Elliott in 1907, "have I stood at the door to watch him as he walked down the street, and have wondered whence would come that supple ease of motion, which seemed to do everything by mere volition."

However immaculate in his external appointments and his carriage, by the age of sixty-three, Bret Harte was a physical wreck. For years he had been suffering from a catalog of ills—none of them fatal, all of them painful and chronic. In addition to the stomach trouble and neuralgia in his face that had plagued him ever since his Crefeld days, he was constantly suffering from colds. Old age brought him gout, sciatica, and lumbago; the latter prevented him from "standing upright before the meanest of my species, and makes me go doddering round from room to room like the old stage peasant who is visiting the scenes of his childhood." The increasing years also brought him rheumatism, of which we have no more poignant evidence than the deterioration of his once beautiful handwriting into an almost illegible, miniscule, crabbed scrawl. The joint of his little finger would swell up so badly that it reminded him "of my poor mother's hand in the later years of her life." Yet he had to keep on writing.

On January 1, 1900, he makes the first ominous complaint of an "irritated throat," which forced him to give up Mary Boyd's New Year's luncheon. It was downhill from there. Though he had the best Harley Street doctors, they diagnosed his case as being one of "acute laryngitis" and did not realize the seriousness of his condition until Francis King Harte called in an Austrian specialist, who happened to be in London for a medical conference. By then it was too late. Taking Frank aside after the consultation, the doctor regretted that the disease had been allowed to progress beyond hope and said that his father only had a few months left to live. Harte had been smoking cigars for most of his life. In 1899, he admitted to A. P. Watt that he smoked so much he could only use very mild brands. While he entered the final stages of terminal throat cancer, he was puffing away at Punch cigars from Valle and Company, Havana.

Bret Harte was not told that he was dying. His friends and family were nevertheless convinced that he knew the end was near. He could hardly speak or eat. As if cancer were not enough, Harte had spent excruciating weeks in the dentist's chair both during the winter of 1900 and in December 1901, having what remained of his teeth removed and being fitted for plates. He did not take gas, the only painkiller at the time, preferring the pain to "that dreadful stuff!" The dentures cost £42 ($200) and did not even fit him, and he wished he had never gone to the dentist in the first place. On February 1, 1901, he wrote to Anna: "I would have infinitely preferred to have had nothing done— and have lived on slops, soups, and jellies!" He added prophetically: "My wretched body is scarcely worth the sum I am spending on it." He still had not lost his sense of humor when he wrote one of his last letters to Mary Boyd on November 3, 1901, to thank her for the "Versailles Christmas Book." Boyd had written a book based on her experience of her son being dangerously ill with scarlet fever at Versailles. "How 'blessed among women' are you," Harte wrote, "to be able to turn your domestic tribulations to such delightful account! I wish I could make something as charming out of 'Nine Months with a Dentist,' or, 'In Surrey with a Sore Throat and an Unfinished Manuscript.'"

On December 1, 1901, he wrote to Frank that he had come to town from Camberley to see the dentist and was oscillating between him and the doctor. He had received Ethel's letter with "all the hopeless enclosures and disclosures" concerning Wodie, but he saw nothing to alter his opinion or his expectancy of being able to do anything more for his eldest son. "I am myself becoming an invalid, and am scarcely able to work more than an hour or two a day." Ten days later, on December 11, he received a telegram from Frank to say that Griswold had died of tuberculosis the preceding night. His widow needed money to bury him. Harte himself was now in such a poor state that a week before he had had to stop writing. To Frank, now living in Battersea Park, he wrote the following from 74 Lancaster Gate: "I have received your letter and telegram. I enclose a cheque for £10, which should be more than sufficient with what your mother has already got to meet this emergency. I feel too hopeless to say more;

I am, and have been quite ill for the last month and unable to work." He had not written to Anna since the explosive letter of September 15. On December 22, he wrote to her: "God knows it is a sorrowful Christmas—for you—for both of us. Happy only to the *one who has gone*—but I hope you will not forget the living for all that." Apart from the note to Frank, it was his only allusion to Griswold's death.

For the first time, he was too ill to go on his customary round of shopping for Christmas presents for friends and family. He was engaged to go to Miss Spenceley and her family for Christmas, as he had been the previous year. When Christmas Day came around, he felt too unwell to go anywhere, no matter how wretched it was to spend his Christmas alone. By coincidence he received an electric lamp for Christmas both from Frank and from the Pembertons. We may picture Bret Harte on his last Christmas, alone in his study at Lancaster Gate, wrestling with the new contraption, for which there were no written instructions, and ending up with the trigger coming off in his hand. He thought that electric lamps were "wretched humbugs got up to sell," he wrote to Frank that day, and was sending both back. Hoping maybe for a little sympathy, he added that he did not think Frank realized how sick he was.

One who was ever ready with sympathy, even after all he had put her through, was his wife, Anna. While at Tunbridge Wells she received a letter from her husband in mid-January 1902. She had not seen him since August 29, 1900, when he had come to Caversham for an afternoon. He realized, he wrote, that she would do all she could for him if she had the opportunity. Yet the doctor felt he needed a more decided change than Tunbridge Wells could offer, and he was going to Southsea the next day for a few days. He ended this, his last letter to Anna, in a vein by now so familiar it had become a settled habit: he hoped he would be able to visit her soon.

In his last known letter to Frank, enclosing, as always the monthly check, he wrote that he had had to borrow the money to send them. "Tell your mother this and impress upon her the necessity of being careful of the little I am still able to give her." He would write to her again when he saw what the specialist said and what must be done: "I should only bother her now with my fear and depressions." He thought, quite rightly, that his case had been mismanaged from the beginning.

Harte saw Arthur Collins for the last time in March. They dined at the Royal Thames Yacht Club, and Collins found his "poor old friend" "sadly aged and broken, but genial and kind as ever." They sat an hour at a music hall and Harte wrote afterwards to thank Collins for having "forced him out." That same month, one of his tonsils was excised. He wrote to Pemberton: "Tell your medical student son that the operation and the instrument were so fascinating that they delighted even the victim!" He rallied and was able to pay what would be his final visit to Anna and Frank and his family. Frank had sold Warren Heights and moved his family to Richmond. It was probably Frank who took the last photograph we have of Bret Harte. In the only photo in which his impeccable facade was allowed to drop, we find a small wizened man, his face heavily lined, almost being swallowed up by the overstuffed armchair he is seated in.

From Richmond Bret Harte went to the Red House, "hoping to benefit from the sun and the fresh air." But his final spring was cold and sunless, and he wrote to Pemberton from Camberley on April 12: "I am still very poorly; everything is against me— even this smileless, joyless, 'sere and yellow' spring! I get no stimulus from it. I can scarcely write a letter. The grasshopper is indeed a burden!"

Saying he felt better, he sat down five days later to write a new story. He got no further than the title and the first few lines. On Monday, May 5, 1902, while still at the Red House, he suffered a sudden hemorrhage in his throat. A second hemorrhage in the late afternoon rendered him partially unconscious, and at about six o'clock in the afternoon Bret Harte died. Madame Van de Velde issued a statement to the press: Bret Harte was on a long visit to the Red House—none of his family were present, his son and daughter arriving too late—and surrounded only by intimate friends (one of them herself), he had "passed away without struggle or pain."

Geoffrey Bret Harte would never forget the morning of Tuesday, May 6. His father and mother had rushed off the preceding night in answer to an urgent telegram. The next morning, early, his father had entered his room, still wearing his overcoat and gloves: "[H]e stood me up and told me that I would never see my grandfather again. His face looked haggard, tears ran down his cheeks. It was the first time I had ever seen him cry and the sight was so shocking that it brought home the meaning of the words much more acutely than the words alone could have done." To Geoffrey's big brother, Richard, his grandfather's death was also the momentous event of their years in Richmond. His grandmother and Aunt Ethel had not appeared at breakfast, and when he asked why, he was told that his grandmother was ill. On the floor he discovered a copy of the *Daily Telegraph* with the glaring headline: "Bret Harte Dead."

On Thursday, May 8, 1902, in the squat, mid-Victorian church of St. Peter's in the Surrey village of Frimley, a group of about twenty people had come to show their final respects to Francis Bret Harte. Outside it was raining steadily. In the subdued light from the stained-glass windows, one could discern a small group at the front of the church consisting of Anna Harte, her son Frank, her daughter-in-law Aline, and her daughter Ethel. Another small group was formed around Madame Van de Velde, including one of her unmarried daughters, Miss Norris (the sister of her son-in-law Richard Norris), and Mrs. Clavering Lyne. Of Harte's closest friends, only Arthur Collins and Alexander Stuart Boyd were present. Pemberton had written to Frank the day before that he wished to attend the funeral but that in his "deplorable state of health" it was impossible for him to travel. Beside the small group of family and old friends, the rest of the people who heard the service conducted by the rector of Frimley, Reverend W. Basset, were recent acquaintances from among the local gentry. As one newspaper noted: "The funeral was of the simplest possible character and the phrase 'this our brother' had a peculiar poignancy, for, though a group of villagers stood in the rain under the trees as the hearse arrived, there were few in the church, who had not the right to call Mr. Bret Harte friend." The simplicity of the service was in keeping with Bret Harte's wishes.

A large hole had been dug in the ground not far behind the church, right next to the orange-red brick wall of the churchyard. Covered with beautiful wreaths, the coffin was conducted to the side of the grave and the service continued. On the card appended to the flowers from Frank and Aline was written: "Devoted in the past, now, and in the long future." One final offering was a bunch of beautiful cowslips bound in a black ribbon. Cowslips were not obtainable in the area, so someone had gone to a lot of trouble, noted one newspaper. As the group huddled by the graveside, the final words of the service were accompanied by the falling of the cold rain, almost hail, and the blowing of a bitter wind, yet there were thrushes and blackbirds singing in the trees. The body was committed to the earth, and in a few minutes the service had ended. After a last look into the ivy-lined grave, the little group of mourners dispersed.

Anna Bret Harte and Hydeline Rodolphine Emma Van de Velde met at Harte's graveside for the first and last time. We can be sure they were civil to each other at this meeting, but inside they must have felt a tumult of emotions. What Anna thought of the foreign woman who for twenty years had made a home for her husband in her place we will never know. As for Madame Van de Velde, she was determined that in death she would be linked to her oldest and dearest friend as closely as she had been in life. She was appalled that, with the exception of William Waldorf Astor and the Bohemian Club of San Francisco, not one token from America was vouchsafed to Bret Harte's last resting place. Back at 109 Lancaster Gate two weeks after his death, Madame sat down and wrote a letter to John Hay, who was now secretary of state and whom she had not seen since "the good old days in London." "Would it not be a graceful act of justice," she asked, "if America paid a public, tangible homage to a man who was her son, a genius, a worker, a patriot and rarer still a *good man?*" She also expressed her opinion of Anna Harte in indirect but no uncertain terms:

> You more than any one perhaps—know what a failure our friend's domestic life was; how to ensure the continuance and perfection of his literary career, his friends procured for him a Consulship in Germany, and how he lived in exile for 28 years, never complaining, working hard to meet the exhaustive claims made on his resources, too chivalrous and generous to repudiate them even when flagrantly excessive. His son, living in England, has often recognized the fact that a return to America and the old conditions would have been

disastrous. Nevertheless, there is much bitterness in such a life to such a man, and that his end was mercifully sheltered from disturbing elements is a source of thankfulness.

She closed her letter: "Dear Mr. Hay believe me when I say that I have written in all sincerity, in all confidence and that I will not for one moment think that you can either misunderstood [sic] or misapply this communication." When Hay failed to respond, Madame put into action the plan she had surely been contemplating all along. *She* would give Bret Harte his monument. It would be the final symbol of the endurance and purity of their friendship.

She instructed that on a base of white granite weighing two and a half tons, a large rectangular slab of red Aberdeen granite should be placed, its sides beveled so that they met in a Roman cross. Around the base should be a chain link held up by small iron balusters topped with spurlike ornamentation. On the stone's southern side were to be inscribed Harte's name, the year of his birth and death, and a line from his poem "Reveille": "Death shall reap the braver harvest." Small fir trees were to be planted on three sides of the grave. Only Madame could have given Bret Harte such a lavish monument, as Harte had died without assets.

When Hay, who had been ill, finally wrote back in July 1902, Madame could reply that she had already completed her instructions for the stone she intended to place on the grave: "[I]n the absence of anybody else here to undertake it, I value the privilege of rendering this last tribute of regard, regret and affection to so dear a friend." By the coming of the new year, the monument was in place.

Today the chain link is broken, a corner of the cross chipped off, the tombstone covered with dust and grime, and the black paint long since worn away from the engraved letters, but one can still read the inscription on the stone's western end: "In faithful remembrance M. S. Van de Velde."

AAAL	American Academy of Arts and Letters, New York
ABA	American Biographical Archive (microfiche)
APWP	Alexander Pollock Watt Papers, Alderman Library, University of Virginia (microfilm)
Bancroft	Bancroft Library, University of California, Berkeley
BMFA	Belgian Ministry of Foreign Affairs, Brussels
Brown	John Hay Library, Brown University, Providence, Rhode Island
Colby	Miller Library, Colby College, Waterville, Maine
Columbia	Rare Book and Manuscript Library, Columbia University, New York
Cornell	Rare and Manuscript Collections, University Library, Cornell University, Ithaca, New York
Diary-1	Bret Harte's manuscript diary from Oct. 19, 1857 to March 5, 1858, Bancroft Library, University of California, Berkeley
Diary-2	"Things that happened. 1881, 1882, 1883, 1884, 1885, 1886, 1887, 1888." Bound diary in the handwriting of M. S. Van de Velde transcribed from Bret Harte's diaries. Dated Feb. 24, 1888. Berg Collection, New York Public Library
Duke	Special Collections Library, Duke University, Durham, North Carolina
FWT	Notes from George Stewart's interview with Harte's niece, Florence Wyman Taylor, Stewart Papers, Bancroft Library, University of California, Berkeley
Hayes	Rutherford B. Hayes Library, Fremont, Ohio
H-B	Hampden-Booth Theatre Library, New York
Houghton	Houghton Library, Harvard University, Cambridge, Massachusetts
HRC	Harry S. Ransom Humanities Research Center, University of Texas, Austin
Huntington	Henry E. Huntington Library, San Marino, California
JBH	In the private possession of Harte's great-grandson John Bret-Harte

Knox	Knox College Archives, Henry M. Seymour Library, Knox College, Galesburg, Illinois
LC	Library of Congress (Manuscript Division), Washington, D.C.
MA	Municipal Archives, Division of Old Records, 31 Chambers St., New York
MC	In the private possession of Marian Collins Surtees
MHS	Massachusetts Historical Society, Boston
MiHS	Minnesota Historical Society, Saint Paul
Morse	Willard S. Morse Collection, Research Library, University of California, Los Angeles. Newspaper clippings in this collection have been pasted up in such a way that the page numbers have been removed.
MTL	Notes from George Stewart's interview with Mary Tingley Laurence, Stewart Papers, Bancroft Library, University of California, Berkeley
Nissen	In the private possession of Axel Nissen
NYPL	New York Public Library, New York
NYU	Fales Library, Elmer Holmes Bobst Library, New York University, New York
RBDM	Registry of Births, Deaths and Marriages, St. Catherine's House, London, England
Reading	Chatto and Windus Papers, University of Reading Library, Reading, England
Richmond	Reference Library, Richmond, Surrey, England
Rochester	Rush Rhees Library, University of Rochester, Rochester, New York
SFPL	San Francisco Public Library, San Francisco
Somerset House	Principle Registry, Family Division of the High Court, Somerset House, London, England
Stanford	Stanford University, Stanford, California
SUL	Syracuse University Library, Syracuse, New York
UCLA	Research Library, University of California, Los Angeles
UVa	Alderman Library, University of Virginia, Charlottesville
WACML	William Andrews Clark Memorial Library, University of California, Los Angeles
Yale	Beinecke Rare Book and Manuscript Library, Yale University, New Haven, Connecticut

NOTES

A Note on Editing

Bret Harte's unpublished letters are given as written, with one exception. Apostrophes have been added in s-genitives and in contractions, where Harte most often omits them.

A Note on the Notes

The notes are intended to inform the reader about the source of factual information or evaluations that are not those of the author. When the key words from the main text are followed by three dots, it means that all information in the remainder of the sentence or passage is taken from the stated source. When a note says that a passage is "based on" or "taken from" a given source, this means that all facts, descriptions, and evaluations have been taken from that source. The key words are usually the first words of a sentence or passage. If the sentence in the main text contains a quotation, then the first words of the quotation are used as key words.

Anonymous reviews and articles from newspapers and journals, and unpublished manuscript sources, are not listed in the bibliography. Instead full bibliographical information is given in the notes, including their location (in parentheses) in the case of unpublished sources. Some of the letters quoted have been published in *Selected Letters of Bret Harte,* ed. Gary Scharnhorst (Norman and London: University of Oklahoma Press, 1997). References to letters published in this collection have been added for the convenience of the reader, though the quotations are from the original manuscripts.

All quotations from Harte's works are taken from the "Argonaut Edition" of *The Works of Bret Harte,* 25 vols. (New York: P. F. Collier, 1906) unless otherwise stated.

Introduction

"Now death has come . . ." Howells 1903, 159.
"Stockton was bad . . ." Howells 1929, 157.
"What is to be done . . ." etc. Clemens-Howells 1960, 776.

"You have written . . ." etc. Ibid., 775.

"By ancient training . . ." Clemens 1959, 309.

"the most contemptible . . ." Ibid., 306.

Henry Adams thought . . . See Adams 1938, 391.

"one of the most . . ." Ina Coolbrith to Laurie Haynes Martin, Feb. 9, 1912 (Huntington).

"a fugitive . . ." *Athenæum* (Mar. 30, 1912): 357.

As Donald Glover . . . See Glover 1966, 5.

"Harte led . . ." Morrow 1973, 129.

"Waves of influence . . ." Canby 1926, 717.

"the first American realist." "Bret Harte and the Short Story," *New York Times Saturday Review of Books and Art* (June 9, 1900) (Morse).

"the last American . . ." Boyesen 1894, 66.

"though they were . . ." Watts-Dunton 1902, 659.

"I love Browning . . ." Meredith 1970, 462.

In a passage . . . See Clemens 1975, 11–12.

"although being . . ." etc. Harte to Eliza Knaufft, October 23, 1873 (Bancroft); Harte 1997, 84–85.

"the Bret Harte Mystery . . ." Howells 1929, 157. "Biography, in its fear . . ." Edel 1973, 152.

"What one chiefly . . ." Skidelsky 1988, 8.

"fiction is not needed . . ."; "How is one . . ."; "both biography and fiction . . ." Petrie 1981, 58, 121, 182.

"Facts do not speak . . ."; "in the unprocessed . . ." White 1978b, 125.

"gain part of . . ."; "the encodation . . ." White 1978a, 83.

"investigating the documents . . ." White 1987, 27.

"[w]hat gives . . ." Nadel 1985, 151.

"is that of having patience . . ." Honan 1985, 651.

Edel uses the term . . . See Edel 1973, ch. 5.

"a character's mental . . ." Cohn 1978, 14.

"Of the various . . ."; "this most distanced . . ." Cohn 1989, 9.

" 'must-have' school of biography." John Updike quoted in Cohn 1989, 10.

"consistent narration" etc. Uspensky 1973, 89.

"an accumulation . . ." Boswell quoted in Altick 1965, 61.

"hanging up . . ."; "in unexpected places." Woolf and Strachey quotes from Clifford 1962, 121, 133.

Chapter 1

"we suppose . . . and poems." Howells 1871, 42.

He had sent . . . See Howells 1929, 1.158.

Not only that . . . See Elinor Howells 1988, 137.

"Mrs. Howells requests . . ." The invitation is quoted in a letter in Elinor Howells 1988, 138.

Miss Sedgwick had been . . . Sara Sedgwick's reply to Mrs. Howells's "thrilling" invitation is quoted in a letter in Elinor Howells 1988, 138.

"Mr. Bret Harte arrived . . ." The notice is quoted in Howells 1929, 1.159.

Henry James to Elizabeth Boott, Friday [Feb. 24, 1871], James 1974, 255.

Their progress . . . compared to California. See Howells 1903, 154.

Saturday Club. Dating and guests from Lilian Woodman Aldrich 1921, 135.

"Why, you couldn't . . ." Harte quoted in Howells 1903, 154.

"I would this . . . when he arrived. Harte to William Dean Howells, Jan. 24, 1871, Booth 1948, 322.

It was true . . . extreme fashion. Based on Howells 1903, 154.

According to Mrs. Howells . . . See Elinor Howells 1988, 134; Howells 1903, 155.

Harte was a most . . . laugh at himself. Based on Howells 1903, 155–57.

Success had clearly not . . . See Howells 1929, 1.159.

sounded Jewish. Lowell's opinion referred to in Howells 1903, 155.

Regardless . . . Lowell's opinion referred to in Elinor Howells 1988, 138.

He feared . . . Lowell's opinion referred to in Fields 1922, 117.

At the Howellses' party . . . thru the air.' " Conversation related in Howells 1903, 155.

Talking with his old . . . See Howells 1900, 231.

Elinor Mead Howells to "Dear girls," Mar. 17, 1871, Elinor Howells 1988, 137, 139.

After sitting up . . . See Howells 1900, 159.

Andrew Anthony. See Merwin 1912, 11–12.

At unhappy times . . . astonishment. See "Ran Away," Harte 1914, 77.

Louis Agassiz . . . See Howells 1900, 272.

"When Messrs. Roman . . ." Howells 1871, 43.

Just think . . . Harte's opinion of his own poem quoted in Sherwood 1897, 192.

The visit . . . on his face. Based on Howells 1903, 155, 159.

Chapter 2

Scene commencing "Frank held his father's hand" (pp. 13–14):

In an article in the *New York Times* in early 1906, Clement Shorter was the first person to make the connection between Bernard Hart and Bret Harte public. Shorter wrote: "Bret Harte recalled that he was once taken by his father to the stock exchange in New York, of which his grandfather, Bernard Hart, was the first president, and the old man was pointed out to the young Bret Harte as his grandfather, but he never spoke to him nor saw him again" (quoted in Davis 1931, 105 n. 14). Merwin 1912, 17, repeats the story, possibly having corroborated it with Harte's sister, Eliza Knaufft.

23 White St. . . . New York City directories 1847–1855. For the residents of the house, see the 1850 New York Census.

Born in London . . . age thirteen. See Merwin 1912, 4.

In 1792 . . . See Stedman 1969, 36.

Three years later . . . See Merwin 1912, 5.

On August 13, 1806 . . . See *American Antiquarian Society Index* 1952, n. pag.; "Items Relating to the Seixas Family" 1920, 163.

Hart installed . . . See New York City Directory 1806; "Items Relating" 1920, 164.

Hart became . . . See Merwin 1912, 5.

"A distinguished trait . . ." Philips quoted in Davis 1931, 109.

"with your usual delicacy . . ."; "both amused and gratified . . ." Booth 1948, 322–23.

"Upon the hearsay . . ." Howells 1871, 42.

Legend has it . . . See Simonhoff 1956, n. pag.

Catharine Brett. Biographical information from Merwin 1912, 8–10.

According to legend . . . at Kingston. See Merwin 1912, 6, 8, 10.

As it turns out . . . two daughters. See records on Catharine Brett and Thomas Jackson in the International Genealogical Index, Family History Library, Church of Jesus Christ of Latter-Day Saints, Salt Lake City. Both Merwin 1912 and Davis 1931 confuse Catharine Brett with her paternal aunt of the same name (b. 1739).

Sixteen years later . . . "Catharine Hart." See Merwin 1912, 10.

at the Bretts. See Stewart 1931, 9.

Henry Philip Ostrander. See Merwin 1912, 10–11.

Abigail Truesdale. See Harte 1926, 444. Elizabeth Ostrander's parents were married on October 7, 1804, which makes it likely that Mrs. Hart was at least five years younger than her husband. See Dahl 1989, 217.

The couple was married . . . See Kelly n.d., 50.

1831. The inscription on her gravestone in Greenwood Cemetery gives her birthdate as August 15, 1831.

Two years later . . . See Albany Directory 1833.

There Henry Hart taught . . . See Merwin 1912, 11.

The growing family . . . See Albany Directory 1833; Merwin 1912, 13.

By 1835 . . . See Albany Directory 1835; Stewart 1931, 9.

August 25, 1836. Merwin 1912, 1. For other evidence in favor of the year 1836, see Stewart 1929 and Werner 1939.

Within a year . . . See Merwin 1912, 11; Stewart 1931, 10.

They returned . . . See Merwin 1912, 12.

A daughter . . . See Stewart 1931, 69–70.

For the rest . . . See Merwin 1912, 12.

One of Bret Harte's . . . See Harte 1990, 78.

Shortly before . . . undergone. See Merwin 1912, 12.

"want of balance . . ." See ibid.

His father . . . See ibid.

According to family tradition . . . See ibid., 1 n. 1.

Family legend . . . Elizabeth Harte's family. See ibid., 12, 13.

Howells remembered . . . See Howells 1890, 126.

"when that company marched . . ." . . . twelve or thirteen. Clemens 1959, 75–76.

May 13, 1846 . . . September 1847. See Merwin 1912, 13–15. In his account of Henry Hart Jr., Merwin quotes a letter from Eliza Knaufft at length.

weakly child. See Pemberton 1903, 1; Merwin 1912, 16.

"at a sickly . . ." "Ships" (1860), Harte 1914, 113. "unable to lead . . ."; Legend has it . . . See Merwin 1912, 16.

"the children took . . ." Adams 1918, 36.

Washington Irving. See Pemberton 1900, 38; Merwin 1912, 16.

summer vacations . . . mountain air. See Harte to Anna Harte, 15 August 1886 (UVa); Stewart 1931, 15–16.

While Frank's father . . . See Merwin 1912, 11.

Bret Harte to Minnie Jackson, 6 April 1899, Pemberton 1903, 330.

"Horace and Montaigne . . ."; "true appreciator . . ." Fields 1922, 238–39.

When there was company . . . See "Ran Away," Harte 1914, 77.

At age eleven . . . another line of verse. See Harte 1894, 42. The journalist who relates this story thought Harte was born in 1841, so it is possible that Harte's print debut took place in 1852, when he was sixteen rather than eleven.

Bret Harte to Bessie Ward, Sept. 19, 1874 (UVa).

Harte's sister . . . son's request. See Merwin 1912, 16–17.

It is interesting . . . See "Ran Away," Harte 1914, 77, 79.

Mrs. Harte's younger sister May . . . The real-life counterparts of the aunt and uncle in the sketch have not hitherto been known. I was able to identify them through a visit to the Kutzemeyer-Knaufft-Harte burial plot in Greenwood Cemetery, Brooklyn, and the examination of the records of interment.

When Henry was a baby . . . See Harte to Francis King Harte, Jan. 15, 1888 (UVa).

Ellington Institute. See Harte to Bessie Ward, 19 September 1874 (UVa).

His formal education . . . See Merwin 1912, 17.

She had wondered . . . Fanny!" See Coolbrith's introduction to Harte 1924, n. pag.

After . . . In 1851. See Merwin 1912, 13, 15, 17.

Frederick Ferdinand Knaufft. See *New York Times* (Apr. 30, 1892): 4.

Towards the end . . . See Merwin 1912, 17.

On the day . . . See Stewart 1931, 8, 29.

21 Irving Place. See New York City Directory 1853.

Not quite three weeks . . . See Stewart 1931, 29.

"Had he been born . . ." Adams 1918, 3.

His solution . . . Bret Harte's daughter, Ethel Bret Harte, was under the impression that Henry Harte lived at odds with his father. See Davis 1931, 105 n. 14.

"never made a secret . . ." Quoted in Davis 1931, 105 n. 14.

"a general interest . . ."; "decidedly incomplete." Havelock Ellis to Rupert L. Joseph, Mar. 15, 1935 (NYPL).

Bret Harte to Havelock Ellis, Dec. 21, 1889 (HRC), Harte 1997, 363–64.

"he [Harte] hides his Jewish birth . . ." Mark Twain to William Dean Howells, June 27, 1878, Clemens-Howells 1960, 235.

"clean daft . . ."; "was amazed . . ."; "now believes . . ." Hay quoted in Clymer 1971, 347; Mayo 1988, 57.

James Russell Lowell's . . . descended from Jews . . ." See Mayo 1988, 57.

William Dean Howells recalled . . . of the name." See Howells 1900, 26; Howells 1903, 155.

"these lying . . ." Harte to Rudolph Schneider, June 22, 1880 (UVa).

"no Israelite . . . the well-bred." *New York Times* (June 19, 1877): 1.

"subtile distinction . . . in his world. "That Ebrew Jew" (1877), Harte 1914, 393–94.

Lydia Maria Child wrote . . . See Mayo 1988, 32.

"America can boast . . ." Parton 1870, 398.

Chapter 3

Scene commencing "In London" (pp. 31–34):

This scene is based on Harte 1894a with two exceptions. The description of the exterior of 109 Lancaster Gate is based on a visit to the site. The description of how Harte looked is taken from Harte 1894a, 38–39 (including a sketch) but also from contemporary photographs not reproduced in the article.

"should as soon . . ." Harte to Minnie Jackson, Apr. 2, 1900, Pemberton 1903, 333.

"There are so many . . ." Harte to Douglas W. Sladen, Nov. 7, 1896 (Richmond).

Harte to Ethel Bret Harte, Sept. 14, 1889 (UVa).

"[a] very singular . . ." etc. Elliott 1907, 125.

"Bret Harte was . . ." . . . let her go. See Hare 1908, 20.

"Many of his later friends . . ." Pemberton 1903, 81.

"sincere; never a poseur . . ." Ethel Bret Harte cited in Fassett 1924, 247.

"First, and before everything . . ." Besant quoted in Graham 1965, 26.

Thus it was shocking . . . See Howells 1903, 156.

Equally, readers . . . See, for example, Murdock 1921, 87.

"Bret Harte wrote . . ." Van de Velde 1881, 233.

After an arduous . . . See Stewart 1931, 31, 32.

There they had built . . . Frank's home. See Stewart 1931, 54 and Shumate and Lewis 1967, n. pag. (including photograph).

"Colonel Williams . . ." McCrackin 1902, 222.

Fred Knaufft. See Haskell 1892 (Morse).

"with no better . . ." Harte 1894a, 40.

"a skylighted locker" Stoddard 1897, 673.

No one was allowed . . . See "Bret Harte's Early Days in San Francisco," *San Francisco Morning Call* (May 25, 1902) (Morse).

Legend has it . . . See Stewart 1931, 54.

He had something . . . whitewashed fence. See "Bret Harte's Early Days in San Francisco," *San Francisco Morning Call* (May 25, 1902) (Morse); Stoddard 1897, 673.

"It was only . . ." "How I Went to the Mines," copy of typescript in the Stewart Papers (Bancroft).

Mary Tingley . . . See MTL.

Family tradition . . . See FWT; Stewart 1931, 55; Pemberton 1900, 32.

"It was not possible . . ." Henry Kirk Goddard, "Francis Bret Harte," eleven-page autograph ms. dated Aug. 7, 1908 (Bancroft).

Abner Bryan. Information on the ages of the various members of the Bryan family taken from the California Census 1860.

"The house is stuck . . ." This letter is quoted in full in a typescript by Ida S. Hall entitled "Bret Harte in Contra Costa" in the Linnie Marsh Wolfe Papers (Bancroft).

One bright spring . . . woods and disappeared; "representing perhaps . . ."; "With only his name . . ."; In the end . . . "How I Went to the Mines" (1899), Harte 1906, 9.335–41, 346.

This young man . . . back to San Francisco. See interview with Steve Gillis in *Town Talk* (Jan. 8, 1915) (Morse); Clemens 1959, 124.

"a very literal . . ." A. P. Watt, Harte's agent, quotes Harte in a letter to William H. Rideing, editor of *Youth's Companion,* Nov. 24, 1897 (APWP).

"dusty and tired . . ." *Town Talk* (Jan. 8, 1915) (Morse).

Steve Gillis's testimony . . . See Clemens 1959, 124.

George Stewart claims . . . See Stewart 1931, 52–53; Gillis 1930, n. pag.

Charles Murdock . . . See Murdock 1921, 72.

"bright May morning." "How I Went to the Mines," Harte 1906, 9.335.

"I have taught . . ." Diary-1 (entry for Dec. 31, 1857).

March 1st or April 5th; left for distant . . . See Stewart 1931, 59, 62.

he told Henry Dam . . . See Harte 1894a, 41.

Harte states that . . . See "How I Went to the Mines," copy of typescript in the Stewart Papers (Bancroft).

Steve Gillis was sure . . . See *Town Talk* (Jan. 8, 1915) (Morse).

Scene commencing "It was New Year's Eve" (p. 46):
With the exception of the first sentence, this scene is a transposition into indirect free style of Harte's diary entry for Dec. 31, 1857 (Diary-1). The final quotation is from the same source.

"a change of clime," etc. Bret Harte, "Up the Coast," *Golden Era* (Nov. 1, 1857).

Benjamin Henry Wyman. See California Census 1860.

"The cradle . . ." Stoddard 1897, 675.

"He was simply . . ." Murdock 1921, 79.

On a regular . . . to read and write. See Diary-1 passim.

"I am improving . . ." Diary-1 (entry for Dec. 10, 1857).

"Bones." Ibid. (entries for Jan. 21 and Feb. 16, 1858).

"vapid"; "trite"; "commonplace." Ibid. (entries for Nov. 27, 1857 and Jan. 3, 1858).

"*very blue* . . ." Ibid. (entry for Nov. 9, 1857).

"very much annoyed"; "incontinently." Ibid. (entry for Nov. 26, 1857).

"What the d——d . . .," etc. Ibid. (entry for Dec. 25, 1857).

disapproved of card-playing. See Boyd 1902, 775.

"a matter of conscience." Diary-1 (entry for Nov. 30, 1857).

Charles Murdock . . . See Murdock 1921, 74.

Genial and witty . . . "the general." Murdock 1902, 301; Murdock 1921, 73.

Jacob Hartley . . . See Hartley 1898 (Morse).

From a different . . . serious attention." See Root 1932 (Morse).

On October 29th . . . to his sister. See Diary-1 (entries for Oct. 31 and Nov. 1, 1857).

That same month . . . Iowa City. See Diary-1 (entry for Jan. 6, 1858).

Ten days later . . . Ibid. (entry for Jan. 16, 1858).

On February 2, 1858 . . . Floy. See Diary-1.

Harte was growing . . . Ibid. (entry for Mar. 4, 1858).

Mrs. Jas. Todd . . . Notes from this interview are in the Stewart Papers (Bancroft).

Charles Murdock writes . . . See Murdock 1921, 73.

The latter job . . . See Root 1932 (Morse).

In his own . . . See Murdock 1902, 301.

Justus Wyman had brought . . . joke. See Root 1932 (Morse).

"a mechanical . . ." Harte 1914, 118-19.

"Will you please . . ." etc. "How I Went to the Mines," Harte 1906, 9.344.

"The sentiment . . ." etc. *Northern Californian* (Oct. 19, 1959).

At midnight . . . any provocation. My account of the massacre is based on Duckett 1954.

"humiliating fact . . ." etc. *Northern Californian* (Feb. 29, 1860).

Charles Murdock recalled . . . danger." See Murdock 1921, 78-79.

"Mr. F. B. Harte . . ." etc. *Northern Californian* (Mar. 29, 1860).
"[a] great mass of . . ." etc. Harte 1894a, 41.

Chapter 4

315 Second St. See San Francisco Directory 1861.

He had boarded . . . The San Francisco Directory for 1860–61, published in July 1860, gives his occupation as "printer Golden Era" and his dwelling as 148 Commercial St. We also know he lived with a distant cousin, who owned a restaurant further up in Commercial St.

Frank's brother Henry . . . "Deaths," *San Francisco Bulletin* (Jan. 18, 1861).

As the Fourth . . . homemade quality. Information from Harte's niece, Maud Williams, recorded in letter from David Magee Book Shop and in undated article from the *Oakland Tribune* (Bancroft). The description of the flag based on an examination of same in the Bancroft Library.

"If it came . . ." Daggett quoted in Henry Kirk Goddard, op. cit.

Noah Brooks recalled . . . See Brooks 1899, 447.

One who certainly . . . California. See Rather 1974, 34, 45.

Jessie Frémont's new home . . . Description based on Rather 1974, 24–33.

"As my hands . . ." Frémont 1993, 234.

"I had to insist . . ." Frémont 1887, 205.

"Though I weigh . . ."; "a She-Merrimac . . ." Wendte 1921, 87, 180, 190–91.

"A man cannot . . ." Frémont 1887, 205.

After a little over . . . See San Francisco Directory 1862.

August 11, 1862; San Rafael. See Merwin 1912, 33.

Reverend Harry Gilbert. See Pemberton 1903, 71.

"peerless creature." "Neighborhoods I Have Moved From," *Californian* (May 28, June 4 and 11, 1864); Harte 1906, 17.253.

fair Circassian . . . "From a Back Window," *Golden Era* (Mar. 8, 1863); Harte 1906, 7.248.

"Psyche-my soul," etc. "Town and Table Talk: A Bohemian's New Year's Retrospect," *Golden Era* (Dec. 30, 1860).

"brilliantly clever . . ." See Rather 1974, 53.

Augusta Atwill. Information on the Atwills from California Census 1860 and San Francisco Directory 1859.

"I'm like the native . . ." The original pages from Augusta Atwill's autograph album containing "Lines by an Ex-Schoolmaster" and "What unto thee I can haply tell . . ." are in HRC. Facsimile of "Lines" in Harte 1991, n. pag.

"usual spirited manner." Harte to Miss Wills, Wednesday AM (Bancroft). This is the first extant letter from Harte's hand.

"simple, guileless figure." "Question," *Golden Era* (June 17, 1860); Harte 1914, 297–98.

"both young and fair; "Dewy eyes . . ." "Effie," *Golden Era* (Nov. 25, 1860); Harte 1914, 303–4.

"a courting." Francis King Harte to T. Edgar Pemberton, July 20, 1902 (JBH).

"My Soul to Thine." Harte 1914, 304–5.

by 1862 . . . giggles. See Henry Kirk Goddard, op. cit.

Anna lodged . . . See San Francisco Directory 1861.

524 Sutter St. See San Francisco Directory 1862.

daughter of . . . See Merwin 1912, 33.

born in Florida on January 9, 1835. Her date of birth is made clear by Harte 1926, 17. According to her death certificate, she was 85 when she died in Aug. 1920 (RBDM). Her place of birth is given in Ethel Bret Harte's certificate of death dated Nov. 13, 1964.

sometime in 1860. She first appears in the San Francisco Directory for 1861–62.

sister Georgiana . . . Information on the Leaches is from the California Census 1860; the San Francisco directories for 1860–70 and Wendte 1928, 117.

518 Bush St. San Francisco Directory 1861.

Anna also had . . . Information on the Zanders from Harte to Zander, June 5, 1872 (Bancroft); San Francisco Directory 1861; "Bret Harte's Early Days in San Francisco," *San Francisco Call* (May 25, 1902) (Morse).

her father had been . . . First Unitarian Church. See Elinor Howells 1988, 137.

Joseph Harrington. See San Francisco Directory 1861, under entry for the First Unitarian Church.

"her family . . ." Elinor Howells 1988, 137.

Regardless . . . approve of it. See FWT; McCrackin 1902, 223.

His friends . . . See McCrackin 1902, 223; Harte 1924, n. pag.

the same sense of humor. See Harte 1924, n. pag.

On the other hand . . . See MTL.

"Kiss the chickens . . ." See, for example, Harte 1926, 32, 34, 38, 47, 68. Lystra 1989 shows that nineteenth-century American married couples were much freer in their expression of love and sexual attraction than has hitherto been perceived.

"[I]n California . . ." Harte to Mary Sherwood, Oct. 1, 1875 (Bancroft).

"The higher passions . . ." Clemens 1959, 303.

"wanted to fall . . ." Rothman 1987, 105.

The newlyweds . . . The address was 312 Post St., on the block now occupied by Saks Fifth Ave. and Tiffany's. See San Francisco Directory 1862.

"I can't realize . . ." Frémont 1993, 356.

"Our Privilege." *Golden Era* (Sept. 28, 1862); Harte 1906, 8.12.

He got him involved . . . See *San Francisco Bulletin* (Aug. 13, 1861).

At the close . . . preceded them. Henry Kirk Goddard, op. cit.

On May 2, 1863 . . . San Francisco Directory 1863, entry for the U.S. Branch Mint.

From the windows . . . cousin of his. San Francisco Directory 1863. The U.S. Branch Mint was at 610 Commercial St. on the northern corner of Montgomery, while Clayton's Saloon was on the southern corner.

By the summer of 1863 . . . The List of Officers, Clerks and Laborers Employed in the U.S. Branch Mint, July 1st, 1863 (compiled by Francis Bret Harte) (Bancroft).

It was raised . . . See pay Roll for Dec. 1863 (Bancroft).

"I am sure . . ." Thomas Starr King to James T. Fields, Jan. 31, 1860 (Huntington).

"his is a fresh . . ." etc. Frémont 1993, 334–35.

"Your young friend . . ." Fields quoted in Frémont 1892, 18.

In the course . . . See Frémont 1993, 337, 341, 342.

"has something flaming . . ." Frémont 1993, 342.

"something to make . . ." etc. Frémont 1993, 341.

limited means . . . bar in Montgomery St.; Frank Harte did not like . . . that way. Based on "Bret Harte's Early Days in San Francisco," *San Francisco Call* (May 25, 1902) (Morse).

Anna would complain . . . See MTL.

One observer . . . See McCrackin 1902, 223.

March 5, 1865. See Pemberton 1903, 78.

they were living . . . San Francisco Directory 1865.

"I think you have misunderstood . . ." Harte to Ruth Watrous, June 10, 1880 (LC).

"the peculiar . . ." "Sidewalkings," *Californian* (June 24, 1865); Harte 1906, 17.216–23.

"one of the best . . ." Harte to Laurence Barrett, Sept. 22, 1875 (Knox), Harte 1997, 114–16.

When he fell . . . parted forever. The description of King's death and burial based on Wendte 1921, 213–17.

Harte to Rev. E. B. Walsworth, Mar. 2, 1864 (WACML).

this quaint . . ." Harte 1926, 41.

"a thing of booty . . ."; "she is best . . ."; "rested upon . . ." Walker 1939, 134, 169, 180.

"prodigally fine." Cummins 1893, 141.

"The 'Californian' . . ." Twain quoted in Morrow 1979, 39.

"always either unsuccessful . . ."; "always so unanimous . . ." "A Few Operatic Criticisms." *Californian* (May 13, 1865); Harte 1991, 73–76.

"His head . . ." Harte 1894a, 47.

Harte hired . . . See Walker 1939, 179.

Harte and others . . . See Clemens 1959, 152; Harte 1894a, 47; Mark Twain to Harte, May 1, 1867, reprinted in Phelps 1939, 492.

My account of the "Outcroppings Scandal" is based on Harte's sketch in the series "My First Book" for the *Idler* (Harte 1894b); MTL.

"*Outcroppings* is the offspring . . ."; "a Bohemian advertising . . ." "beneath contempt." *San Francisco Bulletin* (Jan. 6, 1866) (Morse) quoting the *Pajaro Times* and the *American Flag.*

The book was doubtless . . . See *San Francisco Bulletin* (Jan. 6, 1866) (Morse).

The chief criticism . . . Goodman. See Walker 1939, 214.

"a good deal . . ." etc. *Californian* (Dec. 23) 1865; Harte 1991, 101.

According to the *Enterprise* . . . See *San Francisco Bulletin* (Jan. 6, 1866) (Morse) quoting the *Territorial Enterprise.*

The *Union's* chief . . . See Walker 1939, 217.

It is also notable . . . See "Outcroppings Come Again," *Californian* (Jan. 20, 1866); Harte 1991, 103–7, which quotes Eastern reviews.

"most entertaining . . ." etc. *Springfield Republican* (Nov. 3, 1866); Harte 1990, 104.

When it came time . . . ; "full of damnable . . ." etc. See Mark Twain to Harte, May 1, 1867, reprinted in Phelps 1939, 492.

The manuscript . . . See Harte to Fields, Osgood and Co., May 30, 1870 (Stanford), Harte 1997, 35–36.

"publishing with . . ." etc. Clemens 1990, 2.14.

Only a few months . . . See Clemens 1959, 152–53.

"Harte's book . . ." Charles Henry Webb to Charles Warren Stoddard, Oct. 7, 1867 (UVa).

He even felt . . . See Harte to Mr. Bush, Nov. 22, 1867 (MHS).

"in every way . . ." etc. *Atlantic Monthly* 21 (1868): 128.

"malformed . . ." Harte to James T. Fields, Oct. 30, 1868 (Huntington), Harte 1997, 24–25.

"of a somewhat . . ." Quoted in "Mr. Harte's New Book," *Californian* (Nov. 16, 1867); Harte 1991, 108.

"His taste fetters . . ." Review reprinted in the *Californian* (Nov. 23, 1867).

"characterized by . . ." Quoted in "Mr. Harte's New Book," *Californian* (Nov. 16, 1867; Harte 1991, 108.

the most elegant . . .; "One of the author's . . ." etc. *Californian* (Dec. 21, 1867); Harte 1991, 116.

Henry Goddard was . . . from memory." Henry Kirk Goddard, op. cit.

"the very best . . ." Harte to Samuel Bowles, Aug. 9, 1867 (Bancroft), Harte 1997, 22.

"labored" . . . mainstay." *Nation* [Apr. 23, 1868?] (Morse).

"breed of scribblers" etc. Clemens 1988, 1.328.

When Clemens came back . . . See Clemens 1990, 2.232 n. 1.

Mark Twain to Thomas Bailey Aldrich quoted in Merwin 1912, 46.

Chapter 5

Had we been . . . nr. 619. Harte to John Ross Browne, Dec. 23, 1870 (Bancroft) gives the address. The dating is based on Joaquin Miller to Charles Warren Stoddard, July 22, 1870 (Huntington).

a three-story . . . The description of the building is from an illustration in an advertisement for the Savings and Loan Society in the issue of the *Overland Monthly* for July 1870.

His commanding . . . See Stoddard 1903, 224.

His guide . . . offices of the *Overland*. See Stoddard 1903, 225.

To the despair . . . See the Overland Monthly Papers (Bancroft). He was a spare . . . as a girl," See Miller 1902 (Morse).

This apparent . . . tall or robust." See Pratt 1924 (Morse); Harte 1924, n. pag.

"You do not want . . . ." Harte 1926, 5.

Harte to Henry Whitney Bellows, Sept. 15, 1866 (MHS), Harte 1997, 20–21.

Harte to Charles Warren Stoddard, Mar. 16, 1868 (UVa).

"exceedingly pained" etc. Ina Coolbrith to Charles Warren Stoddard, Jan. 1, 1869 (Huntington).

"to get in amongst . . ." Stoddard to Walt Whitman, Apr. 2, 1870, reprinted in Katz 1992, 507. On Stoddard's homosexuality, see also Austen 1991.

Josephine Clifford. Biographical details from McCrackin 1915; George Wharton James n.d.

Hattie L. Dolson . . . continued to doubt it. See McCrackin 1902, 222, 223; McCrackin 1915, 14.

Anna lost . . . See "Deaths," *San Francisco Daily Bulletin* (Oct. 28, 1867).

Harte had given . . . See Stewart 1931, 173.

As a publisher . . . yearly contracts. My account of the inception of the *Overland Monthly* is based on Roman 1898; Roman 1902; Bartlett 1898; and Brooks 1898.

The "Etc." section . . . Pacific Coast. "Etc.," *Overland Monthly* 1 (1868): 99–100.

"the only reliable . . . ." Advertising circular for the *Overland Monthly* (Bancroft).

"worthy of Hawthorne" etc. Tom Hood, *Fun* (Feb. 27, 1869): 249.

Another eager . . . moved." See Forster 1876, 1.143.

Only a few . . . See Pemberton 1900, 16.

"I see nothing . . ." . . . in the future. Harte 1926, 8.

"to his [Harte's] criticism . . ." Stoddard 1897, 676.

Another who trusted . . . See letter from Ambrose Bierce to Harte [c1870] (Yale), published in Williams 1941, 179.

"reminiscent of foreign travel." Brooks 1898, 9.

"Readers who were amazed . . ." *Atlantic Monthly* 25 (1870): 633.

Harte to James T. Fields, Oct. 30, 1868 (Huntington).

A year later . . . See Harte to Fields, Osgood and Co., Sept. 8, 1869 (UCLA).

By this time . . . See Harte to James T. Fields, Jan. 27, 1870 (Bancroft).

"the sketches have . . ." etc. "First Appearance in Book Form of Bret Harte's California Sketches," *Chicago Times* (May 4, 1870) (Morse).

"very correct photography . . ." etc. *Alta Californian* (May 15, 1870) (Morse).

"It is a fault . . ." etc. *Nation* (Aug. 18, 1870) (Morse).

"Nothing so thoroughly . . ." *Buffalo Express* (Apr. 30, 1870) (Morse). This review may possibly have been written by Mark Twain.

"Mr. Harte knows . . ." etc. *Spectator* 43 (1870): 1587.

"To my mind . . ." Watts-Dunton 1902, 659.

"the intense sensibility." Chesterton 1902, 432.

"Mr. Harte possesses . . ." *Spectator* 53 (1880): 1193.

"to illustrate an era . . ." Harte 1906, vol. 7, n. pag. "Harte saw . . ." Morrow 1979, 128–29.

"a parable . . ." Morrow 1973, 128.

"He has taken . . ." "The First Appearance in Book Form," op. cit.

"No, reader . . ." *Spectator* 43 (1870): 1587.

"the family state . . ." Beecher 1869, 19.

"a blueprint for colonizing . . ." Tompkins 1985, 144.

"Woman's profession . . ." Beecher 1869, 14.

"the great stimulus . . ." Ibid., 19.

As Catharine Beecher . . . See ibid., 268.

"The first . . ." etc. Ibid., 43, 49.

"Both the health . . ." Ibid., 150.

"If men will give . . ." Ibid., 157.

"There is no more important . . ." Ibid., 285.

"being supposed to have . . ." Ibid., 296.

direct sunlight . . . See ibid., 269.

"to form such habits . . ." Ibid., 271.

"A child who . . ." Ibid.

"the chief educator . . ." Ibid., 149.

"Christian house" etc. Ibid., 24.

"outdoor labor for all" etc. Ibid.

"typical male protagonist" etc. Fiedler 1970, 25.

"increasing agitation . . ." Ibid., 16.

"a great social . . ." Ibid.

Harriet Beecher Stowe's . . . See Sklar 1973, 263.

Whether in the shape . . . See Beecher 1869, 91, 95, 98, 102.

Ivy is the thing . . . See ibid., 96.

"If you live . . ." Ibid., 94.

Mrs. Stowe's mundane . . . See ibid., 101–2.

"Surrounded by . . ." etc. Ibid., 94.

"learn to enjoy . . ." Ibid., 102.

"grottoes from bits . . ." Ibid., 101.

"a fragment . . ." Ibid., 103.

"*one fourth* . . ." Ibid., 54.

"to embody . . . from domestic forms." Sklar 1973, 167.

"Chinese cheap labor . . ." Head 1909, 30.

"From the persecutions . . ." Harte 1906, 7.246.

Harte's satirical poem was copied . . . See Moore 1909, 410; Scharnhorst 1995.

"no poem has appeared . . ." *Alta California* (Jan. 2, 1871) (Morse).

"Bret Harte's 'Heathen Chinee' . . ." etc. "The Political Influence of
Humor in America," *Spectator* 44 (1871): 1523.

"admirable good sense" etc. "Harte's Poems," *North American Revue*
(1871): 234–35.

Harte to James T. Fields, Apr. 1, 1871 (Huntington), Harte 1997,
51–52.

To this effect . . . a half later. See Stewart 1931, 183–84.

The first six editions . . . See *Alta California* (Jan. 2, 1871) (Morse);
Blanck 1959, 3.418.

"with such a blaze . . ." Cummins 1893, 126.

Chapter 6

"The recent transit . . ." "Notes," *Every Saturday* 2 (1871): 235.

"Transatlantic Genius." *London Daily News* (Mar. 21, 1871): 5.

"crossed the continent . . ." Clemens 1959, 125–26.

"the newspapers . . ." Lilian Woodman Aldrich 1921, 133.

"It is nothing . . ." *Every Saturday* 2 (1871): 235.

Harte wrote to Ambrose Bierce . . . Booth 1948, 324.

"for the exclusive publication . . ." Harte 1926, 12.

"Bret Harte is brighter . . ." Bowles quoted in Merriam 1970, 2.170–71.

"He is a dramatic . . ." Fields 1922, 243.

"It has been a very pleasant . . ." Howells 1929, 1.159.

"Those were gay years . . ." Clemens-Howells 1960, 3.

"Wasn't he entertaining . . ." Howells 1929, 1.158.

"all the most exacting . . ." Gilder 1905, 203.

"satisfying" etc. Young 1952, 44.

"What a hit . . ." Howells 1929, 1.157.

"wrote Bret Harte . . ." etc. Howells 1903, 157, 159.

Josephine Clifford well . . . See McCrackin 1902, 224.

"representative American . . ." Murphy and Monteiro 1979, 94.

He said no . . . graduates want? See Harte to Edward Everett Hale, Aug.
21, 1870 (UVa); Harte to James Russell Lowell, Mar. 27, 1871, Booth
1948, 326.

What Harte came up with . . . See "Recent Literature," *Atlantic Monthly*
29 (1872): 107–8.

"a jingle . . ." Howells 1903, 158.

"did not recognize . . ." etc. Lilian Woodman Aldrich 1921, 141–42.

"he took the whole . . ." Howells 1903, 158.

"unfortunate experience . . ." "Bret Harte Explains," *New York Times* (July 6, 1871): 6.

"exceedingly neat . . ." Harte to James T. Fields, Apr. 4, 1874 (UVa).

"rather provoking . . ." Harte to James R. Osgood, Apr.11 [1874] (Yale).

Harte to William Dean Howells, May 15, 1871, Booth 1948, 327.

"that breeding place . . ." Clemens 1959, 295.

Edgar Cottage. See Newport Directory 1871; Wilkins 1988, 156.

He entertained . . . left undone . . ." Fields 1922, 236–39.

"Yesterday Bret Harte . . ." Emerson 1939, 183.

Harte and Emerson had also . . . religious effects." Emerson 1982, 6.247.

Harte was not . . . See Howells 1900, 62.

Harte to Josiah Gilbert Holland, Sept. 20, 1871 (NYPL).

"poor stuff." Harte 1926, 15.

he was in debt. See Harte to James R. Osgood, Sept. 24, 1871 (UVa).

"curious to see . . ." etc. Fields 1922, 239.

"Think how awkward . . ." Harte to Jessamy Harte, June 5, 1883, Harte 1926, 229.

late March 1871. See Dr. Barker to John Hay, Mar. 25, 1871 (Brown).

Harte to Anna Harte, Jan. 10, 1872 (UVa).

"Bret Harte has a queer . . ." Fields 1922, 240.

When Howells questioned . . . mutual friends. See Harte to William Dean Howells, Mar. 25, 1872, and Mar. 30, 1872, Booth 1948, 329, 331.

Howells came . . . See Howells 1929, 1.168–69.

Harte said . . . See Harte to William Dean Howells, Mar. 30, 1872, Booth 1948, 331.

"one of half a dozen . . ." Harte 1926, 70.

"This morning . . ." Harte to Mrs. Spring, June 21, 1872 (Stanford).

"obliged to fly . . ."; "a walker of hospitals . . ." Harte to Marina Godwin, July 7, [1872] (NYPL).

"the only combination . . ." "Maruja," Harte 1906, 1.118.

"He was always . . ." Clemens 1959, 125.

"He wore . . ." Parton 1936, 44.

"be quits . . ." Harte to John Spencer Clark, Sept. 27, 1872 (UVa).

Holland had been . . . See Harte to Josiah Gilbert Holland, Nov. 17, 1870 (NYPL).

"The sudden death . . ." "Etc.," *Overland Monthly* 2 (1869): 479.

$1,000. See Booth 1948, 333.

The lecture was . . . no longer." Harte 1909, n. pag.

"I have met . . ."; "tip-toppers . . ."; "artists, clergymen . . ." Fields's letter quoted in Pemberton 1903, 134–35.

little did they know . . . See Howells 1903, 157.

"late on a stormy . . ." etc. Lilian Woodman Aldrich 1921, 136–37.

"Bret Harte's Lecture . . ." "The Argonauts of '49," *New York Times* (Dec. 17, 1872): 3.

Scene commencing "As he had ridden" (pp. 127–29):

As he had ridden . . . each other. Based on Harte to Anna Harte, Oct. 16, [1873], Harte 1926, 36.

Miraculously . . . Based on Harte to Anna Harte, Oct. 31, 1873, Harte 1926, 31.

This evening . . . best sentences. Based on Harte to Anna Harte, Oct. 19, 1873, Harte 1926, 26.

The twilight hour . . . closer to home. Based on Harte to Anna Harte, Oct. 26, [1873], Harte 1926, 35, 37.

He had been reminded . . . Based on Harte to Anna Harte, Oct. 19, 1873, Harte 1926, 26.

He had left . . . The hotel was Stevterant House. See Harte to H. C. Harriot, Jan. 1, 1873 (NYU) and envelope of Harte to Anna Harte, Feb. 26, 1873 (UVa).

She had almost been . . . See Harte to Anna Harte, Feb. 26, 1873 (UVa).

The tour . . . at any rate. See Harte 1926, 20–22.

They had had . . . The first extant letter from this address is dated Apr. 2, 1873.

The summer . . . See Harte to Whitelaw Reid, [June 8, 1873?] (LC).

The plan was . . . "moated-grange." Based on Harte to Anna Harte, Oct. 29, 1873, and Oct. 26, [1873], Harte 1926, 29, 35.

The summer season . . . for their own. Based on Harte to Anna Harte, Oct. 26, [1873] (UVa).

"I always enter . . ." Harte 1926, 37.

The reviews . . . furious. Based on Harte to Anna Harte, Oct. 19, 1873, Harte 1926, 26.

He had had the honor . . . he was working on. Based on Harte to Anna Harte, Oct. 19, 23 and 29, 1873, Harte 1926, 26, 27, 28, 30.

"bigoted, self-righteous . . ." Harte to Anna Harte, July 9, 1880, Harte 1926, 181.

Harte to Jeannette Gilder, Nov. 18, 1873 (UVa).

"as a nationally distinctive . . . produced." Based on "American Humor," *New York Times* (Jan. 27, 1874): 5; Harte 1909, n. pag.

received $500. See Booth 1948, 333.

As it happened . . . See Harte to James R. Osgood, Sept. 20, [1873] (UVa).

This in combination . . . See Harte to Mark Twain, Dec. 24, 1875 (Bancroft), Harte 1997, 125–26.

In June 1874 . . . "How am I to live?" Harte to Elisha Bliss, July 21, 1874, Booth 1944, 135.

He had been to see . . . he came back. See Harte to Anna Harte, Wednesday am [Aug. 26, 1874] (UVa).

They only offered . . . that price. See Harte to Anna Harte, [Sept. 5, 1874] (UVa).

Howells's answer . . . us or not." William Dean Howells to Harte, Sept. 1, 1874, Sheick 1976, 277.

"I want to leave . . ." Harte to William Dean Howells, Sept. 2, 1874 (Hayes).

"I shall have to take . . ." Harte to Anna Harte, [Sept. 5, 1874] (UVa).

Maybe sensing . . . See William Dean Howells to Harte, Sept. 1, 1874, Sheick 1976, 277.

Harte was livid . . . selling it to him. See Harte to William Dean Howells, Sept. 8, 1874, Booth 1948, 332-33.

Harte responded . . . criticism." Harte to William Dean Howells, May 14, 1874, Booth 1948, 331-32.

In addition to . . . over a month. See Harte to Elisha Bliss, Sept. 16, 1874 (UVa); Harte 1926, 43.

By October 5, 1874 . . . in Morristown. See Harte to Elisha Bliss, Oct. 5, 1874 (SUL).

$150 a month. Harte to Elisha Bliss, Oct. 5, 1874 (SUL); information from Tom Coulter, Fosterfields.

"I want you to see . . ." Harte to Anna Harte, Nov. 7, 1874, Harte 1926, 39.

"I have had occasion . . ." Harte to Anna Harte, Nov. 4, 1874, Harte 1926, 38.

"You wonder . . ." Harte to Anna Harte, Nov. 7, 1874, Harte 1926, 40-41.

Seeming a bit . . . grievances." Harte to Anna Harte, Nov. 8, 1874, Harte 1926, 43.

"Bret Harte, is said . . ." etc. "Plain Language from Mr. Bret Harte," *New York Times* (Jan. 17, 1875): 5; Harte 1997, 108.

"Pay Rosen and Cooper . . ." Harte 1926, 38. See also Harte 1926, 32, 43, 49, and Harte to Eliza Knaufft, Oct. 27, 1873 (Bancroft).

If they won . . . See Harte to James R. Osgood, Apr. 18, 1875 (Columbia), Harte 1997, 110-11.

"How comes . . . hanging over him. Harte to James R. Osgood, May 26, 1875, Harte 1926, 52-53.

"I shall not . . . gouging." Harte to James R. Osgood, Apr. 18, 1875 (Columbia), Harte 1997, 110-11.

"the shorter the title . . ." Harte 1926, 50.

For the American . . . book form. See Clemens-Howells 1960, 92.

The final pages . . . See Harte to Elisha Bliss, June 8, 1875 (Stanford).

Harte to Frank Mason, Sept. 30, 1875 (NYU), Harte 1997, 120.

"an absolute change . . ." Harte to Elisha Bliss, May 24, 1875 (AAAL).

Harte to Lawrence Barrett, July 11 and 14, 1875 (H-B).

Ethel Bret Harte . . . See "Certificate of Death," State of California Dept. of Health Services.

Elizabeth Ostrander Harte Williams . . . See *New York Times* (Apr. 6, 1875): 7.

"There has been . . ." Harte to Lawrence Barrett, Sept. 22, 1875 (Knox).

"has been very patient . . ." Harte to Lawrence Barrett, Sept. 22, 1875 (Knox).

On March 18th . . . 1875–76 season. See "Memorandum of Agreement. March 18, 1875" (H-B).

The third act . . . the scissors." See Harte to James R. Osgood, Sept. 3, 1875 (Brown); Harte to Lawrence Barrett, Sept. 22, 1875 (Knox).

He had felt confident . . . See Harte to John Carmany, Sept. 13, 1875 (Bancroft), Harte 1997, 113–14.

Chapter 7

Scene commencing "At 351 Farmington Avenue" (pp. 139–42):

Harte could report . . . "horrible egotism and stubbornness." Transcription into free indirect style and direct quotation from Harte to Mark Twain, Dec. 16, 1876 (Bancroft), Harte 1997, 143–44.

early October . . . that fall. Based on Mark Twain to William Dean Howells, Oct. 11, [1876], Clemens-Howells 1960, 157.

At the end . . . got through. Based on Clemens 1959, 297.

He himself . . . Based on Mark Twain to William Dean Howells, Oct. 11, [1876], Clemens-Howells 1960, 157.

Harte wrote . . . ought to be." Based on Harte to Mark Twain, Dec. 16, 1876 (Bancroft), Harte 1997, 143–44.

All that fortnight . . . been paid for." Free indirect style and direct quotation from Clemens 1959, 298–99.

Twain recalled . . . from books. Based on Clemens 1959, 303–4.

December 9, 1876. Dating from Clemens 1959, 298 and Harte to James R. Osgood, Dec. 5, 1876 (Huntington), Harte 1997, 142.

It took place . . . was completed. See Clemens 1959, 296–97.

"could never persuade . . ." Ibid., 296.

$3,600, including interest. See Clemens 1959, 299; Harte to Mark Twain, Mar. 1, 1877 (Bancroft), Harte 1997, 145–48.

loaned him $750. See Harte to Mark Twain, Mar. 1, 1877 (Bancroft), Harte 1997, 154–48.

He was also wont . . . Eugene Field." Mitchell 1924, 283–84.

"Poor fellow . . ." Dickinson quoted in Young 1952, 45.

"To think . . ." Harte to Mark Twain, Jan. 2, 1876 (Bancroft), Harte 1997, 127.

Though he had . . . See Harte to Mark Twain, Dec. 24, 1875 (Bancroft), and Jan. 2, 1876 (Bancroft).

"more difficult to open . . ." Charles Dudley Warner to Charles Henry Webb, Oct. 27, 1876 (Bancroft).

In the spring . . . See "Bret Harte Interviewed," *Washington Capital* (Oct. 1, 1876): 1. See also Harte to Eliza Knaufft, Sunday am [Apr. 2, 1876] (Bancroft).

Harte to Eliza Knaufft, Sunday am [Apr. 2, 1876] (Bancroft).

Harte had gone . . . the Blaines. See Garfield 1973, 264 and n. 152.

Scene commencing "As he issued" (pp. 146–48):

Harte reflected . . . traditional customs." Based on the sketch "Morning on the Avenue," Harte 1906, 1.268. Originally published in the *New York Sun* (Mar. 4, 1877).

His finances . . . Based on Harte to Mark Twain, Mar. 1, 1877 (Bancroft), Harte 1997, 145–48.

After finishing . . . "My Friend the Tramp," *New York Sun* (Mar. 11, 1877); Harte 1906, 1.229–39.

He often met . . . There are several examples in "Morning on the Avenue."

This frosty . . . Delmonico's. "Morning on the Avenue," Harte 1906, 1.268–69, 271.

Uppermost in his mind . . . Harte's letter of Mar. 1, 1877 was written in response to one from Mark Twain, which has been lost.

He had deliberately . . . despise him for it. Based on Harte to Mark Twain, Mar. 1, 1877 (Bancroft), Harte 1997, 145—48.

The plan seemed . . . See Harte to Mark Twain, July 25, 1872 (Bancroft).

When he had asked . . . plays with Mark Twain. Based on Harte to Mark Twain, Mar. 1, 1877 (Bancroft), Harte 1997, 14548.

Harte had been incensed . . . See Mark Twain to Charles Henry Webb, Nov. 26, [1870] (UVa).

"I must and will . . ." Clemens 1967, 58.

"The struggle after . . ." etc. Clemens-Howells 1960, 261.

"[N]o human being . . ." Clemens 1880, 850–51.

"stood at the head . . ." Adams 1918, 234.

"and those not in dialect . . . no living writer. Nadal 1877, 81–85.

"at the very top . . ." Clemens 1959, 297.

Whitelaw Reid to John Hay, Jan. 30, 1877 (Brown).

His dealings . . . unseen manuscript. See Harte to Mark Twain, Aug. 8, 1874 (Bancroft), Harte 1997, 97–99.

From Dana . . . See Harte to E. A. Buck, Oct. 16, 1877 (Bancroft).

As Harte also . . . with Mark Twain. See Harte to Mark Twain, Aug. 8, 1874 (Bancroft).

"Why, fellows, this is the dream . . ." See Howells 1903, 156; Howells 1910, 6–7; Howells 1929, 2.157.

"I never thought . . ." Harte to Mark Twain, Aug. 8, 1874 (Bancroft).

"I cannot say . . ." Howells 1910, 47.

Howells said . . . rest of us." See Clemens 1959, 295, 296.

"You ought to be . . ." Harte to Mark Twain, June 17, 1872 (Bancroft), Harte 1997, 67.

"not caring . . . way of warning." Hooker's diary quoted in Andrews 1950, 86–87.

"Business has its laws . . ." Clemens 1959, 260.

"to give 'Sandy Bar' . . ." Leonard Grover to Albert M. Palmer, Aug. 7, 1876 (H-B).

"an object . . ." etc. "Bret Harte's New Drama," *New York Times* (Aug. 29, 1876): 4.

"as brilliant . . ." etc. "The 'Two Men of Sandy Bar,' " *New York Herald* (Aug. 29, 1876): 5.

"essentially undramatic" etc. Leonard Grover to Albert M. Palmer, Aug. 7, 1876 (H-B).

Harte had meant . . . See Cevasco and Harmond 1988, 60–61.

"the function . . ." Harte to A. C. Wheeler, Sept. 3, 1876 (UVa), Harte 1997, 132.

"Give the Names!" See, for example, *New York Sun* (Sept. 9, 1876): 2 and *New York World* (Sept. 10, 1876): 4.

"It seems to me . . ." Harte to Mark Twain, Sept. 5, 1876 (Bancroft), Harte 1997, 133.

"approving Mr. Robson's . . ." *New York Post* (Sept. 4, 1876): 2.

"As the case now stands . . ." *New York World* (Sept. 17, 1876): 4.

had dismissed the man. "Bret Harte Interviewed," *Washington Capital* (Oct. 1, 1876): 1.

"If, after all this clamor . . ." *New York Daily Graphic* (Sept. 22, 1876): 568.

"acted crazily . . ." etc. Clemens-Howells 1960, 162.

"I have nothing . . ." Harte to Anna Harte, [July 10, 1877] (UVa).

"Charles Sumner . . ."; "for weeks . . ." Harte to John Hay, Dec. 12, 1878 (Brown).

"one more advertisement . . ." etc. *Atlantic Monthly* (1878) (Morse).

"savagery"; "If Harte could . . ." Hill 1968, 523.

"The plot . . ." etc. Lang 1876, 235.

"The reader . . ." etc. *Athenaeum* (June 3, 1876): 762.

The London *Times* . . . failure." *Times* (June 21, 1876): 5.

Mark Twain to William Dean Howells, June 21, 1877, and late June 1877, published in Murphy 1985, 89–90.

William Dean Howells to Mark Twain, June 30, 1877, Clemens-Howells 1960, 185.

Birchard A. Hayes to Elinor Howells, July 9, 1877, reproduced in Clemens-Howells 1960, 190.

Harte to Anna Harte, Sunday evening [June 24, 1877] (UVa), Harte 1997, 151–52.

Harte to Anna Harte, July 8, 1877, Booth 1944, 135–36.

Harte to Anna Harte, [July 10, 1877], Harte 1926, 59–60. Dating from internal evidence.

Harte to Anna Harte, July 27, [1877], Harte 1926, 55–56.

Olivia Clemens to Mark Twain, July 29, 1877, Clemens 1949, 203.

"When our play . . ." The speech is reproduced in Daly 1917, 235–36.

Mark Twain to William Dean Howells, Aug. 3, 1877, Clemens-Howells 1960, 191.

Harte to Donn Piatt, Aug. 20, 1877 (Hayes), Harte 1997, 157.

Harte to Anna Harte, [Oct. 18, 1877], Harte 1926, 62. Dating from internal evidence.

Mark Twain to William Dean Howells, Oct. 15, 1877, Clemens-Howells 1960, 206.

Harte to Anna Harte, [Mar. 26, 1878], Harte 1926, 64–66; Harte 1997, 171–72 (misdated Apr. 23, 1878). Dating from internal evidence and postmarked envelope.

Rutherford B. Hayes to William Dean Howells, Apr. 5, 1878 (Houghton). Shelfmark bMS Am 1784(216). By permission of Houghton Library, Harvard University.

William Dean Howells to Rutherford B. Hayes, Apr. 9, 1878, Howells 1929, 251–52.

Harte to Anna Harte, Apr. 19, 1878, Harte 1926, 66–68. Dating from internal evidence.

"[T]here is a prospect." Harte 1926, 10. This is the first extant letter from Harte to his wife.

Harte to Anna Harte, n.d. [June 27, 1878] (UVa).

Harte to Griswold Harte, Nov. 4, 1873 (Bancroft), Harte 1997, 88.

On June 27, 1878 . . . See Harte 1997, 173 n. 1.

Chapter 8

"nearly four hundred . . ."; "only seemed to me . . ." Harte 1926, 78, 79.

"about the most uninteresting . . ."; "a cramped Philadelphia . . ." Harte 1926, 86.

Harte to Anna Harte, Oct. 16, 1878 (UVa), Harte 1997, 191–96.

In the latter position . . . $3,000 a year. See Harte 1926, 82, 83.

"to uphold the flag . . ."; "Oddly enough . . ." "Unser Karl," Harte 1906, 13.5–6.

"showing the Rainfall . . ." State Dept. Letters, Oct. 8, 1879, reprinted in Sears 1954, 18.

"as full and exact . . ." Appraiser of the Port (New York) to Bret Harte, Apr. 16, 1879, State Dept. (George Stewart's Notes, Bancroft).

"a very old . . ." Pemberton 1903, 174.

"a gorgeous picnic . . ." Pemberton 1903, 174.

"quiet bachelor den." Harte to Clara Schneider, Aug. 11, 1880 (UVa).

134 Drüsberger strasse. See Harte to Consul General Crowe, written from 134 Drüsberger strasse, Düsseldorf, Monday am (UVa).

86 Neue Linnerstrasse. See, for example, Harte to Rudolph Schneider, May 31, 1879 (UVa).

"very preoccupying." Harte to Helena Stanton, Dec. 15, 1878 (SFPL).

dearly remembered . . . ourselves with." Harte to Clara Schneider, Aug. 29, 1882 (UVa).

He fondly . . . played piano. See Harte to Clara Schneider, June 19, 1885 (UVa).

"I miss our old . . ." Harte to Clara Schneider, Aug. 11, 1880 (UVa).

"*I* ought to have had . . ." Harte to Clara Schneider, June 19, 1885 (UVa).

"Uncle Bret Harte." Harte to Rudolph Schneider, Nov. 1, 1888 (UVa).

Callie studied German . . . See Harte 1926, 124; correspondence Harte to Marie Wilhelmi (Cornell) and Marie Wilhelmi to Callie Cooper, n.d. (Bancroft).

"the gentleman . . ." etc. Belle Flower to Callie Cooper, Nov. 1, [1879] (Bancroft).

27 Rue Baudin. See Harte to Gertrude Griswold, Jan. 17, 1879 (Huntington).

Anna's brother . . . See F. O. Jones. *A Handbook of American Music and Musicians,* 1886 ("Gertrude Griswold," ABA).

"like an intelligent . . ." Harte 1926, 102.

"Dora is the same . . ." etc. Harte to Anna Harte, n.d. [late Oct. 1879] (UVa).

"although she belongs . . ." Murphy and Monteiro 1979, 98.

Harte first met . . . See Harte to Professor V. Botta, Dec. 25, 1872 (Yale).

He first me Lord Houghton . . . See Harte to Annie Fields, Sept. 27, 1875 (Huntington), Harte 1997, 117–19.

"dear old noble fellow" etc. Harte 1926, 91.

The eldest daughter . . . dare ask. See Harte to Gertrude Griswold, Aug. 18, 1878 (Huntington).

"No visitor . . ." MacDonald 1915, lix.

"No one is made . . ." McCarthy 1899, 69.

"about *Rules.*" Joaquin Miller to Lord Houghton, Wednesday [Aug. 1878] (Duke).

Harte's and Miller's host . . . English hospitality. See Harte 1926, 93, 98–99.

On September 4 . . . Duchess of St. Albans. See Harte to Rudolph Schneider, Sept. 4, 1878 (UVa).

"[a] sweet, bright . . ." etc. Harte 1926, 95–96.

"that brilliant . . . abhorrence." *Times* (Nov. 19, 1926): 17.

It was this . . . a Household." Queen Victoria 1930, 56, 57. "You'll see she . . ." Harte 1926, 112.

"We are very good friends—" Ibid., 108.

"I am asked out . . ." Ibid., 131.

"Americans are very . . ." Harte to Samuel Barlow, July 22, 1880 (Huntington), Harte 1997, 264–65.

"it would be quite . . ." Harte to Anna Harte, Oct. 16, 1878 (UVa), Harte 1997, 191–96.

It was while . . . single lecture. See Harte 1926, 107.

He had had . . . See Harte 1926, 113; Harte to Gertrude Griswold, Dec. 10, 1878 (Huntington).

"old nervous dread." Harte to Anna Harte, Nov. 23, 1878 (UVa).

a week to recover . . . See Harte to Helena Stanton, Dec. 15, 1878 (SFPL).

went off very nicely. See Harte to Rudolph Schneider, Jan. 29, 1879 (UVa).

"It's been a wretched . . . immediately. Harte to Rudolph Schneider, Feb. 8, 1879 (UVa), Harte 1997, 204–5.

After three weeks . . . See Harte 1926, 132.

"shocking state." Harte to Anna Harte, Mar. 4, 1879 (UCLA).

offered eighty-five pounds. See Harte 1926, 134.

"she needs . . ." See Harte to Georgiana Cooper, Mar. 16, 1879 (Bancroft).

"a most decided hit . . . collect the rest. Harte to Rudolph Schneider, Mar. 29, 1879 (UVa), Harte 1997, 204–5.

gave a dinner . . . See Cornélie Trübner to Callie Cooper, Monday evening [Mar. 31, 1879] (Bancroft); see also Harte 1926, 113.

"[N]o one could get up . . ." Fiske 1917, 2.138. Consul Byers . . . enough for him . . ." Byers 1903, 291, 293, 294, 426–30.

"it smelt . . ." Harte to Rudolph Schneider, Aug. 4, 1879 (UVa).

"inveterate comparison-monger." Reid 1902, 258.

The Paris exposition . . . Harte to Griswold Harte, Sept. 14, 1878 (Bancroft), Harte 1997, 187–89.

"one of the greatest . . ."; "was not as fine nor as noble . . ." Harte to Anna Harte, n.d. [late Oct. 1879] (UVa).

"a great, ugly, pretentious . . ." Harte to Rudolph Schneider, Sunday pm [Oct. 1879] (UVa).

"the California mountains . . . failed to impress him. Harte 1926, 150, 152, 218–19.

"was really the only 'sight' . . ." Pemberton 1903, 215.

"Germany is no place . . . record was good. Harte 1926, 134.

One of the friends . . . Harte to Charles A. Dana, Oct. 1, 1879 (MiHS), Harte 1997, 238–39.

In late 1878 . . . spring and summer. See Harte 1926, 97, 115, 116, 140, 141, 144, 145.

He blamed . . . condition." Harte to Charles A. Dana, Oct. 1, 1879 (MiHS); quote from Harte to Anna Harte, May 29, 1879, Harte 1926, 144.

Hay had encouraged . . . own writers." Murphy and Monteiro 1979, 88–89.

"one of the all-time . . ." Luedtke and Morrow 1973, 101. On Harte's literary reputation in Germany, see also Timpe 1965.

By 1885 . . . See Lilienthal, "Bret Harte in Germany," *Critic* (Feb. 21, 1885). Noted by George Stewart (Stewart Papers, Bancroft).

109 separate editions . . . See Luedtke and Morrow 1973, 102.

So much more absurd . . . Prussia." Murphy and Monteiro 1979, 88–89.

"the great swell . . . British author. See Harte 1926, 136, 140.

"in a vexed dilemma" etc. George H. Boughton to Nicholas Trübner, Apr. 18, 1879 (Brown).

Harte dallied . . . See Harte to Sir Frederick Leighton, Apr. 30, 1879 (UVa).

Besides dreading . . . Harte's place. See Harte 1926, 138–39, 140.

The following year . . . little result." Ibid., 170–71, 175, 178.

"To his great . . ." *New York Tribune* (May 17, 1880) (Morse).

"crowded with fashionable . . ." etc. Harte to Rudolph Schneider, June 22, 1880 (UVa).

Bret Harte's Monthly . . . See Harte 1926, 184, 189, 192; Murphy and Monteiro 1979, 93.

By the time . . . See Harte 1926, 172.

" 'pitched into Evarts' " etc. Harte 1926, 170.

"in every way better . . ." etc. Murphy and Monteiro 1979, 90.

Glasgow had . . . See Harte 1926, 173.

On June 17, 1880 . . . See Harte 1926, 185.

"living in his trunks." Harte to Rudolph Schneider, July 21, 1880 (UVa), Harte 1997, 262–63.

"an awful old fogy." Harte to Rudolph Schneider, July 8, 1880 (UVa). hung on . . . coal brokerage." Murphy and Monteiro 1979, 92.

retain the services . . . See Harte to Rudolph Schneider, July 21, 1880 (UVa); Harte 1926, 205.

He went . . . See Harte to Rudolph Schneider, July 21, 1880 (UVa).

Gertrude Griswold had just won . . . See Harte to Mrs. Schneider, Aug. 11, 1880 (UVa); Harte 1926, 186.

"anxious to get . . ." Harte to Rudolph Schneider, Aug. 4, 1880 (UVa).

"The Scotch folk . . . commute from Innellan. Harte to Mrs. Schneider, Aug. 11, 1880 (UVa).

"a lovely little . . ." Harte 1926, 190.

"*this* is not . . ." etc. Harte to M. S. Van de Velde, Sept. 10, 1880, Pemberton 1903, 214–15.

"close to . . ." etc. Harte to Rudolph Schneider, Sept. 10, 1880.

On Monday, September 13, 1880 . . . nearly drowned. Harte 1926, 188, 191; Harte to Gertrude Griswold, Sept. 25, 1880 (Huntington); Harte to Clara Schneider, Sept. 9, 1880 (UVa); Murphy and Monteiro 1979, 94.

"far from strong." Harte to Clara Schneider, Oct. 7, 1880 (UVa).

"helplessly ill" etc. Harte 1926, 191. See also Harte to Rudolph Schneider, Nov. 5, 17 and 18, 1880, and Dec. 3, 1880 (UVa).

The doctors said . . . See Harte 1926, 191.

"the vapors . . ." Ibid., 187–88.

January 12, 1833. See Diary-2 (entries for Jan. 12, 1882, 1884, 1886, and 1888). Hydeline Rodolphine Emma Van de Velde's death certificate from 1913 gives her age as eighty (RBDM).

the daughter of . . . See *Recueil de généalogie vaudoises* 1940, 1.126.

her mother's remarriage . . . See ibid., 1.126.

who was attaché . . . This and all other facts about Arthur Van de Velde's diplomatic career are from the notes of the Royal Belgian Ministry of Foreign Affairs (Brussels).

She gave birth . . . Berthe Emma Josephe Van de Velde was born in Jan. 14, 1864 (RBDM).

Her last child . . . Marcel Arthur Maurice Van de Velde was born on Aug. 1, 1879 (RBDM).

"stayed with some kind . . ." etc. See Harte 1926, 196.

He did not mention . . . Diary-2 (entry for Sept. 21, 1881). The entry reads: "Start for Glasgow by pullman at 8 p.m. with Madame V. de V. as my guest."

"His wife got . . ." Harte to Anna Harte, Oct. 11, 1882 (UVa); Harte 1926, 216.

"vagabond condition." Harte to Anna Harte, May 24, 1880 (UVa).

Scene commencing "At the beginning of a day" (pp. 185–86):

At the beginning . . . See Diary-2 (entry for June 10, 1882).

He was writing . . . See Harte to J. Usher, June 10, 1882 (UVa).

At midnight . . . General Washington. Based on "Longfellow," Harte 1914, 249–54.

They had parted . . . on his way. See conversation with Harte recorded in Fields 1922, 243.

"living by gaslight . . . his first lodgings. See Harte 1926, 215.

"some one's 'folly' . . . apartments." Ibid., 216.

He wrote to Anna . . . Ibid., 194.

Ass. Secretary of State to Harte, Nov. 15, 1882, State Dept. (George Stewart's Notes, Bancroft).

"As I do not keep . . ." Glasgow Letters 66 (Dec. 2, 1882) (George Stewart's Notes, Bancroft).

As he noted . . . country-man." Harte 1926, 274.

"dying for a breath . . ." Murphy and Monteiro 1979, 93.

"I am so longing . . ." Harte to W. A. Searn, May 26, 1880 (UCLA).

"rather a good Consul" etc. Harte 1926, 205.

"For the last five . . ." Harte to Anna Harte, Jan. 15, 1884 (UVa).

"not to see . . ." Harte to Anna Harte, Mar. 18, 1880, Harte 1926, 170.

"all the ugly things." Harte to Anna Harte, July 17, 1878, Harte 1926, 80.

" 'was sick of Germany . . .'" The *Röhmische Zeitung* article is quoted by Harte in Harte to Anna Harte, Apr. 17, 1880, Harte 1926, 176.

"abominable and filthy slander." Harte to Rudolph Schneider, Mar. 27, 1880 (UVa).

at once wrote to demand . . . See Harte to Anna Harte, Apr. 17, 1880, Harte 1926, 176.

Harte's doctor . . . Ibid.; see also reference to Van Köhlwalter's letter in Harte to Rudolph Schneider, Apr. 3, 1880 (UVa).

"not only was not . . . absurd." See Harte to Anna Harte, Apr. 17, 1880, Harte 1926, 176.

"almost every form . . ." Harte to Anna Harte, Oct. 5, 1878, Harte 1926, 104.

Consul Byers . . . jolly." Byers 1903, 294.

"Give up whiskey . . ." Ibid. (entry for Apr. 13, 1883).

"quite a blue-ribbon man"; "not touched . . ." Harte to Anna Harte, Feb. 5, 1884, Harte 1926, 248.

"almost a teetotaller." Harte to Anna Harte, Feb. 14, 1885, Harte 1926, 267.

"a lodging-house . . ." etc. William Black to Harte, May 25, [1884] (JBH).

"*slander came* . . ." Harte to Anna Harte, Apr. 17, 1880, Harte 1926, 177.

"Harte is a liar . . . never pays." Clemens-Howells 1960, 235–36.

In Heidelberg . . . avoided him. See Harris 1924, 161–63.

"Yes, I know . . ." Dunne 1963, 244.

"sham and shoddy." Kaplan 1966, 334.

while he was composing . . . See Higginson 1921, 330.

"the paragraph fiend." Murphy and Monteiro 1979, 94.

"[t]he attitude of the press . . ." Harte 1926, 286.

"unless by some . . ." Harte to Anna Harte, Nov. 5, 1884 (UVa).

As so often . . . See "Latest Intelligence," *Times* (July 18, 1885): 7.

"was quite unprepared . . ." etc. Harte 1926, 284.

"the office . . ."; "this is the kind . . ." Ibid., 271.

"[I]t has come . . . able to find him." F. Marion Tower to William C. Endicott, Mar. 14, [1885] (Brown).

"I believe . . ." Murphy and Monteiro 1979, 107.

"I have been . . ." James E. Blaine to John Hay, Dec. 31, 1889 (Brown).

"sanguine of success." Harte to Anna Harte, Sept. 17, 1890 (UVa).

Chapter 9

"The public of both . . ." Van de Velde 1881, 236.

"I have at least . . ." See Harte 1926, 202.

"I suppose . . ." etc. Ibid., 215.

In November 1889 . . . at the legation. See Minister Baron Greindl to Monsieur le Prince de Chimay, Nov. 15, 1889 (BMFA).

The reply . . . Belgian minister. See "Note confidentielle," Nov. 19, 1889 (BMFA).

"M. de S.—Madame Van de Velde's letters." Harte to Mr. Robinson, Mar. 18, 1889 (HRC).

The only other . . . Ludolph Bacon. See *Receuil de généalogie vaudoises* 1940, 1.126.

"he could not . . ." Pemberton 1903, 213.

She [Madame Van de Velde] and her family . . ." Harte to Anna Harte, Apr. 19, 1886 (UCLA).

"It has been . . ." Van de Velde 1889, 2.1–2.

"My dear friend . . ." Published in Pemberton 1903, 239–40.

"kind care . . ." Sherwood 1902, 308.

"I am only too . . ." Harte 1926, 206–7.

He sold . . . volume rights. See Diary-2 (entry for May 2, 1882).

By 1895 . . . See A. P. Watt to E. L. Burlingame, May 31, 1895 (APWP). For a detailed discussion of Harte's later literary career, including tables showing his income and publishing outlets, see Nissen 1997.

When Mr. Bret Harte . . ." Payne 1885, 124.

"that his popularity . . ." *Book Buyer* 15 (1897), 11.

The Heiress of Red Dog . . . $365 for it. See Chatto and Windus to Harte, July 4, 1879 (Reading).

This time . . . See Chatto and Windus to Harte, July 11, 1879 (Reading).

"is not selling . . ." Chatto and Windus to Harte, Oct. 3, 1879 (Reading).

The figures on the number of copies printed that follow and those quoted above are taken from Chatto and Windus's production ledgers (Reading).

For the 3,400 words . . . See list of payments, "Overland Monthly Papers" (Bancroft).

"It is one thing . . ." Stevenson 1882–83, 73.

"the old dispute . . ." etc. Lang 1887, 684–85, 693.

"As I live . . ." Stevenson quoted in Graham 1965, 66.

"It must be . . ." Harte 1926, 358.

"true concern . . ." Caine quoted in Graham 1965, 68.

"private doubts . . ." Harte to unknown recipient, Jan. 19, 1888 (UVa).

"But 'Monte Cristo' . . ." etc. "My Favorite Novelist and His Best Book," Harte 1914, 275.

"A marked feature . . ." Hannigan 1894, 33, 35.

"We keep . . ." Purcell 1885, 40.

"These stories . . ." Payne 1885, 124.

"a relief" etc. Payne 1888, 269.

"We could say nothing . . ." Payne 1903, 372.

"One might almost . . ." "Trent's Trust," *Times Literary Supplement* (May 8, 1903), 144.

"a not very successful . . ." etc. *Athenæum* (Dec. 26, 1896), 901.

"harried perpetually." Harte to Anna Harte, Aug. 4, 1883 (Bancroft), Harte 1997, 296–99.

"It is simply . . ." Harte 1926, 308.

"God knows . . ."; "*I* haven't lost . . ." Ibid., 322–23.

"*almost* secured . . . economical." Harte 1926, 243–44.

"even though . . ." Harte to Gertrude Griswold, May 28, 1895 (Huntington).

"I hasten . . ." Harte 1926, 316–17.

"Don't let's play . . ." Ibid., 381.

"Don't expect . . ." Ibid., 391.

"Am I not . . ." Ibid., 374.

"It has not fallen . . ." Pemberton 1900, 17.

"chained to the oar." Harte to Clara Schneider, Dec. 20, 1892 (UVa).

We know from another . . . Harte to Clara Schneider, Aug. 30, 1894 (UVa).

"I have a very good . . ." Harte 1926, 310–11.

Watt took a flat rate . . . See Hepburn 1968, 54; "BH Income" [brief overview in Harte's handwriting showing his income and expenses for three years in the late 1890s] (JBH).

"[W]e know nothing . . ." Murphy and Monteiro 1979, 98.

Just two months before . . . as his style is." Harte 1926, 158–59, 163.

"A singularly . . ." Harte 1926, 163.

Three years later . . . See Hardy 1978, 1.121.

"absurdly offended . . ." Diary-2 (entry for Oct. 26, 1883).

In a letter . . . See Harte to Nelly Goodrich, Dec. 15, 1879 (Colby).

The Woodlanders . . . See Van de Velde 1903, 539.

"thought better . . ." Harte to Gertrude Griswold, Mar. 1, 1880 (Huntington).

"I was very pleasantly . . ." Harte 1926, 163.

Wilde had a keen . . . See Wilde 1923, 136.

"in fulfilment . . ."; "Much depressed . . ." Ibid., 284, 285.

"greatly lionized"; "This to all . . ." Harte 1926, 331.

"The spectacle . . . he was recalled. Harte 1926, 272–73, 277–78, 342–43.

Hyndman had met . . . See Hyndman 1911, 188.

"poor starving devils . . . sheer starving." Harte 1926, 231, 302–3.

"usual violent . . ." Murphy and Monteiro 1979, 105.

"I am an earnest . . ." Harte 1926, 321.

Scene commencing "Staring out into the gathering gloom" (pp. 220–21):

he would have liked . . . See Harte to Anna Harte, Jan. 23, 1892, Harte 1926, 361; Harte to Florence Henniker, Feb. 3, 1892 (UVa).

"City of Dreadful Night" . . . stricken down. Based on Harte 1926, 362.

It was partly . . . Based on Harte to Anna Harte, Jan. 23, 1892, Harte 1926, 362; Harte to Florence Henniker, Feb. 3, 1892 (UVa).

He had been . . . like midnight. Based on Harte to Anna Harte, Jan. 23, 1892, Harte 1926, 361, 362.

For the last . . . go away with Maurice. Based on Harte to Florence Henniker, Feb. 3, 1892 (UVa).

Christmas had been . . . See Harte to Joseph Hatton, Dec. 25 and 30, 1891 (HRC).

George B. Burgin . . . been done! Based on Harte to George B. Burgin, Dec. 31, 1891 (UCLA).

A week ago . . . See Harte to Mary Stuart Boyd, Wednesday pm [Jan. 27, 1892] (UCLA).

A telegram . . . dying father! Based on Harte to Anna Harte, Feb. 20, 1892, Harte 1926, 363–64; Harte to Clara Schneider, Feb. 13, 1892 (UVa).

Arthur Van de Velde . . . See Harte to William Walter Phelps, Feb. 7, 1892 (Huntington).

"It was a sad . . ." Harte 1926, 363.

For Madame . . . See Harte to Clara Schneider, Feb. 13, 1892 (UVa).

Monsieur Van de Velde was laid . . . See extract from "The Register of Burials in St. Mary's Cemetery," Feb. 15, 1995 (Nissen).

Chapter 10

Scene commencing "In between revising" (p. 222–23):

In between revising . . . See Harte to T. Edgar Pemberton, Sun. eve. [Mar. 24, 1895] (Yale).

February 27th . . . See typescript of Geoffrey Bret Harte's memoirs, p. 11 (JBH).

He had been . . . was gone! Based on Harte to Anna Harte, Mar. 30, 1895 (SFPL), Harte 1997, 396–97.

Harte was skeptical . . . See Harte 1926, 396–97.

"a distinct reputation . . ."; He managed . . . than expected. Harte to Mary Stuart Boyd, Thursday pm [Jan. 31, 1895] (UCLA).

"Well received . . ." Frohman's cable quoted in Harte to Aline Harte, Sunday [Sept. 20, 1896] (JBH).

Harte, ever suspicious . . . See Harte to T. Edgar Pemberton, Friday pm [Sept. 18, 1896] (Yale).

His old naval . . . enthusiastic about it." Tobin quoted in Harte to Francis King Harte, Oct. 12, 1896, Harte 1926, 431.

"a dear good fellow . . ." Harte to T. Edgar Pemberton, Oct. 9, 1896 (Yale).

"perfect play" etc. Anna quoted in Harte to T. Edgar Pemberton, Oct. 9, 1896 (Yale).

"still very uncertain . . ." etc. Harte 1926, 429.

Early on . . . grey monotony." Harte to T. Edgar Pemberton, Friday pm [Feb. 8, 1895] (NYPL).

"The plot is faulty . . ." Scharnhorst and Bales 1985, 138.

stayed two weeks . . . old fogy." Harte to Clara Schneider, Jan. 1, 1889 (UVa).

"He lives . . . would save him. Harte to Anna Harte, Sept. 17, 1889 (Bancroft), Harte 1997, 360–62.

Aline Bouton Smith . . . See Harte to Clara Schneider, Aug. 30, 1894 (UVa), Harte 1997, 392–93; Typescript of Geoffrey Bret Harte's memoirs, pp. 12, 28 (JBH). Aline Harte was born in 1862 (RBDM).

In September 1890 . . . I don't see it!" Harte to Eliza Knaufft, Sept. 14, 1890 (Bancroft).

"He was to her . . ." etc. Typescript of Geoffrey Bret Harte's memoirs, p. 22 (JBH).

"the chocolate girl." Harte 1926, 457.

"healthy taste." Harte to Aline Harte, Wednesday pm [Nov. 1900?] (JBH).

Harte had written . . . See Harte 1926, 367; Harte to Anna Harte, Jan. 21, 1893 (UVa), Harte 1997, 382–83.

"the *household* . . ." Harte to Gertrude Griswold, May 28, 1895 (Huntington), Harte 1997, 397–99.

Madame continued . . . See Van Zeller 1950, 61.

We know . . . See Van Zeller 1950, 73; Van Zeller 1965, 235.

Long after . . . See Van Zeller 1950, 61.

"little cottage" Harte 1926, 424. Description of Arford House from visit.

"the monkish seclusion" etc. Harte 1926, 428.

"But really! It *is* . . . to Arford. Harte to Mrs. Kingham, Tuesday [late Nov. 1896] (JBH).

"Poor Madame . . . father-in-law B.H." Harte to Aline Bret Harte, Sunday [Sept. 20, 1896] (JBH).

"our mighty intellect." Harte 1926, 386.

"I like the freshness . . ." Harte to Florence Henniker, Saturday pm [Apr. 5 or 12, 1890] (UVa), Harte 1997, 366.

"[A] small edition . . ." etc. Harte 1926, 387.

"an ideal house." Harte to Clara Schneider, Aug. 29, 1898 (UVa).

"We are, if we consult . . ." Harte to T. Edgar Pemberton, Nov. 2, 1898 (Yale), Harte 1997, 425–26.

"I think he was . . ." Clemens 1959, 125.

"probable that . . ." etc. Stegner 1961, xiv.

"your dear good . . ." etc. Harte 1926, 346.

"[Henry] Adams began . . ." Adams 1918, 385.

"the strongest . . ." Harte 1906, 14.220. The story is "The Judgement of Bolinas Plain," the basis for *Sue.*

"The virginal dew . . ." Canby 1909, 295.

"[o]ne of the most common . . ." Thomas 1973, 93, passim.

" 'mebbe he don't . . .' " Harte 1883, 89.

"you really ought . . ." etc. Harte 1906, 23.412.

"You know best . . ." Harte to Charles A. Dana, Apr. 6, 1882 (NYPL).

"As a general thing . . ." Harte to Anna Harte, Apr. 19, 1886 (UCLA).

"By temperament . . ." Van de Velde 1903, 540.

"In Bret Harte's stories . . ." etc. Merwin 1912, 157.

"California was . . ." MacDonald 1915, lxxv.

"the brotherly love theme . . ." Morrow 1979, 18.

"seems to have founded . . . " Stoneley 1996, 199.

His *Cecil Dreeme* . . . See Martin 1991.

"They were splendidly . . ." etc. Harte 1995, 272, 273.

"above all faithful . . ." Harte 1909, n. pag.

"as intense . . ." MacDonald 1915, lxv.

"the story of a love . . ."; "Reading those tales . . ." Van de Velde 1881, 235. "I want . . ." John Hay to Bret Harte, Mar. 21, 1881 (JBH).

Harte quoted . . . See Harte to Anna Harte, Apr. 22, 1881, Harte 1926, 194.

"quite the snell . . ." Harte to Clara Schneider, Jan. 6, 1886 (UVa).

"my Schneider." Harte to Rudolph Schneider, July 21, 1880 (UVa) and Apr. 19, 1881 (UVa).

voluminous in his praises . . . See Harte to Rudolph Schneider, Aug. 8, 1879 (UVa).

After his departure . . . off the rose. See Harte to Clara Schneider, Dec. 14, 1880 (UVa); May 8, 1887 (UVa); Apr. 23, 1892 (UVa), Harte 1997, 378–79; and Nov. 3, 1893 (UVa).

"I am afraid . . ." Harte to Clara Schneider, Nov. 20, 1894 (UVa), Harte 1997, 394–95.

"engaged in a series . . ." Hoffman 1995, 25.

"Is it possible . . . were romances." Ibid., 36.

"relates much of . . . " etc. Stoneley 1996, 196, 197–98.

"hard, thorny . . . " Harte to Mark Twain, June 17, 1872 (Bancroft), Harte 1997, 67.

Arthur Collins. Biographical information from Collins's obituary in the *Times* (Nov. 23, 1911): 11.

Collins had long . . . See Arthur Collins, "Bret Harte: A Personal Appreciation," undated clipping in Arthur Collins's scrapbook (MC).

Beefsteak Club . . . See Diary-2 (entry for Dec. 17, 1885). Harte became an official member on July 12, 1886. See Beefsteak Club to Axel Nissen, Nov. 16, 1994 (Nissen).

Harte was among . . . true regard." Arthur Collins, "Bret Harte: A Personal Appreciation," undated clipping in Arthur Collins's scrapbook (MC).

"never prone . . . understood him." Pemberton 1903, 213, 280.

When, in the summer . . . 'the cure.' " See Harte 1926, 404, 410–11; Harte to Florence Henniker, Aug. 31, 1895 (UVa).

"a very charming . . ." etc. Harte 1926, 343.

In 1898 . . . See Davies 1978.

Collins liked to be . . . From His Father." Several of the photos may be found in Collins's scrapbook (MC).

Collins's obituary notes . . . "Lieutenant-Colonel Collins," *Times* (Nov. 23, 1911): 11; Testament of Arthur Collins (Somerset House).

Harte to Francis King Harte, Dec. 14, 1898 (UVa), Harte 1997, 427–28.

Harte to Arthur Collins, Dec. 15, 1898. Published in Pemberton 1903, 280–81.

On August 2, 1920 . . . 7 days." See death certificate of Anna Bret Harte (RBDM).

unmarked grave . . . Hove Borough Council Cemeteries Office to Axel Nissen, Mar. 9, 1995 (Nissen).

Anna Harte to Mrs. Rudge, Apr. 8, [1901] (Yale).

"had he made . . ." Ethel Bret Harte to George Stewart, Dec. 12, 1931 (Stewart Papers, Bancroft).

"Alas! I have been . . ." etc. Harte 1926, 455–56.

"I will come . . ." Harte to Francis King Harte, Sunday [Jan. 1899] (UVa), Harte 1997, 429–30.

Harte's youngest grandson . . . was heartfelt." Typescript of Geoffrey Bret Harte's memoirs, p. 18 (JBH).

"that other . . . to enjoy it!" Typescript of Geoffrey Bret Harte's memoirs, pp. 26–27 (JBH).

His earliest . . . back upstairs. See Van Zeller 1965, 3.

"typified . . ." etc. Ibid., 25.

He recalled . . . See Van Zeller 1950, 89; Van Zeller 1965, 46.

She frowned . . . Bret Harte." Van Zeller 1950, 59–61.

Claude could never . . . her.' " Ibid., 174.

In retrospect . . . Bret Harte." Ibid., 60–61.

"Unfortunately I am not . . ." Harte to Miss Chappell, Jan. 2, 1899 (Rochester).

"a kind friend . . ." Harte to Francis King Harte, Dec. 22, 1901 (UCLA).

"heroine ghost . . ." etc. Harte 1926, 479.

"delightful book" etc. Harte to Lady Augusta Gregory, Wednesday am (Bancroft).

Harte's opinion . . . a writer of romance!" Harte 1926, 382–83.

"It thoroughly . . ." Harte to James Anthony Froude, May 22, 1889 (UCLA).

To Harte . . . trace of humour." Harte to Florence Henniker, Oct. 3, 1890 (UVa).

"a stick of clothing . . ."; "when I am . . ." Harte 1926, 425, 446.

"It may be . . ."; "Do you keep . . ." Pemberton 1903, 322–23.

If we are to believe . . . See Boyd 1902, 776. William Dean Howells . . . "Two Men of Sandy Bar"? Based on Garland 1930, 445, 447.

Harte to Hamlin Garland, May 3, 1899 (USC), Harte 1997, 432–33.

On the appointed day . . . said good-bye. See Garland 1930, 447–49.

We know that . . . See Garland 1930, 445.

"[T]he secret of the American . . ." etc. Harte 1899, 8.

"He was affable . . ." Garland 1968, 143.

Yet walking down . . . ever saw him. See Garland 1930, 449.

He writes . . . bounty of a patron." Ibid., 448, 449.

The occasion . . . discounted the charges. See Garland 1931, 178–82.

when Harte died . . . See Garland 1930, 449.

$185,500. For a detailed account of Harte's income during the last twenty years of his life, see Nissen 1997.

By 1897 . . . recovery of the money. See indenture of May 30, 1899 (APWP).

The advances . . . economic independence. Harte to Anna Harte, July 29, 1896 (UCLA), Aug. 31, 1896 (UCLA).

In mid-September . . . that I do it." Harte to Anna Harte, Sept. 15, 1901 (UVa), Harte 1997, 441–43.

Griswold Harte married . . . parish priest. See marriage certificate (MA).

They do not show . . . See May Pemberton 1922 (Morse).

"walked with short . . ." See Atherton 1932, 181.

"was something . . ." etc. Elliott 1907, 122.

Old age brought him . . . See Harte to Anna Harte, Apr. 3, 1900 (UVa).

"standing upright . . ." Harte to Minnie Jackson, Apr. 6, 1899, Pemberton 1903, 329.

The joint . . . See Harte 1926, 423.

On January 1, 1900 . . . See Harte to Mary Stuart Boyd, Monday night [Jan. 1, 1900] (UCLA).

Though he had the best . . . left to live. See typescript of Geoffrey Bret Harte's memoirs, p. 33 (JBH).

An operation . . . See Harte to Francis King Harte, Feb. 1, 1902 (UVa).

Bret Harte was not told . . . See typescript of Geoffrey Bret Harte's memoirs, p. 33 (JBH).

He did not take . . . spending on it." Harte 1926, 482, 486.

On December 1 . . . two a day." Harte to Francis King Harte, Dec. 1, 1901 (UVa).

Ten days later . . . to bury him. Death certificate (MA); Record of Interment, Cypress Hills Cemetery (Nissen).

"I have received . . ." Harte to Francis King Harte, Dec. 11, 1901 (NYPL).

"God knows . . ." Harte 1926, 500.

He was engaged . . . sick he was. See Harte to Francis King Harte, Dec. 25, 1901 (UCLA).

She had not seen him . . . visit her soon. See Harte 1926, 480, 503.

In his last . . . the beginning. See Harte to Francis King Harte, Feb. 1, 1902 (UVa).

Harte saw Arthur . . . "forced him out." Arthur Collins, "Bret Harte: A Personal Appreciation," undated clipping in Arthur Collins's scrapbook (MC).

That same month . . . the victim!" Pemberton 1903, 338; Harte to Francis King Harte, Feb. 1, 1902 (UVa).

He rallied . . . to Richmond. Typescript of Geoffrey Bret Harte's memoirs, pp. 28, 31.

"hoping to benefit . . . new story. Pemberton 1903, 96–97, 338.

On Monday . . . Harte died. See Pemberton 1903, 340; typescript of
Geoffrey Bret Harte's memoirs, pp. 31–32 (JBH).

Madame Van de Velde . . . struggle or pain." Madame's statement
quoted in the *Times* (May 9, 1902): 10.

His father . . . could have done." Typescript of Geoffrey Bret Harte's
memoirs, p. 30 (JBH).

To Geoffrey's big brother . . . "Bret Harte Dead." Richard Bret Harte
1916, 529.

On Thursday, May 8, 1902 . . . *Times* (May 9, 1902): 10; "Funeral of
Mr. Bret Harte," undated newspaper clipping from the scrapbook of
Arthur Collins (MC). All the persons I mention as being present are
mentioned in one or both of these newspaper accounts. Description
of church from visit to site.

Pemberton had written . . . See T. Edgar Pemberton to Francis King
Harte, May 7, 1902 (JBH).

"The funeral . . ." "Funeral of Mr. Bret Harte," op. cit.

The simplicity . . . See Pemberton 1903, 340.

Covered . . . long future." "Funeral of Mr. Bret Harte," op. cit.

One final offering . . . one newspaper. See ibid.

As the group . . . dispersed. *Times* (May 9, 1902): 10; "Funeral of Mr.
Bret Harte," op. cit.

She was appalled . . . misapply this communication." M. S. Van de Velde
to John Hay, May 21, 1902 (LC).

When Hay . . . so dear a friend." M. S. Van de Velde to John Hay, July
19, 1902 (LC).

BIBLIOGRAPHY

Adams, Henry. 1918. *The Education of Henry Adams: An Autobiography*. Ed. Henry Cabot Lodge. Boston and New York: Houghton Mifflin.

———. 1938. *The Letters of Henry Adams (1892–1918)*. Ed. Worthington Chauncey Ford. Boston: Houghton Mifflin.

Aldrich, Lilian Woodman. 1921 [1920]. *Crowding Memories*. London: Constable.

Aldrich, Thomas Bailey. 1907. *The Writings of Thomas Bailey Aldrich: The Story of a Bad Boy, The Little Violinist, and Other Sketches*. Boston and New York: Houghton Mifflin.

Altick, Richard D. 1965. *Lives and Letters: A History of Literary Biography in England and America*. New York: Alfred A. Knopf.

American Antiquarian Society Index of Marriages and Deaths in New York Weekly Museum, 1788–1817. 1952. N.p. Vol. 2.

Andrews, Kenneth R. 1950. *Nook Farm: Mark Twain's Hartford Circle*. Cambridge: Harvard University Press.

Atherton, Gertrude. 1932. *Adventures of a Novelist*. London: Jonathan Cape.

Austen, Roger, and John W. Crowley. 1991. *Genteel Pagan: The Double Life of Charles Warren Stoddard*. Amherst: University of Massachusetts Press.

Barnett, Linda Diz. 1980. *Bret Harte: A Reference Guide*. Boston: G. K. Hall.

Bartlett, William C. 1898. "Overland Reminiscences." *Overland Monthly* 32:41–46.

Baym, Nina. 1981. "Melodramas of Beset Manhood: How Theories of American Fiction Exclude Women Authors." *American Quarterly* 33:125–39.

Beecher, Catherine [sic] E., and Harriet Beecher Stowe. 1869. *The American Woman's Home or, Principles of Domestic Science; Being A Guide to the Formation and Maintenance of Economical, Healthful, Beautiful, and Christian Homes*. New York: J. B. Ford.

Beer, Gillian. 1970. *The Romance*. London: Methuen.

Besant, Walter. 1899. *The Pen and the Book*. London: Thomas Burleigh.

Booth, Bradford A. 1944. "Unpublished Letters of Bret Harte." *American Literature* 16:131–42.

———. 1948. "Bret Harte Goes East: Some Unpublished Letters." *American Literature* 19:318–35.

———. 1954. "Mark Twain's Comments on Bret Harte's Stories." *American Literature* 25:492–95.

Boyd, Mary Stuart. 1902. "Some Letters of Bret Harte." *Harper's Monthly Magazine* 44:773–76.

Boyesen, Hjalmar Hjorth. 1894. *Literary and Social Silhouettes.* New York: Harper.

Brooks, Noah. 1898. "Early Days of 'The Overland.' " *Overland Monthly* 32:3–11.

———. 1899. "Bret Harte in California." *Century Magazine* 36:447–51.

Byers, Samuel. 1903. "Bret Harte in Switzerland." *Overland Monthly* 42:291–97, 426–32.

Canby, Henry Seidel. 1909. *The Short Story in English.* New York: Henry Holt.

———. 1926. "The Luck of Bret Harte." *Saturday Review of Books* 2:717–18.

Cevasco, G. A., and Richard Harmond. 1988. "Bret Harte to Robert Roosevelt on *Two Men of Sandy Bar:* A Newly Discovered Letter." *American Literary Realism* 21:58–62.

Charvat, William. 1968. *The Profession of Authorship in America, 1800–1870: The Papers of William Charvat.* Ed. Matthew J. Bruccoli. Columbus, Ohio: Ohio State University Press.

Chesterton, Gilbert Keith. 1902. "The Ways of the World: Bret Harte." *Pall Mall Magazine* 27:428–32.

Clappe, Louise Amelia Knapp Smith. 1933. *California in 1851: The Letters of Dame Shirley.* Intro. and notes by Carl I. Wheat. San Francisco: Grabhorn.

Clemens, Samuel L. 1880. "The Contributor's Club." *Atlantic Monthly* 45:849–51.

———. 1949. *The Love Letters of Mark Twain.* Ed. Dixon Wechter. New York: Harper.

———. 1959. *The Autobiography of Mark Twain.* Ed. Charles Neider. New York: Harper.

———. 1960. *Mark Twain-Howells Letters: The Correspondence of Samuel L. Clemens and William D. Howells, 1872–1910.* Ed. Henry Nash Smith and William M. Gibson, with Fredrick Anderson. Cambridge: Harvard University Press.

———. 1967. *Mark Twain's Letters to His Publishers, 1867–1894.* Ed. Hamlin Hill. Berkeley and Los Angeles: University of California Press.

———. 1975. *Mark Twain's Notebooks and Journals.* Vol. 2, *1877–83.* Ed. Frederick Anderson, Lin Salamo, and Bernard L. Stein. Berkeley and Los Angeles: University of California Press.

———. 1988. *Mark Twain's Letters.* Vol. 1, *1853–66.* Ed. Edgar Marquess

Branch, Michael B. Frank, and Kenneth M. Sanderson. Berkeley and Los Angeles: University of California Press.

———. 1990. *Mark Twain's Letters*. Vol. 2, *1867–68*. Ed. Harriet Elinor Smith and Richard Bucci. Berkeley and Los Angeles: University of California Press.

Clifford, James L., ed. 1962. *Biography as an Art: Selected Criticism, 1560–1960*. London: Oxford University Press.

Clymer, Kenton J. 1971. "Anti-Semitism in the Late Nineteenth Century: The Case of John Hay." *American Jewish Historical Quarterly* 60:344–54.

———. 1975. *John Hay: The Gentleman as Diplomat*. Ann Arbor: University of Michigan Press.

Cohn, Dorrit. 1978. *Transparent Minds: Modes for Presenting Consciousness in Fiction*. Princeton: Princeton University Press.

———. 1989. "Fictional *versus* Historical Lives: Borderlines and Borderline Cases." *Journal of Narrative Technique* 19:3–24.

Cummins, Ella Sterling. 1893. *The Story of the Files: A Review of Californian Writers and Literature*. San Francisco: World's Fair Commission of California, Columbian Exposition.

Dahl, Barbara, and Emmett Ostrander. 1989. *Ostrander Family Vital Records*. Decorah, Iowa: Ostrander Family Association.

Daly, Joseph Francis. 1917. *The Life of Augustin Daly*. New York: Macmillan.

Dam, Henry J. W. 1894. "A Morning with Bret Harte." *McClure's Magazine* 4:38–50.

Davies, Celia. 1978. *Brian Hatton: A Biography of the Artist (1887–1916)*. Lavenham, Suffolk: Terence Dalton.

Davis, Helen I. 1931. "Bret Harte and His Jewish Ancestor, Bernard Hart." *Publications of the American Jewish Historical Society* 32:99–111.

Dennett, Tyler. 1933. *John Hay: From Poetry to Politics*. New York: Dodd, Mead.

Duckett, Margaret. 1953. "Bret Harte's Portrayal of Half-Breeds." *American Literature* 25:193–212.

———. 1954. "Bret Harte and the Indians of Northern California." *Huntington Library Quarterly* 18:59–83.

———. 1964. *Mark Twain and Bret Harte*. Norman: University of Oklahoma Press.

Dunne, Finley Peter. 1963. *Mr. Dooley Remembers: The Informal Memoirs of Finley Peter Dunne*. Ed. Philip Dunne. Boston: Little, Brown.

Edel, Leon. 1973 [1959]. *Literary Biography*. Bloomington: Indiana University Press.

Elliott, S. F. 1907. "Glimpses of Bret Harte." *Reader* 10:122–27.

Ellmann, Richard. 1988 [1987]. *Oscar Wilde*. Harmondsworth, England: Penguin.

Emerson, Ralph Waldo. 1939. *The Letters of Ralph Waldo Emerson*. Ed. Ralph L. Rusk. New York: Columbia University Press.

————. 1982. *The Journals of Ralph Waldo Emerson.* Vol. 16, *1866–1882.* Ed. Ronald A. Bosco and Glen M. Johnson. Cambridge, Mass., and London: Belknap.

Fassett, Mary Weymouth. 1924. "Bret Harte's Daughter." *Overland Monthly* 82:247.

Fiedler, Leslie. 1970. *Love and Death in the American Novel.* London: Paladin.

Fields, Annie A. 1922. *Annie Adams Fields: Memoirs of a Hostess: A Chronicle of Eminent Friendships.* Ed. M. A. DeWolfe Howe. Boston: Atlantic Monthly.

Fiske, John. 1917. *The Life and Letters of John Fiske.* Ed. John Spencer Clark. Boston and New York: Houghton Mifflin.

Forster, John. 1876. *The Life of Charles Dickens.* London: Chapman and Hall.

Frémont, Jessie Benton. 1887. *Souvenirs of My Time.* Boston: D. Lothrop.

————. 1892. "What makes literary success?" *Ladies' Home Journal* 9:18.

————. 1993. *The Letters of Jessie Benton Frémont.* Ed. Pamela Herr and Mary Lee Spence. Urbana and Chicago: University of Illinois Press.

Frye, Northrop. 1990 [1957]. *Anatomy of Criticism.* Harmondsworth, England: Penguin.

Garfield, James A. 1973. *The Diary of James A. Garfield.* Vol. 3, *1875–1877.* Ed. Harry James Brown and Frederick D. Williams. East Lansing: Michigan State University Press.

Garland, Hamlin. 1930. *Roadside Meetings.* New York: Macmillan.

————. 1931. *Companions on the Trail: A Literary Chronicle.* New York: Macmillan.

————. 1968. *Hamlin Garland's Diaries.* Ed. Donald Pizer. San Marino, Calif.: Huntington.

Gilder, Jeannette. 1905. *The Tomboy at Work.* London: Doubleday, Page.

Gillis, William Robert. 1930. *Gold Rush Days with Mark Twain.* New York: Albert and Charles Boni.

Gittings, Robert. 1990. *Young Thomas Hardy/Thomas Hardy's Later Years.* New York: Book-of-the-Month-Club.

Glazener, Nancy. 1997. *Reading for Realism: The History of a U.S. Literary Institution, 1850–1910.* Durham and London: Duke University Press.

Glover, Donald Ellsworth. 1966. "The Later Literary Career of Bret Harte: 1880–1902." Ph.D. diss., University of Virginia.

Graham, Kenneth. 1965. *English Criticism of the Novel, 1865–1900.* Oxford: Clarendon.

Haight, Gordon S. 1968. *George Eliot: A Biography.* Oxford: Clarendon.

Hannigan, D. F. 1894. "The Decline of Romance." *Westminster Review* 141:33–36.

Hardy, Evelyn, and F. B. Pinion. 1972. *One Rare Fair Woman: Thomas Hardy's Letters to Florence Henniker, 1893–1922.* London: Macmillan.

Hardy, Thomas. 1978. *The Collected Letters of Thomas Hardy.* Ed. Richard Little Purdy and Michael Millgate. Oxford: Clarendon.

Hare, John. 1908. "Reminiscences and Reflections." *Strand* 36:20–21.

Harris, Frank. 1924 [1923]. *Contemporary Portraits*. Fourth Series. London: G. Richards.

Harte, Francis Bret. 1883 [1876]. *Gabriel Conroy*. Boston: Houghton Mifflin.

———. 1892. "Francis Bret Harte. Two Interviews with Him on Somewhat Dissimilar Lines." *Idler* 1:301–11.

———. 1894a. "A Morning with Bret Harte." By H. J. W. Dam. *McClure's Magazine* 4:38–49.

———. 1894b. "Californian Verse." *My First Book*. Intro. by Jerome K. Jerome. London: Chatto and Windus.

———. 1899. "The Rise of the 'Short Story.' " *Cornhill Magazine* 7:1–8.

———. 1906. *The Works of Bret Harte*. Argonaut Edition. New York: P. F. Collier.

———. 1909. *The Lectures of Bret Harte*. Ed. Charles Meeker Kozlay. Brooklyn, N.Y.: privately printed.

———. 1914. *Stories and Poems and Other Uncollected Writings by Bret Harte*. Compiled by Charles Meeker Kozlay. Boston and New York: Houghton Mifflin.

——— 1924. *Plain Language from Truthful James*. Intro. Ina Donna Coolbrith. San Francisco: John Henry Nash for his Friends.

———. 1926. *The Letters of Bret Harte*. Ed. Geoffrey Bret Harte. London: Hodder and Stoughton.

———. 1990. *Bret Harte's California: Letters to the* Springfield Republican *and* Christian Register, *1866–67*. Ed. Gary Scharnhorst. Albuquerque: University of New Mexico Press.

———. 1991 [1926]. *California Sketches: Mark Twain and Bret Harte*. New York: Dover.

———. 1995. *Selected Stories and Sketches*. Ed. David Wyatt. Oxford and New York: Oxford University Press.

———. 1997. *Selected Letters of Bret Harte*. Ed. Gary Scharnhorst. Norman and London: University of Oklahoma Press.

Harte, Francis Bret, and Samuel Clemens. 1961. *Ah Sin*. Ed. Frederick Anderson. San Francisco: Book Club of California.

Harte, Richard Bret. 1916. "Grandpa." *Overland Monthly* 68:529–29.

Hartley, Jacob. 1898. "Characteristics of Twain and Harte." *Sacramento Bee* (Jan. 29, 1898): n. pag.

Haskell, Mabel Percy. 1893. "Bret Harte in London," *San Francisco Examiner* (Feb. 12, 1893): n. pag.

Head, Franklin H. 1909. "Bret Harte's First Strenuous Revolt." *Second Book of the Dofobs*. Chicago: Society of the Dofobs. 27–30.

Hepburn, James. 1968. *The Author's Empty Purse and the Rise of the Literary Agent*. London: Oxford University Press.

Herr, Pamela. 1987. *Jessie Benton Frémont: A Biography*. New York: F. Watts.

Higginson, Thomas Wentworth. 1921. *Letters and Journals of Thomas Wentworth Higginson, 1846–1906.* Ed. Mary Thatcher Higginson. Boston: Houghton Mifflin.

Hill, Hamlin. 1968. "Mark Twain and His Enemies." *Southern Review* 4:520–29.

Hoffman, Andrew J. 1995. "Mark Twain and Homosexuality." *American Literature* 67:23–49.

Honan, Park. 1985. "Beyond Sartre, Vercors, and Bernard Crick: Theory and Form in Literary Biographies." *New Literary History* 16:639–51.

Howells, Elinor Mead. 1988. *If Not Literature: Letters of Elinor Mead Howells.* Columbus: Ohio State University Press.

Howells, William Dean. 1871. "Mr. Francis Bret Harte." *Every Saturday* 2:42–43.

———. 1890. *A Boy's Town.* New York: Harper.

———. 1900. *Literary Friends and Acquaintance: A Personal Retrospect of American Authorship.* New York and London: Harper.

———. 1903. "Editor's Easy Chair." *Harper's Monthly Magazine* 47:153–59.

———. 1910. *My Mark Twain.* New York: Harper.

———. 1929. *Life in Letters of William Dean Howells.* Ed. Mildred Howells. London: William Heinemann.

———. 1960. *1960. Mark Twain-Howells Letters: The Correspondence of Samuel L. Clemens and William D. Howells, 1872–1910.* Ed. Henry Nash Smith and William M. Gibson, with Fredrick Anderson. Cambridge: Harvard University Press.

Hubbell, Jay B. 1933. "George Henry Boker, Paul Hamilton Hayne, and Charles Warren Stoddard: Some Unpublished Letters." *American Literature* 5:146–65.

Hyndman, Henry Mayers. 1911. *The Record of an Adventurous Life.* London: Macmillan.

"Items Relating to the Seixas Family." 1920. *Publications of the American Jewish Historical Society* 27:161–74.

James, George Wharton. n.d. [1911?]. "The Romantic History of a Remarkable Woman: Josephine C. McCrackin." *National Magazine,* pp. 91–114. Off print in Bancroft.

James, Henry. 1974. *Henry James Letters.* Vol. 1, *1843–1875.* Ed. Leon Edel. Cambridge: Harvard University Press.

Jones, Gareth Stedman. 1984 [1971]. *Outcast London: A Study of the Relationship between Classes in Victorian Society.* New York: Pantheon.

Kaplan, Justin. 1966. *Mr. Clemens and Mark Twain: A Biography.* New York: Simon and Schuster.

Katz, Jonathan Ned. 1992. *Gay American History: Lesbians and Gay Men in the U.S.* New York: Meridian.

Kelly, Arthur C. M., ed. n.d. *Death, Marriages, and Miscellaneous from Hudson, New York, Newspapers: Marriages 1802–1851.* N.p.

Lang, Andrew. 1876. "New Novels." *Academy* 10:235.

———. 1887. "Realism and Romance." *Contemporary Review* 52:683–93.

Longfellow, Henry Wadsworth. 1982. *Letters of Henry Wadsworth Longfellow*. Vol. 5. Ed. Andrew Hilen. Cambridge: Harvard University Press.

Luedtke, Luther S., and Patrick Morrow. 1973. "Bret Harte on Bayard Taylor: An Unpublished Tribute." *Markham Review* 3:101–5.

Lystra, Karen. 1989. *Searching the Heart: Women, Men, and Romantic Love in Nineteenth Century America*. New York and Oxford: Oxford University Press.

McCarthy, Justin. 1899. *Reminiscences*. London: Chatto and Windus.

McCrackin, Josephine Clifford. 1902. "A Letter from a Friend." *Overland Monthly* 40:222–25.

———. 1915. "Reminiscences of Bret Harte and Pioneer Days in the West." *Overland Monthly* 67:7–15.

MacDonald, William. 1915. "Introduction." *Stories and Poems by Bret Harte*. London: Oxford University Press.

Mayo, Louise A. 1988. *The Ambivalent Image: Nineteenth Century America's Perception of the Jew*. London and Toronto: Associated University Press.

Meredith, George. 1970. *The Letters of George Meredith*. Vol. 1. Ed. C. L. Cline. Oxford: Clarendon.

Merriam, George Spring. 1970 [1885]. *The Life and Times of Samuel Bowles*. New York: Da Capo.

Merwin, Henry Childs. 1912 [1911]. *The Life of Bret Harte. With Some Account of the California Pioneers*. London: Chatto and Windus.

Miller, Cincinnatus Heiner. 1902. "Joaquin Miller: He Writes for the *Saturday Review* His Reminiscences of Bret Harte." *New York Times Saturday Review of Books and Art* (May 31, 1902): 360.

Mitchell, Edward P. 1894. "Mr. Dana of 'The Sun.' " *McClure's Magazine* 3:371–97.

———. 1924. *Memoirs of an Editor: Fifty Years of American Journalism*. New York: Charles Scribner's.

Moore, Isabel. 1909. *Talks in a Library with Laurence Hutton*. New York and London: G. P. Putnam.

Morrow, Patrick. 1973. "Bret Harte, Popular Fiction, and the Local Color Movement." *Western American Literature* 8:123–31.

———. 1979. *Bret Harte: Literary Critic*. Bowling Green, Ohio: Popular.

Murdock, Charles Albert. 1902. "Bret Harte in Humboldt." *Overland Monthly* 40:301–2.

———. 1921. *A Backward Glance at Eighty*. San Francisco: Elder.

Murphy, Brenda, and George Monteiro. 1979. "The Unpublished Letters of Bret Harte to John Hay." *American Literary Realism* 12:77–110.

Murphy, Francis. 1985. "The End of a Friendship: Two Unpublished Letters from Twain to Howells about Bret Harte." *New England Quarterly* 58:87–91.

Nadal, Ehrman Syme. 1877. "Writings of Bret Harte." *North American Review* 124:81–90.

Nadel, Ira B. 1985. *Biography: Fiction, Fact and Form.* London: Macmillan.

National Cyclopædia of American Biography. 1900. New York: James T. White. Vol. 10.

Nissen, Axel. 1997. "Lord of Romance: Bret Harte's Later Career Reconsidered." *American Literary Realism* 29:64–81.

Parton, Ethel. 1936. "A New York Childhood: The Seventies in Stuyvesant Sq." *New Yorker* (June 13, 1936): 32–46.

Parton, James. 1870. "Our Israelitish Brethren." *Atlantic Monthly* 26:385–403.

Payne, William Morton. 1885. "Recent Fiction." *Dial* 6:124.

———. 1888. "Recent Fiction." *Dial* 8:269.

———. 1903. "Recent Fiction." *Dial* 34:372.

Pemberton, May. 1922. "Recollections and Letters of Bret Harte." *New York Herald* (Oct. 15, 1922): N.p.

Pemberton, T. Edgar. 1900. *Bret Harte: A Treatise and a Tribute.* London: Greening.

———. 1903. *The Life of Bret Harte.* London: C. Arthur Pearson.

Petrie, Dennis W. 1981. *Ultimately Fiction: Design in Modern American Literary Biography.* West Lafayette, Ind.: Purdue University Press.

Phelps, William Lyon. 1939. *Autobiography With Letters.* New York: Oxford University Press.

Pratt, Harry Noyes. 1924. "The Man Bret Harte." *Step Ladder* 8:134–38.

Purcell, E. 1885. "New Novels." *Academy* 28:40.

Queen Victoria. 1930. *Letters of Queen Victoria: A Selection from Her Majesty's Correspondence and Journal Between the Years 1886 and 1901.* Vol. 1. Ed. George Earle Buckle. London: John Murray.

Rather, Louise. 1974. *Jessie Frémont at Black Point.* Oakland, Calif.: Rather.

Recueil de généalogie vaudoises. 1940. Lausanne: G. Bridel. Vol. 1.

Reid, Thomas Wemyss. 1890. *The Life, Letters, and Friendships of Richard Monckton Milnes, First Lord Houghton.* London: Cassell.

———. 1902. *William Black, Novelist: A Biography.* London: Cassell.

Rhodehamel, Josephine, and Raymond Wood. 1973. *Ina Coolbrith: Librarian and Laureate of California.* Provo: Brigham Young University Press.

Richardson, James. 1874. "The New Homes of New York: A Study of Flats." *Scribner's Monthly* 8:63–76.

Roman, Anton. 1898. "The Beginnings of the *Overland*: As Seen by the First Publisher." *Overland Monthly* 32:72–75.

———. 1902. "The Genesis of the *Overland Monthly.*" *Overland Monthly* 40:220–22.

Root, Sophia Whipple. 1932. "Three Lost Years of Bret Harte's Life." *Overland Monthly* 90:229–39, 240, 249, 253.

Rothman, Ellen K. 1987. *Hands and Hearts: A History of Courtship in America*. Cambridge: Harvard University Press.

Scharnhorst, Gary. 1992. *Bret Harte*. Boise, Idaho: Twayne.

———. 1995. *Bret Harte: A Bibliography*. Lanham, Md.: Scarecrow.

Scharnhorst, Gary, and Jack Bales. 1985. *The Lost Life of Horatio Alger, Jr.* Bloomington: Indiana University Press.

Sears, Louis Martin. 1954. "Bret Harte as Consul." *Mark Twain Journal* 9:17–24.

Sheick, William J. 1976. "William Dean Howells to Bret Harte: A Missing Letter." *American Literary Realism* 9:276–79.

Sherwood, Mary E. W. 1897. *An Epistle to Posterity, Being Rambling Recollections of Many Years of My Life*. New York: Harper.

———. 1902. "Bret Harte." *New York Times Saturday Review of Books* (May 10, 1902): 308.

Shumate, Albert, and Oscar Lewis, ed. 1967. *Homes of California Authors*. San Francisco: Book Club of California.

Simonhoff, Harry. 1956. *Jewish Notables in America, 1776–1865*. New York: Greenberg.

Sims, George R. 1904. *Among My Autographs*. London: Chatto and Windus.

Skidelsky, Robert. 1988. "Only Connect: Biography and Truth." *The Troubled Face of Biography*. Ed. Eric Homberger and John Charmley. London: Macmillan. 1–16.

Sklar, Kathryn Kish. 1973. *Catharine Beecher: A Study in American Domesticity*. New Haven: Yale University Press.

Spingarn, Lawrence. 1952. "The Journey of Bret Harte." *Yale Review* 41:591–93.

Stedman, Edmund Clarence. 1969 [1905]. *The New York Stock Exchange*. New York: Greenwood.

Stegner, Wallace. 1961. "Introduction." *The Outcasts of Poker Flat and Other Tales*. New York: New American Library.

Stevenson, Robert Louis. 1882–83. "Gossip on Romance." *Longman's Magazine* 1:69–79.

Stewart, George R. 1929. "The Year of Bret Harte's Birth." *American Literature* 1:78.

———. 1931. *Bret Harte: Argonaut and Exile*. Boston: Houghton Mifflin.

Stoddard, Charles Warren. 1897. "Early Recollections of Bret Harte." *Atlantic Monthly* 78:673–78.

———. 1903. *Exits and Entrances*. Boston: Lothrop.

Stoneley, Peter. "Rewriting the Gold Rush: Twain, Harte and Homosociality." *Journal of American Studies* 30 (1996): 189–209.

Timpe, Eugene F. 1965. "Bret Harte's German Public." *Jahrbuch für Amerikastudien* 10:215–20.

Thomas, Jeffrey F. 1973. "Bret Harte and the Power of Sex." *Western American Literature* 8:91–109.

Tompkins, Jane. 1985. *Sensational Designs: The Cultural Work of American Fiction, 1790–1860.* New York and Oxford: Oxford University Press.

Trudgill, Eric. 1976. *The Origins and Development of Victorian Sexual Attitudes.* New York: Holmes and Meier.

Uspensky, Boris. 1973. *A Poetics of Composition.* Trans. Valentina Zavarin and Susan Wittig. Berkeley and Los Angeles: University of California Press.

Van de Velde, M. S. [Hydeline Rodolphine Emma]. 1881. "Francis Bret Harte." *Belgravia* 45:232–36.

———. 1888. *Random Recollections of Courts and Society by a Cosmopolitan.* London: Ward and Downey.

———. 1889. *Cosmopolitan Recollections.* London: Ward and Downey.

———. 1903. "Bret Harte: First and Last Tales of the Argonauts." *Gentleman's Magazine* 195:535–44.

Van Zeller, [Claude] Hubert. 1950. *Family Case-Book.* London: Collins.

———. 1965. *One Foot in the Cradle.* London: John Murray.

Walker, Franklin. 1939. *San Francisco's Literary Frontier.* New York: Alfred A. Knopf.

Watts-Dunton, Theodore. 1902. *Athenaeum* (May 24, 1902): 658–60.

Wendte, Charles W. 1921. *Thomas Starr King: Patriot and Preacher.* Boston: Beacon.

———. 1928. *The Wider Fellowship.* Boston: Beacon.

Werner, W. L. 1939. "The Year of Bret Harte's Birth." *American Literature* 2:298–99.

White, Hayden. 1978a. "The Historical Text as Literary Artifact." *Tropics of Discourse: Essays in Cultural Criticism.* Baltimore: Johns Hopkins University Press. 81–100.

———. 1978b. "The Fictions of Factual Representation." *Tropics of Discourse: Essays in Cultural Criticism.* Baltimore: Johns Hopkins University Press. 121–34.

———. 1987. "The Question of Narrative in Contemporary Historical Theory." *The Content of the Form: Narrative Discourse and Historical Representation.* Baltimore: Johns Hopkins University Press. 26–57.

Who Was Who 1897–1915. 1953 [1920]. London: Adam and Charles Black.

Wilde, Oscar. 1923. *The Complete Works of Oscar Wilde.* Garden City, N.Y.: Doubleday, Page.

———. 1962. *The Letters of Oscar Wilde.* Ed. Rupert Hart-Davis. London: Rupert Hart-Davis.

Wilkins, Thurman. 1988. *Clarence King: A Biography.* Albuquerque: University of New Mexico Press.

Williams, Stanley T. 1941. "Ambrose Bierce and Bret Harte." *American Literature* 13:179–80.

Young, James Harvey. 1952. "Anna Dickinson, Mark Twain, and Bret Harte." *Pennsylvania Magazine of History and Biography* 76:39–46.

INDEX

Abinger, Lord, 217

Adams, Henry, xiii, xiv, 19, 21, 24–25, 26, 143, 230, 233

Agassiz, Louis, 7, 11

Age of Innocence, The (Wharton), 117, 120

Airlie, Lady, 217

Aldrich, Lilian Woodman, 114, 116–17, 126–27

Aldrich, Thomas Bailey, xiii, 19, 86, 115, 252

Alger, Horatio, 225

American Woman's Home, The (Beecher and Stowe), 100–09

Anthony, Andrew, 9

Arthur, Chester A., 208

Arthur, T. S., 78

Astor, William Waldorf, 230, 231, 264

Atherton, Gertrude, 258

Atwill, Augusta, 65

Atwill, Joseph, 65

authorship, conditions of, 198–202

Autobiography of Mark Twain, The, 142, 151

Avery, Benjamin P., 92, 94

Bacon, Ludolph, 195–96

Baker, Colonel, 81

Bancroft, Hubert Howe, 36

Baring, Lord, 217

Barlow, Samuel, 143, 173, 178

Barnes, George, 74, 79

Barrett, Lawrence, 136–37, 138, 216, 225

Bartlett, William C., 92, 93, 94

Basset, W., 263

Beale, Fitzhugh, 64

Beecher, Catharine E., 100–09

Beecher, Henry Ward, 61, 125

Beer, Gillian, 203

Bellew, Frank, 84

Bellows, H. W., 89

Benton, Thomas Hart, 61

Besant, Sir Walter, 38, 198, 201, 213, 214

Bierce, Ambrose, 94, 114

Bierstadt, Albert, 107

Biglow Papers, The (Lowell), 9

Billings, Josh (Henry Wheeler Shaw), 130

Bing, Lady, 217

biography, the "scenic method" in, xx–xxii

biography, theory and practice of; biographical narrative, xvii–xxiii

Bismarck, Otto, Count von, 188

Black, William, 176, 182, 190

Blaine, James G., 145, 192–93

Bleak House (Dickens), 135

Bliss, Elisha, 131, 133, 134, 136, 145, 147, 148

Blunt, Arthur, 240

Boileau, Nicolas, 126

Booth, Edwin, 225

Boswell, James, xxiii

Bouch, Lady Margaret, 216

Boucicault, Dion, 89, 137, 185

Boughton, George, 179

Boutelle, James, 48

Bowles, Samuel, 82, 114

Boyd, Alexander Stuart, 211–12, 249, 263
Boyd, Belle, 78
Boyd, Mary Stuart, 211–12, 221, 224, 230, 233, 249, 250, 251, 259, 260
Boyd, Stuart, 211, 260
Boyesen, Hjalmar Hjorth, xv
Braddon, Mary, 78
Brannan, Sam, 76
Brett, Catharine (grandmother), 15–16, 25, 272
Brett, Roger, 16
Brett, Sir Balliol (Viscount Esher), 16
"Bringing the Good News to Aix" (Browning), 216
Brontë, Emily, 78
Brooks, Noah, 60, 74, 92, 93
Browning, Robert, xv, 169, 215–16
Bruin, Ashbel, 134
Bryan, Abner, 41–43
Bryan, George, 42–43, 65
Bryan, Jonathan, 42
Bryan, Tom, 42
Bryan, Wise, 42
Buchanan, James, 18, 61
Bunyan, John, 22
Burgin, George B., 221
Byers, Samuel, 175–76, 189, 216
Byron, Lord George Gordon, 171

Caine, Hall, 205
Canby, Henry Seidel, xv, 233
Carleton, G. W., 83, 84
Carloss, M. R., 243
Carlyle, Jane Welsh, 170
Carlyle, Thomas, 169–70
Carmany, John H., 88
Carson, Kit, 62
"Casabianca" (Hemans), 22
"Cathedral, The" (Lowell), 9
Cecil Dreeme (Winthrop), 235
Cellier, Alfred, 240
Celtic Twilight (Gregory), 250
Cervantes, Miguel de, 22, 96
Chapin, E. H., 61

Chappell, Miss, 249–50
Chappell, William, 249
Charles II, King, 173, 178
Chesterton, G. K., 98
Child, Lydia Maria, 29
Chopin, Kate, xv
Clapp, Charles A., 144
Clark, John Spencer, 124
Clarke, Sir John, 216
Clay, Henry, 18, 19
Clemens, Clara, 142
Clemens, Olivia Langdon (Livy), 139–41, 152, 159
Clemens, Samuel Langhorne (Mark Twain), xiii, xiv, xvi, 19, 20, 26, 28, 43–44, 68, 77, 79, 82, 83, 85–86, 94, 114, 116, 121, 124, 125, 130, 131, 133, 139–61, 178, 190–91, 194, 230, 232, 239–40, 251, 254, 282
Clemens, Susy, 152
Cleveland, Grover, 191
Clifford, Josephine. *See* McCrackin, Josephine Clifford
Cody, William Frederick "Buffalo Bill," 216
Cohn, Dorrit, xxi
Collins, Arthur, 239, 240–42, 249, 263
Collins, Ferdinando, 240
Collins, Wilkie, 78, 194
Connaught, Duke of, 247
Coolbrith, Ina Donna (Josephine D. Smith), xiv, 24, 80, 88–90, 91
Cooper, Callie, 168, 174, 175–76, 179
Cooper, David Mack, 168
Cooper, Georgiana Thacher, 168, 174
Cooper, James Fenimore, 78
Cooper, Samuel F., 180
Corelli, Marie, 250
Cornbury, Lord, 16
Count of Monte Cristo, The (Dumas), 22, 205
Cowper, Earl, 217
Cowper, Lady, 217
Crane, Stephen, xv
Crewe, Robert, Earl of, 231

Cross, John, 215
Cross, Nigel, 201

Daggett, Rollin M., 60
"Daisy Miller" (James), 214
Daly, Augustin, 159
Dam, Henry, 31–34, 39, 44, 45
Dame, Hannah, 117
D'Amour, Mr., 51
Dana, Charles Anderson, 143, 150, 177, 208
Dana, Richard Henry, 7
David Copperfield (Dickens), 137, 180
Daw, Annie, 51
"De Sauty" (Holmes), 10
Delepierre, Octave, 175
Derby, Earl of, 179
Dickens, Charles, 21, 27, 40, 78, 93, 96, 114, 137, 171
Dickinson, Anna, 115, 125, 144–45, 184
Disraeli, Benjamin, 179
Dolson, Hattie L., 90–91
Dombey and Son (Dickens), 21
Don Quixote (Cervantes), 22, 40
Dove, Benjamin, 20
Dreiser, Theodore, xv, 200
Du Maurier, George, 214, 240
Dumas (*père*), Alexandre, 22, 78, 96, 205
Duncan, Isadora, 80
Duncan, Joseph Charles, 80
Dunham, Caroline, 67
Dunraven, Lord, 217
d'Usedom, Monsieur, 195
Dutton, E. P., 144

Edel, Leon, xviii, xx–xxi
Eliot, George (Marian Evans), 215
Elliott, S. R., 259
Ellis, Havelock, 25–26
Emerson, Ellen, 118
Emerson, Lidian, 118
Emerson, Ralph Waldo, 7, 118
Endicott, William C., 192
Eugénie, Empress, 247
Evarts, William Maxwell, 158, 160, 161, 177

Fern, Fanny (Sarah Payson Willis Parton), 30, 124
Field, Eugene, 144
Fields, Annie Adams, 22, 111, 114, 118, 120, 122, 137, 186
Fields, James T., 7, 71–72, 84, 95, 111, 118, 126
Fiske, John, 175
Flower, Belle, 168
Foiled (Henniker), 230
Ford, John T., 146, 157
Forgie, Peter, 191
Forster, John, 93
Foster, Stephen, 130
Franklin, Benjamin, 29
Frémont, Charles, 61, 62
Frémont, Frank, 61, 62
Frémont, Jessie Benton, 61–64, 66, 68, 69, 71–72, 74, 182, 234
Frémont, John Charles, 61, 64
Frémont, Lily, 61, 62, 65
Frith, William Powell, 175
Frohman, Charles, 224
Froissart, Jean, 40, 96
Froude, James Anthony, 169–71, 174, 179, 213, 250
Frye, Northrop, 203
Fulford, Helen Harte (granddaughter), 256, 258

Garfield, James A., 145, 183, 208
Garland, Hamlin, xv, 251–54
Gateless Barrier, The (Corelli), 250
George, Henry, 94, 253
Gibson, William, 180, 187, 188, 192
Gilbert and Sullivan, 210
Gilbert, Harry, 64
Gilded Age, The (Twain), 151, 159
Gilder, Jeannette, 115, 129
Gilder, Richard Watson, 121, 129
Gillis, Bill, 45
Gillis, Jim, 43–46, 79
Gillis, Steve, 44, 46
Gladstone, William, 172
Glazener, Nancy, 204

Glover, Donald, xv, 202

Goddard, Henry Kirk, 41, 66, 69, 85

Godwin, Parke, 121

Goldsmid, Lady Louisa, 216

Goodman, Joe, 81

Goodman, Lyman R., 81

Graham, Kenneth, 203–04

Granville, Lord, 172, 217

Gray, Thomas, 78

Gregory, Lady Augusta, 250

Greindl, Baron, 195

Greindl, Madame, 195

Griswold, Charles, 67

Griswold, Daniel S., 66–67

Griswold, Gertrude (Gertie), 168–69, 170, 180–81, 210, 215, 227

Griswold, Henry, 67

Griswold, Mary Dunham, 66

Griswold, Medora (Dora), 168, 210

Grover, Leonard, 153

Gwynne, Nell, 173

Haggard, Rider, 204

Hale, Edward Everett, 116

Haliburton, Thomas Chandler, 130

Hallam, A. H., 169

Hannigan, D. F., 206

Hardy, Thomas, 194, 214, 215, 230, 250, 251

Hare, John, 36, 240

Harland, Henry (Sidney Luska), 254

Harrington, Joseph, 67

Harris, Frank, 190

Harrison, Benjamin, 192

Hart, Bernard (grandfather), 14–16, 18, 25, 30, 271–72

Hart, Emanuel B., 14, 18, 30

Hart, Henry, 18

Hart, Rebecca Seixas, 14, 15, 18, 30

Harte, Aline Bouton Smith (daughter-in-law), 225–27, 229, 244, 246, 262, 263, 264, 298

Harte, Anna Griswold Bret (wife), 7, 9, 64, 65–68, 73, 91, 112, 117–18, 119, 121, 122–24, 127–28, 129, 131–32, 133–34, 135, 136–37, 140–41, 158–62, 165–66, 168, 170, 172–73, 174, 177, 179, 182, 184, 186, 187, 188, 189, 195, 196–97, 199, 207–10, 212, 215, 216, 217, 221, 222–23, 224, 225, 232–33, 234, 241, 242, 243–47, 251, 255, 256–58, 260, 261–62, 263–65, 278, 290

Harte, Elizabeth. *See* Knaufft, Elizabeth Harte

Harte, Elizabeth Ostrander (mother), 16–18, 19, 20, 21, 23, 24, 25, 40, 41, 67, 91, 133, 137, 272

Harte, Ethel Bret (daughter), 25, 35, 133, 137, 162, 244, 245, 246, 260, 263, 274, 278

Harte, Francis Brett (Bret)

    Life: and African Americans, 75–76; agent, use of literary, 213; and alcohol, 49, 142, 152, 158, 161, 189–90; ancestry of, 14–17; appearance of, 5, 7–8, 24, 31–32, 41, 88, 124, 144, 252–53, 258–59; artistic strengths of, 57; and *Atlantic Monthly*, 71–72, 118–19, 121–22, 132–33; audience of, 201–02; and authorship as profession, xvi; bachelorhood, return to, 210; birth of, 17; books, sales figures of, 200–01; California, journey to, 39; California correspondent for East coast newspapers, 82–83; and *Californian*, 77–79, 82; Cambridge, Mass., visit to, 6–12; charisma of, xiii, 8, 114–15, 151, 175–76; child, loss of, 9; childhood, 10, 17–24; and Chinese Americans, 109–11; and Civil War, 58–59, 63–64, 69–70; Civil War poetry of, 69–70; and class, 146, 212, 217–20; club memberships of, 240, 242; courtship of, 66–68; Crefeld, life in, 165–68, 177–78; death of, 262–63; and depression, 49, 176; diplomatic appointment of, 142, 145, 157–58, 160–61; diplomatic career of, 165–67, 177–78, 180, 186–89, 191–93; double life of, 186–88, 191–92; dress, mode of, 124, 176, 252, 258; East coast, triumphant return to, 6–7, 112–14; education of, 23; and English aristocracy, 169–74, 214, 216–17, 230–31, 249; enigmatic personality of, xvii; fame of, xiii–xiv, xvi, 34, 113–14, 116; father, death of, 19; father, relationship with, 13–14, 23; fatherhood of, 68, 73, 91, 122–23, 137, 162, 223, 225–27, 245, 256–58; financial difficulties of, 73, 124–27, 131–32, 135, 143, 147–48, 152, 155, 208; first book, 83–85; first novel, 131, 133, 135–36, 138, 145, 147–48, 155–56; first play, 136–38, 145, 152–55; first poem, 22, 273; first story, 59, 62–63; funeral of, 263–64; and gender, 99–109, 233–42; and Germany, 165–68, 177–79; Glasgow, life in, 181–82, 186–88; gold mining experience of, 43–46; and *Golden Era*, 59–60, 62, 70, 77; grave of, 265; health, state of, 158, 177, 181–82, 184, 189, 256, 259–62; homes of, 58–59, 68, 73, 77, 129, 133–34, 227–29, 247; and homoeroticism, 42–43, 65, 234–42; humanitarian attitudes of, 55–56, 75–76, 109–11, 125; humor, sense of, 7, 22, 50, 129–30; and hunting, 48, 181–82; illness, final, 256, 259–62; illnesses, 21; income of, 10, 114, 131–33, 147, 150, 199–200, 208, 255–56; and Indian massacre, 55–56; and influensa epidemic, 220–21; Jewish ancestry of, 8–9, 13–16; Jewish ancestry, concealment of, 25–26, 30; Jews, attitudes toward, 27–30; kindness of, xiv, 176; laziness of, 143; and lecturing, 125–31, 134, 174–75; legend, creation of own, 35–37, 53–54; lit-

erary career, beginning of, 46–47, 50–51; literary career, later, 199–207, 213; literary career, revival of, 194–95; London, life in, 170–71, 175, 183–86, 195–97, 212–13, 220–21, 226–28, 249, 255–56; masculinity, lack of, 54–55; mentor role of, 78–80, 88–91, 92–93, 230; modesty of, 7, 175; Morristown, N.J., life in, 123, 128–29, 133–34; mother, death of, 137; mother, relationship with, 23; and Native Americans, 48, 55–56, 119; New York, life in, 117, 119–21, 144; and *Northern Californian*, 52–53, 55–56; Oakland, life in, 39–41; and *Outcroppings* scandal, 80–82; and *Overland Monthly*, 11, 87–94; *Overland Monthly*, inception of, 92–93; and "Overland Trinity," 89–90; parents, marriage of, 17; passion, lack of, 142; patriotism of, 176–77, 217–18; photography, as hobby, 251; political views of, 134, 141–42, 217–20; popularity of, xvi, 11; poverty, fear of, 209; and the press, 5, 31–34, 135, 152–55, 188–91; privacy, need for, 34–35; professorship at University of California at Berkeley, 111–12; and race, 24–30, 55–56, 75–76, 109–11; reading, 22, 40, 214, 250–51; religion, attitudes to, 21–22; reputation of, 72–73, 254; and romantic friendship, 42–43, 65, 234–42; and Royal Academy dinner, 179–80; San Francisco, life in, 58–59, 61–62, 66, 68, 72–74; satirical tendency of, 75–78, 109–11, 139–41, 150; scandals involved in, 7, 80–82, 116–17, 152–55, 184, 191, 254; sex appeal of, 6, 8; sexual history of, 42–43, 46, 50, 64–68, 232–42; and shooting accident, 181–82; shyness of, 62, 116; siblings of, 17, 20–21, 23–24, 47, 50–51,

59, 144; and smoking, 49, 259; son, death of oldest, 260–61; and the South, 134; surname, change in spelling of, 18–19; Switzerland, travels in, 175–77; tardiness of, 12; theater, enjoyment of, 240, 242; and tutoring, 41–43, 46–48; "Uncle Bret Harte," role as, 167, 210–11; Uniontown, life in, 46–56; U.S. Branch Mint, work in, 70–71; U.S. Marshal's Office, work in, 64; U.S. Surveyor General's Office, work in, 64; wedding of, 64; wife, relationship with, 66–68, 73, 91, 123–24, 127–28, 131, 141, 207–10, 232–33, 242, 243–47, 256–58, 261; and women, 182, 234

Literature: assessment of, contemporary, xiv–xv, 95–96, 115, 149–50, 206–07; assessment of, modern, xv, 202; "Bret Harte Country" in, 97, 99, 254–55; care in writing, 60; cross-dressing in, 119; and domesticity, 99–109; immorality of, 23; New Historicist approach to, 99–109; originality of, xv, 94–109; "power of sex" in, 233; realism, lack of, 149, 156; realism vs. romance in, xv, 33, 37–39, 202–06; sentimentality in, 149

Individual works: "Adventures of John Longbowe, The," 202; "After the Accident," 125; Ah Sin (with Mark Twain), 139–40, 146–47, 149, 155, 156–60; "Angelus, The," 109; "Argonauts of '49, The," 126–27, 236–37; "Argonauts of North Liberty, The," 233; "Arsenical Spring of San Joaquin, The," 109; "At the Sepulchre," 75; "Autumn Musings," 22; "Ballad of the Emeu, The," 77; "Bell-Ringer of Angel's, The," 200, 233; "Bohemian Days in San Francisco," 53–54; "Brown of Calaveras," 97; By Shore and Sedge, 206; "Captain Jim's Friend," 236–37; "Chicago," 119; "Clarence," 35, 231; "Complete Letter Writing," 77; "Concepcion de Arguëllo," 122, 129, 133; "Condensed Novels," 72, 78, 83–84, 230; "Conspiracy of Mrs. Bunker, The," 221; "Copperhead, The," 69; "Coyote," 109; "Cressy," 216; "Crusade of the Excelsior, The," 200, 204, 212; "Dolores," 50–51; "Don Diego of the South," 130; Drift from Two Shores, 149; East and West Poems, 119; "Episode of Fiddletown, An," 125; "Executive Committee to the Colored Population, The," 75–76; "Fate," 109; "Few Operatic Criticisms, A," 77; "Flip," 199; Flip and Other Stories, 201; "Fool of Five Forks, The," 132; "For the King," 133; "Found at Blazing Star," 195, 234; "Friar Pedro's Ride," 109; Gabriel Conroy, 131, 133, 135–36, 138, 143, 145, 147, 148, 149, 156, 178, 212, 233–34; "Gentleman of La Porte, A," 194; "Ghost that Jim Saw, The," 130; "Grandmother Tenterden," 121; "Grayport Legend, A," 119; "Great Patent Office Fire, The," 150; "Grizzly," 109; "Half an Hour Before Supper," 122; Heiress of Red Dog and Other Tales, The, 200; Held Up, 231; "Her Letter," 110; "Heritage of Dedlow Marsh, The," 200, 233; "High-Water Mark," 63, 97; "His Pen," 75; "Homecoming of Jim Wilkes, The," 221; "How Are You, Sanitary?," 69; "How I Went to the Mines," 44–46, 53–54, 56, 202; "How Santa Claus Came to Simpson's Bar," 121; "Hudson River, The," 23; "Idyl of Red Gulch, The," 95, 97; "Iliad of Sandy Bar, The," 38, 97, 111; "In the Tules,"

237–38; "In the Tunnel," 110; "Indiscretion of Elsbeth, The," 201, 207; *Jeff Briggs's Love Story and Other Sketches,* 201; "Jim," 110; "John Chinaman," 110–11; "Judgment of Bolinas Plain, The," 223; "Legend of Monte del Diablo, The," 71–72, 83; "Letters from 'Icabod'," 47; "Lonely Ride, A," 96; "Lost Beauty, The," 116; "Lost Galleon, The," 85; "Lothaw," 119; "Luck of Roaring Camp, The," 95, 99–109, 113, 185, 238, 243, 252; *Luck of Roaring Camp and Other Sketches, The,* 11, 63, 95, 99, 201; "Madroño," 109; "Mæcenas of the Pacific Slope, The," 231; "Man of No Account, The," 63, 78, 95, 97; "Maruja," 200, 201; "Mary's Album," 80; "Miggles," 95, 97; "Mliss" ("The Work on Red Mountain"), 63, 70, 78, 95, 97; "Monte Flat Pastoral," 140; "Morning on the Avenue," 146; "Mountain Heart's-Ease, The," 109; "Mr. McGlowrie's Widow," 200; "Mr. Thompson's Prodigal," 153; "Mrs. Judge Jenkins," 82; "My Favorite Novelist and His Best Book," 205–06; "My First Book," 221; "My Metamorphosis," 59–60; "My Soul to Thine," 66; "Mysterious Drum, The," 77; "Neighborhoods I Have Moved From," 77; "Newport Romance, A," 119; "Night at Wingdam, A," 97; "Notes by Flood and Field," 42–43, 70, 78, 95, 97, 237; "Ode," 82; "On a Vulgar Little Boy," 77; "On the Decay of Professional Begging," 77; "Our Privilege," 69; "Outcasts of Poker Flat, The," 95, 97, 131, 238; "Passage in the Life of Mr. John Oakhurst, A," 131, 132, 150, 233; "Patagonian Lyric," 51; "Phyllis of the Sierras, A," 172; "Plain Language from Truthful James" ("The Heathen Chinee"), 11, 28, 38, 70, 75, 107, 109–11, 112, 113, 219; "Poet of Sierra Flat, The," 119; "Princess Bob and Her Friends," 119; "Progress of American Humor, The," 130; "Ramon," 132, 133; "Relieving Guard—March 4th, 1864," 75; "Reveille, The," 69–70, 265; "Right Eye of the Commander, The," 96; "Rise of the Short Story, The," 253; "Romance of Madroño Hollow, The," 119; "Rose of Tuolumne, The," 130, 132, 150; *Rushbrook,* 231; "San Francisco, By the Poets," 78; "San Francisco (From the Sea)," 109; "Snow-Bound at Eagle's," 231; "Society Upon the Stanislaus, The," 11, 110; "Stage-Driver's Story, The," 119; "Stories Three," 230; "Story of a Mine, The," 155; *Sue,* 223–25, 231–32, 245; "Susy," 213; *Tales of the Argonauts and Other Sketches,* 135, 138; "Tennessee's Partner," 95, 109, 202, 236, 237, 238; "Thankful Blossom," 142, 143, 147, 149; "That Ebrew Jew," 28–29, 76; "Three Partners," 200, 206; "To the Pliocene Skull," 10; "Trent's Trust," 256; *Trent's Trust and Other Stories,* 207; "Trip Up the Coast, A," 49; "Twins of Table Mountain, The," 201; *Two Men of Sandy Bar,* 136, 137–38, 140, 145, 149, 152–55, 191, 252; "Two Saints of the Foothills," 150; "Uncle Jim and Uncle Billy," 109, 236–37; "Unser Karl," 166; "Valentine, The," 47; "Volunteer Stocking, A," 69; "Waif of the Plains, A," 39, 201; "Wan Lee, the Pagan," 111; "What Happened at the Fonda," 233; "What the Bullet Sang," 143; "With the Entrées," 36–37

Harte, Francis King (Frank) (son), 7, 9, 73, 75, 112, 137, 161–62, 166, 208, 223, 225–27, 229, 242, 244, 245, 246, 247, 257, 259, 260, 261, 262, 263, 264

Harte, Geoffrey Bret (grandson), 226, 232, 246, 247, 248, 262–63

Harte, Griswold (Wodie) (son), 7, 9, 68, 77, 112, 137, 161–62, 244, 256–58, 260

Harte, Helen. *See* Fulford, Helen Harte

Harte, Henry (father), 10, 13–14, 15, 16–19, 21, 22, 23, 24, 25, 271–72, 274

Harte, Henry (brother), 10, 17, 20–21, 23, 24, 40, 51, 59

Harte, Jennie Astoria Chapin (daughter-in-law), 256–58, 260

Harte, Jessamy (Tottie) (daughter), 119, 122–23, 136, 137, 152, 162, 244, 245

Harte, Margaret. *See* Wyman, Margaret Harte

Harte, Richard Bret (grandson), 226, 263

Hartley, Jacob, 50

Haskell, Mabel, 39

Hatton, Brian, 241

Hatton, Joseph, 221, 252

Hawthorne, Nathaniel, 22, 93, 96, 216

Hay, John, xvii, 26, 121, 150, 155, 169, 178, 180, 187, 192–93, 219–20, 238, 239, 264–65

Hayes, Birchard A., 157–58

Hayes, Rutherford B., 142, 157, 158, 160–61, 180

Hayes, Webb, 157–58

Heine, Heinrich, 8, 169

Hemans, Felicia, 22

Henniker, Hon. Florence Ellen Hungerford Milnes, 229–31, 250

Henniker, Lord, 230

Henniker-Major, Hon. Arthur Henry, 229–30

Henry IV (Shakespeare), 28

Higginson, Thomas Wentworth, 191

Hill, Hamlin, 155

Hilton, Henry, 28–29

Hilton-Seligman scandal, 28–29

Hoffman, Andrew J., 240

Holland, Josiah Gilbert, 118

Holmes, Oliver Wendell, 7, 10, 11

Holy War, The (Bunyan), 21–22

Honan, Park, xx

Hood, Tom, 93

Hooker, Isabella Beecher, 152

Hope, Anthony (A. H. Hawkins), 207

Horace, 22

Houghton, Annabel, Lady, 231

Houghton, Henry O., 132–33

Houghton, Richard Monckton Milnes, Lord, 169, 170–71, 213, 229, 230, 231

Howe, Dr., 243

Howells, Elinor Mead, 6, 9, 67, 157–58

Howells, William Dean, xiii–xiv, xvii, 6–8, 10, 11, 12, 15, 19, 20, 26, 27, 28, 38, 114–15, 116, 117, 122, 126, 132–33, 149, 151, 157, 158, 159, 160, 161, 190, 207, 250, 251, 252, 254

Hutchinson, Mr., 221

Hyndman, Henry Mayers, 219

Innocents Abroad, The (Twain), 86, 148

"International Episode, An" (James), 214

Irving, Washington, 21, 96

Jackson, Andrew, 18, 29

Jackson, Minnie, 250

Jackson, Thomas, 16

James, Henry, xx, 6, 190, 214–15, 227

Jenny, 46, 48

Jentges, Wilhelm, 166

Jerome, Jerome K., 221

Jews, nineteenth-century attitudes toward, 26–30

John, Goscombe, 241

John Brent (Winthrop), 235

Jude the Obscure (Hardy), 230

Kearney, Dennis, 110

Keeler, Ralph, 151

Kerr, Orpheus C. (R. H. Newell), 130
King, Clarence, 94, 121, 178, 180, 238
King, Edith, 61
King, Julia, 61
King, Thomas Starr, 60–64, 68, 69, 70, 71, 72, 74–75, 215
Kingham, Mrs., 228, 229
Kingsley, Charles, 170
Kipling, Rudyard, 38, 216, 230
Knaufft, Dora, 144
Knaufft, Elizabeth Harte (Eliza) (sister), xvi, 10, 16, 17, 21, 23, 24, 40, 128, 141, 144, 145, 225, 244, 272, 273
Knaufft, Ernest, 144
Knaufft, Frederick F., 10, 24, 40, 123, 144, 244
Knaufft, Frederick, Jr., 144
Knaufft, Nina, 144
Knaufft, Sarah, 144
Knaufft, Wilhelmina, 144
Kutzemeyer, Henry (uncle), 10, 23, 273
Kutzemeyer, Mary Ann Ostrander (aunt), 10, 23, 273

Lambert, 256
Landor, Walter Savage, 169
Lang, Andrew, 156, 204, 205
Langdon, Olivia Lewis, 139–40
Latham, Milton S., 73
Launay, Edouard, Count de, 182–83, 188, 221, 227
Launay, Emma de Hallwyl, Countess de, 182–83, 195, 221, 227
Lawrence, Joe, 59, 62, 79
Leach, Georgiana, 66
Leach, Stephen W., 66
Led Astray (Boucicault), 137
Leighton, Sir Frederick, 179
Lewes, George Henry, 215
Lincoln, Abraham, 18, 63
Liscomb, Charles, 47, 49–50
Liscomb, Charles H., 46, 47–48, 50
Liscomb, Frank M., 46, 47–48, 50
Livingstone, David, 171
Londonderry, Lady, 217

Longfellow, Henry Wadsworth, 7, 10–11, 21, 28, 185–86, 205
Louisa, Princess (Marchioness of Lorne), 240
Lowell, James Russell, 7, 8–9, 10, 11, 26–27, 116, 130, 179, 184, 185, 205, 218
Lyne, Mrs. Clavering, 263
Lystra, Karen, 278

McCarthy, Justin, 171
McCrackin, Josephine Clifford, 90, 91, 116
Manxman, The (Caine), 205
Martin, Cassie, 65
Mary Garnett (Henniker), 230
Mason, Frank Holcomb, 136, 145, 160–61
Mason, Jennie Birchard, 145, 160–61
Menken, Adah Isaacs, 76
Meredith, George, xv
Merrill, George B., 74, 92, 94
Merwin, Henry C., 16, 235, 273
Miles, Frank, 183
Miller, Joaquin (Cincinnatus Hiner), 87–88, 93–94, 171
Milnes, Richard Monckton. *See* Houghton, Richard Monckton Milnes, Lord
Mitchell, Edward P., 144
Mitchell, Laura, 158
Monckton, Lady, 216
Montaigne, Michel de, 22
Morrow, Patrick, xv, 99, 235
Munger, 88
Murdock, Albert H., 52
Murdock, Charles, 50, 51–52, 55

Nadal, Ehrman Syme, 149
Nadel, Ira B., xx
narrative, in biography, xvii–xxiii
Nasby, Petroleum V. (David Ross Locke), 125
Nast, Mrs., 131
Nemesis of Faith, The (Froude), 169

Neville, Lady Dorothy, 216
Newman, John Henry, 169
Nightingale, Florence, 229
Norris, Frank, xv
Norris, Miss, 263
Norris, Richard, 228, 263
Northampton, Lord and Lady, 231, 249

Ogden, Dick, 74
Ogden, Isabella, 74
Ogelvie, Lady, 217
"Old Folks at Home" (Foster), 130
Oliver Twist (Dickens), 27
Osborne, Ralph Bernal, 172
Osgood, James R., 10, 114, 119, 121,
    122, 124, 125, 135, 136, 147, 150,
    162, 175
Ostrander, Abigail Truesdale (grand-
    mother), 17, 272
Ostrander, Henry Philip (grandfather),
    17, 272
Ouida (Marie Louise de la Ramée), 194

Paget, Lord Alfred, 217, 240
Parks, Sir Henry, 217
Parrott, John, 73
Parsloe, Charles T., 139, 147, 160
Parton, Ethel, 124
Parton, James, 29–30, 124
"Passionate Pilgrim, The" (James), 6
Payne, William Morton, 206–07
Peabody, Sarah, 27
Pease, Mrs., 17
Pemberton, May, 251, 258
Pemberton, T. Edgar, 37, 212, 222–25,
    229, 231–32, 240–41, 247, 249, 251,
    261, 263
Pembroke, Lord and Lady, 217
Pendennis (Thackeray), 241
Petrie, Dennis, xviii
Philips, Jonas B., 15
Phillips, Wendell, 61
Piatt, Donn, 158–60
Picture of Dorian Gray, The (Wilde),
    250–51

Plain Tales from the Hills (Kipling), 230
Poe, Edgar Allan, 78
Polk, James, 19
Pollock, Edward, 80
Pollock, Sir Frederick, 214
Purcell, E., 206

Rabelais, François, 214, 215
Reade, Charles, 194
realism vs. romance in literature, 37–39,
    202–06
Reid, Whitelaw, 121, 150
Revere, Joseph Warren, 133–34
Revere, Paul, 133
Ridge, John R., 81
Roberts, Frederick Sleigh, 230
Robertson, T. W., 223
Robson, Stuart, 137–38, 145, 152–54
Rogers, Bob, 74
Rogers, Henry Huttleston, 152
Rogers, Lydia, 74
Roman, Anton, 80, 83, 92, 94, 96–97
Rombout, Francis, 16
Roosevelt, Robert Barnwell, 153
Root, Sarah Whipple, 50
Rothman, Ellen K., 68
Rothschild, Ferdinand, Baron de, 217
Roughing It (Twain), 140
Rudge, Mrs., 244
Russell, Annie, 224, 231

St. Albans, Grace (*née* Osborne), Duch-
    ess of, 172–73, 174, 214, 216
St. Albans, William Amelius Aubrey de
    Vere Beauclerk, Duke of, 172–73,
    174, 216
Saintsbury, George, 204
Sawyer, Warren, 82
Schneider, Clara, 167, 168, 181, 211,
    212, 225, 231, 239, 247
Schneider, Rudolph, 166, 167, 168, 172,
    176, 180, 181, 189, 211, 238–39, 247
Schurz, Carl, 160
Scott, Sir Walter, 78, 185
Scoville, Joseph, 14

Sedgwick, Sara, 6

Seigneux, Charles-François-Fréderic de, 182

Seixas, Benjamin Mendes, 14

Seligman, Joseph, 28–29

Seward, Frederick William, 161

Shakespeare, William, 27, 153

Shelley, Percy Bysshe, 89

Shorter, Clement, 271–72

Shrewsbury, Lady Theresa, 217

Siam, Crown Prince of, 247

Skidelsky, Robert, xviii

Sklar, Kathryn Kish, 108–09

Smelmann, Mr., 256

Smith, Charles, 226

Smith, Sidney, 226

Sothern, Edward Askew, 223

Soulé, Frank, 81

Spenceley, Miss, 249, 251, 261

Spenser, Edmund, 78

Stanley, Lady, 217

Stebbins, Horatio, 85

Steele, Henry Milford, 245

Steele, Jessamy Harte. *See* Harte, Jessamy

Stegner, Wallace, 232

Stephen, Leslie, 27

Stevenson, Robert Louis, 204, 205

Stewart, George, 45, 51

Stoddard, Charles Warren, 79–80, 83, 84, 87–90, 94, 239

Stone, A. L., 85

Stoneley, Peter, 235, 240

Stowe, Harriet Beecher, 100, 107–08, 116, 152

Strachey, Lytton, xx

Sullivan, Arthur, 240

Sumner, Charles, 155

Swain, Robert Bunker, 70

Swett, John, 81

Swinburne, Algernon Charles, 98, 169, 194

Tatnall, Commander, 20

Taylor, Bayard, 121

Taylor, Florence Wyman (niece), 51, 59

Tennyson, Alfred, Lord, 21, 78, 169, 170

Teulon, S. S., 173

Thackeray, William, 21

Thomas, Jeffrey F., 233

Tilden, Samuel J., 142

Tilly, George, 51

Tingley (Laurence), Mary, 41

Tobin, John, 224

Todd, Mrs. Jas, 51

Tompkins, Jane, 101

Tower, F. Marion, 192

Traveller from Altruria, The (Howells), 250

Trübner, Cornélie, 175, 183, 184

Trübner, Nicholas, 175, 183, 184, 215

Trudgill, Eric, 236

Twain, Mark. *See* Clemens, Samuel Langhorne

Two Chiefs of Dunboy, The (Froude), 250

Underwood, Francis, 191–92

Updike, John, xxi

Usher, J., 185

Uspensky, Boris, xxii

Van de Velde, Arthur, xvii, 183–85, 186, 187, 195–97, 208, 209, 211, 216, 220–21, 227, 255

Van de Velde, Beatrice, 191, 227, 246

Van de Velde, Berthe, 228, 294

Van de Velde, Hydeline Rodolphine Emma de Seigneux ("M. S."), xvii, 182–85, 186, 187, 188, 189–90, 191, 194–98, 208, 209, 211, 216, 221, 226, 227–29, 232, 234, 235, 238, 242, 246, 247–49, 255, 262, 263–65, 294

Van de Velde, Marcel, 183, 294

Van de Velde, Marguerite, 191, 221

Van de Velde, Maurice, 220, 221

Van de Velde, René, 228, 229

Van den Steen, Count, 226

Van Köhlwalter, Dr., 189

Van Zeller, Claude (Dom Hubert), 248–49

Victoria, Queen, 172, 240

Wales, Albert, Prince of (King Edward VII), 179

Walker, Franklin, 82

Walpole, Horace, 46

Walsworth, E. B., 74

Ward, Artemus, 79, 130

Ward, Bessie, 22

Warner, Charles Dudley, 145

Washington, George, 129–30, 186

Washington, Martha, 129–30

Watrous, Charles, 73–74, 239

Watrous, Ruth, 73–74

Watt, A. P., 199, 208, 209, 213, 255, 259

Watts-Dunton, Theodore, xv, 97–98

Webb, Charles Henry, 76, 77, 80, 81, 82, 83, 84

Webb, Geraldine, 171, 216

Webb, William Frederick, 171, 216

Weston, Willie, 241

Wharton, Edith, 117

Wheeler, A. C., 153–54

Whipple, Stephen G., 52, 53, 55–56

White, Hayden, xviii–xix, xx

Whitman, Walt, 233

Wilde, Lady Jane, 216

Wilde, Oscar, 215–16, 236, 238, 241, 250–51

Wilhelmi, Marie, 168

Williams, Andrew (stepfather), 24, 39–40, 41, 133, 137

Williams, Elizabeth Ostrander Harte. *See* Harte, Elizabeth Ostrander

Williams, Maud Wyman Eberts (niece), 59, 277

Williams, Sam, 74, 94

Willow Copse, The (Boucicault), 89

Wills, Miss, 65

Wings of the Dove, The (James), 227

Winthrop, Theodore, 235

Woodlanders, The (Hardy), 215

Woolf, Virginia, xxiii, 27

Woolson, Constance Fenimore, xv

Wyman, Benjamin Henry, 47, 59

Wyman, Justus, 48, 52

Wyman, Margaret Harte (Maggie) (sister), 10, 17, 24, 38, 41, 47, 48, 49, 50–51, 59, 77

Zander, L. T., 66

Zander, Mattie Griswold, 66

Zangwill, Israel, 252

Zola, Émile, 26